Dear Dr Smith —

How appreciative I am of all your guidance, service and care. You saved my life for which I am extremely grateful. Thank you so much.

(They interviewed me for this book and included it in chapter X Chronicles of Leadership, page 220)

Thanks,

Neal

SANTA CLARA COUNTY

American Historical Press
Sun Valley, California

SANTA CLARA COUNTY
HARVEST OF CHANGE

AN ILLUSTRATED HISTORY

STEPHEN M. PAYNE

Library of Congress Catalogue Card Number: 2008929775

ISBN: 978-1-892724-57-1

Bibliography: p. 296
Includes Index

CONTENTS

FOREWORD

The last few decades have seen the dawn of the "Information Age," and more than a few economists, politicians, seers, and pundits have linked America's future to its computer industry. Thus the eyes of this nation and the world turn repeatedly to the birthplace of this remarkable high technology—Santa Clara County—known worldwide as Silicon Valley.

But before Silicon Valley there was the Valley of Heart's Delight, famous the world over for its orchards, open spaces, friendly towns, profound universities, and its lifestyle. Still further back we find a plain inhabited by generous, hospitable natives living without fear of starvation or want, so bountiful was the land. Santa Clara County has been all of these and more; *Harvest of Change* is its story.

Gaspar de Portolá and Father Junípero Serra could scarcely have imagined the wealth, struggles, and tremendous potential of the quiet valley that lay before their tired, sick party of explorers more than 200 years ago. Generations of Ohlone had lived without war or starvation, just hunting, fishing, and gathering as their ancestors had done.

The Spanish conquered and converted, and brought the Indians and land under their empire. The Mexicans rebelled, but ruled California for only a short time. Manifest destiny and the lure of gold brought the Americans and a new government. In the new county of Santa Clara, San Jose became, for a short time, the capital of the nation's thirty-first state.

The promise of California and the Santa Clara Valley held constant. Rich land, plentiful water, and the mild climate brought merchants, miners, and farmers. They found that whatever was planted—grain, fruit, vegetables—grew larger here than anywhere else.

Orchards and vineyards spread. Within a century of its discovery Santa Clara County boasted fruit and wine industries that were the envy of the nation. The Valley of Heart's Delight bathed itself in pastel blossoms each spring; each fall its harvest helped feed the world.

Industry, too, grew at an incredible pace. Canneries, foundries, machine shops, and railroads served the swelling small towns and cities.

The nation's wars brought profound changes. The technology of flight and space exploration, both anchored in our Valley, bred ventures never before imagined. Ideas and solutions became the valley's commodities as orchards gave way to industrial parks.

Expanding populations and shifting economies have carried new challenges: protecting our water and air, open spaces, and hillsides. But Silicon Valley's prosperity continues to attract refugees and immigrants, seekers and dreamers.

Today Santa Clara County is perhaps famous more for its engineers than its farmers, more for its tiny silicon miracles than for its once-abundant blossoms.

But the past doesn't fade entirely. Its traces need not be sought in musty archives or books yellowed with age. They live still in the names of streets and parks,

in neighborhoods and family histories and the collective memory of more than 1.7 million citizens. Look sharp and you can still see small orchards among the factories. Hike the hills and you'll be among the redwoods and oaks that built our towns and the creeks that continue to provide them water. Drive our back roads and you'll likely as not travel the same route used by conquistadores, revolutionaries, cowboys, and fortune-seekers hundreds of years before.

Like them, you'll join the valley's inventors, trades people, venture capitalists, and environmentalists in inheriting great resources and ideas. Our challenge today lies in enjoying the bounty, while continu-

ing to protect and enhance Santa Clara County's legacy for the generation of the this new millennium; our Valley's next group of explorers.

We're all new arrivals, heirs to those who came in search of the future. Stay long enough and you'll know what they learned. To live here is to inherit dreams as old as our hills; to work here is to give life to imagination. Santa Clara County is indeed unique in all the world.

Rod Diridon, Sr., Supervisor District 4 (ret.)
Chair, 1978, 81, 85, 89, 91, and 94
Santa Clara County Board of Supervisors

Mission Santa Clara's Father Catala employed 200 Indians to plant three rows of willows on the four-mile Alameda between the Pueblo of San Jose and the mission in 1799. The mission served as San Jose's parish church and the father hoped the pleasant journey along the cool and shaded road would encourage the worldly inhabitants of the pueblo to regularly attend Sunday mass. Painting by Andrew P. Hill, courtesy, San Jose Historical Museum

PREFACE

Santa Clara County is in a state of perpetual change. As much as its citizens feel that things will stay as they are, change gradually seeps into the fabric of the county. During the beginning of some eras, change suddenly sweeps the old away.

Throughout the past few decades several publications concerning individual cities in the county have been published. This study will not delve into histories of individual cities, except where that history directly affects Santa Clara County as a whole.

This book is an introduction to the history of Santa Clara County and should not be viewed as an attempt at a definitive history. With this in mind, most readers will find that this quick impressionistic canvas will provide a basic overview of Santa Clara County's past.

To understand local history is one of the most important things that an individual can do to develop a sense of belonging to a place. Since most of the county's families arrived in the latter part of the twentieth century, a sense of place is needed. I hope that this publication will encourage other historians to step forward and add to the knowledge of Santa Clara County, correcting where necessary and adding material to its gaps.

This project would not have occurred without the support and effort of many people. I alone, however, am responsible for errors and omissions. While a student at San Jose State University I was fortunate to have taken courses in local history from professors Benjamin F. Gilbert and David Eakins. Over the years the chairmen of SJSU's History Department, James Walsh and George Moore, and the Dean of Social Science Charles Burdick, were kind enough to allow me to teach courses in local and public history, which were invaluable for this effort. My uncle, Perley B. Payne, Jr., was an invaluable help in sorting out the details of farming techniques during the county's agricultural era. I would also like to thank Beth Wyman, a Santa Clara County Historical Heritage commissioner and former mayor of Morgan Hill, for her efforts in selecting and encouraging me for an earlier version of *Santa Clara County: Harvest of Change.* County Supervisor Rod J. Diridon was a crucial ally of this project. He kept a constant interest in the work. Supervisor Diridon directed Michael Holm, one of his staff members, to assist with researching and writing about county government. Michael did a tremendous job in a short time. The late Glory Anne Laffey was brilliant at finding and captioning the photographs for this volume and helping, through pictures, to fill in some of the many historical gaps.

In the twenty years since that publication a plethora of books were published that focused on Silicon Valley and covered themes as divergent as: technology and medicine; women leaders in

the technology industry; the businesses of Silicon Valley; the influence of key individuals; as well as globalization and the impact of the various immigrant communities. In addition, several authors have added to the rich local history of the county, including the late Glory Anne Laffey and her nephew, Robert G. Detlefs, who coauthored a much needed history, *County Leadership: Santa Clara County Government History*. This edition of *Harvest of Change* is fortunate to have Charlene Duval, Laffey's sister, as the historic photo editor. I am also proud to note that my youngest son, Kevin, is responsible for the color photographs of this edition. I am very much in debt to James C. Williams for reviewing the chapter, "Second Harvest." I owe a debit of gratitude to Amber Avines, who initiated this edition for the American Historical Press, and Carolyn Martin, who completed the process. Finally, I need to once again thank Carol for her patience and support.

On May 12, 1908, during Admiral Dewey's tour with the Pacific Fleet, naval officers approach Meridian Corners (Saratoga Avenue and Stevens Creek Road). Courtesy, San Jose Public Library, California Room

CHAPTER ONE

VALLEY OF THE OAKS

Mission Santa Clara de Asis, founded in 1777 by Father Junípero Serra, is pictured here as it may have appeared in 1849. Painting by H.G. Peelor after Andrew P. Hill, courtesy, San Jose Historical Museum

The Santa Clara Valley's first inhabitants, the Ohlone or Costanoan Indians, settled at least 1,000 years before the Spanish arrived. Before the Ohlone, other Indian cultures lived in the area for thousands of years. The name Costanoan comes from the Spanish word "Costenos," meaning "people of the coast." The word "Ohlone" is favored by the descendants of the native population and most anthropologists, although historically the term referred to either a small tribelet living on the San Mateo coast, or to the Miwok word meaning "the western people."

The Ohlone lived in a territory that extended from the southern edge of San Francisco Bay south to Point Sur, and from the Pacific Ocean east to the crest of the Diablo Mountains. The Ohlone were part of the Penutian-speaking people that included the Miwok, Wintun, Maidu, and Yokuts. These other Penutian tribes resided along the coast in present-day Marin County and in California's central valley. The Ohlone comprised from 7,000 to 26,000 people before contact with the Spanish. These figures vary widely due to the fact that the only census taken for the local native population occurred fifty years after the initial Spanish contact.

This group of California Indians lived in forty scattered villages and spoke approximately twelve dialects and several sub-dialects. Streams, ridges, canyons, and other natural features served to divide the tribes. The separation was such that people living within a short distance spoke different dialects. No more than 1,000 people spoke each dialect, while each village com-

prised up to 250 people and often held much smaller numbers. Those Ohlone living in Santa Clara County are considered, by anthropologists, as part of the northern interior Ohlone.

The Ohlone tribes living within the modern geographic area of Santa Clara County were the Puichon (or Puichun), who lived near Palo Alto. The Pojoron were located in the Mountain View-Los Altos area—the main village, Posolomi, was located where Moffett Field is now. The Puichon lived in the foothills near Cupertino; the Retocsi along Stevens Creek; the Quiroste in Saratoga; the Tha-

mien or Tamien along the banks of the Coyote Creek near present-day downtown San Jose; the Matalan in the south county area near Coyote; and the Unijaima near the boundary of Santa Clara, Santa Cruz, San Benito, and Monterey counties.

The valley's Ohlone lived in small, round half-sphere dwellings. The Ohlone built huts out of redwood and other wood branches that the people covered with a thatch of more branches, grasses, and earth. Several huts formed a small tribelet of between fifty and 100 people. A tribelet chief lived in the largest cluster of huts and exercised some nominal control over

Left:
Old Chief Ynigo of Mission Santa Clara was granted title to Rancho Posolmi in 1844, one of the few natives so honored. Although the Mountain View Rancho was purchased by Robert Walkinshaw, Ynigo lived there until he died in 1864 at the age of 104. Ynigo was a gifted musician and singer who often participated in the choir services at the mission. Courtesy, Santa Clara University Archives

Far left:
This photograph of James Bohohi, the last Mission Santa Clara Indian, was taken by Mrs. Fremont Older in about 1920. Courtesy, Santa Clara University Archives

the group. Each group, however, owned its own lands and remained basically independent. The groups shared the same dialect and traded goods with other tribelets in the area. The chief's authority was passed from father to son, or to a sister or daughter if the chief did not have a son.

Families lived in the huts and took care of their own needs. The family unit made their own bows, arrows, baskets, nets, and whatever else they needed in order to survive. The men pierced their ears and dressed in short rabbit-skin capes, or went without clothes. The women tattooed their faces and wore tule reed or deer skin skirts around their waists.

Acorns from the abundant oak trees provided the staple food of the valley's tribelets. After gathering the nuts the women used a pestle and mortar to grind the acorns before leaching the tannic acid from the meal in water. Great quantities of acorns were gathered and stored to insure a source of food during the winter months.

The Ohlone also lived on fish, deer, elk, antelope, rabbits, rodents, water fowl, nuts, berries, and seeds. In addition to the food collected in the valley, archaeological evidence indicates that tribelets ventured over the Santa Cruz Mountains in search of various forms of sea food. In the tidepools of Monterey Bay the Ohlone found fish and shellfish readily available. The Ohlone used shells from the *saxidomus nuttalli,* a clam, as money. The ethnographic record indicates that the Ohlone had plenty of food to eat and did not fear starvation.

This nineteenth-century painting depicting Califor- nio vaqueros tangling with an uncooperative bull was done by Augusto Ferran in about 1840. Courtesy, The Bancroft Library

The 1860 dedication of the Enrequita quicksilver mine on Capitancillos Creek was depicted in this painting by A. Edouart. This mine was considered one of the richest in the cinnabar range. When the operation of the mines was taken over by the Quicksilver Mining Company in 1863, this mine was only partially worked in favor of developing the ore beds in closer proximity to the New Almaden Hacienda. Courtesy, The Bancroft Library

Mission Santa Clara is shown as it appeared in 1842. Secularized in 1836, the mission became the home of American settlers during the war with Mexico in 1846. Courtesy, Santa Clara University Archives

The only crop that the Ohlone cultivated was tobacco. The natives mixed tobacco leaves with lime from seashells and ate the mixture. Although those who partook often vomited, another side effect was intoxication. Unfortunately, researchers do not know if the tobacco and ground shell mixture was taken for a religious rite. In fact, little is understood about the religious beliefs of the Ohlone. Twentieth-century anthropologists have spoken with a few Ohlone who remembered what they were told about their culture from their parents. From these conversations scholars have pieced together details of the Ohlone society.

One feature of the Ohlone religion revolved around the Kuksu cult. The Kuksu held dance ceremonies in large roundhouses. These structures could be as large as sixty feet in diameter. Dancers dressed in colorful costumes designed to gain favor with Kuksu, the South God, who was believed to renew the world each spring and insure that the people would be able to hunt and gather plenty of food.

In addition, the Ohlone believed in a sun spirit. Each morning the people faced the east and prayed to the sun. Furthermore, since the Ohlone were hunters, they worshiped animal spirits. The social life of the Ohlone revolved around animal clans. In dance the people imitated the animals they depended upon for food.

The life-style of the Ohlone remained fairly constant until the arrival of the Spanish. Fearful of foreign encroachment in Alta California, in 1769 José de Gálvez, visitador general to New Spain, ordered Gaspar de Portolá and Father Junípero Serra to establish presidios and missions at San Diego and Monterey in what became known as "The Sacred Expedition."

Portolá organized two land and two sea expeditions to ensure success. The first sea expedition included twenty-five Catalan volunteers, under the command of Lieutenant Pedro Fages, who left Baja California on January 9, 1769, on the *San Carlos.* The second sea expedition left aboard the *San Antonio* on February 15.

On March 22, 1769, the first land expedition left Baja California. Captain Fernando Rivera y Moncada, with twenty-five leather-jacket soldiers, forty-two Christian Indians, and Fray Juan Crespi, became the first land expedition to reach Alta California. Portolá and Serra left Baja for San Diego on May 15, 1769.

The *San Antonio's* crew became the first segment of the sacred expedition to reach San Diego, anchoring in the bay on April 11. Eighteen days later the *San Carlos* arrived. The voyage of the *San Carlos* lasted 110 days and resulted in twenty-four deaths. Even after their arrival in San Diego, the men continued to fall sick. La Pinata de los Muertos, or Dead Men's Point, in San Diego became the first cemetery in Alta California, as two-thirds of the *San Carlos'* crew fell to the scourges of scurvy and dysentery and were buried there.

When Captain Rivera and his band arrived in San Diego on May 14, 1769, they quickly erected a few huts to shelter the sick and then awaited Portolá and Serra, who arrived at the end of June.

After securing San Diego, Portolá marched north on July 14, 1769, to find Monterey, which, although identified by Sebastián Rodrígues Cermeño in 1595, had never been visited by land. Portolá took Captain Rivera, Lieutenant Fages, Miguel Costansó, the expedition's engineer and cartographer, Fray Juan Crespí—whose diary details the exploration—and several other men, including, Sergeant José Francisco Ortega, Pedro Amador, Juan Bautista Alvarado, Antonio Yorba, and José María Soberanes, who would become key figures in California's history.

On November 6, 1769, a company of Spanish explorers reached what is now known as the Santa Clara Valley near the present Palo Alto. Captain Gaspar de Portolá and his men camped on the north bank of Arroyo San Francisquito, not far from this giant redwood tree that took the name *El Abra Palo Alto.* Courtesy, San Jose Historical Museum

Viceroy Antonio Bucareli of New Spain wrote to the Minister of the Indies in 1774 that "it now appears necessary to explore the land still further, and to establish a presidio at the port of San Francisco." Bucareli commissioned an expedition led by Captain Don Juan Bautista De Anza to transport the first non-military settlers to California. Courtesy, The Bancroft Library

was the expedition's supply ship. On November 1, 1769, Ortega's party reached the top of the Santa Cruz Mountains between the present location of Pacifica and Millbrae and became the first Spaniard to see San Francisco Bay. Interestingly, Portolá did not recognize the significance of the discovery, as the giant bay was clearly not Monterey Bay. However, Fray Crespí wrote in his diary: "It is a very large and fine harbor, such that not only all the navy of our Most Catholic Majesty but those of all Europe could take shelter in it."

Realizing that they had made a mistake and missed Monterey Bay, the group headed south in search of the famed, although unexplored, port. From November 6 to 11, 1769, the explorers camped on the northwest bank of San Francisquito Creek, the current site of Menlo Park. The expedition faced chilly nights and dreary days. The grass was still brown, as November is only the beginning of the rainy season, which lasts until April. Fray Juan Crespí wrote in his diary:

We pitched camp in a plain some six leagues long, grown with good oaks and live oaks, and with much other timber in the neighborhood. This plain has two good arroyos with a good flow of water, and at the southern end of the estuary there is a good river, with plenty of water, which passes through the plain mentioned, well wooded on its banks (Guadalupe River) . . . This entire port is surrounded by many and large villages of barbarous heathen who are very affable, mild, and docile, and very generous.

The weary group camped beneath a tall redwood called *palo alto,* the name used today for the northern Santa Clara town. The "barbarous heathen" were the Posolmi, a *rancheria* (village) of the Po-

The group traveled up the coast, naming Santa Margarita, Santa Ana, Carpinteria, Gaviota, and Cañada de los Osos, before reaching the mouth of the the Salinas River. However, Portolá and his men did not recognize Monterey Bay from the description left by Cermeño, as they were looking for a well-protected landlocked harbor. The body of water that the expedition looked over from the mouth of the Salinas was hardly a great harbor.

Pressing north along the coast the expedition crossed the Pajaro River and soon came upon *palo colorados,* or redwood trees. Local Indians indicated that a ship was anchored further north and Portolá sent Sergeant José Ortega and a group of scouts to search for what Portolá assumed

joron tribelet. The Castro Indian Mound, located on the San Francisco Bay, was part of the Pojoron tribelet's lands. This mound is the largest in present-day Santa Clara County, measuring 290 feet by 450 feet and standing ten feet high. Archeologists from Stanford University and the University of California, Berkeley, have uncovered seashells, bones, mortars, pestles, beads, soapstone, obsidian tools, and other goods left from several generations of Pojoron Ohlone. The obsidian, used for arrow points, shows that the Ohlone traded with Indians from the Santa Rosa, Clear Lake, and St. Helena areas. The presence of soapstone—used to make pipes, beads, and other ornaments—indicates trading with northern groups and Indians from the Sierra Nevada.

While most of the men camped, José Francisco de Ortega traveled east around the bay in search of the expedition's supply ship, the *San José*. Upon Ortega's return, Portolá pressed south in search once again for Monterey Bay. Portolá and his men trudged back along the way they came. Several men tried to eat acorns like the natives to stave off hunger pains and became ill. The party erected a cross at Carmel Bay and another cross near Monterey Bay, which they still did not recognize, before heading back to San Diego on December 9, 1769. Portolá finally recognized Monterey Bay the following June 3, when he and his party found the oak tree marked by the Vizcaíno expedition in 1602. Fray Serra conducted a mass and founded Mission San Carlos Borroméo, the second mission in Alta California.

On November 12, 1770, Viceroy Antonia de Bucareli, Gálvez's replacement, sent a letter to Pedro Fages, the Spanish governor of California, in the new settlement of Monterey. He ordered Fages to explore the newly discovered Bay of San Francisco and, in cooperation with Fray Junípero Serra, establish a mission to protect the bay for Spanish interests. Bucareli, like his predecessor, was fearful of foreign invasion. Six months later, Fages received the letter. With Fray Crespi, twelve soldiers, a mule skinner, and an Indian, Fages set out northward on May 20, 1771.

The next day they reached the southern end of Santa Clara Valley, near Hollister, and named the area San Bernardino de Sena. Marching on, they camped north of Gilroy on March 22 and named the surrounding valley *Llano de los Robles del Puerto de San Francisco* (Plain of the Oaks of the Port of San Francisco).

Traveling up the west side of the valley through the narrows near San Martin, the small band of men continued on the shore of lake San Benvenuto (now called Venito), which feeds Coyote Creek. On March 24 they continued on and named Penitencia Creek. The following day, the group reached the San Lorenzo Creek in Alameda County.

Turning eastward at San Pablo Bay, the men marched until they could see the Sacramento Valley before them. At this point the tired party turned around and started back. By April 3 the explorers were in the foothills of San Martin near the origins of Coyote Creek and the Pajaro River.

On August 17, 1773, Viceroy Bucareli sent a letter to Francisco Rivera, the new commandant of Monterey, ordering him to explore San Francisco and, with Serra's approval, establish a mission there. Rivera, with sixteen soldiers, two servants, Fray Francisco Palou, and a mule team with provisions for forty days set out for San Francisco on November 23, 1774.

Fray Palou wrote that the party retraced Fages' steps to the Hollister and Gilroy area before turning up the western edge of the valley. On November 28 they

In October 1775 Don Juan Bautista De Anza left Mexico with the first large overland party of California settlers. Leaving the exhausted colonists at Monterey in March 1776, De Anza and a small party of men traveled north to explore the Santa Clara Valley and to choose sites for the mission and presidio at San Francisco. Courtesy, The Bancroft Library

stopped at the old Spanish camp on the San Francisquito Creek. Finding that the Puichons were friendly, the padre and his servants erected a cross at a good place for a mission. The following day the small band of explorers traveled further north, reaching the area of the Cliff House in present-day San Francisco on December 4, 1774. On their return to Monterey, the group reported finding six possible sites for missions, including San Francisco, Santa Cruz, and San Juan Bautista.

In 1775 Juan Bautista De Anza received orders from the viceroy to establish a mission at San Francisco. De Anza's party left from Monterey for San Francisco on March 22, 1776, taking Fray Moraga and Fray Font, a corporal, ten soldiers, and provisions for twenty days. The party camped first on Llagas Creek, then reached and named the Coyote Creek. De Anza and his men traveled on the west side of the valley, reaching Arroyo de San Josef Cupertino on March 25. The following day they reached the Palo Alto tree. In the area of the Guadalupe River and the present location of Moffett Field, the De Anza party came upon three large Ohlone rancherias. After surveying the Palo Alto area, De Anza decided that the San Francisquito Creek area did not have enough water to support a mission.

The explorers found several large villages along a water course they named *Río de Nuestra Señora De Guadalupe*. Near the present location of Moffett field, the explorers met the Ohlone tribelet of the Pojoron people at their village of Posolmi. The well-traveled trail they took became known as El Camino Real, "The King's Highway."

Between January 4 and 6, 1777, José Joaquín Moraga and Fray Tomas de la Pena set out with ten soldiers and their families from the new mission at San Francisco to establish a mission along the banks of the Guadalupe Creek. The Mediterranean climate of the Santa Clara Valley was excellent for the establishment of a mission, as the winters were mild with only a light frost. The dry season, from May through October, was significant for the ripening and harvesting of crops.

Fray Pena conducted the first mass on January 12, 1777, and Fray Junípero Serra named the new mission Santa Clara de Asis in honor of Saint Claire of Assisi, the founder of a religious order, the Poor Clares.

The local Ohlone, the Tares, called the mission area Thamien, or Tamien, although some accounts call the area Socoisuka (abundant laurel trees). The Tares painted themselves with a red dirt they called "mohetka," their word for cinnabar ore (mercury or quicksilver).

Fray Murguia arrived at the new mission site on January 21 with cattle and supplies from San Francisco. The friendly Tares soon acquired a taste for beef and began to steal cattle, which upset the Spanish. The soldiers flogged several Tares before finally killing three people. After this display of force the Tares left the cattle alone, at least for a while.

In May an epidemic at the mission killed several Tares children, most of whom were baptized. The first Spanish baptism was held on July 31, 1777, for the illegitimate son of José Antonia Gonzales and a woman who married another man the following year (the first marriage for the mission). Six months later, in January 1778, José Antonia Garcia became the first recorded Spaniard to die at the mission.

Fray Junípero Serra visited the new site in November 1777 and baptized a Tares boy. The mission fathers baptized sixty-seven Indians, of which only eight were adults, by the end of 1777. That same year the mission recorded twenty-five deaths, most from the epidemic. Thirteen Christian Indians and ten Catechumens lived at the mission while the rest of the baptized children lived at their villages with their parents.

The padres and Indians built the first church with redwood logs. On January 23, 1779, at the height of the rainy season, Mission Santa Clara flooded. After more flooding in February, the fathers moved the mission site south. Fray Murguia designed a new mission in 1781, and the Indians laid a new cornerstone. The new mission's design was the most imposing edifice in Alta California. Unfortunately, Murguia died four days before Fray Serra blessed the new mission, and he was buried within the mission walls.

The friezes on the current replica of the 1781 mission follow patterns of the original, which Indians painted on the front of the smooth walls. Fray Murguia designed the mission to hold 1,000 worshipers. In addition, the compound held two buildings which were used as living quarters for the mission Indians, who divided the buildings into apartments. Two corrals for cattle and sheep completed the rest of the mission grounds. The Indians also constructed a bridge across the Guadalupe River and built a dam to store water for the crops grown by the mission Indians. In 1911, while excavating a trench for a gas main, workers discovered the cornerstone of the 1781 mission complete with artifacts. The site is on the grounds of the Southern Pacific Depot in Santa Clara. The stone and artifacts are on display at the University of Santa Clara Museum.

Under Spanish rule the missions were the core of keeping California safe from foreigners. Presidios, pueblos, and ranchos all had their place, but the Spanish counted on turning the native Indian population into *gente de razon,* or civilized people.

The king of Spain claimed all the land of California and allowed the missionaries to hold that land for the native inhabitants until the Indians were able to take control of their own lives. The Spanish authorities thought that the missions would last for only ten years, during which time the priests were to train the Indians in agriculture, religion, and civilized behavior. After the ten years the Spanish crown would give the mission lands back to Christianized Indians, who would then become Spanish citizens. The role of the missions would then be as parish churches for the new citizens.

According to the Spanish system, the missions would become self-sufficient, and surplus foods grown at the missions would be given to the military presidios to support the soldiers who were keeping California safe from hostile Indians and, more importantly, from foreign intervention.

Scholars maintain two conflicting views of the life-style of missionized California Indians. Basically the two views share the same basic facts: the Indians were baptized, built the mission system, and tended the crops. However, the two views differ in their interpretation as to the hardships endured by the California Indians during the process of becoming *gente de razon.*

Shipping grain and other supplies from Mexico up to Alta California to keep the missions and presidios a viable part of the empire became increasingly difficult for the Spanish. In June 1776 Governor Felipe de Neve and Viceroy Antonio Bucareli decided that Alta California needed settlements to furnish supplies to the presidios. On his trip up the California coast Neve selected sites for a village at Los Angeles and another on the banks of the Río de Guadalupe.

Governor Neve selected Lieutenant-

This humorous Spanish celebration, the "Colgante de Judas," was the symbolic dramatization of the hanging of Judas. The ceremony was preceded by a colorful procession and the gathering of the inhabitants of Spanishtown. Courtesy, Sourisseau Academy

Erected between 1792 and 1800 by mission Indians, this adobe dwelling was originally an apartment in a continuous row of houses built for young Indian couples. It has served as the headquarters and meeting place for the Santa Clara Women's Club since 1907. Courtesy, Santa Clara University Archives

Commander José Joaquín Maraga to escort nine soldiers who knew how to farm, five pobladores, a servant, and some members of Juan Bautista De Anza's colonists living in Monterey to the new pueblo. The ages of the immigrants ranged from two-month-old Juan de Mesa to fifty-eight-year-old Manuel Gonzales, an Apache Indian.

A total of sixty-eight people traveled from San Francisco to the eastern bank of the Guadalupe, about three miles from Mission Santa Clara. In addition the colonists brought their own horses and livestock.

The route to the new Pueblo de San José de Guadalupe was extremely difficult. Seventy-five years after the founding of the pueblo, a Yankee immigrant, William A. Manley, described the journey into San Jose as a constant fight through "willows so thick, and so thickly woven together with wild blackberry vines, wild roses, and other thorny plants, that it appeared at first as if I never could get through." In addition to the natural vegetation obstacles faced by the settlers, grizzly bears freely roamed the valley, remaining a constant threat to the safety of the new pueblo for years to come.

On November 29, 1777, ground was broken, and the new settlement was christened *El Pueblo de San José de Guada-*

lupe in honor of the patron saint of California.

The Santa Clara Valley offered much to the early *pobladores*. The land was the most fertile in Alta California, and the Diablo Range protected the valley from harsh winter winds and storms. To the south the valley closed where the Santa Cruz Mountains, the Diablo Range, and the Gabilan Range drew the valley together just south of Gilroy. The northern portion of the valley touched San Francisco Bay. The valley's warm, dry summers and wet winters and springs reminded Spanish settlers of the climate found in Spain.

The Spanish authorities located the first pueblo close to the mission at Santa Clara to enable the pobladores to have access to the benefits of the padres while expecting the pueblo to supply the mission with excess crops. The pobladores of San Jose were the first settlers in Alta California who were primarily engaged in farming.

The Spanish government gave each new settler a plot of ground to build a house and a field large enough to plant three bushels of maize. In addition, each settler received a regular soldier's pay, the equivalent of ten dollars per month, an allowance of clothing and supplies of $116.17 for each of the first two years, then sixty dollars for each of the next three years, along with daily rations for three years. The Spanish crown provided the heads of families with a loan of two cows, two oxen, two mares, two bulls, two sheep, and two goats, but only one mule. The settlers also received farm equipment and as much land as needed for pasture and timberlands. Furthermore, the government granted the colonists a tax exemption for five years.

The governor required that the settlers build a dam on the Guadalupe for irrigation purposes. They were also required to

Cattle ranching provided a major economic base before and during the American period. Hides and tallow were the medium of exchange in the absence of hard currency. Although perhaps an exaggeration, it is said that early travelers were welcome to the meat, provided the hide was left for the owner. Courtesy, San Jose Historical Museum

sell surplus products to the presidios and to be ready to serve in the defense of the province. They were under probation for five years and were to build homes and irrigation ditches, plant fruit trees as boundary markers, cultivate their land, and keep their farm equipment in order. In addition, each settler was limited to fifty head of cattle, so there would be no monopoly. The excess would go to communal herds. Settlers could not sell their land, nor divide it, but could will their land to one child. Each settler was also required to work on communal projects, such as the dam, ditches, roads and streets, a church, and public buildings, as well as to help till public lands that would provide revenue for the pueblo. The first pueblo was near the present location of the county government building on West Hedding Street.

During the first year the new settlers built a dam and an irrigation ditch, then planted their fields with maize. Personal shelter was quickly thrown together in the first pueblo. Crude thatch huts with an adobe mud coating formed the basic housing in early San Jose. Unfortunately, the

site of the dam was not properly located and winter rains caused flooding and the loss of 350 bushels of corn.

The second year the farmers yielded between 600 and 800 bushels of corn. The second winter, however, was disastrous. The dam collapsed and floods washed away the mud walls of the settlement in January and again in February 1779. The entire valley between the pueblo and the mission turned into a quagmire, and the few miles to the mission became a nine-mile detour.

Not until the pueblo was six years old and numbered eighteen pobladores did the settlers ask to move to higher ground. Change took time under Spanish rule, and the pueblo suffered an additional six winters after the original request before the settlers moved to the present location of downtown San Jose.

The padres at Mission Santa Clara did not appreciate the crown allowing the pueblo to be built in the vicinity of the mission. The padres particularly protested the bad influence the settlers exerted on the Indian neophytes. The settlers were prone to gambling with the Ohlone men and sleeping with the Ohlone women. In addition, the pueblo's cattle wandered onto mission property and mixed with mission cattle. Furthermore, both the mission padres and the pueblo settlers claimed the water in the Guadalupe River. The conflict grew heated enough for the padres to ask the viceroy to move the pueblo out of the area. The viceroy declined and allowed the settlers to stay.

In addition to the conflicts with the padres, the colonists of the young pueblo suffered continual losses from Indian raids on the cattle. The Ohlone had acquired a taste for beef during the founding of Mission Santa Clara and continued to raid the herds. The muddy grounds near the pueblo left the settlers almost helpless to protect their cattle. The only remedy was to stage military expeditions against the offenders.

The pobladores of the young pueblo discovered that corn, beans, and wheat could easily be grown in the valley's favorable climate. The pobladores also planted vineyards and orchards. The first vineyard in the valley was planted by the padres at Mission Santa Clara in 1792, although the first successful vineyard was not planted until 1798. These mission grapes first produced wine in 1802. However, the wine was very poor. By the mid-1820s padres Magin Catala and José Viader transformed the mission's two-acre vineyard into a fairly decent table wine producer.

In addition to wine the padres mixed the fresh unfermented sweet grape juice with aguardiente, a native brandy. The result was Angelica, a California discovery. The brandy was distilled in small copper pot stills.

The pueblo settlers quickly began planting their own family vineyards and produced wine and Angelica. The winemakers crushed grapes with their feet in cowhide vats. After pouring the grape juice into fermenting containers or mixing directly with homemade brandy the settlers added water to any grape pulp left over from the winemaking process and used this mixture to distill more aguardiente.

By the early 1800s the fruit trees planted as field borders began bearing fruit. In addition to wine brandy, the citizens of the pueblo manufactured peach brandy, with or without official sanction. On August 19, 1805, the valley's first horticultural records indicate that Manuel Higuerra was allowed to manufacture "one barrel of peach brandy." Five years later archival records from Mission Santa Clara show that olive orchards and grape vines were in production. Cattle, sheep, and horses quickly multiplied beyond the needs of the small pueblo. During the 1780s the agricultural crops grew to 2,250 bushels, while the livestock increased from 417 to 980. The sheep, however, decreased to a flock of 600.

In 1781 the King of Spain ordered that pobladores in the New World grow hemp and flax as an experiment. In the fall of 1795, Diego de Borica ordered Comisionado Ignacio Vallejo to begin a hemp-growing project in the pueblo. Although the first crop failed during the summer of 1796, the following year proved successful. The pueblo's carpenter constructed machinery to process the hemp, and in 1798 the hemp shipment to San Blas, Mexico, was the equivalent of 625 pounds. Hemp growers in San Jose harvested larger crops than in any other portion of the province. However, when the civil wars errupted in Mexico in 1810 the hemp farmers in San Jose found that their market was cut off.

Although the pobladores in San Jose experienced some early success with hemp production, the settlers were mainly interested in the bare rudiments of survival until they began lucrative trading with foreign merchant and sea otter ships. Until the beginning of the nineteenth century, the pobladores were forced, by royal decree, to limit their commerce to the two yearly ships sent from San Blas. These official trading vessels brought the province manufactured items and the payroll for the soldiers and officials in Alta California. The settlers basically traded wheat for their supplies, although the missions and settlers also shipped tallow to Callao.

In addition to official trading, the pobladores occasionally engaged in some surreptitious trading with foreign trading vessels. The Yankee traders smuggled in luxuries that Spanish authorities refused to authorize aboard the Mexican trading ships. Furthermore, once the revolution against Spain and various Mexican civil wars started in 1810, almost all supplies were cut off from Mexico, and Alta California citizens found that they had to increasingly rely on foreign trading ships.

One American trading ship cost Mexican merchants a loss of $300,000. Finally, after the contraband trade became so intense that Mexican manufacturing firms were losing too much in trade, the Mexico City authorities ordered the illegal trading stopped. However, Governor Pablo Vincent de Solá decided that the only way to raise the needed money to pay his soldiers and to provide the civilian settlers and missions with an outlet for surplus crops was to look the other way from the illegal trading between the Californios and American and Russian hide and tallow traders and sea otter trappers.

After the Mexican takeover in 1822 foreign ships received permission to visit the interior settlements along San Francisco Bay. In the classic book, *Two Years Before the Mast,* Richard Henry Dana, Jr.,

reported that large boats carrying up to 1,000 hides each came out to the trading vessels. With increased trading in hides and tallow, the pobladores of San Jose began cutting back on other agricultural duties until they were working the soil for only two weeks a season—planting and reaping. After secularization of the missions, pueblo residents had a ready supply of inexpensive Indian laborers to work the fields.

Ox-drawn plows made of rough-twisted poles cut shallow grooves into the soil just deep enough to plant vegetables. The Indians cut the ripe wheat high enough to leave enough seed on the stalk to resow the crop naturally. The method worked so well that, if a drought did not kill the plants, the Indians often reaped a third wheat crop.

In addition to trading hides and tallow to the foreign traders, the pobladores traded their surplus wheat with the American fur trappers, as well as with the Russians at Fort Ross. Furthermore, during the 1840s there is evidence of some trade between the pobladores of San Jose and the Sandwich (Hawaiian) Islands.

With the increasing importance of wheat and flour to the economy of the Santa Clara Valley, José María Larios and Juan Balesteros established the first gristmill in the valley in the late 1790s.

In 1806 Meriwether Lewis and William Clark returned to the East Coast after exploring the northwest area from the Mississippi River to the Pacific Coast. They described the west as "richer in beaver and otter than any country on earth." This report played a central role in the development of the North American frontier.

In New France and New England the fur trade grew quickly into one of the first large-scale corporate businesses in the New World. Corporations with headquarters in

London, Paris, New York, Montreal, and St. Louis controlled the fur market. Hiring trappers and supplying the young men with traps, horses, food, boats, whiskey, and trinkets for Indians, the corporation executives sent expeditions into the vast American wilderness to trap beaver and otters. At the end of the season the companies prepared, collected, warehoused, and sold the pelts.

In 1824 the Hudson Bay Company set up operations on the Columbia River in Oregon. The fur market entered a brief period of depression after the War of 1812, but by the 1820 new markets opened up in China and elsewhere, allowing for the expansion of the fur industry. About this time William Ashley, lieutenant governor of Missouri, hired a young trapper to accompany him and his mountain men on Ashley's first trapping venture. The young man was Jedediah Strong Smith, who, while he only spent a decade in the West, was nonetheless one of the most important mountain men during the era of trappers. Dale Lowell Morgan, his biographer, wrote, "he saw and is familiar with the land–from the Missouri River to the Pacific, from Mexico to Canada." Smith discovered the South Pass through the Rockies and was the first white man to travel over the Sierra Nevada.

In November 1826 Smith and his band of trappers set out for California. The following month the explorers arrived in California and were immediately arrested and summoned to San Diego to see the governor, José María Echeandia. Arriving on December 12, Smith met with the suspicious governor three times in four days. The governor felt that the American came into California out of the desert on a military mission, rather than Smith's stated reason, the pursuit of beavers. Smith responded, "I was only a hunter" and that "dire necessity had driven me here."

Echeandia realized that Smith's presence signified the disintegration of the desert barrier against foreigners settling in California. Over the past decade the Spanish Empire broke up and the new Mexican government could not adequately deal with the new threat of foreign settlers.

Finally, the governor allowed Smith and his trappers to leave, but they had to go the way they came, as Governor Echeandia did not want the trappers to explore the northern portion of Alta California. However, once Smith crossed the San Bernardino Mountains and was out of the governor's control, he turned north and entered the San Joaquin Valley looking for beaver.

By the end of April, Smith's men had 1,500 pounds of beaver furs and had explored 350 miles north to the American River area. After an abortive attempt to cross the Sierras, Smith turned south to the Stanislaus to wait until the snow melted.

Smith's presence, however, did not go unnoticed. Father Narciso Duran, president of the missions and living at Mission San José (established in 1789 and located fifteen miles north of the Pueblo San José), wrote a letter to Ignacio Martinez, commandant of San Francisco, on May 16, 1827, reporting that 400 Indians ran away from Mission San José because of pronouncements Smith was making, urging them to return to their old villages. Smith heard of Duran's letter from an Indian, and wrote a letter to the priest on May 19, explaining that he was simply waiting until the snow melted, and then he would leave Alta California.

The Indian uprising at the mission, later investigations revealed, was caused by a disgruntled mission Indian. But Governor Echeandia gave orders "not to let them [Smith's party] advance a single yard, because, though they do not seem to come with any bad intentions, it is not right that they should see what we have and to permit them to map this territory."

The governor ordered Martinez to arrest Smith and bring him into San Jose. When Martinez reached Smith's camp he found the furs and most of the trappers. Smith, however, was blazing the first trail over the Sierra Nevada, while still trying to make the appointed yearly rendezvous in Salt Lake. He became the first white man to cross the Sierras and reached the rendezvous in Utah on July 3, with only a few of his horses still alive.

After recruiting new men and obtaining enough horses and supplies for two years, Smith turned around only ten days after he reached the rendezvous and set out once more for California. Reaching the San Bernardino Valley on August 28, 1827, Smith retraced his old route, finding the California camp two days before his agreed upon deadline of September 20. At this point he decided to travel on to the Mission San José with three of his men to seek new provisions and horses. Upon their arrival at Mission San José, Smith and his men were detained for two weeks before Smith was allowed to travel on to Monterey and talk with the governor.

Governor Echeandia was not pleased to see Smith once again. The governor reminded the trapper that Smith was forbidden to travel outside his original path into California. The governor decided that Smith must leave the country via the same route he originally entered, through the desert and across the Colorado River.

On November 26 Smith and nine trappers, a formidable army of sharpshooters, left San Francisco and traveled through the Santa Clara Valley headed for Mission San José. The trappers drove before them more than 300 horses that

Smith planned to sell to trappers in Salt Lake for fifty dollars apiece; they had cost him ten dollars. After more delays, partly to get his horses in better shape, the group left Mission San José on December 30, 1827.

Rather than returning the way he promised, however, Smith immediately turned northward and began trapping along the Buenaventura (Sacramento River). By this time Smith realized that there was no river cutting through the Sierras to Salt Lake. Finally, on June 14 they reached Crescent City, and nine days later entered Oregon. After being attacked and his party reduced to two men, Smith finally reached the Hudson Bay Company's Fort Vancouver.

Before Smith's travels, California was still a semi-mythical land. Smith was able to shed some light on its mission system, government, and people, but, more importantly, he also knew information about the interior of California, about which even the Californios knew little. The Hudson Bay Company's agent sent dispatches to London filled with information Smith provided. However, this information was purposely misleading, especially regarding Oregon, which Smith described as an inhospitable land to the British agents. In his own dispatches, written to United States government authorities, Smith gave a much different picture, one that helped set in motion a whole generation of settlers who crossed the plains and mountains and settled in Oregon and California.

The Hudson Bay Company quickly reacted to Smith's reports of beaver in California, and by 1829 agents of the company had collected 1,500 beaver skins from the Ohlone living in Santa Clara Valley. The company sold the skins for three United States dollars per pelt to launches sent to Mission San José from trading ships anchored in San Francisco Bay.

CHAPTER TWO

TURMOIL AND REVOLUTION

This Wright photograph of a painting by Andrew P. Hill depicts the Santa Clara Mission as it might have looked in 1849. This church building is no longer standing. Courtesy, San Jose Historical Museum

The inhabitants of the Santa Clara Valley witnessed rapid and radical change during the seven decades after the arrival of the first Spanish expedition in 1769. After the Catholic padres converted the native inhabitants, they built four missions in Santa Clara and several others nearby. The Ohlone culture was essentially destroyed by the influx of the Hispanic settlers, who developed a new economy based on cattle. Change, sudden and devastating, also came to the newcomers as they found themselves displaced by even newer settlers—Americans from the United States. Only sixty-nine years elapsed between the establishment of Mission Santa Clara and the end of the Mexican-American War of 1846. While there are many explanations why Hispanic rule was

so short in the Santa Clara Valley, and indeed over all of Alta California, one episode in early California history holds the key to the demise of the Californios.

Juan Bautista De Anza, the famed explorer of Alta California and the Santa Clara Valley, delivered a report in Mexico City to Viceroy Antonia Bucareli in 1776 concerning the conditions in California and the need to establish a mission on the Colorado River for the Yuma Indians in present-day Arizona. De Anza blazed the only overland trail from Mexico to California in 1774 and realized the importance of maintaining good relations with the Yuma Indians, who were instrumental in the success of De Anza's 1775 expedition into Alta California with the new territory's first civilian settlers.

That same year Padre Francisco Gar-

Mission Santa Clara was the town's nucleus. The college of Santa Clara was founded in 1851. In this 1857 lithograph of the town, the old mission and college buildings can be seen in the center background. Courtesy, Santa Clara University Archives

ces traveled among the Indian tribes on the lower Colorado River area in an attempt to find a better river crossing for the California trail. Garces' explorations took him up to the Bakersfield area and Tulare Lake, then through the Tehachapi Pass and as far east as New Mexico. Garces reported to Viceroy Bucareli that several presidios and missions along the Colorado and Gila rivers were needed.

Viceroy Bucareli sent a plan detailing the establishment of two presidios in the Colorado River area to the proper authorities at the Ministry of the Indies in Spain. Before the ministry acted upon Bucareli's plan, the Minister of the Indies died and the new minister decided to give the control over the Spanish possessions north of Mexico to Teodoro de Croix. Croix, however, did little for Alta California and turned down the request for new presidios along the Colorado and Gila rivers.

In July 1777 Croix decided to send Padre Garces and a few other priests into the Yuma area with a few gifts and enough provisions for the missionaries,

rather than spending the money necessary to establish presidios and missions. When the missionaries arrived with scanty provisions, the Yumas, who associated Christianity with gifts and food, were unhappy. Two years later Croix decided to establish a mission among the Yuma Indians.

Padre Garces asked for an army detachment consisting of a dozen soldiers and their families, along with sufficient gifts to keep the Yumas content. When Garces set out once again for the Colorado River area, however, only the soldiers accompanied him; their wives and children remained behind. In 1780 Croix finally decided to allow the establishment of two Spanish settlements, Purísmima Concepción and San Pedro y San Pablo de Bicuñer, in the Colorado River area.

Unfortunately, by 1780 the Yuma Indians were not as receptive to the missions and the Spanish did little to help the Indians adjust. Rather than asking the Indians where the new settlers could live, the Spanish simply took what land they wanted. Furthermore, the Spanish did little

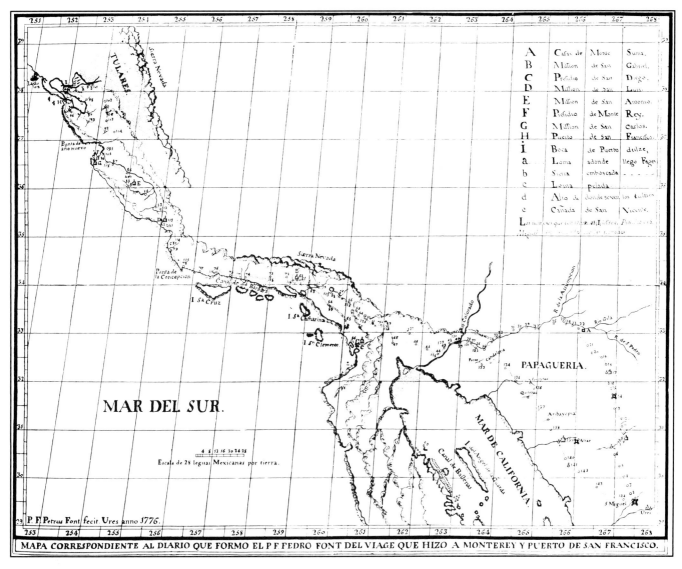

A	Cafas de	Monte	Suma.
B	Mifsion	de San	Gabriel.
C	Prefidio	de San	Diego.
D	Mifsion	de San	Luis.
E	Mifsion	de San	Antonio.
F	Prefidio	de Monte	Rey.
G	Mifsion	de San	Carlos.
H	Puerto	de San	Francisco.
i	Boca	de Puerto	dulce,
a	Loma	adonde	llego Fages
b	Sierra	emboscada	- - - -
c	Loma	pelada	
d	Alto de	donde seven los tulares	
e	Cañada	de San	Vicente.

P. F. Petrus Font fecit Ures anno 1776.

MAPA CORRESPONDIENTE AL DIARIO QUE FORMO EL P F PEDRO FONT DEL VIAGE QUE HIZO A MONTEREY Y PUERTO DE SAN FRANCISCO.

to prevent their cattle from wandering among the Yuma cornfields and pumpkin patches.

Finally, in mid-July 1781 Captain Fernando Rivera y Moncada and a party of forty California-bound settlers arrived in the area. The emigrants allowed their cattle to wander among the Indians' crops before crossing the Colorado and journeying on to the coast. Captain Rivera and his soldiers remained to freshen up the livestock.

On the night of July 17, the Yuma Indians attacked the two Spanish settlements. The attackers killed all the men and enslaved the women and children. The following morning Rivera's party came under attack. During the fight, the Yumas killed Rivera and his men.

The Spanish mounted several punitive expeditions to no avail. However, the Yumas accepted a ransom for the remaining survivors. While Croix tried to blame Captain De Anza for the disaster because he did not warn the Spanish authorities about the possibility of danger, the real problem was the delay in establishing a strong Spanish presence. Croix simply could not see the problem in the same perspective as Captain De Anza, Viceroy Bucareli, and Padre Garces.

Chaplain Pedro Font accompanied Don Juan Bautista De Anza on his explorations in California. Font attended to religious matters as well as keeping a faithful diary of their experiences. This map corresponds to his diary. Courtesy, The Bancroft Library

33

The inability to establish and maintain an overland trail from old Mexico into Alta California prevented both Spanish and Mexican authorities from properly colonizing and communicating with their far-flung outpost. If the Hispanics had been able to colonize Alta California by a land route and if these people had discovered gold in the Sierra Nevadas, more people would have come into California from New Spain. This would have acted as a deterrent to American settlers and the subsequent takeover of Alta California by the United States.

With the closing of the only land route into California, Spanish authorities in Mexico City and in Spain remained adamant that foreigners were not welcome in the northern Pacific Coast colony. The first non-Hispanic and non-Indian to enter the Santa Clara Valley was Captain George Vancouver in 1792. Six years later the explorer published his book *A Voyage of Discovery* describing the Santa Clara Valley as being a swampland, yet possessing excellent potential for agriculture.

In 1806 José Joaquín de Arrillaga, the governor of California, issued an order prohibiting trade with foreign vessels, allowing local authorities to seize and detain crews and vessels from foreign nations. In addition to the governor's stern pronouncement, Fray Estevan Tapis, the president of the mission system, issued orders to the missions prohibiting trade with foreigners.

A few foreigners, however, disregarded Spanish warnings and entered California waters to trade hard-to-find manufactured items from Europe and New England for hides and tallow, sea otter skins, and other raw materials. The sea traders felt that they had a right to trade in California and characterized the actions of Spanish authorities as reprehensible.

The Spanish became increasingly agitated with the arrival of foreigners fearing that reports from the merchants would inevitably contain word of how poorly defended California was. These fears were justified. In the first account of California printed in the United States, Captain William Shaler of the *Lelia Byrd* reported in 1808 to the readers of the *American Register* that California was an easy and desirable prey for some foreign nation.

During the last decades of Spanish rule, a few foreigners did manage not only to trade with the Santa Clara Valley Californios, but to remain in the valley. In December 1808 five American sailors arrived in the Pueblo de San José claiming to be shipwrecked. The alcalde quickly arrested the men and set them to work in the presidio to earn their food. Within a few months the Spanish shipped the Americans, who were really deserters from the American ship *Mercury,* to San Blas.

The first foreign settler allowed to remain in California was John Cameron. Cameron took the name of Gilroy when he ran away from his home in Inverness, Scotland, as a teenager. He arrived in Monterey aboard the English trading ship *Isaac Todd* and was left in port in 1814 to recover from the effects of scurvy. Sometime between 1814 and 1815 Gilroy arrived in the Santa Clara Valley. He and all subsequent foreigners were allowed to remain in California only if they swore allegiance to the Spanish Crown and became baptized as Roman Catholics. During Easter in 1821 Gilroy married Maria Clara de la Asuncion Ortega at Mission San Juan Bautista. Gilroy, who worked as a soapmaker and millwright, settled on a portion of the San Ysidro Rancho inherited by his wife.

In mid-January 1816 two American ships, the *Lydia* under the command of Captain Henry Gyzelaar and the *Albatross* under the command of Captain William Smith, anchored off Pt. Refugio north of Santa Barbara. Soldiers from Santa Barbara under the command of Comandante José de la Guerra, Sergeant Cárlos Carrillo, and Santiago Arguello captured both captains and some crew members who were ashore. The defenseless *Lydia* was quickly seized by the soldiers, but the well-armed *Albatross* managed to keep the Spanish soldiers at bay. Captain Smith refused to surrender his ship and finally the remaining crew, after promising to return in eight days, sailed away. The *Albatross*, however, did not return.

After investigations in Santa Barbara and Monterey, Governor Pablo Vincente Sola decided to allow the *Lydia* to leave with the crew of the *Albatross*. Thomas W. Doak, however, stayed in Monterey, becoming the first American settler in California. Doak began instruction in the Catholic faith and the padres at Mission San Cárlos baptized him on December 22, 1816. Two years later, the Mission San Juan Bautista records indicate, Doak

painted the church. On October 20, 1819, the viceroy permitted him to marry and settle in California. On November 8, 1820, Doak married a daughter of Mariano Castro, the holder of both Rancho Solis and Rancho Las Animas in southern Santa Clara County.

The same year that Doak arrived in Monterey, Robert Livermore, an Englishman, arrived in San Jose. Livermore's arrival in the small pueblo marked the beginning of an era of change as more and more foreigners began settling in and around the Santa Clara Valley. Livermore later married into the Higuera family and moved to their lands in what is now the Livermore Valley in Alameda County.

Perhaps the most influential foreigner to arrive in the valley was Antonio María Suñol. Suñol, a Spaniard, arrived in San Francisco on October 16, 1817, on the *Bordelais,* a French-armed merchantman. The ship remained on the bay waters for three weeks, waiting for several crew members to recover from scurvy. When the *Bordelais* set sail once more, Suñol

During the 1840s and 1850s many Americans made the arduous journey across the plains to California. Some settled in the Santa Clara Valley. In 1914 Andrew P. Hill painted *Crossing the Plains,* a memorial to the pioneer journey. Courtesy, San Jose Historical Museum

This adobe ruin was once the gracious home of Don Antonio Suñol. A prominent and active citizen in both the Mexican and early American periods, Suñol was renowned for his warm and generous hospitality. His residence stood on the west side of Market Street Plaza until 1904. Courtesy, San Jose Historical Museum

and three other sailors stayed behind. Whether these men were still sick or were deserters is unclear. However, a year later on October 20, 1818, after the ship returned once again and prepared to leave for France, Suñol was living in San José. The seaman became the first Spaniard to arrive in the pueblo without traveling through Mexico first as a colonist or soldier.

In addition to being the pueblo's first permanent foreign immigrant, Suñol was the best educated person in the area. As a young boy he left war-torn Barcelona in 1808 and attended school in Bordeaux, France, where he studied engineering and architecture. After serving briefly as a cadet in the French navy, Suñol sailed to the New World.

The young Spaniard soon found his education in great demand. As one of the few people in the pueblo who could write, Suñol often wrote private letters as well as business and legal correspondence for San Jose's citizens. Around 1820 the young man opened the first mercantile store in the pueblo on the plaza. In addition to selling various trading goods the Spaniard distilled and sold liquor in the first such establishment in the valley.

Although Governor Luis Arguello asked San Jose's alcalde, Juan Alvires, to investigate Suñol's establishment and report on any harmful effects from the Spaniard's liquor sales, Suñol continued to expand his liquid product.

In addition to liquor and dry goods, Suñol sold redwood lumber—operating probably the region's first lumber yard, he obtained the split and whipsawed lumber from Americans working in the Santa

Cruz Mountains.

In 1822, the year after Mexico secured independence from Spain, Suñol joined other San Jose citizens in swearing allegiance to the new government in Mexico City. On September 7, 1823, Suñol married Maria de los Dolores Bernal, daughter of one of the pueblo's leading citizens, José Joaquín Bernal. Bernal owned an extensive herd of cattle on lands south of the pueblo that became known as the Rancho de Santa Teresa. Bernal, an ex-soldier, quickly recognized the business skills of his new son-in-law and let the young man manage the Bernal herd. As the Spaniard spoke both French and Spanish, he was better able to conduct business with foreign hide and tallow traders than his fellow citizens. Soon Suñol found himself as the negotiator for many other rancheros.

Furthermore, Suñol's own store generated many hides during the year, hides being the accepted medium of trade since few people had cash. Whenever a trading ship ventured into the San Francisco Bay waters near Alviso, Suñol shipped all available hides down the Guadalupe River out to the waiting vessel.

In addition to being the pueblo's semi-official middleman, Suñol also acted as San Jose's banker. Although the pueblo's citizens did not have much money, occasionally Suñol took in hard currency and stored the silver or gold in a redwood strongbox at the store. The store was the only place to safely keep valuables. Furthermore, Suñol's customers often asked for loans of hard money, and thus Suñol found himself in the banking business.

Suñol began purchasing the land surrounding his store, located on the western side of the plaza. Suñol soon became the wealthiest man in the pueblo, but rather than being a miser, the storekeeper seemed to extend credit quite liberally. A devout

Catholic, Suñol also donated a lot on the northeast corner of the plaza to the padres at Mission Santa Clara for the establishment of a new church for the pueblo.

In addition to Suñol's contributions to the pueblo church, he became a frequent contributor to Mission Santa Clara. Through his good will and position as a leading businessman, Suñol became politically prominent. When the Mexican government established the pueblo's first post office in 1826 the authorities elected Suñol to the post he held until 1829. In the 1830s Suñol became the attorney and registrar, or sindico, for the pueblo. The following decade Suñol became the subprefect and had the responsibility of enforcing the laws and ordinances of Governor Juan Bautista Alvarado, maintaining order, imposing fines, supervising local elections, and serving as the liaison between the district and the government in Monterey. Suñol's district ranged from north of San Juan Bautista to the pueblo de Branciforte and the Pueblo de San José. In addition, when the citizens did not elect an alcalde in the elections of 1841, Suñol assumed that role as well.

Although considered a foreigner and as such coming under the Mexican government's 1830 proclamation demanding that Spaniards leave California, a provision of the order allowed Suñol to remain in San Jose. While a few foreigners did settle in California before the Mexican Revolution of 1821, most foreigners settled after the change of government. While the Mexico City authorities did not really want foreigners, they did realize that if foreign governments were to be kept out of California, Mexico needed more people. Civilian settlers were always a problem in Alta California from the days of Fray Junípero Serra.

The period after the Spanish gave up control of Alta California, the Mexican era, can be seen as a period of transition from one rule to another. Mexico did little in the province, other than to send governors and a few soldiers. During the twenty-five years that Mexico City controlled the territory, French, English, American, and other traders increased their presence as they searched for sea otters or were engaged in the hide and tallow trades. Furthermore, the greater numbers of ships led to more sailors deserting or being left behind to recover from the scurvy that plagued seamen until the British discovered the use of lime juice in 1795.

California settlements such as Yerba Buena, New Helvetia, and Sonoma became strongholds for foreigners during the Mexican era. The new settlers found that if they could prove their good intentions, swear allegiance to Mexico, and convert to Catholicism they could stay.

On April 21, 1828, the Mexican government passed a colonization law authorizing foreigners to live in California. The law opened up the province for settlers with the provisions of allegiance to the government and baptism into the Catholic faith. By 1830, 150 foreigners resided in California. Many of these men converted and became naturalized citizens of Mexico. However, few had any strong attachment to the government in Mexico City. The young men married California women and a few acquired vast acres of land. Other immigrants became quite active in commercial affairs.

William Willis, who arrived in California between 1827 and 1828, settled in the Pueblo de San José in 1828. After gaining a large herd of cattle, Willis applied for a land grant, but the governor turned down his request. The commandant of San Francisco granted Willis a rancho, but the governor fined the impetuous Willis, who was

The first town hall, or "juzgado," which was probably erected in the late 1820s, stood in the intersection of Market and Post streets until 1850. It consisted of three rooms: the alcalde's office, a courtroom, and a jail. The city council declared it a public nuisance in 1850 and it was dismantled. The adobe bricks were used by J.D. Hoppe to construct a two-story store at Market and Santa Clara. Courtesy, Sourisseau Academy

living in San Jose in 1841 with a wife and child.

The year after Willis arrived, John Burton settled in San Jose. Burton, the captain of the *Juan Battey,* was forced to settle in California after his ship sunk near San Diego in 1825. Burton managed to blend into the fabric of San Jose quite well. In 1831 he married Juana Galindo and six years later became a regidor for the pueblo. He served as San Jose's alcalde for the first two years after the American takeover.

One of the most important foreigners during the Mexican period was James Alexander Forbes. Forbes, a Scot, arrived

in California in 1831 aboard the whaler *Fanny* after living in Chile for a number of years. The following year Forbes was appointed majordomo at Mission Santa Clara and two years later, in 1834, was both married and naturalized. By 1836 he served as the Hudson Bay Company's agent in Alta California and held a few positions in San Jose government. In 1841 Forbes moved to Monterey, where he became the British vice-council. After the Mexican-American War, Forbes returned to San Jose to supervise the Almaden quicksilver mines.

James W. Weeks also arrived in California on the whaler *Fanny.* After deserting

in San Francisco, Weeks wandered to the Pueblo de San José, where he later married Ramona Pinto.

Of the approximately 700 people who lived in the Pueblo de San José by 1835, forty were foreigners, mostly Americans and Englishmen. The pueblo possessed about forty homes. While the number of foreign settlers in California began to rise in the decade of the 1830s due to the colonization law, only about fifty men came overland into the province before 1841, a dozen of whom came with the intent of living permanently. Of the various overland parties, only two crossed the Sierra Nevada before the Bartleson-Bidwell party of 1841, Jedediah Smith and Joseph Redeford Walker. The rest of the overland parties came into the region from Oregon or by the southern route via New Mexico. However, as newspapers reported what the fur trappers had to say about California, adventuresome young men began looking westward.

The overland emigrants typically came from small-town rural farming backgrounds in the Midwest and upper South and were looking for better farmland. Other emigrants came to California to further their professional careers. As adults they were forced to move on when older brothers inherited the family farm. An émigré usually came from the middle class and had to work in order to accumulate the average of $600 for the cost of the trip to California. Further, once they crossed the Sierras and found a place to settle they needed at least another $500 to survive until they harvested their first crop.

Newspapers throughout the United States speculated on the future boundaries of the nation during the late 1830s and into the 1840s. During this period the term *Manifest Destiny* became a part of the American language. Under this doc-

trine expansion was believed to be prearranged or preordained in heaven. While the exact area for national expansion was not clearly defined, some people felt that the Pacific Ocean would be the proper border of the United States. Other people thought in terms of the whole of the North American continent. Still others looked at the entire hemisphere. Basically Americans felt that the United States was a nation that other people would want to join in the great democratic experiment.

James Alexander Forbes had an active career: grantee of Rancho El Potrero de Santa Clara; British Vice-Consul; superintendent of the New Almaden Quicksilver mines; and the builder and operator of the Santa Rosa Brand Flour Mill, in what is now Los Gatos. Courtesy, William A. Wulf Collection

Martin Murphy, Sr., joined forces in 1844 with Dr. John Townsend and Captain Elisha Stephens to bring the first wagon train through the Sierra Nevada, opening the most practical overland route into California. Murphy and his sons owned large tracts of land in the county, including present-day Sunnyvale and Morgan Hill. Courtesy, San Jose Historical Museum

As the American expansionists began looking at California, they reported on Mexico's failure to improve this modern-day Eden. Editors wrote that the local government was almost in a state of anarchy and that the local population remained content to do as little as possible to better their lives. Newspaper readers came to believe that Americans could teach the Californios how to properly develop their lands.

These proclamations did not go unnoticed by authorities in Mexico City and Monterey. In an effort to discourage Yankee immigration, the Mexican government sent orders that all foreigners must possess a legal passport. The events in Texas of 1836 were very much in the thoughts of Mexican officials.

In the fall of 1840 California fever hit Platte County, Missouri. In public meet-ings, 500 people signed a pledge to meet the following May at Sapling Grove, Kansas, to journey overland to California. However, in the spring only one pledge signer, John Bidwell, left Missouri for Kansas. Bidwell, a twenty-one-year-old former school teacher, managed to talk three other young men into joining him: Robert H. Thomes, George Henshaw, and Michael C. Nye. The four adventurers set out for the gathering place in May and met up with other small parties along the Kansas River. John Bartleson headed one of the small groups, in all totaling sixty-three people. In addition, another seventeen, including Catholic and Protestant missionaries, accompanied the California group until they neared Salt Lake in Utah.

On August 27, after traveling all spring and summer, the California group camped in the eastern flank of the Sierras and slaughtered some of the oxen after eating all their provisions. By September 15 the weary travelers faced up to the inevitable and abandoned their wagons. Earlier in their journey the party traveled too far south and was forced to take a detour in search of water.

After more bad luck the travelers found themselves on October 16 with only three half-starved oxen left, and they were still facing the Sierras. Throughout the remainder of October the tired emigrants struggled up the mountains in the Sonora Pass area. Finally, on October 31 the group looked out upon the Stanislaus Valley.

After spending a day hunting deer the refreshed travelers arrived at Dr. John Marsh's rancho at the foot of Mount Diablo. During the previous year Marsh sent many letters of encouragement to friends in Missouri, which editors reprinted in frontier newspapers. However, being a Mexican citizen, Marsh was required to inform the authorities in Monterey of the

Left:
Josiah Belden arrived in San Jose in 1841 as a member of the Bidwell-Bartelson party, and was immediately jailed by suspicious Mexican officials. After his release he successfully engaged in the mercantile business. Belden was elected San Jose's first mayor. Courtesy, San Jose Historical Museum

Far left:
The first organized group of American settlers came to California by land in 1841. These settlers were led by John Bidwell, a twenty-one-year-old schoolteacher, and John Bartelson, a wagon master and land speculator. Courtesy, San Jose Public Library, California Room

arrival of the thirty-one Americans.

After resting for two days, half of the travelers journeyed on to San José, where Sub-prefect Antonio Suñol arrested them for not having proper passports and placed the men in the calaboose. Suñol then referred the matter to General Mariano Vallejo.

On November 13, 1841, the general gave the Americans temporary passes until they took the necessary steps to obtain permanent visas. The only condition placed on the settlers was that they find local citizens of good character to post a bond for their behavior. Vallejo recommended to five of the party that they travel up to his rancho in Sonoma as his guests to see if they might like to settle there.

Due to the relaxed immigration laws under Mexican rule, the population of San Jose jumped from 524 people in 1831 to an estimated 900 by 1845. Most of the new arrivals resided within the pueblo limits and most of the new settlers were Americans.

The Yankees brought with them a distinct feeling that the American form of democracy was superior to any other form of government. They did not feel that Alta California should be governed as a colony by Mexico, and from the onset began working with similarly-minded Californios. The sentiments of the American settlers were echoed by President Andrew Jackson, who in 1835 attempted to purchase the San Francisco Bay area from Mexico. By 1845 Secretary of State James Buchanan wrote Thomas O. Larkin, the American Council in Monterey, that if the Mexican people wanted help in securing their independence and would join the Union, then the United States government would do what it could to help.

Helping the Californios plot revolutions seemed to be a pastime for the transplanted Yankees. In July 1836 the Californios forced Governor Mariano Chico to flee California after a series of disputes erupted between the Mexican governor and the native Californios.

The Californios, especially the younger men in their twenties who held minor positions in the Monterey government, became increasingly upset in the years after the Mexican revolution, as they felt that nothing had really changed for California. Mexico, like Spain before, continued to control the government of California by appointing Mexican officials to the post of governor. In 1836 Juan Bautista Alvarado and José Castro plotted to overthrow Governor Nicholás Gutiérrez, who followed Chico as interim governor.

Both Juan Bautista Alvarado and José Castro were members of the semi-aristocratic families who obtained their education in Monterey. These young men, like all of their peers, identified themselves as Californios, not as Mexicans.

Alvarado was born at Monterey in 1809. He held several posts with the Monterey government from 1827 until 1836. After the revolution Alvarado served as revolutionary governor from December 7, 1836, until July 9, 1837, when he again recognized Mexican rule in California. The Mexican government appointed Alvarado governor on November 24, 1839, and he served until December 31, 1842.

José Castro was the grandson of Sergeant Macario Castro, who was a very prominent settler in the Santa Clara Valley. Sergeant Castro arrived in California in 1784 and held various posts in the Pueblo de San José from 1788 through 1807. José Castro's father, José Tiburcio Castro, came to California with his father in 1784, and he too became a soldier. José Tiburcio Castro served as alcalde for the Pueblo de San José twice and held several other government posts.

After Governor Gutiérrez dissolved the *diputacion* Alvarado quarreled with the governor, who threatened to lock the young man up for insubordination. At this point Alvarado and Chico decided that they had to raise an army to overthrow Mexican rule. Alvarado traveled to So-

noma to gain the support of his uncle, General Mariano Guadalupe Vallejo, the ranking Mexican military officer in California. Vallejo, however, was non-committal, but sent the young man to San Jose by boat to see if he could muster an army there.

In San Jose, Alvarado found support from the citizens of the pueblo and there met with José Castro, who had raised a small band in San Juan Bautista. Antonio Buelna, a former school teacher in San Jose and Monterey, joined Alvarado and Castro in San Jose, where the two leaders placed Buelna in charge of the volunteers from Pueblo de San José.

Alvarado knew most of the foreigners in Monterey, having acted as translator and clerk for many firms there. Before he was forced to flee, he received encouragement from the foreigners, especially the Americans. Now when he needed to raise an army he was able to call upon the leader of the American mountain men, Isaac Graham, for support.

Isaac Graham was a native of Kentucky who was raised in the wilds of Tennessee. A fur trapper and mountain man, Graham followed Jedediah Smith's trail into Southern California between 1833 and 1835. He established a whiskey distillery at Natividad, near Salinas, and was the leader of the American mountain men in Northern California. In later years Graham claimed that Alvarado told the mountain men that as governor he would sever ties with Mexico, and California would become an independent state. Furthermore, according to Graham, Alvarado made a promise to give Graham and his sharpshooters land and horses.

Although Alvarado later denied Graham's claims, there is no doubt that Alvarado wanted Graham and his mountain men to join the revolution since they were unquestionably the best riflemen in Califor-

nia. Furthermore, in 1839 Alvarado rewarded Antonio Buelna for his part in the
revolution by granting him Rancho San
Francisquito. The 1,500-acre rancho started
at the famed redwood El Palo Alto and
included land that later became Stanford
University.

On November 3, 1836, Graham and a
force numbering between thirty to fifty
sharpshooters joined Alvarado's force that
included a few Indians and about 100 Californios. The rebels gathered at the outskirts of Monterey and after one shot of
Castro's cannon Governor Nicholás Gutiérrez surrendered.

Although Alta California was free from
Mexican rule for the next few years, political harmony did not exist. Internal squab-
bles continued to erupt between the politicians residing in the southern portion of
the province and those residing closer to
Monterey. In 1840 a local priest told Alvarado that Isaac Graham and his American followers planned to overthrow the
government, which was once again loyal
to Mexico.

On the morning of April 7, 1840, a
party of Californios under the leadership of
José Castro surrounded Graham's shack at
Natividad. The Californios kicked in the
door and quickly placed Graham and a
few of his followers under arrest. Throughout the rest of the month the Californios
arrested 120 foreigners.

In an effort to rid the province of potential revolutionaries, Alvarado charged
Graham and forty-six of his fellow trappers
and other foreigners with conspiracy to
overthrow the government. The Californios
placed the men on the next available boat
for Mexico. The governor's actions met
with the approval of many of California's
foreign residents. Graham and his mountain men were felt to be a menace to society.

After they had been in a Mexican jail

José María Hernandez,
one of the grantees of the
Rancho Rinconada de los
Gatos, posed with one of
his sixteen children in this
1855 photograph taken in
San Jose. Sebastian Peralta
and Hernandez were
granted the rancho in 1840
by Governor Juan Bautista
Alvarado, although they
occupied the rancho as
early as 1824. Courtesy,
William A. Wulf Collection

for several months, the British minister in Mexico took up the case of Graham and his followers. After a few more months the Mexican court acquitted the men, released them, and gave them free passage back to California. In July 1841 the citizens of Monterey were surprised to see Graham and twenty-four of his fellow trappers disembark from a ship.

The Mexican and Californian governments had good cause to suspect the Americans. In September 1842 the American commander of the Pacific naval squadron, Commodore Thomas Ap Catesby Jones, heard a false report that the United States and Mexico were at war. Acting under established orders to capture Alta California in the event of war, Commodore Jones sailed into Monterey and seized the province on October 19, 1842.

When word of the American occupation of Monterey reached Santa Cruz, a group of Americans gathered together and raised the American flag. James Weeks, later the alcalde in San Jose, was a member of the crowd, as was Josiah Belden, San Jose's first mayor under American rule. Belden climbed the flagpole and attached the stars and stripes.

After a few hours Jones realized his mistake and offered his apology to the Monterey authorities. The new governor of California, Manuel Micheltorena, happened to be in Los Angeles during the incident and Jones sailed south to explain the situation in person. Although the incident was quickly over, Mexican and Californian authorities were put on notice as to the intentions of the Americans.

In July 1844 Governor Micheltorena received dispatches from Mexico stating that Texas had signed an annexation treaty with the United States of America— Mexico and the United States would soon be at war. Micheltorena quickly placed California on a war footing. The governor ordered the evacuation of Monterey, as the seaside city would be too hard to defend, and reestablished the government inland at San Juan Bautista. He ordered all male citizens between the ages of fifteen and sixty, including naturalized citizens, into the army. Finally, Micheltorena established nine military companies. He named Antonio Maria Pico as the captain of the San Jose company.

However, the citizens of San Jose were not willing to join Governor Micheltorena. They, like other Californios, were outraged with the governor for bringing 300 *cholos* (ex-convicts) into California to act as the governor's guards. These men were a menace to society, as they seemed to establish their own laws. They took whatever they wanted and now, after several complaints to the governor with no results, the Californios were ready to revolt once again.

Manuel Castro organized his own army in San Jose and quickly found volunteers from the Santa Clara Valley, as well as other pueblos and ranchos in the northern district of California. Merchants in San Francisco sent military supplies to Castro, and Charles Weber and William Gulnac set out to raise a company of American sharpshooters.

Weber owned a store in the pueblo and was more than willing to aid in any attempt to rid the province of Micheltorena's thieving men. Gulnac, a native of Hudson City, New York, arrived on the *Volunteer* in 1833. The following year after settling in San Jose, Gulnac converted to Catholicism and was naturalized. Gulnac married Isabel Cesena, and they had six children. By 1838 he was engaged as a surveyor, and the following year he became a regidor. Gulnac served on the first jury in San Jose in 1848, before passing away in 1851.

The foreign citizens of San Jose took John Sutter into their confidence, telling him of their plans. Sutter, however, wanted no part of a revolution and after traveling to Monterey to inform Governor Micheltorena about the conspirators' plans, the Swiss landholder returned to his rancho to raise an army to fight the rebels.

In the meantime Castro and Alvarado conferred with General Vallejo. The general then spoke with the governor, informing him that there would not be a revolution if the cholos left California. Micheltorena, however, refused to take the Californios' instructions and, with the information supplied by Sutter, decided to march with an army of 150 men on San Jose and the rebels on November 22. By November 27 the governor's army was only twelve miles southeast of San Jose. That night and throughout the following day the army camped on Juan Alvires' Laguna Seca Rancho.

Scouts for the rebel army, numbering 220 men, including Weber's sharpshooters, alerted Castro to the moves of Micheltorena's army. The insurgents quickly gathered at Santa Clara on November 28. That evening, during a rain storm, Castro's force moved down the valley. Castro and Weber planned to surprise Micheltorena's men during the night. Weber's two companies of riflemen, numbering between forty and sixty men each, sneaked to within 200 yards of Micheltorena's camp when one of the sharpshooter's rifles accidentally discharged. At this point, with surprise no longer in their favor, the Americans scattered into the nearby woods.

Rather than risk a head-on skirmish, the two sides spent November 29 and 30 negotiating. The two armies drilled during the daylight hours in an effort to show their respective military strength. In the end, although Micheltorena had the advantage of two or three field pieces, the governor decided against risking his men to the abilities of the American riflemen and agreed to send the cholos back to Mexico.

During the evening of December 1, 1844, both sides signed the Treaty of Campo de Santa Teresa, also known as the Treaty of Rancho de Alvires or Treaty of Laguna Seca. In any war there is a loser, even in a war with no casualties. In the case of the November revolution, the loser was Juan Alvires, who was forced to host Micheltorena's army. The expenses were not reimbursed by the governor, and the following year Alvires' rancho was auctioned to pay the debts amassed by Micheltorena's cholo army. William Fisher bid an unheard of sum of $6,000 for the 23,040 acres comprising Rancho Laguna Seca.

In the meantime John Sutter returned to the Sacramento Valley and raised an army of 220 men complimented with a brass cannon. On January 1, 1845, Sutter and his army set out for the Pueblo de San José, which Sutter determined to be the center of rebellion in Alta California.

When the citizens of San Jose heard about the approaching army, they realized that the pueblo was unprotected. The rebel army had disbanded a month earlier and San Jose now had only fifty men for defense. In an effort to avert needless bloodshed, Charles Weber rode out to negotiate with Sutter. Sutter, however, was in no mood to discuss anything with an enemy of Mexico and placed Weber in irons.

The fears of the merchants in San Jose were well-founded, for when Sutter's army entered Mission San José they began looting. When word reached the Pueblo de San José of the capture of Weber and the havoc at the mission, the citizens panicked. The remaining rebels fled while the merchants and shopowners locked their doors.

Charles M. Weber, a member of the Bidwell-Bartelson Party, settled in San Jose in 1841. He took a prominent part in the conflict between the United States and Mexican forces. A merchant and large landowner, he became very wealthy. In 1850 he founded the town of Stockton, which he named after Commodore Robert F. Stockton. Courtesy, San Jose Public Library, California Room

When Sutter and his army reached the pueblo, James Forbes, Antonio Suñol, and William Gulnac attempted to talk Sutter out of joining Governor Micheltorena, who had returned to Monterey after signing the Treaty of Campo de Santa Teresa. Sutter, however, refused any peace overtures and rode south down through the Santa Clara Valley.

Riding out in front of Sutter's main force in the southern Santa Clara Valley a group of scouts managed to capture the rebel commander, Manuel Castro, near John Gilroy's rancho. Fortunately for Castro, some of his men managed to surround Castro's capturers, who agreed to let Castro free in return for their own freedom.

Governor Micheltorena decided to regroup his army after learning of the approach of Sutter's forces. On January 9, 1845, the two armies joined forces on the Salinas River. The combined army numbered 400 men and was clearly the dominant military force in California.

Alvarado and Castro realized that now Governor Micheltorena would never recognize the Treaty of Campo de Santa Teresa. The rebel leaders quickly raised a small 100-man army. A force of this size would be powerless against Micheltorena's army with four times the manpower, and the rebels decided on a forced march through the Salinas Valley along El Camino Real to Los Angeles. There in the southland the rebels would raise an army capable of facing the governor's army.

The small force managed to elude Micheltorena in the Salinas Valley and reached Southern California in February. After joining Pío Pico, who became the rebel governor after recruiting 300 men from the southern portion of the province. Castro remained in his accustomed role as the rebel commander. The new army, now consisting of about 400 mounted men, rode out to the Cahuenga Pass to challenge the governor's army.

On February 20, 1845, the armies began a two-day artillery battle, in addition to the usual parades and military maneuvers. During the bloodless battle, foreigners from both sides held a meeting. Pío Pico agreed that all of Governor Micheltorena's promises, including land grants, would be awarded to the foreigners fighting with the loyal army. At this point John Sutter, to whom Micheltorena had promised a land grant in Santa Barbara, arrived and tried to convince his men to rejoin the loyalists. The foreigners, however, had had enough of California politics and decided to let the Mexicanos and Californios do what they wished.

Governor Micheltorena realized that his force was much too small to face the Californios. On February 22, 1845, he signed another treaty and agreed to leave California. Micheltorena turned the governorship over to Pío Pico, while Castro became the military commandant of Alta California.

Although the Californios once again controlled their province, the basic internal sectional problems between the northern and southern Californios did not vanish. The natural animosity between the two sections of the province was heightened when Governor Pico moved the capital south from Monterey to Los Angeles.

In an attempt to ease the growing tensions between the north and south, General Mariano Vallejo wrote to the President of Mexico expressing his opinion that Los Angeles was not the best place for the capital of California. Instead Vallejo promoted the city of Santa Clara which, he wrote, was far more suitable and more central than the City of Angels.

With all the uncertainty over governors and the location of the province's power

base, California's foreign-born population began to realize that the current situation would not lead to stability. On March 27, 1845, Charles Weber, William Gulnac, John Marsh, James Weeks, and many other foreigners, most of whom lived in the Santa Clara Valley, issued a "Call to Foreigners," which set a meeting for all foreigners in California in San Jose on July 4, 1845.

Charles Weber, one of the leaders of the proposed meeting, wrote that the foreign leaders represented:

. . . a more systematic organization, the ultimate effects of which should, when they become sufficiently strong, result in wresting from Mexican rule that portion of California lying north and east of the San Joaquin River, and north and west of the bays of San Francisco, San Pablo, and Suisun, and making it, like Texas, an independent state.

Texas and the fight for independence in the southwest was a topic of discussion for all foreigners in California, as well as for the Californios. The date of July 4 had more overt meaning than simply a convenient date for the meeting, although at the actual meeting no real plan for revolution was discussed.

Throughout the rest of 1845 and into 1846 the possibility of war with the United States was discussed by California officials in letters sent throughout the province. Governor Pico and Military Commandant Castro continued to assess their role in the event of war. In April 1845 Castro appointed his old revolutionary friend, Charles Weber, to be a militia captain in San Jose in case of the outbreak of hostilities. Californians realized that war was inevitable—when and where were the only unknown variables.

WAR AND THE AMERICANIZATION OF THE VALLEY

Several factors in the mid-1840s resulted in the American take-over of California. The two principal causes were the expansionist mood in the United States and a new wave of immigration into California.

The concept of Manifest Destiny, the idea that the United States should expand beyond the Mississippi River to the Pacific Ocean, was hotly debated by Americans during the late 1830s and 1840s. One result of this expansionist mood was the Texas Revolution of 1836. Americans had settled into the Texas territory of Mexico and, rather than accepting their host country's customs and traditions, they rebelled. During this time the United States Congress and the President were pursuing expansion. The Americans were worried that California might fall into the hands of Russia, England, France, or Prussia, since Mexico was too weak to defend the region. In 1842 Commodore Thomas Ap Catesby Jones invaded Monterey under the mistaken belief that the United States and Mexico were at war. Although American occupation was short-lived, it served as a notice to others that if any nation was going to take over California, that nation would be the United States.

The incident that kindled the fire of expansionism occurred between the Mexican Army and the Republic of Texas. Although Texas was an independent republic, Mexico had never been satisfied with losing the area and, on April 25, 1846, Mexico entered disputed territory between the two countries. President James K. Polk already had General Zachary Taylor and his troops stationed in the area, and he quickly asked Congress to declare war. On May 12, 1847, Congress consented, and General Taylor moved into action as soon as he received the news.

In the meantime John C. Frémont arrived in California with sixty-two soldiers

John C. Frémont visited the Santa Clara Valley during his mapping expedition of California in 1846. He camped for a time on the unoccupied Rancho Laguna Seca near Coyote, and visited the New Almaden Mines and the Santa Cruz Mountains. From Charles Wentworth Upham, *Life, Explorations and Public Services of John Charles Frémont,* 1856

and six Delaware Indians. Frémont's stated reason for entering California was that he was on a scientific expedition, but in reality he was ready to help Americans in California take over the area if the opportunity presented itself.

After receiving permission to winter in California from General José Castro, military commander of Alta California, on the condition that he keep away from settled areas along the coast, the brash young Frémont moved his men to Gabilan Peak, erected a log fortification only twenty-five miles from Monterey, and raised the American flag. After receiving a warning letter and seeing that Castro was prepared to back his threats with force, Frémont moved his men northeast into the San Joaquin Valley.

After they reached Oregon, Frémont's party was overtaken by Lieutenant Archibald H. Gillespie, a Marine officer, and presented with secret dispatches from Washington. The party then turned south and rode into the Sacramento Valley, where they were met by Americans near Sutter's Fort who had heard rumors that the Mexicans were planning to force settlers out of the territory.

Throughout the 1840s emigrants arrived in increasing numbers from areas outside of Mexico. American citizens made up the largest influx of the new settlers, but others, including British subjects, Italians, and Scandinavians, all journeyed to California in order to take advantage of its growing reputation as fertile agricultural land.

In June 1846 the settlers intercepted a herd of horses destined for Castro and turned them over to Frémont. Soon the Americans felt bold enough to try a Texas-style revolution, and on June 14, under the leadership of Ezekiel Merritt and William B. Ide, the Americans took General Mariano Guadalupe Vallejo prisoner at the general's Sonoma rancho. Vallejo, one of the most respected citizens in California, was taken to Sutter's Fort along with two other Mexican officers.

The Americans wanted to act under the protection of the United States, but Frémont refused to become involved, so Ide and his followers selected a flag with a grizzly bear and a red star and declared a California Republic. With the capture of Monterey on July 7, 1846, by Commodore John Drake Sloat, the Bear Flag Rebellion ended as the Bear Flaggers joined with the American military.

In the Santa Clara Valley word of the Bear Flag Rebellion and the actions of Sloat in Monterey met with approval by most foreigners, Americans and others. One of the most important of the new immigrants was thirty-two-year-old Prussian Charles David Weber, who arrived in California in 1841. After settling in the Santa Clara Valley Weber became a nationalized Mexican citizen and changed his name to Carlos María Weber. Weber, who had been involved in the Texas Revolution of 1836, became one of the primary causes of the only battle fought in Northern California during the Mexican-American War of 1846—the Battle of Santa Clara.

Upon his arrival in the valley, Weber established a general merchandise store, a blacksmith shop, a flour mill, a bakery, a salt works, a soap and candle business, and the Weber House, a *fonda* (saloon) that catered to foreigners. He also purchased a rancho in the vicinity of the Pueblo de San José. During the initial occupation of California by the United States Navy, Weber supplied the naval forces.

After the outbreak of the Bear Flag Rebellion in Sonoma, Weber gave the appearance of neutrality while giving information to Captain Charles Frémont and

James F. Reed and his family were members of the ill-fated Donner Party, arriving in San Jose in 1846. After a successful visit to the gold fields in 1848, he returned to San Jose and invested heavily in real estate. A large portion of downtown San Jose, south of the university, was originally land subdivided by Reed, who named the streets for family members. Courtesy, Sourisseau Academy

urging other foreigners to join in with the rebels. Word of his activities and the fact that he had a small arsenal in his bedroom reached the citizens of San Jose, who became infuriated with Weber. When Comandante José Castro left San Jose for Mexico, after the United States Navy took Monterey, Weber decided that he would be safer accompanying Castro than remaining behind. After reaching the dry bed of the San Gabriel River near Los Angeles, Weber decided not to continue to Mexico and rode into the City of Angels.

Weber returned to Northern California with Lieutenant William Alfred Truman Maddox's battalion, which was chasing rebellious Californios up the coast after the rebellion in Los Angeles failed. On October 8, 1846, Commodore Robert F. Stockton appointed Weber the sergeant in command of the San Jose volunteer militia. Although Weber was under orders to simply observe what was going on in the Santa Clara Valley region, he quickly

abused his newly found powers. Captain Weber, as he referred to himself (Castro had named him a captain in the Mexican Army during the revolution against Governor Manuel Micheltorena in 1844), enlisted sixty-five men, rather than the ten authorized, and began mounting horse raids on October 25 against the local California ranchos. Weber named his militia the Rangers after the Texas Rangers.

One of the persistent problems faced by Weber was the constant cutting down of the American Flag, which, as sergeant of the militia, Weber was supposed to keep flying. After receiving orders "to take charge of all arms found in possession of Californians residing in the towns of San Jose and Santa Clara," Weber and his Rangers responded by taking horses and livestock.

Unfortunately for the Californios, when they appealed to the military governor in Yerba Buena, now known as San Francisco, they received a less than satisfactory

This drawing purports to show the first United States flag-raising in San Jose. On July 13, 1846, Captain Thomas Fallon is shown in front of the town hall. The flag was sent at Fallon's request by Commodore John D. Sloat, U.S.N., commanding the Pacific Squadron. Courtesy, Sourisseau Academy

answer. Even British Vice-Consul Alexander Forbes could not get the military to understand the severity of the problems that Weber was causing in the Santa Clara Valley.

Approximately 6,000 horses were rounded up by Weber and a few other overzealous "patriots," yet when Frémont needed horses to mount an expedition into Southern California Weber could only find about 300 head. However, Weber managed to amass a large herd of horses and cows on his San Joaquin rancho in the summer of 1847.

Weber's raids took him from San Juan Bautista in the south up to the contra costa in the East Bay and along the San Francisco Peninsula in the northwest. One of the ranchos raided was the Sánchez family's Buri-Buri. Although the Sánchez family had decided not to oppose the American takeover, after their herds of horses were taken without their consent in October and November, they became

rightfully upset—but continued to cooperate with the military government in Yerba Buena. The patience of the Californios was starting to wear thin when Weber's Rangers took saddles, work mules, and blankets from rancho Indians, and even killed milk cows. In the process the raiders threatened and humiliated the Californios.

Shortly after Weber's raids started, Yerba Buena began suffering from a lack of meat, as the Californios had no means by which to round up their cattle. An interesting feature of the raids and their effect was that, while Weber claimed to have received orders for the raids from various military authorities, including Frémont and Stockton, there is no proof that he ever had orders from any military commander to collect horses and livestock.

On the evening of December 11, 1846, Manuel Sánchez and Ramón Aguila were arrested for spying and confined aboard the USS *Savannah* due to wild rumors that Californios were gathering to-

Saratoga's Banks Mill wa constructed in 1865 by Charles Maclay. It replaced an earlier frame mill across the road, which was destroyed by fire in 1862. By 1867 the mill was producing seventy-five barrels of flour per day. The structure was severely damaged in the 1906 Earthquake and the stone walls were dismantled and used in the construction of the Paul Masson Winery. Courtesy, Sourisseau Academy, SJSU

gether an army to attack Yerba Buena. Manuel Sánchez was a member of the Rancho Buri-Buri Sánchezes. When Manual was arrested, his older brother, José de la Cruz Sánchez, felt completely betrayed. His family had agreed to help the Yankees, and the outcome was raids on their livestock and Manuel's unjust imprisonment.

Three days later Yerba Buena's alcalde, Lieutenant Washington Allon Bartlett, set out with a party of six seamen to scout the countryside in search of the Californio army. Bartlett announced that he and his men were going out in search of meat. When the party reached Mission Dolores, Bartlett met with José de la Cruz Sánchez, Manuel's brother, and arranged to purchase some cattle from Rancho Buri-Buri. Although under orders not to travel further south than Mission Dolores, Bartlett and his men pressed on to the rancho to round up the cattle.

The group reached the rancho, now located in San Mateo County, on December 15 and began rounding up the herd the following morning. In order to help drive the twenty or so head of cattle into the stone corral, Bartlett had his men stack their arms. Within a few minutes José de la Cruz Sánchez and his Californio vaqueros took the men as prisoners.

Unlike the actual rebellion going on in the southern portion of California, the Californios living in the San Francisco Bay area did not wish to fight the Americans and rejoin Mexico. They had simply had enough of Weber and his Rangers' constant raids on their livestock and did not like the way they were being treated by the foreigners.

When the news of Bartlett's capture reached other Californio rancheros José de la Cruz Sánchez's force was joined by three companies of men. Although the men were excellent horsemen, they were

not a real fighting unit, as most of their arms and ammunition had been seized in earlier raids by Weber and his Rangers. The thirty-eight rifles and one pistol that the Californios gathered were useless without powder. Their only real weapons were nineteen lances made from willow poles, with knives tied on the ends. In addition, ten of the Californios had served in the Mexican army and carried swords. These weapons, however, were useful only in close combat, leaving the Californios with one strategy: their excellent horsemanship.

The Californios took their hostages from Rancho Buri-Buri over the Sierra Azul to Francisco Sánchez's Rancho San Pedro. From Rancho San Pédro the men moved south of Half Moon Bay and then recrossed the mountains near present-day Woodside and moved south around both Mission Santa Clara and the Pueblo de San José, before turning north to José Higuera's Rancho los Tularcitos, where present-day Milpitas is located. There Sánchez's men met reinforcements from Contra Costa.

Word of Bartlett's capture reached Yerba Buena on December 17, 1846. Captain William Mervine immediately sent a warning to Lieutenant Robert F. Pinkney, who was in command of San Jose, urging him to be on guard "day and night." Interestingly, Captain Mervine released Manuel Sánchez on December 21, five days after Manuel Sánchez's relatives and friends captured Bartlett.

Although Lieutenant Pinkney was under orders from Captain Mervine to stay close to the pueblo, Pinkney drew up a plan to capture the rebels and enlisted the help of Second Lieutenant William Maddox of the United States Marines, who was commander of the Middle Department in Monterey.

Maddox set out with fifty from Monterey on December 22. Pinkney sent a letter to Captain Joseph Bartine Hull of the USS *Warren* asking for reinforcements to help round up Sánchez's men. When Mervine was informed of Pinkney's plan he was furious that the junior officer instituted a plan without authority from his commanding officers. The captain quickly ordered his insubordinate officer to cancel the plans.

Later Weber had a meeting with Mervine and the information provided by Weber changed Mervine's mind about the campaign to rescue Bartlett. On December 26, 1846, the captain issued his own orders, which essentially enacted Pinkney's plans. Captain Hull gathered together 101 men under the command of Marine Captain Ward Marston.

The Santa Clara Expeditionary Force set out from Yerba Buena in the afternoon of December 29, 1846, and headed for the Red Woods (now Woodside). Although Weber and his Rangers had been scouring the countryside for weeks, only about half the company was mounted. The enlisted sailors and marines had to trudge through the mud while the six-pound cannon was a burden on the entire company, as the makeshift gun carriage kept bogging down in the muddy, brush-covered countryside.

On January 2, 1847, Weber's scouts entered the Olhone village of Posolmi and were informed that the Californios were between them and Mission Santa Clara. At about the same time the main party, which was marching toward the mission, saw traces of the Californios and fired a shot into the air to call Weber and his men back to the main force.

The men advanced after the rancheros along the muddy *camino del dedio* (dry road). Weber and his Rangers advanced on the right flank, while the Yerba Buena volunteers rode on the left. The sailors came along the road with the cannon, while the Marines marched in front of the cannon.

As the two opposing forces got closer to the mission, the Californios staying out of shooting distance, the cannon suddenly became stuck in the mud, near the point that the present-day El Camino Real crosses el Arroyo Quito, about two miles from the Mission Santa Clara. Seeing that the main armament of the Americans was stuck, the Californios came closer to the expeditionary force. The American Marines and volunteers fired their rifles, while the sailors fired grapeshot from the cannon three times. None of the shots or cannon fire hit the Californios, who quickly rode out of danger.

The following morning, a Sunday, Marston and Forbes along with Marius Duvall, a naval surgeon, and William Smith, a volunteer from Yerba Buena who could speak Spanish, rode out of the mission and met with Francisco and José de la Cruz Sánchez, Domingo Féliz, a brother-in-law of the Sánchezes, and Lieutenant Bartlett.

The Californios explained that they were upset only with the way they were being treated by Weber and his Rangers. They were not in rebellion, were not carrying a flag, and did not wish to see Mexico back in control of Alta California. They simply did not want their property taken without payment, and they were afraid that the Rangers might harm their families. The only person that the Californios were rebelling against was Captain Carlos Weber.

Marston quickly arranged a truce and sent a letter to his superior, Captain Mervine. To show their good faith the Californios released Lieutenant Bartlett and remained camped in the area with the rest of the naval detail they had captured. That afternoon the Californio camp was surprised by the appearance of Captain Maddox and his Monterey contingent, who, being unaware of the truce, charged at the ranchero's camp. Fortunately Maddox was intercepted before any bloodshed occurred, and Forbes was able to quell the fears of the Californios.

On the morning of January 7, 1847, Marston, Duvall, William Smith, Forbes, and Bartlett rode out of the mission under a truce flag. The representatives of the Californios, Francisco Sánchez, José de la Cruz Sánchez, Domingo Féliz, and Julio Valencia, met with the Americans near Mission Santa Clara. Marston gave the rancheros an ultimatum from Captain Mervine, demanding the release of the American prisoners, the cessation of hostilities, and the surrender of all arms. In return the United States government would respect the rights of the Californios by giving them receipts for any livestock the military might need and would pay the rancheros in due time.

After some reluctance the Californios agreed to the terms of the treaty, and that afternoon a ceremony signaled the end of the Battle of Santa Clara and the war in the Northern Department of California.

With the end of the Mexican-American War in the Santa Clara Valley, life returned to normal. Cattle were tended to, crops planted, and commerce continued, as new immigrants entered the valley. Little changed in California or in the Santa Clara Valley in the months following the Battle of Santa Clara, until the outbreak of gold fever in 1848.

From the discovery of gold to the present day, California has been identified with the precious yellow metal. Historians have speculated as to why the Spanish or Mexicans did not discover *el dorado* before John Marshall did in 1848. Had Hispanics discovered the substance, the Spanish and later Mexican authorities would not have had such a difficult time in finding settlers willing to come to this far outpost of Spanish civilization. Furthermore, had either Spain or Mexico gained a stronger foothold in Alta California, the United States would have found the conquest of California much more difficult, if not impossible, to achieve.

That neither Spanish nor Mexican prospectors discovered gold in Alta California was not due to a lack of exploration. In 1842, six years before Marshall's discovery, a Mexican prospector found gold at Placerita Creek, about thirty-five miles northwest of Los Angeles. Miners, however, quickly panned the area clean and interest in the area as a gold field soon dwindled. Interestingly, the first gold sent to the United States Mint from California came from the Placerita site.

Gold prospecting was not limited to the southern sector of Alta California. Several prospectors searched for gold and silver in the foothills of the Sierra Azul (Santa Cruz Mountains). In the early 1820s Secundio Robles of San Jose found a red ore while prospecting for gold in the foothills above the Almaden area. Although he is credited with being the first white man to discover cinnabar in Santa Clara County, Robles did not know how to identify the mineral and thus did not know what he had discovered.

Robles, however, did tell San Jose residents Antonio Suñol and Luis Chabolla about the red ore in the foothills. Suñol and the others collected their own samples in 1824. Unfortunately, Suñol and Chabolla knew little more about metals than Robles did, and the valuable ore remained both undiscovered and untapped.

In the fall of 1845, Captain Andres Castillero of the Mexican Army visited Mission Santa Clara and picked up some reddish rock piled in the mission yard. The captain also saw some of the red color that the Ohlone painted on the mission buildings. Although he did not have the time to investigate the curious rocks in a rigorous manner during his initial visit, he decided that the rocks warranted a closer examination.

After a trip to Monterey and another journey through the Santa Clara Valley, Castillero returned once again to Mission Santa Clara. Castillero's curiosity was quite natural, as he was trained in geology, chemistry, and metallurgy at the College of Mines in Mexico City. In addition the captain was interested in an offer by the Mexican government of the equivalent of a $100,000 reward for the discovery of valuable minerals.

Castillero talked with Fray José Maria del Real, a padre at Mission Santa Clara, and found that the local Indians used the ore to paint their bodies a vermillion color. Fray del Real told Castillero that some of the mission Indians could guide him to the source of the rocks located fifteen miles to the southwest in the foothills of the Sierra Azul, which was on part of José Reyes Berryessa's Rancho.

Although Castillero, like Robles, Suñol, and Chabolla before him, hoped the rocks contained either gold or silver, after several tests he realized that the rocks could not contain either of the valuable metals. However, in addition to his formal education in Mexico City, the captain once traveled to the La Mancha, Spain, site of the greatest quicksilver mines in the world, and the rocks Castillero collected and tested resembled the Spanish ore. After further tests Castillero collected small silver globs of mercury and uncovered the secret of the red ore.

Castillero filed a claim to the mining site, which he named Santa Clara. Fray

del Real received four shares, as did General José Don Juan Castro and Secundino and Teodora Robles. The captain retained twelve shares for himself. During his stay in the Pueblo de San José, Castillero met William Chard, a foreigner, who was a general handyman. The pair discussed the problems of separating the quicksilver from the ore and after some tinkering, Chard devised a way of using old gun barrels and whaling pots to extract the mercury ore from the cinnabar ore.

On December 30, 1845, the alcalde of San José, Antonio Maria Pico, granted Castillero "three thousand varas of land in all directions" around the mining claim. After eight months of working the ore with little to show for his efforts, Castillero recognized that he would have to obtain better finances for equipment and supplies in order to make the venture pay off. After bidding farewell to William Chard and Fray del Real, the captain set out for Mexico, where he intended to seek a government subsidy for the venture.

Upon Castillero's arrival in Monterey, Mexico, the captain quickly established the legality of his claim, but before he obtained help from his government, Mexico and the United States were at war. As an active duty army captain, Castillero soon found that he had to report to wartime duty. Realizing that he could not realistically complete his mining project, Castillero sold his shares in the Santa Clara Mine to the Barron, Forbes Company of Tepic, Mexico. Castillero's name does not appear on any records after 1847, but he should be remembered as the discoverer of quicksilver in Alta California and the first person to file for a legal mining claim in Alta California.

In the meantime Fray del Real placed James Alexander Forbes in charge of the day-to-day activity at the mines. He was

Captain Henry W. Halleck, a West Point graduate, was hired by the Barron, Forbes Company as the first general manager of the New Almaden Mines in 1850. Halleck instituted changes in the mining operations by designing and constructing the first experimental furnace of brick and cement. He served as the mine manager until the change of ownership in 1863. Courtesy, The Bancroft Library

not related to the Barron, Forbes Company. Forbes immediately began to explore the possibilities of mining the quicksilver. However, once Eustace Barron and Alexander Forbes obtained Castillero's shares, they managed to have James Forbes evicted and placed Robert Walkinshaw in charge.

In 1847 Alexander Forbes arrived in San Jose to arrange the expansion of the mines, which he renamed Nuevo Almaden (or New Almaden) after the famous Almaden mine in Spain. Forbes hired John Young as the first superintendent of the mine.

By 1848 the mine was producing between 100 and 150 pounds of mercury a day. But, while Alexander Forbes and John Young experienced success with the mine operations, Forbes soon found himself facing serious legal challenges to the ownership of the mines.

Two other events affected the mine operation. The first was the takeover of 1846, which placed further complications on land ownership throughout the new territory. The second event was the discovery of gold.

Quicksilver, or mercury, was used primarily to extract gold and silver from impure ores. Reduction workers washed the crushed ore with the liquid metal, which combined with the two precious metals. Then the workers fired the amalgam in giant kilns, which vaporized the quicksilver and left the gold or silver behind. The gold rush created a heavy demand for the mineral and meant giant profits for the quicksilver mines at New Almaden.

To take advantage of the possibilities presented by the gold rush, Alexander Forbes hired an English reduction expert, Dr. Tobin, to take over the reduction operation and a lawyer, who specialized in California land titles, Captain Henry W. Halleck, a West Point graduate who had

Civil and mining engineer Sherman Day graduated from Yale University in 1826. Coming to California in 1849, he explored the Johnson Cutoff (now U.S. 50) in 1855, recommending it as a more practicable route for winter travel. He surveyed the town of San Jose as well as serving as the superintendent of the New Almaden Mines. Courtesy, Sourisseau Academy

The New Almaden Quicksilver mines were a major producer of mercury. Shown in 1880, these miners are working 1,500 feet down into the Randol Shaft. Courtesy, San Jose Historical Museum

been secretary of state under the military government and who became President Abraham Lincoln's chief of staff during the Civil War. Halleck arrived at the mines to take over the general management of the mine operations and serve as the legal representative for the firm.

Halleck began construction of the Main Tunnel on Mine Hill, and by 1851 the miners reached 807 feet into the mountain. To further modernize the operations Halleck installed machinery and mule-drawn ore carts to haul the ore to the surface, replacing the Hispanic *tanateros* or ore haulers. In addition, Halleck introduced the use of black powder to quickly tunnel into the mountainside. A side benefit of using black powder was that the explosions helped to pulverize the ore.

The increased efficiency of the mine rendered the reduction process obsolete. Halleck and Young designed a brick fur-

nace to heat and separate the quicksilver from the ore. By 1854 thirteen brick furnaces were operating day and night. The reduction workers stored the refined quicksilver in flasks made in England that were eighteen inches long, eight inches in diameter, and one-quarter-inch thick. The flasks contained seventy-five pounds of quicksilver kept in place with a plug. Teamsters hauled the flasks in wagons to Alviso, where launches ferried the quicksilver to San Francisco for shipment to the gold fields within California, or to Mexico and South America. Although the ore yielded 36 percent quicksilver the profit margin was affected by the expenses of modernization.

During the modernization period Alexander Forbes hired civil engineer Sherman Day to become the superintendent and surveyor for the company. Day came from a prominent East Coast family. His father,

Jeremiah Day, was the President of Yale University and his grandfather, Roger Sherman, was a signer of the Declaration of Independence. Day graduated from Yale in 1826, then received a master's degree before coming west in 1849. In the mid-1850s he surveyed roads over the Sierra Nevada, before becoming a California state senator in 1856. A lack of capital forced his resignation from the senate, and subsequent employment with Barron, Forbes. Day's main accomplishment at New Almaden was the construction of the much needed Day Tunnel that drained water from the 600-foot level of the mine shafts.

While the company modernized the mine, the workers in the Hacienda and Spanishtown were working and living in very poor conditions. Dr. W.S. Thorne of San Jose gave an account of his visit to the mine in 1858:

Upon my first visit to Nuevo Almaden in 1858, the general environment and its population was not too favorable. The general conditions in the settlement were somewhat unrestrained, turbulent and with little concern for law and order. Many renegades, murderers and thieves were frequent visitors to the locality. However, the standard of living was comparable to other mining camps throughout the West. During the early years, most of the workers were peons from Mexico, and renegades from justice. Almaden was a publicized rendezvous for some of the worst element in the state.

Although the miners suffered from diseases and accidents, few of San Jose's phy-

This 1870 view of the New Almaden Mine Hacienda shows the reduction works, or ore furnaces, where the ore was roasted after being brought down from the mine on the hillside. Here the ore was pulverized, heated, and the precious mercury condensed from the escaping vapor. The main thoroughfare and small dwellings of the Hacienda village can be seen in the distance. Courtesy, Sourisseau Academy

sicians would venture the twelve miles to the mines, as often the miners could not afford to pay the doctors for their time or medicine.

Soon after Thorne's visit, the United States District Court issued an injunction, closing the mine until legal ownership could be determined between the many claimants. During the course of the ensuing court case 125 witnesses gave testimony that filled 3,584 pages. Eighteen prominent Mexican nationals traveled to San Francisco and gave testimony. After an initial favorable decision in the district court, the Supreme Court heard the case and rejected the Barron, Forbes Company claim. California's eminent nineteenth-century historian Hubert Howe Bancroft reported that the decision was completely

unjust. The company, however, continued to operate the mines until 1863, when President Lincoln signed an eviction order to remove Barron, Forbes Company from the property.

The United States government sent Leonard Swett, a special agent, to take over control of the mines. Swett brought Samuel Butterworth, president of the Quicksilver Mining Company, and U.S. Marshal C.W. Rand out to the mines to post the notice, but the miners, in no uncertain terms, forced the trio off the property. At this point local newspapers took up the miners' cause and President Lincoln received hundreds of letters and telegrams protesting his action. Rather than face a loss of support from the western states, Lincoln, who was in the midst of the Civil

War, decided to withdraw the eviction notice. Finally in April 1864, the Quicksilver
Mining Company of New York and Pennsylvania purchased the Barron, Forbes
Company holdings and improvements for
$1,750,000. Between 1847 and 1864 the
Barron, Forbes Company produced fifteen
million dollars worth of quicksilver from
the mines at New Almaden.

Under the new leadership of Samuel
F. Butterworth, the president of the Quicksilver Mining Company, the mine reached
a peak annual production of $2,166,304 of
quicksilver, which represented 47,149
flasks of quicksilver. Butterworth also improved the conditions at the mines and the
mining settlements. Dr. W.S. Thorn became the first resident physician; a school
district offered classes for the first time to
the miners' children; and the company
opened a tollgate to keep undesirable elements off the property. They also operated
a tramway in the mines. By 1865 the
mine property consisted of a village with
houses scattered throughout the hills, 700
buildings with 1,800 people working at the

mine, and 600 people living at the Hacienda representing twenty-eight nationalities. In addition, Butterworth decided to
move the main offices to Jackson and
Front streets in San Francisco to be in the
heart of the trading center of the west.

In 1870 James Butterworth Randol replaced the retiring Samuel F. Butterworth
as General Manager of the Quicksilver
Mining Company. Under Randol the miners' living conditions continued to improve.
Dr. A.R. Randol, James Randol's brother,
replaced Dr. Thorn and Dr. Randol was
replaced, in turn, by Dr. S.E. Winn. The
company provided a complete health service by charging all miners one dollar a
month. The miners also started a Helping
Hand Society to aid miners and their families in times of need.

In addition to social improvements,
Randol increased production, paid off
debts, and began paying dividends to
shareholders. Unfortunately, prosperity for
the mines lasted only a decade. By 1881
the annual production began decreasing as
the miners produced only 13,000 flasks of

One of the most colorful and popular employees at New Almaden Mines was Chinese Sam. Many Chinese were employed at the mines, engaged in the more menial tasks such as brick-making, woodcutting, and housekeeping. Chinese Sam had a young wife and a daughter who returned to China upon Sam's death in 1889. Courtesy, Sourisseau Academy

quicksilver, and the stockholders did not receive their dividend checks. In 1889 Randol left the mine operations, and the company continued to decline until it filed for bankruptcy in 1912. The only new shaft built on the mine property during this period was the Harry shaft, which operated until the mines finally closed in the 1970s.

After the Quicksilver Mining Company dissolved, George H. Sexton obtained a twenty-five-year lease and built a new furnace and equipment in 1916. The following year the United States government purchased all the production for the war effort, as mercury was a vital ingredient in the manufacture of bombs. The company was quite profitable during World War I, and the company made one million dollars in a few years. However, with the signing of the armistice the mines once more hit hard times before closing again in 1926.

The Great Depression years were hard at the mine, with only small amounts of ore refined between 1927 and 1935. In 1940 the New Almaden Corporation leased the property and C.N. Schuette became the General Manager. The war in Europe and soon the war in the Pacific resulted in high prices once again and miners produced 7,000 flasks. The company engaged primarily in open pit mining and refining old dregs, although the new company did reopen the Sherman Day Tunnel. However, from the end of World War II in 1945 until the outbreak of the Korean War, the mine produced very little quicksilver.

The Korean War brought prices up once again, and workers returned to surface drilling, but could not locate any new ore. In 1953 underground crews reopened the Sherman Day Tunnel, but again the miners could not locate new ore and the mine floundered once again.

Gene Allen obtained a five-year lease

in the mid-1950s, and miners came back to work during the next decade. On July 20, 1965, the *San Francisco Chronicle* reported that the mine was once again in production under the direction of the Thornburg Mine Company. Geology crews again began probing the site in 1975, and when they did not discover new quicksilver deposits, the mine closed, thus ending one of the last direct links with the Costanoan, Spanish, Mexican, and early American eras.

At the onset of the War of 1846 the population of *el Pueblo de San José* was between 600 and 800 people. By 1850 this figure had reached about 1,000. The population of the county increased from 935 in 1841 to near 4,000 by 1849.

The official United States Census of 1850 was lost, but the gold rush and subsequent events in San Jose and the valley caused the population to rise to 2,500 in

San Jose and an overall population of 6,764 for the County of Santa Clara by the 1852 census.

With the growth of the new United States Territory of California and the subsequent discovery of gold, a regular means of transporting people from the Santa Clara Valley to San Francisco was needed. In autumn of 1849 John Whistman established the first stage service in California, with a nine-hour run between San Jose and San Francisco. The service cost thirty-two dollars, or "two ounces." Mustangs and mules pulled Whistman's French omnibus until the winter rains turned El Camino Real into an impassable quagmire. Whistman then provided service to Alviso, where the *Sacramento,* took passengers to San Francisco, Oakland, and Sacramento.

In the spring of 1850 Whistman again established his route up the peninsula. In April, Ackley and Maurison established

A *First Night's Camping* was illustrated in *Hutching's Illustrated California Magazine* in 1857. The "young hopefuls'" first night on the prairie consisted of singing California gold songs with glee and hilarity until bedtime. They retired at a late hour with a boot for a pillow, hugging the cold ground, forgetting bad roads and contrary oxen. From *Hutchings' Illustrated California Magazine,* 1857

Visitors to California were impressed by the lack of class consciousness among the population. Wealth was expressed by nothing more than a certain ostentation in dress—a silk dress, a lace shawl, or a satin sash of brilliant colors. The men's trousers had metal buttons from hip to ankle, left unbuttoned from the knee to expose a colorful lining. From *Hutchings' Illustrated California Magazine,* 1857

service three times a week. That summer Whistman sold his business to Warren F. Hall and Jared B. Crandall, two experienced stage operators from Mexico.

In 1851 Hall and Crandall purchased a ranch at Mountain View, where they placed their herd of 500 horses. The pair ordered several Concord coaches at a cost of between $1,200 and $1,500 each. In May 1851 the entrepreneurs were awarded a four-year contract worth $6,000 annually to carry the United States mail between San Jose and San Francisco three times weekly.

On July 2, 1851, Hall and Crandall reduced the fare to sixteen dollars and established service to Monterey twice a week. In April 1853 the pair sold their stage business to Dillon, Hedge and Company. By the end of the decade Dillon, Hedge and Company sold their line to the California Stage Company, the largest in the state, and passengers leaving San Jose could reach any destination in California served by stageline or boat.

Along with the establishment of stage and boat routes to San Francisco and beyond, there existed a need to travel from Santa Clara County to Santa Cruz County. In the 1850s the only roads through the Santa Cruz Mountains belonged to Charles "Mountain Charley" Henry McKiernan, the first permanent settler in the summit area. McKiernan operated a toll road down an old Indian trail near his home on the summit that wandered down through the Moody Gulch area to the turnpike toll road of the Santa Cruz Gap Joint Stock Company, of which he was a stockholder. The first mail delivered to the summit area was by stage over Mountain Charley's road.

On March 12, 1853, the Santa Clara County Supervisors authorized a turnpike road, but the supervisors were unwilling to undertake the operation of a mountain road to Santa Cruz. In 1857 the Board of Supervisors passed an ordinance to allow the construction of toll roads owned and operated by private companies. Under the new ordinance the Santa Cruz Gap Joint Stock Company built the Santa Cruz Gap Turnpike. The stock company was formed on November 1, 1856, with $20,000 worth of stock purchased by shareholders from both Santa Clara and Santa Cruz counties. Adolf Pfister was elected president and D.B. Moody became the secretary, while the officers were L.A. Whitehurst, E.H. Evans, R.S. Smith, A.S. Logan, and J.Y. McMillin.

The surveyors, or "viewers," as they were called, were Sheriff John M. Murphy, L.B. Healy, and W.M. Hoy from Santa Clara and Harry Rice, George Evans, and Henry W. Peck from Santa Cruz. Freeman and Company received the contract to build the road to Soquel in Santa Cruz County. The road was completed on May 5, 1856.

The *Alta Californian* described the road on December 22, 1860, as having a moderate grade that allowed horses to trot the seven miles to the summit. The road was cut into the side of steep hills and was so narrow and crooked that turnouts were provided to allow wagons to pass. While these were an improvement, travelers were involved in a number of accidents, resulting in the loss of both horses and wagons. Although a tremendous sum of money was spent on the road, it was always, and still remains, in danger of being washed out by winter storms.

The first stage service from Santa Clara County to Santa Cruz County went around the Santa Cruz Mountains from San Jose to Gilroy and San Juan Bautista, then along the Pajaro River to Watsonville and on to Santa Cruz. In 1855 the California Stage Company received the United

Arriving in San Jose in 1847, Adolf Pfister was a prominent merchant. He also took an active role in local government, serving as mayor of San Jose from 1870 to 1872. As mayor he is remembered for the creation of the San Jose Public Library and Alum Rock Park. Courtesy, Sourisseau Academy

States mail contract between San Jose and Santa Cruz, which paid $1,000 annually, and when the company went out of business, employees in Santa Cruz formed the Pacific Express Company and continued operating the route.

In 1857 a mountain route was established from Santa Cruz to Scotts Valley, then up Mountain Charley Road to the summit. The route then moved down the mountain to Patchen, Alma, Lexington, Los Gatos, and on to San Jose.

The following year a route was established on the San Jose-Soquel Turnpike road. These early stages were "gaudily painted" and pulled by four horses that were changed every fifteen miles at a saloon or hotel, and handled by lively drivers. The coaches, horses, and drivers that traveled the Santa Cruz Mountain stage routes from the 1850s to the 1880s were a part of a wild and exciting era and were replaced only by the encroachment of the railroad. However, a certain amount of transfer occurred. George Lewis Colegrove, the last of the stagecoach drivers, became the first conductor on the South Pacific Coast Railroad when it was completed on May 1, 1880.

CHAPTER FOUR

VALLEY OF HEART'S DELIGHT

The orchards provided seasonal work for women and children during the harvest. Here is a group cutting apricots in preparation for drying. The cutters halved the fruit and laid it out on wooden trays that were stacked and carted to the sulfur house. After a time in the sulfur house, the cut fruit was put out in the sun to dry. Courtesy, California History Center Foundation, De Anza College

In 1851 an American farmer in what is now southern Alameda County grew an economically successful wheat and barley crop. This proved to other Americans in Santa Clara County that the Yolo loam soil found in the northern center portion of the Santa Clara Valley could sustain grain farming and the valley's commercial farming period began. The following season farmers throughout the area began to plant grains. The soil was so rich that in one field five barley crops were harvested from one sowing, as each successive crop came in from volunteer grain lost during the previous harvest. The yields were so high that without any fertilization the fields fifth crop brought forty-three bushels per acre. Fields on the Commodore Robert F. Stockton ranch, *Rancho El Potrero de Santa Clara,* pro-

duced grain for ten years without any soil supplement. (In the 1880s, however, the wheat crop declined to about sixteen bushels per acre, no doubt due to a lack of fertilizer.) It is no wonder that by the turn of the century Santa Clara County was known as the "Valley of Heart's Delight."

Throughout the 1850s and into the next three decades wheat and other cereals were the dominant crop grown in the Santa Clara Valley, as farmers concentrated on the single cash crops of wheat, barley, and oats. In 1852 valley farmers cultivated 19,066 acres of grain, and four years later farmed 24,500 acres.

Santa Clara County's wheat crop by 1868 was 1,188,137 million bushels, "sufficient to feed the entire state," according to the *San Francisco Argus.* By 1874 Santa Clara County was California's fifth

Teams haul the hay to a central location to be stacked by a mechanical "buck rake" in about 1890. This location is probably in the Santa Teresa area south of San Jose. Courtesy, Sourisseau Academy

largest producer, with 1,701,132 bushels of wheat harvested. In 1878 the county's wheat farmers harvested 2,875,120 bushels on 56 percent of the county's cultivated acreage. In all, the valleys farmers planted wheat, barley, oats, rye, corn, and hay on just less than 185,000 acres. The last large grain harvest occurred in 1881, when wheat farmers reaped 2,312,600 bushels. After this the grain production declined, as midwestern wheat farms, located closer to eastern markets, came into production.

By 1899 the wheat harvest was cut to 175,230 bushels, enough to supply the Sperry Flour Company in San Jose. The company, located between Third and Fourth streets, was the location of the old R.G. Moody Brothers mill, built in 1858. Sperry incorporated and bought out the Central Milling Company in 1892, which remained in operation until the mid-1920s.

The boom days of wheat and grain farming in Santa Clara County occurred at a time when farm laborers charged a rate of pay based on what they felt they could

earn in the gold fields. The high cost of labor forced the valley's farmers into purchasing or renting mechanical harvesters.

The first threshing machine and reaper in the state was used by Lorenzo Dowe Stephens in Santa Clara County in 1850. This machine was probably a McCormick combine harvester, a machine that cut the wheat and stripped the grain from the

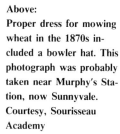

Above:
Proper dress for mowing wheat in the 1870s included a bowler hat. This photograph was probably taken near Murphy's Station, now Sunnyvale. Courtesy, Sourisseau Academy

Left:
To pay the bills while their young orchards reached maturity, many ranchers planted row crops between the young trees. On the Weston Ranch near Santa Clara in the 1880s, strawberries were planted in this young pear orchard. Courtesy, California History Center Foundation, De Anza College

stalks. These early harvesting machines required twenty horses and cut a swath twelve feet wide. After stripping the grain from the stalks, the wheat went into sacks hanging on the side of the machine. The chaff blew out behind the machine.

While the mechanical reaper was an improvement over hand methods, the development of steam and gasoline farm equipment did much to improve the farmers' lot. In 1875 the Joseph Enright Foundry of San Jose patented the Patent Wood and Straw-Burning Portable Engine. This machine used the grain stalks for fuel and was quite successful. Other companies such as the San Jose Foundry made sowers, gang plows, and horse-drawn threshing machines.

In the years immediately preceding the Mexican-American War of 1846, American settlers trickled into the Santa Clara Valley supplanting the old rancho system with small family farms. In the years immediately following the American takeover, the trickle turned into a flood. On May 3, 1848, the *Californian,* a San Fran-

cisco newspaper, published an account of the Santa Clara Valley's agricultural potential:

Corn grows well here. I have seen some grown upon sandy soil, unaided by irrigation, the ears of which were fourteen inches long . . . . Cabbage grows the year round.

During the latter half of the nineteenth century Santa Clara County became known as "The Eden of the World," and the City of San Jose was known as the "Garden City."

The early Anglo-American farmers found that virtually everything they planted came up bigger and better than anything they had ever seen. The *Reports of the United States Commissioner of Patents* for 1851 show that Isaac Branham grew a sixty-three-pound beet in addition to forty-pound carrots that were three feet long. Valley farmers also harvested three-pound potatoes, twenty-two-inch onions, and twenty-six-inch tomatoes.

Although wheat remained the prime

Wheat is being threshed using an Enright Straw-Burning Steam Engine in 1887. Cut grain was fed from the pile to the thresher with the help of the derrick. Grain emerged to be sacked at the side of the thresher at right. Courtesy, Sourisseau Academy

Pioneer nurseryman and silk culturist Louis Prevost arrived in San Jose from France in 1849. Prevost's nursery and garden became a favorite park and picnic spot during the 1850s. The Pioneer Horticultural Society, the forerunner of the Santa Clara Valley Agricultural Society, was organized in Prevost's garden in 1853. Courtesy, Sourisseau Academy

The Santa Clara Valley Agricultural Society Fair in 1874 displays locally produced pears, grapes, wine, canned goods, flour, and indoor plants. Courtesy, Sourisseau Academy

concern of farmers in the first three decades of American rule, as early as 1852 some farmers began planting orchards and vineyards. By the end of that year 17,739 fruit trees and 16,800 grapevines were growing in the county. The farmers had real incentives for planting orchards and vineyards, as apples grown in the old mission orchard brought one dollar each in the gold fields. Four years later farmers tended to 106,000 fruit trees and 150,000 grapevines.

The establishment of several nurseries provided farmers with the needed fruit trees and wine grape stock to begin the transformation of Santa Clara Valley from grain fields to orchards and vineyards. One of the first of these nurseries was the Fox

Nursery, established by Bernard S. Fox in 1852. By the late nineteenth century the Fox Nursery became the largest nursery on the West Coast, developing pears and other orchard trees for California's farmers.

The best French nursery in the valley was Antoine Delmas' French Gardens. Delmas followed the French immigrant pattern of buying his property from Suñol, and in 1852 imported the first European grapevines into the state. His foreign grapes won the first award in that category at the 1855 California State Agricultural Society fair held in San Jose. Delmas repeated his successes at the 1857 Santa Clara County Fair and at other fairs and agricultural meetings for the next several years. Delmas also introduced the technique of using sul-

Above:
German immigrant Joseph Hartmann established the Eagle Brewery in 1853, producing six gallons of beer. In 1856 he moved the operation to the corner of Market and San Carlos, building the factory pictured here. Upon Hartmann's death in 1877, the business was purchased by George Scherrer, who, in 1881, employed five brewers and produced 5,000 barrels. The St. Claire Hilton Hotel now stands on this site. Courtesy, Sourisseau Academy

Right:
Forty-niner Louis Pellier settled in San Jose in 1850. A native of France, Pellier established a nursery, the City Gardens, on San Pedro Street near St. James Street, where he introduced the French prune to San Jose in 1856. Pellier and other pioneer horticulturists in the area formed the Horticultural Society in 1853. Courtesy, San Jose Historical Museum

Frenchman Pierre Sainsevain settled in San Jose about 1844. As his father-in-law, Antonio Suñol, had done, Sainsevain found many business opportunities in the developing settlement. In addition to viniculture, he was also involved in flour milling and real estate speculation. He participated in the Constitutional Convention in Monterey and built the hotel that became the first State House. Courtesy, San Jose Historical Museum

fur gas on grapes to fight mildew and he imported the first European winery and distillery equipment in 1860.

In addition to the European grape cuttings imported by Delmas, Bernard Fox brought many East Coast varieties of vineyard and orchard cuttings with him when he arrived in the valley in 1852. Before coming west Fox, an immigrant from Ireland, was the superintendent of Hovey and Company, Boston's largest nursery. Fox and a partner established the San Jose Valley Nursery in April 1853, three miles north of San Jose on Milpitas Road.

Of all the early nurseries in the valley perhaps the most important was that of Louis Pellier, who established his City Gardens Nursery on San Pedro Street in 1853. In December 1856 Louis' brother Pierre returned from France after journeying home to marry and brought with him two large trunks filled with cuttings and seeds for his brother's nursery. Some cuttings from *Le petit prune d'Agen,* were grafted on local plum trees and provided the base for the giant prune industry

of the late 1800s.

Between 1849 and 1852 viniculturists in Santa Clara County planted their vineyards using mission grape cuttings from the old Santa Clara mission vineyard. During these years Santa Clara County attracted between 1,000 and 1,500 French settlers, who immediately realized the potential of the valley and foothills for an important wine district.

One of the first French viniculturists was Pierre Sainsevain, the son-in-law of Antonio Maria Suñol, San Jose's leading citizen. Suñol, himself a Francophile, was pleased to see the arrival of Frenchmen and began selling them good vineyard sites at reasonable prices. By the end of the 1850s Sainsevain began promoting the Santa Clara Valley as the best wine-growing area in the new state.

In 1849 Suñol gave his daughter and son-in-law one-third of the 2,219-acre Rancho de los Coches that he bought in 1847. After selling fifty-five acres to Captain Stefano Splivalo, Sainsevain planted several varieties of grapes and began making red table wines by 1865 at his Belle Vue vineyard. Three years later at the Santa Clara County Fair Sainsevain won the top award for red wine with his *Menlo Park* brand of claret. Sainsevain also produced a sparkling wine he called *Sparkling California* in the late 1850s.

After spending several years in Central America from the mid-1870s to the early 1880s, Sainsevain returned and began producing a better sparkling wine. The pioneer wine maker also invented a successful steam-powered stemmer-crusher in 1882. However, when his wife Paula died in 1889 Pierre decided to return home to live out his days in his native France, where he died in 1904.

While several farmers established vineyards during the 1850s and 1860s, the most important wine maker was Charles Lefranc. In 1857 Lefranc married Marie Adele Thée, daughter of Bernard Edmond Thée, who had property on the Narvaez Rancho along the Guadalupe Creek. Thée had already planted mission grapes on his land in 1851. The year following their marriage the Lefrancs became half owners in the property and began making wine from the mission grapes. Not satisfied with the wine produced from these grapes, Lefranc imported French cuttings to graft onto the mission roots for his Sweet Grape Vineyard, later named the New Almaden Vineyard. By 1862 Lefranc had 40,000 vines and was making good wine from his French grafts, now in full production. Over the years Lefranc continued to experiment, winning many prizes at various county fairs. The commercial success of his New Almaden Vineyard enabled Lefranc's vineyard to expand to seventy-five acres, while his winery developed to a 100,000-gallon capacity.

Lefranc's success inspired other farmers in the area to begin planting vineyards. In 1861 Isaac Branham established a fifty-acre vineyard that produced about 5,000 gallons of wine by 1865. Dr. N.H. Stockton established the Live Oak Vineyard, while his brother Stephenson established the Gravel Ridge Vineyard.

Another of Lefranc's neighbors, Santa Clara County Assessor David M. Harwood, planted a forty-acre vineyard in 1865 north of Blossom Hill Road on the south side of Lone Hill, along Harwood Road. By 1868 Harwood's Lone Hill Vineyard was the largest vineyard in the valley with its 115 acres producing 20,000 gallons three years later.

Lefranc and his neighbors sold most of their wine by the barrel or half barrel at their wineries, or to San Jose stores and other community grocery stores. Customers simply brought their own bottles and filled them directly from the wine barrels.

While several viniculturists were responsible for making Santa Clara County the leading wine producer in California, one man was responsible for making Santa Clara County into the leading brandy center in California. General Henry Morris Naglee first came to California during the War of 1846. In 1852 he purchased land in the valley and moved there in 1858 before reenlisting in the army during the Civil War.

Before coming home after the war Naglee visited France, where he studied brandy making in Cognac. Upon his return he planted a vineyard, and in 1868 the general established a winery and distillery on the east side of town. By the mid-1870s Naglee was producing the best brandy outside of France. At the Centennial Exposition of 1876 the general's *Naglia* brandy won a special award as the "only American brandy on exhibit that approached the fine French spirits in flavor." Professor Eugene Hilgard, the American wine expert, gave a rating of 100 on a scale of one to 100 to Naglee's *Burgundy Brandy* and rated Naglee's *Riesling Brandy* an eighty-five, this at a time when most brandy in California rated a twenty-six. In the 1940s, when the last of Naglee's brandy had been consumed, two prominent wine critics felt that the general's brandy was still a superior product.

However successful the county's other agricultural products were, Santa Clara County became best known for the vast fruit orchards that filled the valley's floor with a pageant of color during the spring months. Orchards did not really become important until after the 1880s, but as early as the 1850s several farmers began experimenting with small orchards on their grain farms. Commodore Stockton's farm workers planted peach, pear, apple, plum, nectarine, and apricot seedlings as well as strawberry plants on his ranch. D.C. Vestal and a Frenchman named Lavalle planted orchards on the outskirts of town. Vestal's orchard was located on Twelfth Street near Berryessa Road. In 1856 Sylvester Newhall built a nursery and planted an orchard in the Willows section of the county, later known as Willow Glen.

With the advent of Pellier's d'Agen French prunes, Santa Clara County farmers began planting this fruit. Although they also tried other varieties, such as the Sugar and Imperial prunes, 85 percent of the valley's prunes were the French variety. By the turn of the century the valley was known as the "Prune Capital of the World." One of the first farmers to experiment commercially with prunes was E.L. Bradley, who planted ten acres in 1875. Six years later, when Bradley's prune orchard came into production his success proved that prunes could be commercially viable, as the crop brought a return of $2,500 to $4,000 each season. This encouraged other orchardists to follow suit, and during the 1880s farmers began putting more of their acreage into prunes.

During the valley's wheat days ranches sold for between fifteen and twenty dollars per acre, but with the success of orchard crops the subdivided acreage began selling at prices ranging from forty to sixty dollars per acre. By the new century good orchard acreage brought as much as $200 to $300 per acre.

Another orchardist, eye specialist Dr. George Handy, moved to the valley from New York and bought a 450-acre grain ranch between Los Gatos and Saratoga in 1883. During the 1890s the ranch, under the supervision of Handy's son-in-law Frank H. Hume, had 350 acres planted in prunes that brought in $35,000 to $44,000

annually.

The success of the prune depended on the ability of farmers to get their fruit to market. California's population was too small in the 1880s to support a large-scale orchard industry, and shipping fresh fruit by train was costly. The only real solution was to dry the fruit in evaporators or dehydrators. Much too frequently, however, the fruit would not dry fast enough and the fruit would ferment.

Two orchardists, John Ballou and George W. Tarleton, began dipping the prunes in boiling lye water. This process allowed the skin to crack and hastened the drying process, while preventing fermentation of the fruit. The real success of the prune industry occurred after 1889, when the evaporators could not dry out the season's crop and farmers resorted to sun drying the prunes.

Although the sun-drying process worked well for prunes, orchardists who tried to dry apricots, peaches, or pears found that their fruit turned black. Henry Coe, a Santa Clara Valley farmer, found that by gassing the fruit with sulfur fumes the color of the fruit was preserved and insects kept out of the fruit. Fruit treated in this manner could not only be shipped to the East Coast, but on to Europe as well.

In addition to prunes, apricots, peaches, and pears, farmers in the valley began experimenting with other crops. As early as 1868 W.C. Geiger planted fourteen acres of cherries alongside the Los Gatos Creek in The Willows. Twenty years later his crop was bringing him $6,000 annually. When other farmers joined Geiger and planted cherries, the area became known as The Cherries. After the turn of the century, the area was renamed Willow Glen.

The Reverend William D. Pollard arrived in the valley in 1876 from Indiana and purchased forty acres in Saratoga on Pollard Road. Reverend Pollard's peaches brought him $300 an acre, while his prunes brought him $550 an acre.

W.H. Rogers and Dr. W.S. McMurtry planted a 400-tree orange and lemon grove next to Forbes Mill, which they purchased in 1868. In the 1870s Harvey Wilcox also found that citrus crops would grow in the temperate zone along the west foothills and planted 160 acres of oranges near Los Gatos. Soon other orchardists were planting citrus trees, to the extent that in 1887 the valley's citrus farmers held the San Jose Citrus Fair to show off their products.

During the 1870s valley orchardists branched out into nuts. Orchards from fifty acres to 140 acres were planted in almonds, and by 1875 nearly 3,000 almond trees were growing in the valley floor. In 1875 James Frederick Payne planted a small walnut orchard on his 126-acre ranch on Payne Avenue near Campbell. These walnuts were part of the 2,703 walnut trees in cultivation in Santa Clara County that year. James Payne's son, George Carlton Payne, who worked with California's premier horticulturist Luther Burbank, later developed the Payne walnut. George Payne was also the first successful commercial walnut grafter in the state. The last few acres of the Payne Ranch were sold in 1972 and merged into another subdivision.

During the 1890s valley grain farmers suffered serious losses due to increased competition from the Midwest. By 1895 only 15,000 acres were planted in barley, while the acreage planted in wheat dropped to 14,000. Orchard acreage, however, doubled from 1890 to 1895, with the valley's farmers cultivating 4,454,945 fruit and nut trees.

Along with their success with orchard crops farmers continued planting vineyards and making table wines. Two important developments helped Santa Clara County viniculturists during the 1870s. The first was the disaster in French and other European vineyards, as the phylloxera root louse destroyed vineyard after vineyard. The result of the root disease was that between 1877 and 1889 French wine production dropped by 59 percent. At the same time in America a protectionist Congress saw fit to raise import duties on foreign wines. This meant that wine lovers, unless they were very rich, began to look for American wine sources. The best American wine sources were found in California, and the best California wine sources were in Santa Clara County.

By the late 1870s California wine prices began rising. People like Jean Baptiste Jules Portal, Joseph C. Merithew, and John T. Doyle, who named the area Cupertino, established the west side as a premier wine-growing area.

Doyle's Cupertino Wine Company at McClellan Road and Foothill Boulevard was one of the valley's most important wineries. The Cupertino Wine Company's clarets were well received. In 1890 Doyles Cabernet Franc was a winner at the Columbian Exposition, and five years later his clarets won a silver medal in Bordeaux, France, as well as being honored at the 1895 Berlin Exposition. The 1906 earthquake, however, shattered both the Cupertino Wine Company and Doyle, who died later that year.

In the foothills above Cupertino and Mountain View, Vincent Picchetti, an Italian immigrant who arrived in the county in 1872, established a winery, now part of the Midpeninsula Regional Park District, in the famous Chaine d'Or, the golden chain. This area remains one of the finest wine areas in the United States today.

The Los Gatos & Saratoga Wine Company was established in 1858. Pictured here in about 1895, boxes of grapes are being unloaded onto a conveyor belt. By the turn of the century, the winery's annual production reached 350,000 gallons. Courtesy, California History Center Foundation, De Anza College

There in the foothills of the Santa Cruz Mountains, Osea Perrone, a San Francisco physician, established the Montebello Vineyards. Perrone's wine maker, Pierre Klein, an Alsatian, purchased 160 acres on the ridge and established Mira Valle. This winery produced wines that won honorable mention at the 1895 Bordeaux Exposition and medals at the 1896 Atlanta and Brussels wine tasting. Klein's biggest achievement, however, came when his Mira Valle Cabernets won the gold medal at the 1900 Paris Exposition.

The Los Gatos-Saratoga area produced such a large vintage that in two years' time local entrepreneurs built two major wineries. At Austin Corners the Los Gatos-Saratoga Winery was established in 1858. Four seasons later the capacity was at

120,000 gallons, and by 1900 the winery's production reached 350,000 gallons. The major wines were clarets, which were shipped to England. In Los Gatos, against the hillside in back of the present library, local viniculturists built the Los Gatos Cooperative Winery in 1886. The cooperative's capacity reached 300,000 gallons by 1889, and by the end of the century this winery was the largest producer in Santa Clara County.

Also in Los Gatos above the town was the Sacred Heart Novitiate. The Jesuit order established the Novitiate in 1886, and in 1888 Father Masnata made the first vintage. Although the Novitiate initially made only sacramental wines, in 1892 the Jesuits decided to enter the lucrative table wine industry. The Novitiate produced quality wines for almost 100 years, making it the oldest winery in California. However, on January 5, 1986, the Novitiate closed its doors. Changing needs dictated that the order sell the business.

Santa Clara County's largest winery was the Casa Delmas, owned by district attorney Delphin M. Delmas. This winery, located along the El Camino Real had more than 300 acres of wine grapes and a facility with a capacity of 500,000 gallons.

Further north, at Santa Clara County's northern boundary, was the winery of the country's most famous personality in the wine business. United States Senator and former California Governor Leland Stanford's farm had more than 10,000 acres with 158 acres devoted to wine grapes. The old brick winery built in 1888 later served as a student dormitory, a dairy barn, and more recently as a commercial building.

During most of the late nineteenth century and all of the twentieth century three wineries best represented the commercial success that Santa Clara County wines continue to enjoy: Paul Masson, New Almaden, and Mirassou. One of the most notable men in the history of the Santa Clara County wine industry was Paul Masson. Masson emigrated from Burgundy, France, in 1878. After meeting the dean of the valley's wine makers, Charles Lefranc, Masson returned to France, but the devastation of phylloxera convinced the young man to return to the Santa Clara Valley where he began working for Lefranc in 1880. Soon after Lefranc died while trying to stop a runaway horse in 1887, Masson married Lefranc's daughter Louise and entered into a partnership with her brother, Henry Lefranc.

Masson soon began working with champagnes. His first big success came with his displays at San Francisco's Mid-

winter Fair of 1894. Two years later the budding champagne maker purchased property in Saratoga's Mount Eden district above Pierce Road. Finally, in 1898 Masson's success allowed him to incorporate the Paul Masson Champagne Company. His sparkling wine caught on and by 1900 Masson's showroom in the cellar of the San Jose's famed Hotel Vendome had 500,000 bottles.

The earthquake of April 18, 1906, destroyed Masson's San Francisco showroom, along with thousands of bottles stored in the Palace Hotel, and broke 62,428 bottles of champagne in the Hotel Vendome. The following year, however, Masson's winery had 500,000 bottles of champagne ready to sell, and in 1908 the Palace used Masson's champagne to celebrate the hotel's reopening.

Henry Lefranc and his family were involved in an accident when their automobile was hit by an interurban trolley in 1909. Both Lefranc and his wife, the daughter of nurseryman Antoine Delmas, were killed. The couple's daughter survived and, along with both her aunts, inherited the New Almaden Winery. Masson became the winery's supervisor, while still running his successful champagne business.

During Prohibition Masson's champagne winery and the New Almaden winery, like other Santa Clara wineries, sold grape juice in bulk to East Coast distributors. The distributors sold the unfermented product to home wine makers who were allowed, under the law, to produce up to 200 gallons for home consumption. Masson was also fortunate to have the only federal patent to produce medicinal champagne.

In 1930 Masson traded the New Almaden Winery and vineyards for a 26,000-acre ranch east of Gilroy. The new owners quickly sold the winery and its

Frenchman Paul Masson arrived in San Jose in 1878, going to work for Charles LeFranc at the New Almaden vineyards. He married Lefranc's daughter, Louise, and carried on the business upon Lefranc's death in 1887. Pictured here at "La Cuesta," his Saratoga estate, Masson remained active until his retirement in 1936. Courtesy, California History Center Foundation, De Anza College

After their father's death in 1889, Peter, Herman, and John Mirassou continued to operate their grandfather Louis Pellier's winery with their mother and stepfather. The brothers continued to expand their holdings, establishing the Mirassou Winery in 1911, which continues to be a successful family business today. Courtesy, California History Center Foundation, De Anza College

350 acres to a new group, the Almaden Vineyard Corporation, headed by Charles M. Jones. Because Masson continued making bonded wines during Prohibition and the new concern added to the stock on hand, when the government repealed the anti-liquor laws under President Franklin D. Roosevelt, the New Almaden Winery had about one million gallons of wine ready to sell. This was undoubtedly the largest stock of quality wine in California.

After selling the New Almaden Winery, Paul Masson continued making champagne at his Saratoga plant, but finally in 1936 he decided to retire and sold the winery to Martin Ray, a businessman and friend. Masson died in 1940 and the following year, on July 7, the Masson Winery burned to the ground. Martin Ray then sold the Champagne Cellars to a non-valley firm, the giant Joseph E. Seagram and Sons, in 1943. Seagram became the first of many large distillers to buy into California wineries.

The advent of new capital allowed the Masson winery to open the Paul Masson Champagne Cellars in 1959 at Saratoga. The old winery remained part of the operation and is currently used to sponsor a summer musical festival.

In the meantime the new owner of the Almaden Winery, Charles Jones, passed away, and in 1941 Louis Benoist and Brayton Wilbur, both businessmen from San Francisco, purchased the winery from Jones' estate. The new owners immediately began to improve the business. They planted new vines, introduced Almaden's first champagne, and began purchasing vineyards outside of Santa Clara County. During the 1950s and 1960s Almaden grew into one of the best-known wineries in the United States.

Like the Paul Masson Winery, Almaden came under the scrutiny of a large national distillery corporation, and in 1967 Louis Benoist sold the Almaden Winery to National Distillers. After the takeover nothing really changed, and during the next decade National continued Almaden's expansion. By 1980 Almaden was the third largest winery in the United States and was ranked as the nation's number one premium winery.

The valley's third largest winery is Mirassou, which got its start, like so many other aspects of agriculture in Santa Clara County, from one of the Pellier brothers, Pierre. The Pellier vineyard was well established when Pierre H. Mirassou married Henriette Pellier in 1880. With the retirement of Pierre Pellier in 1885, his daughter and son-in-law continued to manage the winery. Four years later, however, Pierre Mirassou passed away unexpectedly, leaving Henriette Mirassou with five children and a large debt on the ranch. Henriette Mirassou remarried to Thomas Casalegno, and the two of them, with help from the Mirassou boys, kept the business going.

Two of the several Mirassou brothers, Peter and Herman, purchased a 100-acre wheat farm on Aborn Road in 1911, planted a vineyard, and established the Mirassou Winery over the next few years. Mirassou wine soon became known as a premium product, allowing the winery to continue expanding. Shortly after World War I the Mirassou brothers partnership broke up, with Peter keeping the winery site and the other brothers beginning a new vineyard. Peter Mirassou, joined by his sons Norbert and Edmund, built a 130,000-gallon capacity winery in 1937.

Although Peter died in 1941, his sons kept improving the winery and vineyards while weathering many of the same storms that endangered other valley wineries throughout the following decades. In the

1960s the Mirassous, like their other successful competitors, branched out into Monterey County, where so many of the older wineries were relocating.

One of the key elements in the establishment of an orchard and vineyard economy in the Santa Clara Valley was the availability of inexpensive farm labor. During the valley's grain period the requirement for farm hands was minimal. However, once farmers began planting orchards the need for farm hands increased. The bulk of the laborers were recruited from Chinese immigrants. In 1870 the county had 104 Chinese farm workers, but as more orchards were established the numbers rose to 689 Chinese farm laborers by 1880, which represented 48 percent of the agricultural workers in the county.

The first Chinese entered the valley as railroad workers on the San Jose-San Francisco Railroad in 1864. The Chinese were the only workers who would work for less than one dollar a day. Once the Chinese completed the railroad they took up the task of clearing the foothills of chaparral for farmers, while providing fuel for the trains. These hillsides were later planted in vineyards. San Jose became one of the first California towns to have a non-mining Chinese population.

In 1851 Thomas Shelton of Santa Clara brought the first strawberries into the valley, starting the commercial berry industry that was soon picked up by Chinese and later Japanese farmers. Berry crops were grown by Chinese farmers in Alviso on land considered unsuitable for grain farming. Most of the Chinese remained farm laborers and sharecroppers. They often made arrangements on the large grain farms to grow fruits and vegetables for local consumption.

Most of the early Chinese in the valley, however, were non- agricultural work-

ers who found employment with the various railroads as land clearers, domestics, and occasionally as miners. However, as the orchards were labor-intensive some Chinese farm workers also provided the labor to plant and tend the new orchards in the 1880s. The Chinese were highly desired as farm labor, as they worked harder for less money than comparable white help and they remained dominant in orchard work until the turn of the century. In addition, they packed all fruit in the valley until 1903, when Portuguese and Italian women began packing fruit, and their husbands, brothers, and sons worked as laborers for the various packinghouses in the valley.

The number of Chinese in Santa Clara County climbed from twenty-two in 1860 to a high of 2,723, mostly men, in 1890, the year that twenty-seven Japanese entered the valley. From this point on the Chinese workforce began decreasing, while the Japanese laborers increased in numbers. As the Chinese left the valley orchards, due to the Chinese Exclusion acts of the 1880s, the Japanese began entering orchard work. By 1908 farmers hired very few Chinese workers to harvest crops, their jobs being filled by Japanese men and white women and children. The 1915 prune harvest was done almost exclusively by Japanese workers, who earned two dollars per day. White men were reluctant to work for such low wages, and the prune industry began relying more and more on the Japanese migrants. This situation changed a bit during the 1920s and 1930s, as Filipino and Mexican migrants were used to keep the wages low. Poor whites, escaping the effects of the Depression, also entered the orchard workforce during the 1930s.

Most of the seasonal workers were migrants who entered the Santa Clara Valley

Paul Masson successfully produced the first champagne in the area in 1888. Obtaining vineyard stock, equipment, and skilled champagne makers from France, he cleared forty acres above Saratoga for the vineyard and winery, pictured here around 1900. Gaining wide recognition, Masson won the first Grand Prix ever awarded to an American champagne in 1914. Courtesy, California History Center Foundation, De Anza College

Japanese-owned businesses gradually spread beyond the cultural nucleus in San Jose's Japantown to the outlying communities in the valley. This Japanese laundry was owned by Hata-keyama in Saratoga. Courtesy, California History Center Foundation, De Anza College

to pick strawberries between April and June and to harvest apricots, pears, and prunes between July and August. The Japanese migrants arriving in Alviso on barges were recruited on the spot by white farmers. During the harvest the migrants lived in bunkhouses on the various valley ranches. There were also migrant farm labor colonies at Alviso and Agnew.

In addition to providing valley farmers with an inexpensive yet dependable workforce, some Japanese managed to get into vegetable and berry farming. By the early 1920s Japanese farmers in the Agnew and Alviso area cultivated 60 percent of the valley's canning tomatoes, more than 80 percent of the spinach grown in the county, and essentially 100 percent of all other vegetables grown for resale. The county's strawberry crop was dominated by Japanese and Chinese horticulturists who mostly leased the farms north of the Berryessa area.

Farmers found that they were not only at the mercy of nature to bring in a good crop, but they were often at the mercy of man to bring in a good price for their crops. After the completion of the San Jose-San Francisco Railroad in 1864, valley farmers began using the fast services of the railroad to ship their produce to the San Francisco Produce Market, the largest produce wholesale market on the West Coast. However, in 1872 the railroad refused to run a night train that would allow fruit picked during the day to arrive in the produce market the following morning and, in addition, began raising the rates for freight.

In an effort to combat the railroad, valley farmers established the San Jose Farmers Club and Protective Association and hired a steamer to leave Alviso for San Francisco at four in the morning. Not only were the farmers able to get their produce to market in time for the morning auction, but the rates for shipping a small chest of fruit dropped from one dollar to sixty cents. The railroad managers quickly realized that they were outmaneuvered and offered a night train at the lower prices.

In 1874 some of the valley's farmers started the Farmers Union Corporation. The union spread to most of the valley's towns and continued operations in San Jose on the northwest corner of San Pedro and Santa Clara streets until the early 1960s. The union supplied everything the farmers needed to buy, other than clothing. It also arranged credit on the following season's crops. The old buildings are now converted into restaurants, offices, and antique shops.

In addition to the Farmers Union, valley farmers established Orchard Supply Hardware in 1931. Albert Smith managed OSH before becoming mayor of Los Gatos in 1977. Smith's brother, Loren, ran OSH until the W.R. Grace Corporation purchased it in 1979. Grace sold to the Wickes Companies before Sears Holdings took control of the chain in 1996.

In order to obtain higher prices and lower shipping costs, Santa Clara County fruit growers joined together to form the California Fruit Union in 1885. The membership elected Santa Clara pear grower John Z. Anderson as president. The union managed to reduce railroad rates under Anderson's leadership, with the help of United States Senator Leland Stanford, who not only was a partner in the Southern Pacific Railroad, but was a major landholder on what would become Leland Stanford Junior University in the Palo Alto area.

The union introduced the auction system of marketing fresh fruit to the Santa Clara Valley. Produce auctions, first held in Florida, enabled fruit growers to get a fair price by having the farmers ship the fruit to a major city, where it was marketed through the auction, thus eliminating a middleman. By 1889 the union accounted for two-thirds of California's fresh fruit reaching eastern tables.

With the increased interest in orchards during the 1890s, several neighborhood farmers joined together to form fruit growers associations. As early as 1891 two such groups formed: the West Side Fruit Growers Association, established by Colonel Philo Hersey in The Willows district, and the East Side Growers Exchange in the Evergreen area. In June of the following year F.M. Righter formed the Campbell Fruit Growers Union and at about the same time the farmers in Berryessa formed their union.

Colonel Hersey realized that the valley farmers would stand a better chance of getting their prices from eastern buyers if they joined together. In 1892 the Santa Clara County Fruit Exchange, with Hersey as president, incorporated. Their trademark, a spoked wheel, symbolized the strength gained by joining together in one exchange.

The Exchange built a sixty-by-150-foot warehouse on Suñol Street in San Jose and an addition in 1896. Over the years they added other neighborhood unions from Los Gatos, Saratoga, Mountain View, and Santa Clara. At its peak the Exchange boasted 436 grower members, who shipped 7,260 tons of fruit through the Exchange in 1902. In 1916 this organization went out of business as its members, who were not required to sell all their fruit to the Exchange, began competing with the Exchange.

On January 25, 1900, Santa Clara Valley prune growers started the first statewide fruit cooperative by forming the California Cured Fruit Association. One thousand California fruit growers came to San Jose and elected Judge H.G. Bond as the first president of the infant cooperative. Over the next few months the organization quickly

signed about 3,800 farmers, representing 75 percent of the dried fruit growers in the state. After building a packinghouse in Santa Clara, the association quickly established a monopoly over the industry, but their price rose too high to sell the record crops of 1900 and 1901 and they went out of business in 1903.

In 1901 fresh fruit growers in Santa Clara County and throughout the state joined together to form the California Fresh Fruit Exchange. This organization, which later shortened its name to the California Fruit Exchange, is still shipping fruit under the Blue Anchor label. One reason for the success of this cooperative was that they not only negotiated fair prices for farmers, but also purchased standing trees used to make fruit boxes at cost.

Another cooperative venture was the Campbell Farmers' Union Packing Company, established on September 1, 1909. F.M. Righter was the president and Perley Baldwin Payne, Sr., served as the Union's manager. The Union was comprised of ten local unions who sold their produce to the California Farmers' Union of San Francisco, which was part of the National Farmers' Union. The San Francisco operation had Santa Clara County branches in Morgan Hill and Saratoga, as well as Campbell. The packinghouse in Campbell was three stories high and measured fifty-four-by-seventy-five feet.

The Growers Market Cooperative on Seventh and Taylor streets in San Jose was another outlet for fresh fruit and produce. This cooperative allowed farmers to sell directly to local restaurants, grocery stores, roadside stands, and fruit-and-vegetable peddlers.

Fourteen years after the demise of the California Cured Fruit Association, the state's prune and apricot growers decided on May 1, 1917, to attempt another statewide association and formed the California Prune

Buyers from the Earl Fruit
Company and Porter
Brothers canneries came to
Wright's depot in 1893 to
purchase fruit grown in
the Santa Cruz Mountains.
The agents bid for the
fruit, and the loaded cars
of the South Pacific Coast
Railroad were dropped off
at the canneries in Camp-
bell and San Jose. Cour-
tesy, William A. Wulf Collection

Above:
The first fruit canned for market was put up by the Dawson family in their backyard in 1871. The following year they established the San Jose Fruit Packing Company on North Fifth Street. In this photograph, taken in about 1875, fresh fruit can be seen arriving by wagon on the left, while the boxes of canned fruit emerge on the right. Courtesy, Sourisseau Academy

Right:
In the 1870s railroad magnate and State Senator Leland Stanford purchased 8,000 acres near Mayfield to serve as his home estate. He named the farm Palo Alto in honor of a huge redwood that stood at one corner of the estate. Shown here in 1891, Stanford and his wife founded a university in the memory of their son, Leland Stanford, Jr. Courtesy, San Jose Public Library, California Room

and Apricot Growers Association. The new association packed dried fruit under the brand name Sunsweet. This association, like the previous one, was headquartered in San Jose. After gaining 75 percent of the state's acreage, the association's annual business reached fifteen million dollars.

Due to the wartime embargoes and the unpredictable crops of 1918 and 1919, the association reorganized between 1920 and 1921 under H.G. Coykendall. The association retained the brand name of Sunsweet and during the 1920s became the largest state cooperatives engaged in dried apricots, peaches, and prunes. Seventy-five percent of the acreage was under the control of the Prune and Apricot Growers Association, and by 1963 Sunsweet had nine packing plants in the county.

Another farming group was the Pear Growers League, which began with twenty-five growers in Santa Clara and San Benito counties. While the league did not act as a marketing cooperative, they did promote pears and acted as arbitrators between growers and canners. During the 1940s and 1950s the league grew to 2,300 members, marketing seventy tons annually, which represented about 50 percent of California's pear crop. During the 1960s and 1970s, with more pear farmers selling their farms, the membership in the league dropped. Finally, in 1978 with only twenty-two members, the Pear Growers League disbanded.

The county's Japanese farmers remained separate from their white counterparts due to cultural and language differences. They sold their produce to buyers from San Francisco, Oakland, Sacramento, and Los Angeles. The quality of their crops often allowed them to collect cash rather than wait to be paid on consignment. By 1908 Japanese tenant farmers at Agnew's joined together in the Japanese

Agricultural Alliance to promote higher prices, offer loans, and to help those farmers in need. The alliance also served as a social institution and acted as a Japanese cultural organization.

Shortly after the establishment of the alliance, businessmen from Nihonmachi (Japantown), located next to Chinatown on Sixth and Jackson streets, established the San Jose Bushberry Association. This marketing association offered the highest prices for berries for a 6 percent charge.

In addition to these groups, the Japanese celery growers in Alviso formed their own cooperative—the Kobai Kumiai. They erected a storage shed and sold their crops together. This group gave rise to the Celery Growers Association in 1931, established by Tomiju Takeda. In 1914 Takeda was responsible for getting Japanese farmers interested in growing celery after he saw a Chinese farmer growing celery in 1909 at Palo Alto. The Association's twenty-seven members paid one cent per crate membership dues. Celery buyers added another penny per crate to provide enough money for the Association to hire a managing secretary. This group sold their produce throughout the San Francisco Bay area and to midwestern and eastern buyers in Chicago and New York City.

With increasing numbers of farms producing fresh fruit, several entrepreneurs set up commercial fruit-drying establishments in the late 1850s. One of the first fruit dryers was Rose and Hartman, which began preserving fruit commercially in September 1857. In 1867 John Q.A. Ballou shipped 500 pounds of prunes on a sailing ship around Cape Horn to the East Coast. The following year Ballou shipped eleven tons of assorted dried fruits. Profits were clearly there to be made by shipping the fruit to the east, as Ballou netted between eighteen to twenty cents per pound.

After the opening of the transcontinental railroad in 1869, more commercial fruit-drying operations opened in the valley. That year L.A. Gould of Santa Clara shipped the first fruit from California to the east Coast, and the Porter Brothers from Chicago began shipping dried fruit from the Santa Clara Valley east. Both of these developments set in motion the planting of more orchards. One of the largest shippers was the Alden Fruit and Vegetable Preserving Company, established in 1874. Two years later Alden made its first shipment of fifteen tons of preserved dried fruit. During 1875 John Z. Anderson converted a boxcar into a refrigerator car by packing green pears in ice before shipping the fruit to the East Coast. Three decades later the San Jose branch of Porter Brothers shipped fresh cherries to the east in refrigerated railroad cars.

In the 1870s the valley's output of produce reached the stage where fresh fruit could be diverted into the infant canning industry. Santa Clara County's canning industry started in a twelve-foot-by-sixteen-foot woodshed behind Dr. James M. Dawson's home. In 1871 Dr. Dawson, with his wife Eloise Jones Dawson and their son E.L. Dawson, packed 350 cases of fruit. The following year the Dawsons and W.S. Stevens, Dawson's brother-in-law, established a cannery with a 1,000-case capacity at what is now Twenty-first and Julian streets. In 1873 Lendrum, Burns and Company, an early San Jose grocery firm, joined the cannery and the new partners erected the J.M. Dawson and Company plant on S.E. Fifth and Julian streets. This cannery produced 4,000 cases of canned fruit annually. In 1874 Wilson Hayes joined the firm. That year the owners enlarged the plant and introduced can presses, which eliminated much of the hand labor. The venture be-

came so successful that in January 1875 the firm incorporated with $200,000 worth of capital as the San Jose Fruit Packing Company. During the next season the firm packed 25,000 cases of fruit.

Dawson's brother-in-law, W.S. Stevens, quit the firm to build the Golden Gate Packing Company with W.H. Muntz. Stevens and Muntz built their plant at Third and Fourth streets, between Julian and Empire. By 1877 Golden Gate incorporated with George M. Bowman as the manager—a job he held until his death in 1907 when Elmer E. Chase took over.

Three years after the establishment of the San Jose Fruit Packing Company, Dr. Dawson sold his shares and formed the J.M. Dawson Packing Company. Dawson ran the plant until his death in 1885, when Eloise Jones Dawson took over and continued the operation until a fire destroyed the cannery in 1895.

Dr. Dawson's son, Thomas Benton Dawson, became the superintendent of the new California Fruit Canners Association in 1899. When the association joined other canneries as the California Packing Corporation in 1916, T.B. Dawson became the general superintendent. Robert I. Bentley, formally of the Golden Gate Cannery, became the new corporation's president.

In 1890 Sai Yin Chew, a Chinese immigrant, established the Precita Canning Company. Chew's tomato cannery was demolished during the disastrous 1906 earthquake, but rebuilt in Alviso in time for the 1906 crop. The new cannery was named the Bayside Canning Company. That same year Sai Yin's son Tom Foon joined the firm and quickly began expanding the business. Foon was a personal friend of Anadeo Pierro "A.P." Gianinni, a native of San Jose and founder of the Bank of Italy. Gianinni extended Foon money to expand the Chinese firm. By 1924 the firm was a

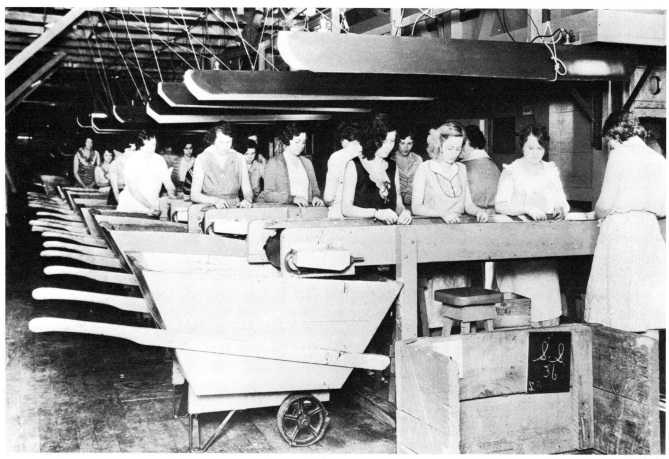

Above:
The fruit packinghouses primarily employed women during the harvest season. In spite of mechanical improvements introduced by 1940, much of the work was still done by hand. Courtesy, San Jose Historical Museum

Right:
Women were a major part of the fruit-packing labor force. In this 1940 Chamber of Commerce photograph, the women are sorting prunes on Monterey Road near Alma. Courtesy, San Jose Historical Museum

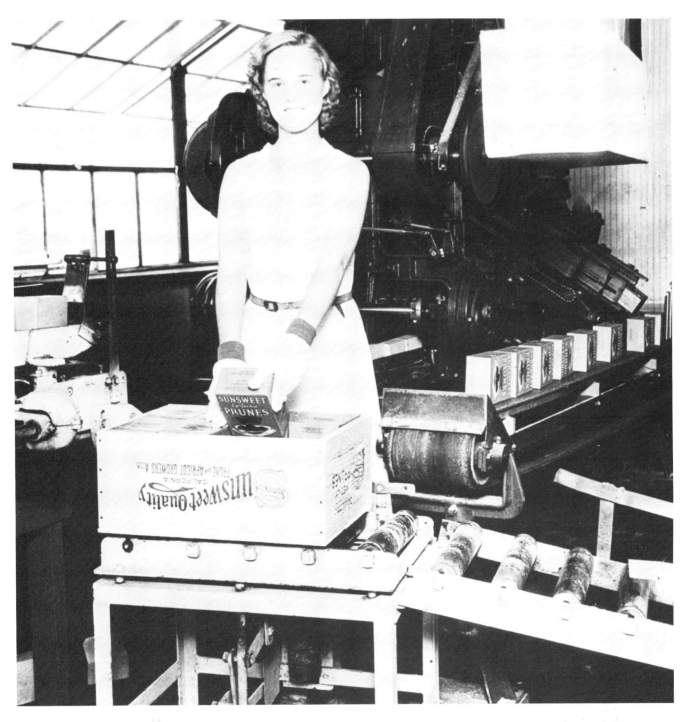

The California Prune and Apricot Growers organized as a cooperative in 1917 and packed fruit under the brand name of Sunsweet. From its Santa Clara Valley headquarters it claimed the participation of 75 percent of the state's bearing-acres of prunes and apricots. Here, in 1940, Santa Clara prunes are being packed for shipping throughout the country. Courtesy, San Jose Historical Museum

three-million-dollar operation, with two additional plants. The company also owned or leased thousands of acres all over Northern California to supply the firm's canneries. One of Tom Foon's most notable achievements was the development of a method to can asparagus without the vegetable turning to mush. This helped launch California's giant asparagus industry. The Bayside Cannery was the only Asian canning operation in the Santa Clara Valley, and shortly after Tom Foon's death in 1931 the plant closed down due to hard times during the Depression years.

Meanwhile, in 1882 fourteen farmers and businessmen had incorporated the Los Gatos Fruit Company. The stockholders established this cannery behind Santa Cruz Avenue and Lyndon Avenue in a sixty-by-eighty-foot building. The plant packed 5,000 cases of fruit during the season. In 1894 George Hooke, the cannery's superintendent, purchased the firm from the second owners. Under Hooke the cannery put up 50,000 cases of fruit a year and employed 250 to 300 workers during the fruit-canning season. In 1906 Hooke sold the cannery to the Hunt Brothers of Hayward, who moved the operation next to the railroad tracks at Santa Cruz and Saratoga avenues. The cannery was finally abandoned in 1955.

Another Los Gatos cannery was the H.D. Curtis Company. The cannery's label *Curtis' Los Gatos Foothill Brand* was known in France, Belgium, England, and Germany. Unfortunately, the company's storage shed housing 200 tons of dried fruit burned down in 1901, resulting in a loss of more than $70,000. Shortly after this disaster the firm went out of business.

Other west valley canners included George N. Herbert, who established his cannery in 1890, and J.C. Ainsley, who started a cannery in Campbell in 1891.

After the turn of the century several more canneries opened. In 1903 F.G. Wool established the Wool Packing Company, which in the mid-1980s was the oldest remaining cannery in the valley.

In the south county, the Bisceglia Brothers established their cannery in 1903. This Morgan Hill plant was a family operation with Pasquale, Joseph, Bruno, and Alfonso Bisceglia running the firm. Ten years later the successful operation moved into San Jose.

In 1905 the Santa Clara firm of Pratt-Low Preserving Company began canning fruit. During 1913 Victor V. Greco founded the Greco Canning Company, while Salvatore and Dominic DiFiore opened the DiFiore Canning Company.

In 1917 Hunt Brothers bought out the Golden Gate Packing Company, which was the oldest canner in the state. Elmer Chase joined the one-year-old E.N. Richmond Company, which incorporated in 1919 as the Richmond-Chase Company and became the largest independent dried fruit and canning company in the United States and one of California's four largest fruit canners.

During the previous year five canners merged into the California Packing Corporation. This giant corporation had sixty-one food-processing plants throughout California, many of them in the Santa Clara Valley.

Most of the valley's canneries were very small operations and as such were adversely affected by local, state, national, and international events. One such cannery was the Orchard City Canning Company, established about 1910 in Campbell by Perley B. Payne, Sr. This company handled fresh and dried fruits. By 1915 the cannery, located in a thirty-by-120-foot building on Harrison Avenue, packed 1,500 cases of canned and dried fruit annually. The cannery operation included

two boilers and employed between forty-five and fifty cannery workers during the season. The plant also handled dried fruit and nursery goods.

During the first years of the war in Europe Great Britain successfully placed a blockade on German sea ports. Unfortunately for Payne his cannery had a standing order with an Austrian firm, and, due to the embargo placed by Great Britain on its wartime foe, Orchard City could not meet its debit obligations and the overcapitalized firm was forced to liquidate its holdings.

In addition to problems suffered by some canners during the early phase of

World War I, other small canners faced insurmountable problems. Most of the small canners were overcapitalized, and their debts forced them to sell their canned products by the end of the packing season, when the market was glutted with canned fruit. The situation was so bad that rival canners found themselves cutting their prices in senseless price wars in order to liquidate their stock.

One of the few canneries still operating in Santa Clara County in the mid-1980s was Sun Garden. Founded by Frank Di-Napoli and Joseph Perrucci in 1941, this small family plant developed into a dried fruit operation—Mayfair—as well as a

Vincent Picchetti, an Italian immigrant, was first employed in 1872 to cultivate the vines of the Jesuit Retreat, Villa Maria. In the 1880s he purchased acreage in the Montebello Ridge and with his family, pictured here in about 1890, began one of the first commercial wineries in the area. Courtesy, California History Center Foundation, De Anza College

canning operation.

Throughout the 1940s and 1950s the fruit-processing business remained one of Santa Clara County's most important industries. In 1960 Santa Clara County remained the world center for fruit and vegetable processing, with 215 fruit-processing operations. Not counting the fruit dehydrators there were eighty-five canneries, twenty-three dried-fruit plants, twenty-five frozen food operators, and eighty-five fresh fruit and vegetable packers.

Twenty-five years later only seven canneries were still in operation in Santa Clara County. Beech-Nut Baby Foods of San Jose is engaged in canning, but all of its fresh produce comes from outside the valley. San Jose's Del Monte Corporation cans fruit it purchases from farmers outside of Santa Clara County, while the Diana Fruit Preserving Company of Santa Clara preserves cherries from Washington and Italy for fruit cocktail as well as maraschino cherries. Gangi Brothers Packing Company, also located in Santa Clara, puts up canned tomatoes from the Salinas Valley. The Stapleton-Spence Packing Company of San Jose cans prunes, dried fruit, and nuts. Sun Garden Packing Company of San Jose cans tomatoes and apricots; some of the apricots come from the valley. Finally, the San Jose firm of F.G. Wool Packing Company puts up canned apricots and pears. Only a few of the canning firms utilize fruit grown in the valley.

Dried fruit processing firms were also hit hard during the 1960s and 1970s. By the mid-1980s only three dried fruit processors remained in business: Benech Farms on McKean Road in the Almaden Valley area, Bonner Packing Company of Morgan Hill, and Mariani Packing Company of San Jose. These firms remain in business because they switched from bulk dried fruit to fancy packs for grocery stores and holiday gift packaging of dried fruit and nuts.

By 1917 most of the cannery workers in Santa Clara County were Italian immigrants. These workers, mostly women, formed a cannery union, the Toilers of the World, which had elements from two unions: the radical International Workers of the World (IWW) or Wobblies, and the American Federation of Labor (AFL). The main complaints of the workers were low wages, long working hours, and the nonrecognition of their union as a bargaining agent by the canners. Their strike was one of the first in California by cannery workers. The strikers were able to gain support from two prominent San Jose churchmen: the Reverend W.L. Stidger of the First Methodist Church and Father William Culligan from Saint Josephs Roman Catholic Church. This support, coupled with the fact that the union began the strike in the midst of the canning season, resulted in most of the union's demands being met. However, the Toilers of the World did not last long, for as soon as the United States entered World War I union activities were considered unpatriotic.

The cannery workers of Santa Clara County remained unorganized after the Armistice until a few months before the 1931 season, when they formed the American Labor Union. This union, like the Toilers of the World, was predominantly Italian in membership. As the canning season approached, the valley's canners offered the cannery workers 20 percent less than the previous year, and in July the cannery workers walked off their jobs. Within a few days recruiters from the Agricultural Workers Industrial Union (AWIU), a union formed by the Communist Party, USA, during the summer of 1929, came to San Jose and quickly gained control of the strike. The leadership of the AWIU re-

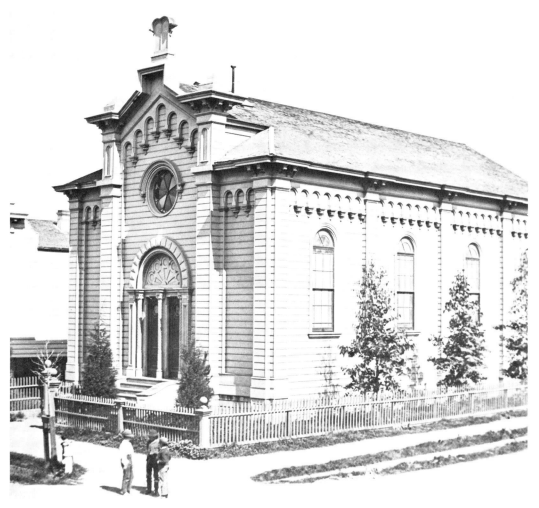

Left:
Dedicated in 1870, Temple Bikur Cholim stood on the corner of San Antonio and South Third streets until it was destroyed by fire in 1940. Members of the Jewish community were prominent in San Jose from the early 1850s, but did not formally organize until 1861. By 1870 the congregation had thirty-five members from San Jose, Santa Clara, Gilroy, San Juan Bautista, and Watsonville. Courtesy, Sourisseau Academy

Below:
In 1906 San Jose boasted a trolley system and mounted police. Both gave way to the automobile, and both are returning as San Jose searches for efficient ways to move more people. St. Joseph's Church (on the right) still stands on Market Street, but the once-famous light tower collapsed in 1915 and was never rebuilt. Courtesy, San Jose Historical Museum

named the union the Cannery and Agricultural Workers Industrial Union (CAWIU).

William Z. Foster, the AWIU organizer, set up mass pickets on August 1, 1931, at the five largest canneries in the county: the Richmond-Chase Cannery, the California Cannery Cooperative, the F.M. Drew Company, and two of California Packing Corporations (CPC) canneries. Almost 2,000 workers were on strike, and the canneries began hiring strikebreakers to fill their manpower shortage.

In order to get the strikebreakers through the picket lines, the canneries called in the San Jose Police Department, who, in turn, deputized American Legionnaires. This led to violent confrontations among the strikers, the police and deputies,

and the strikebreakers. Several CAWIU leaders were arrested during the pitched battles. The CAWIU leadership organized mass marches to protest the arrests. This, however, led to more violence as the strikers and police, along with local vigilantes, clashed once again. After several days of no negotiations, the strikers realized that the canners would not accede to the union's demands, and the workers were forced to return to the lines with no gains. The valley's cannery workers remained unorganized until the American Federation of Labor (AFL) replaced the CAWIU in 1938.

After World War II the cannery workers organized the canneries into closed-shop unions. In addition to the AFL, cannery workers were represented by the Teamsters Union. Over the years the composition of workers changed. More Mexican-Americans entered the workforce, as well as high school and college students, who saw the cannery jobs as summer work instead of permanent jobs.

The Depression of the 1930s hit the valley's farmers extremely hard. Many small farmers simply could not make a living when the canners paid them only two dollars a ton for apricots. For a small farmer the yearly apricot crop might bring sixteen dollars. The prices paid by canners and wholesalers were equally low for other orchard products during the Depression, which forced 629 farmers out of business between 1930 and 1940.

By the 1930s many of the agricultural workers were Mexican braceros, while others were white farmers forced from their lands due to the combined effect of the Dust Bowl years in the 1920s and the Great Depression of the 1930s. In 1933 these migrant workers arrived in the Santa Clara Valley to find that the cherry growers had established a twenty-cents-per-hour wage rate. The CAWIU pointed out that

this was really one-third less than the migrants had earned the previous season. On June 13 the union organized a meeting of several hundred cherry pickers in San Jose. After hearing the details of the growers offer, the membership called for a strike the following day. They demanded thirty cents per hour, an eight-hour day, and union recognition.

Although several small farmers accepted the workers' demands, the valley's larger farmers did not, and 500 cherry pickers went out on strike at a dozen of the largest orchards. After the union set up mass picket lines, the growers called in the police. In addition to the local police and their civilian deputies, Governor James Rolph allowed the use of the California Highway Patrol.

Using pickaxe handles and tear gas, the police managed to break up some of the picket lines. Two days later, on June 16, the foreman of the Spaulding Ranch, the largest cherry ranch in the valley, invited Pat Callahan, the CAWIUs local organizer, to discuss terms. However, when Callahan entered the ranch property he was promptly attacked by deputies who leaped out of the trees onto the unsuspecting union leader. Callahan's jaw was broken in the scuffle and he was generally roughed up. When other strikers saw what was happening and attempted to help they too were attacked then arrested and charged with resisting a peace officer.

On June 17, 250 strikers, both men and women, were attacked by club-swinging deputies and highway patrolmen. At least sixty strikers were beaten and thirty arrested. However, the following day these actions, rather than breaking the back of the strike, served to unify the CAWIU and the growers found 1,000 workers were on strike at twenty ranches.

At this point, after days of confrontation and few cherries picked, the ranchers realized that they were in danger of losing their entire crop. After some discussion the growers gave into the thirty-cents-per-hour demand, but refused to recognize the CAWIU. On June 24, with their principal demand won, the strikers voted to return to work.

A tenuous truce was maintained by both workers and growers for the next few years, but in August 1933 the valley's pear growers set an hourly wage average of between fifteen and twenty cents, which was below what the workers had received in 1932. The CAWIU quickly gained the support of the pear pickers and called a strike on August 14. The strike involved 1,000 pear pickers, who demanded hourly wages of thirty cents, an eight-hour day, and recognition of the union.

Again the strikers engaged in mass picket lines. During this strike the growers turned to the courts and a San Jose judge issued an injunction against interfering with strikebreakers. The CAWIU, however, continued to picket and the police arrested and charged six of the union leaders with contempt of court. The strikers held firm and finally on August 17 the growers, although refusing to recognize the union, did agree to a compromise of a new hourly wage of between twenty-five and twenty-seven-and-one-half cents. The CAWIU recommended the acceptance of the offer, and the workers voted to come back to the pear orchards that day.

The valley's farm workers found that during World War II, with the internment of the large Japanese workforce, the demands of the remaining farm workers were readily met. In addition, due to wartime patriotism, the CAWIU fell from favor and farm workers remained unrepresented until the rise of the United Farm Worker Union in the 1960s.

Fruit growers went on strike in 1939, holding out for $42.50 a ton against the canneries' offer of thirty dollars. Eleven-year-old Irene Munoz reads the sign that growers left on boxes they overturned on Saratoga-Sunnyvale Road near San Jose. The boxes had been delivered to a non-striking grower. Courtesy, Sourisseau Academy

CHAPTER FIVE
THE SURROUNDING WILDERNESS

Irrigation is the key to productivity of the Santa Clara Valley, where there is no reliable rainfall from April to October. Ditches have been used since Spanish times to bring water to the fields. Courtesy, San Jose Historical Museum

Surrounding the Santa Clara Valley are two mountain ranges, the Diablo Range to the east and the Santa Cruz Mountains to the west. These mountains protect the valley floor from harsh winter storms, as well as sheltering the valley from hard frosts. In addition, the winter rains wash the mountain soil down the numerous small creeks and onto the plains below, providing the topsoil for the valley floor. The Santa Clara Valley was once the second most fertile valley in the world, ranking behind the Ganges River Valley in India.

The southern border of Santa Clara County lies along the top of the Santa Cruz Mountains. This area stretches from approximately the intersection of Page Mill Road and Skyline Boulevard at the northwestern corner of the county to the Sargent Hills at the southeast tip of the

county. The altitude varies from an average of 1,800 feet to the peak of Loma Prieta (Dark Mountain) at 3,791 feet above sea level.

The terrain of the mountain area is extremely rough with large canyons, gullies, and washes dividing the mountains into a rugged maze. The giant coastal redwoods, *Sequoia Sempervirens,* are predominant throughout most of the mountains. However, brush and thin scrub pines are all that survive at the higher altitudes around Mount Thayer, above Lexington Reservoir, to the Croy Ridge area near Mount Madonna. In addition to redwoods, Douglas fir, madrone, bay, and various varieties of oaks thrive in the altitudes below 2,500 feet. The annual rainfall of up to fifty inches in the mountains is the highest in Santa Clara County and much of the valley's water supply comes from dams built across the mountain's numerous creeks.

Spanish explorers left the first written record of this area in the late-1700s. The Spanish named the range the *Sierra Azul,* or Blue Mountains. In August 1791 Fray Curta Lasuen became the first non-Indian to cross the mountains between what are now Santa Clara and Santa Cruz counties. He left the valley in the Morgan Hill area and traveled by foot to Santa Cruz to establish a mission there. The padre's journey took him up the Llagas Creek to its headwaters at the base of Loma Prieta, about 3,000 feet above the valley floor. From this vantage point he could look across the blue Monterey Bay to the capital of Alta California, Monterey, to the south. Looking northeast Fray Lasuen could see past the Diablo Range and, if the San Joaquin Valley was not too hazy, Lasuen saw a glimpse of the Sierra Nevada range above the distant horizon.

After pausing for a rest Lasuen continued down the mountainside past Sugar Loaf Mountain and down Hester Creek into the Soquel area and on to Santa Cruz. There he surveyed the area around the proposed mission site and after saying mass, Lasuen returned to Mission Santa Clara on a shorter, but rougher road. The padre decided to have the missionized Indians from Santa Clara clear and improve this path, which was the forebearer of the present State Highway 17, which was recently designated part of the national highway system and renamed Interstate 880.

Although the new mountain road was hardly a thoroughfare, the path served the purpose of linking the two missions together. Indians and donkeys carried supplies, provisions, seeds, tools, and other implements of civilization over the mountain between Mission Santa Clara and Mission Santa Cruz.

The road remained primitive, although passable, until Governor Diego De Borica selected the Santa Cruz area as the site for a new experimental civilian pueblo. On July 23, 1795, the governor ordered Sargeant Pedro Amador to improve the mountain road to enable civilian settlers to establish Branciforte, California's third, and last, pueblo.

With an improved road linking Branciforte and San Jose the new settlers of Branciforte found that they could easily travel to San Jose. On December 31, 1799, after numerous complaints from authorities in San Jose and the padres at Mission Santa Clara, due to the unruly behavior of the Branciforte settlers, Governor Borica ordered the settlers not to use the mountain road for pleasure trips without specific advance approval. The governor wanted his settlers to stay at home and work their land rather than loiter in San Jose.

The mountain road was next written about by Captain John Charles Frémont. Frémont and his band of explorers traveled throughout California in 1846 on a thinly disguised topographical mapping expedition, which, in reality, was a military scouting mission.

On March 22, 1846, Frémont and his party camped above the present site of Los Gatos on the *Cuesta de Los Gatos* (Wildcat Ridge). The following day the party traveled up the mountainside to the summit of the Santa Cruz Mountains. Staying in the area for two days Frémont recorded in his journal the wonders of the giant redwood trees with red fur-like bark and the madrone trees with red bark that curled up in thin, paperlike sections. On March 25, the band of men broke camp before proceeding down the mountain road into Santa Cruz and, eventually, history.

At the time of Frémont's visit, lumbermen used the lower Lexington portion of the mountain road to transport shingles and lumber cut from the mighty redwood giants into the Santa Clara Valley. Although Frémont described the route from San Jose to Santa Cruz as a road, Lyman John Burrell, who moved his family over the route with a wagon in 1851, described it as pure torture. He forced his oxen to trample down the thick underbrush to enable his wagon, which the settlers unloaded at various places, to reach the top of the ridge. Burrell gave an account of the road in his memoirs, published in 1882 in the handwritten journal, *The Mountain Echos:*

No man had ever been known to drive over the summit with a wagon. It was considered not only difficult, but a rather dangerous undertaking. In those days, a man could not safely travel very far alone, unless he was well armed, because bears were not unfrequently seen on the trails, and they had not always the politeness to turn out for a man; but, on the contrary, they would sometimes dispute his passage. The poor conditions remained even after the road to Santa Cruz was improved in the late 1850s.

So dangerous was the road that when Eliza W. Farnham became the first woman to cross the Santa Cruz Mountains alone with a buggy, the main pass at the foot of the Los Gatos Canyon was named after her.

The only other roads in the Santa Cruz Mountain area were built by Charles Henry McKiernan, "Mountain Charley," who settled in the summit area in 1850. In the 1850s and 1860s McKiernan built roads throughout his property on the summit and operated a toll road down an old Indian trail near his home. McKiernan's toll road wound through the Moody Gulch area to the turnpike toll road of the Santa Cruz Joint Stock Company, of which he was a stockholder. A stagecoach delivered the first mail in the mountains over Mountain Charley's road in the 1850s. Later more improved roads supplanted this old road, although Mountain Charley Road is still used by local residents.

The early roads were only six to seven feet wide, just enough for a team and wagon. The roads were not surfaced or even graveled. In the winter the mud was six to ten inches deep, and in the summer the dust was just as deep. The summer dust from wagons hauling fruit and lumber to Santa Clara and Santa Cruz forced the early settlers, who built the roads with pick and shovel in front of their homes, to divert the roads around their dwellings. These roads were the only way for the early mountain settlers to bring up supplies, by mules, from Santa Clara, the nearest post office and general store.

When the first settlers built their homes and ranches in the Santa Cruz Mountains they found the area covered with giant redwood trees. The first redwood tree seen by a non-Indian was on the Corralitos Creek in October 1769, by members of the Gaspar de Portolá expedition. The Olohne Indians used large branches of fallen trees to build their huts. Later, the Spanish and Mexicans used the small trunks as roof beams over their adobe buildings. When Anglo-Americans came into the forested areas above the valley floor, they began one of the most important businesses in Santa Clara County —lumbering.

The lumber industry served two purposes: supplying lumber for the growing valley population, and enabling settlers to come into previously inaccessible regions above the valley to farm the cleared land.

At first the lumbering business was limited by the labor intensive whipsaw

method, which was slow and tedious. Working in pairs the lumbermen dug a pit deep enough for a man to stand in and accommodate sawdust, then the pair selected a nearby redwood. Because the first ten feet of a redwood is hard, with the grain twisted and unusable, the lumbermen errected a scaffold six to ten feet above the ground. The scaffold held the men as the pair used axes, saws, or a combination of the two to fell the giant. Once the tree fell the men stripped the branches and bark before cutting the tree into the desired finished lengths. After the lumbermen dragged the logs over the pit, one man stood on top of the log while the other stood in the pit. Together they pushed and pulled the whipsaw up and down until a plank fell from the log.

Men found that to enter the lumbering business required very little capital. These men lived in cabins close to the pit during the summer and fall, until the rains came. In the winter they cut firewood, stakes, and other split stuff. Unfortunately, little is known about these early lumbermen, for most lived lonely lives in the woods.

Another early lumbering method required felling the redwood and splitting lengths of lumber out of the logs with wedges and malls. Much of the early lumber was split rather than whipsawed. Even after the gold rush began many men found that they could make more money by splitting lumber in the Santa Cruz Mountains than they could in the gold fields. Whipsawed lumber and split lumber brought $100 per 1,000 board feet, or up to five dollars per fourteen-inch plank. Each tree contained about 200 board feet

Teams of oxen were used to drag the heavy redwood logs to the mills. Trees up to ten feet in diameter were cut and hauled out on skid roads. Courtesy, San Jose Historical Museum

of lumber.

In the late 1840s lumbermen began using the first mechanical saws in the Santa Cruz Mountains. Peter Lassen, a Danish blacksmith living in San Jose and discoverer of the Lassen Immigrant Trail, built the first mechanical saw used in the Santa Cruz Mountains. The lumbermen dammed up mountain streams into lagoons or ponds to run the early water-powered sawmills. Using an overshot waterwheel to power an up-and-down "Muley" saw, the men quickly recovered their capital investment in the new mills. Although these early mechanical saws were slow, they were a vast improvement over the old whipsaw or splitting methods. By the 1850s there were very few whipsawyers left in the area due to the fact that the new mills cut up to 5,000 linear feet of lumber a day, equal to the efforts of ten whipsawyers.

Large companies employed between fifty and sixty men. The fallers and strippers worked a long, hard, twelve-hour day, while the teamsters worked fifteen hours a day, as they had the additional responsibility of caring for the work animals. The men earned $1.50 a day with two-bits taken out for room and board. Most of the men worked only during the dry season, but the fallers and strippers worked year-round.

Along with the cost of the mill and mill shed, the mill operators built other buildings to house the large crews necessary for full production. These camps were composed of a cook shed, consisting of a large dining hall with a kitchen and storage facilities, a company store with a post office, a meeting hall in large camps, and stable areas, including a barn for horses, mules, and oxen along with a granary. They also provided bunkhouses or cabins for the crews, a blacksmith shop, and business buildings.

In 1848 Isaac Branham and Julian Hanks built the first operating sawmill and lumber camp in Santa Clara County at Lexington, about two miles above Forbes Mill (Los Gatos). Branham and Hank sold the mill for $3,000 to Zachariah "Buffalo"

Jones, who named the area Jones Mill. In 1860 Buffalo Jones sold the mill to John P. Hennings, who renamed the area Lexington after his hometown in Kentucky. The following year a United States Post Office opened in the Santa Cruz Mountains at Lexington.

By 1867 Lexington became the most important town in the foothill region of the county, surpassing even Forbes Mill in importance. Lexington remained the business center for the foothills throughout the 1860s. In addition to eight sawmills, the town boasted a redwood pipe factory. This enterprise made water pipes that were used throughout Santa Clara County.

In 1862 Lysander Collins built a hotel up the creek from Lexington that he named the Forest House. As the lumbering industry moved up the Los Gatos Creek further into the mountains, more businesses were located at the Forest House. In 1873 the post office in Lexington moved to the Forest House and the area was renamed Alma. Seven years later the South Pacific Coast Railroad, recognizing the importance of Alma as a natural feeder for the lumber industry, established their foothill station at Alma and again Lexington was bypassed.

The advent of the railroad in the 1870s dramatically changed the lives of the lumbermen. Prior to the railroad the young men were by and large forced to live as bachelors because the distance between any real town and the lumber camps precluded having a wife or family. With train service, however, the young men married and lived with their families near the depots. Train service also made transportation of lumber to the markets much faster.

Some of the early pioneer settlers in the mountains above Lexington and Alma cut and split lumber for their own use and sometimes to sell; however, they were not primarily occupied by the lumber business.

The first full-time lumbermen in the summit area were Stephen "Si" Hall Chase and his cousin, Josiah W. Chase.

The Chases arrived in San Francisco on May 18, 1859, from Maine after sailing around Cape Horn on the three-masted schooner *Golden Rucket*. The cousins worked as laborers in the lumber camps around Lexington and Alma for four years. After acquiring enough capital they bought 146 acres further up the mountainside from Lyman Burrell for $100. In the spring and summer of 1863, they built a mill and lumberyard on Summit Road on the northern portion of what was once the Soquel Augmentation Rancho. This rancho was one of the few granted to a woman, Martina Castro, who obtained the property in 1844 by a grant from Governor Manuel Micheltorena. The rancho started in the Soquel area and went up and over the summit, covering 32,702 acres in parts of what became two counties—Santa Clara and Santa Cruz.

In 1878 the Chases moved their finishing mill into San Jose, and by 1885 they had one of the largest industries in Santa Clara County. This mill turned out fruit boxes, drying trays, doors, sashes, and other mill products. Many of the old ranches in Santa Clara County were built with and used products bought from the Chase Mill, located in downtown San Jose.

For many years lumbering remained the most important business in the mountain region. Mills sprang up in the mountains along the creeks above Lexington and Alma. Saratoga, located further north along the foothills, was another lumbering town. The mills above Saratoga turned that town into the center for lumbering all the way up the mountain to the Castle Rock area.

In the first fifty years after the takeover of California by the United States, the

The development of the fruit industry created a demand for boxes. The requirements called for a box that would be light and strong. Albert Lake's San Jose Box Factory was located on San Pedro Street and in 1895 utilized 1.5 million feet of white pine and spruce for the production of suitable boxes for the growers. Courtesy, San Jose Historical Museum

Settling in the Santa Cruz Mountains in 1880, Josephine Clifford was a popular writer for magazines and newspapers. She was responsible for introducing such literary giants as Bret Harte and Samuel Clemens/Mark Twain to the region. She married Jackson McCrackin and in 1901 was one of the founders of the Sempervirens Club of California. Courtesy, The Bancroft Library

Santa Cruz Mountains were stripped of the giant redwoods by both lumberers and fire. In the summer of 1899 a small brush fire got away from a farmer in the Spanish Ranch area of the Santa Cruz Mountains in Santa Cruz County. The blaze quickly engulfed a large portion of the summit area and swept down the hills on the Santa Clara County portion of the old Soquel Augmentation Rancho. One of the many homes that were destroyed belonged to Josephine Clifford McCrackin, a well-known California writer and poet. Her home, *Monte Paradiso,* sat just inside the Santa Clara County border with Santa Cruz County.

After surveying the damage caused by the fire, Josephine McCrackin realized that while the burned-out homes could be replaced, the giant redwoods could not. McCrackin reached the conclusion that throughout the Santa Cruz Mountains the native redwood forests were being destroyed, not only by fires, but by the many logging operations. Deciding to try and save the remaining giants, she wrote an article published in the *Santa Cruz Sentinel* on March 7, 1900, calling for the conservation of the great forests. She enlisted the help of Andrew P. Hill, a noted Santa Clara County artist and photographer, who took photographs of the fire's destruction. McCrackin and Hill, together with many summit residents and nature lovers throughout the world, established the Sempervirens Club of California in Palo Alto. The club, dedicated to the preservation of the redwood forests, gained support from the Native Sons and Daughters of the Golden West and the California Pioneer Society. After lobbying the California State Legislature for the creation of state parks to protect the redwoods, the legislature created the first California Redwood Park in March 1901, at Big Basin, near Boulder

Creek in the northern part of Santa Cruz County.

While the establishment of a state park saved some redwoods, many conservationists felt that not enough was being done to spare the giant trees. In 1906 *The Realty,* the summit area's local monthly newspaper, began a series of articles written by local residents on the subject of conservation. Little heed was paid by the lumbermen, and they continued to log the area. Soon, however, there were no more first growth trees left to cut, and the lumbermen closed their mills and moved out of the mountains.

At the same time that lumbermen cleared the land above the valley floor, settlers began coming into the mountain region above Lexington and Alma. The most famous of the early pioneers was "Mountain Charley" (Charles Henry McKiernan). McKiernan hunted throughout the areas in the 1850s supplying the markets in San Francisco with fresh venison and occasionally bear. Over the years this pioneer experienced several close-hand encounters with the 400- to 1000-pound grizzly bears.

One episode was reported in *The Pioneer,* a San Francisco newspaper, twenty-five years after the event. On May 8, 1854, McKiernan was out hunting deer with John Taylor, a neighbor. After sighting a bear the men decided to kill the beast and started down a trail. However, as the men made their way downhill the bear was heading up the trail, and when the two hunters climbed over a mound they came face to face with the grizzly and her cubs. After a missed shot and a brief scuffle, McKiernan lay with a piece of his skull torn from his head. Satisfied that the man posed no danger to her cubs, the bear went after Taylor's hunting dogs, who posed a real threat. After the bear left,

Taylor managed to get his friend home and hurried down the mountain into San Jose for a doctor.

The next morning Dr. A.W. Bell examined McKiernan and sent Taylor back to San Jose with instructions for Bell's partner Dr. T.J. Ingersoll to make a silver plate to fill the hole. However, the plate was too small, and the next morning Ingersoll returned to San Jose, made another plate, and returned by eight that evening. The two physicians cleaned the wound and completed surgery by eleven that night—without the benefit of anesthetics.

A week later Dr. Ingersoll removed the silver plate that was irritating the wound. The following year the surgeon once again operated to clean an infection in the wound. During this surgery Dr. Ingersoll used chloroform to put McKiernan to sleep—the first reported local use of the new anesthetic. McKiernan recovered and, although disfigured, lived a long life before dying in San Jose on January 16, 1892.

Soon after McKiernan moved into the mountains, other settlers moved up also. In 1851 John Martin Schultheis and Susan Byerly Schultheis settled in the mountains after finding that farming lands in the valley were tied up by litigation over uncertain ownership. After a three-day trip from Lexington to the summit, during which they used oxen to break a trail through the brush, the Schultheises settled about two miles east of McKiernan on a portion of the old Soquel Augmentation Rancho, at the present intersection of Summit Road and the Santa Cruz Highway on the border with Santa Cruz County.

The Schultheises settled next to a lagoon that Ohlone Indians used for centuries during their travels from the Santa Clara Valley to the coast. The Indian trail was probably the same one established by Frey Curta Lasuen sixty years before, to

111

Professional photographer and artist Andrew Putman Hill came to San Jose in 1867 as a boy of fourteen. He attended local schools before enrolling in San Francisco's California School of Design. Among his many contributions was his determined campaign to save the Santa Cruz Mountains' redwood trees from the woodsman's axe. Courtesy, San Jose Historical Museum

travel between the Missions Santa Clara and Santa Cruz. The log cabin that the family built is still standing, although a later owner placed milled lumber over the logs in an effort to preserve the original structure. This is the oldest standing building in the summit area of Santa Clara County.

Over the years the Schultheises planted orchards and vineyards. Susan became a well-known nurse and midwife, often traveling as far as Boulder Creek along the wild roads of the 1850s and 1860s to tend the sick and deliver babies.

At the corner of Mountain Charley Road and just a mile down the Santa Cruz road from the Schultheis ranch was Patchin, the first settlement in the summit area. Patchin was a stage stop on the San Jose to Santa Cruz stageline. On March 28, 1872, the Postmaster General authorized the first United States Post Office above Alma at the Patchin home of a man named Shirley. The post office operated until November 30, 1929, in various homes until finally locating in the Edgemont Hotel in Patchin. The office closed on November 30, 1929.

In 1885 Patchin, then consisting of the post office, a store, and a few hotels, was represented at the American Exposition at New Orleans by D.C. Feely, then the little burg's postmaster. Feely exhibited a soil sample and polished wood collection from his farm, as well as a large exhibit of fresh fruit provided by the Fruit Growers of the Santa Cruz Mountains at the exposition. A state historic marker is all that is left of this early mountain community.

Lyman John Burrell was the first fruit grower in the summit area. Burrell, like John Schultheis, found the land titles in the valley hopelessly unresolved and moved to the summit area in 1851. Burrell thought that he was settling on government land, which would allow him to receive

The Sempervirens Club, organized by Andrew P. Hill, was dedicated to saving the redwoods of the Big Basin. Battling the lumber interests in the California State Legislature, the Sempervirens' unstinting efforts saw the formation of California's first State Park, at Big Basin, in 1904. Courtesy, San Jose Historical Museum

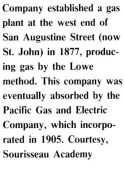

The Garden City Gas Company established a gas plant at the west end of San Augustine Street (now St. John) in 1877, producing gas by the Lowe method. This company was eventually absorbed by the Pacific Gas and Electric Company, which incorporated in 1905. Courtesy, Sourisseau Academy

his land from the federal government by homesteading.

The Burrell family raised pigs, goats, and cattle, which they sold in San Jose. In 1856 Lyman planted an orchard and vineyard, the forbears of the fruit and wine industry that eventually stretched from Alma to the summit. Once the railroad came through Alma up to Wrights, and through the Wrights to Laurel tunnel, the region's farmers shipped tons of fruit, and wine was shipped annually as far as the East Coast.

In 1865 oil promoters Theodore G. McLearan and Henry Palmer leased 2,500 acres from Burrell for oil exploration. Although the men put in a well, the expected bonanza did not materialize. Throughout the 1860s the prospect of oil in the Santa Cruz Mountains remained constantly in the San Jose newspapers as the area boasted the first oil wells in California.

Above Alma, in Moody Gulch near the present-day State Highway 17, a group of lumbermen accidentally discovered oil seeping out of the ground in 1861. This freak discovery began the oil industry in California. Two years later Dr. Vincent Gelcich leased the seepage area to drill for the expected bonanza. Gelcich came to the West Coast as a United States Army surgeon. After settling in California he married the niece of Pío Pico, the last Mexican governor of California.

An active businessman, Gelcich realized the value of oil for lighting homes in the Santa Clara Valley. He was thirty-four years old when he began promoting the oil venture. After organizing the Santa Clara Petroleum Company, Gelcich's drillers worked with a steam drilling rig early in 1865. A year later the well, the first in California, was at the 470-foot level but produced little oil. After two more dry holes the disheartened Gelcich gave up his efforts at Moody Gulch.

Eleven years later Alonza Dillabaugh, an experienced Pennsylvania driller, convinced local investors that oil could be found at the Moody Gulch site, and together the men formed the new Santa Clara Petroleum Company in March 1877.

Alma became a favorite roadside refreshment stop on the old Santa Cruz Highway. Pictured here is an appropriately dressed party out for a Sunday afternoon drive in about 1920. Courtesy, William A. Wulf Collection

Right:
The army's improved cement road over the Santa Cruz Mountains made the trip to Santa Cruz a favorite weekend activity. Here we see an early "traffic jam" near Alma in about 1926. Courtesy, William A. Wulf Collection

Below:
Alma was photographed in 1883 with the passenger cars of the South Pacific Coast Railroad between the Alma Depot and Mr. Floyd's Alma Hotel. Courtesy, William A. Wulf Collection

The company immediately leased 200 acres, including the old Gelcich site. This action sent the local valley newspapers into a frenzy of speculation over the possibilities of a major strike at Moody Gulch. However, by mid-June the well was only sixty feet deep and although the company claimed a daily production of five barrels the newspaper hoopla was a bit overenthusiastic.

Without a major strike the company floundered until Colonel Zaccur P. Boyer, a Pennsylvania promoter and manufacturer of household illuminating gas, bought into the operation and took the reins as manager. Boyer needed oil, as his Garden City Gas Company had recently received a twenty-five-year franchise to supply the citizens of San Jose with illuminating gas.

With renewed activity in the hills above Alma, other promoters became interested in leasing land around the Santa Clara Petroleum Company's sites. One of the new promoters, R.C. McPherson, convinced Boyer and other investors that they should all become partners in the new leases. McPherson turned out not to be the most honest partner. When the leases were recorded, only McPherson's name appeared on the documents. Colonel Boyer, a man of action, finally caught up with McPherson and secured some of the leases at gunpoint. Two other promoters, D.G. Scofield and F.B. Taylor, decided to let the courts settle the matter. Charles N. Felton, a friend of Scofield and Taylor, acted as a liason between the injured parties and McPherson. In a compromise move, McPherson sold the disputed leases to Felton for $500. With the leases back in their control, Scofield and Taylor dropped the lawsuit.

During this time Boyer continued drilling on his separate lease, reaching the 900-foot level without hitting enough oil

The discovery of petroleum depostis at Moody Gulch in the 1860s caused expectations of a Santa Clara County oil boom. Although deposits of oil, bitumen, tar, and natural gas were found from Moody Gulch to Sargent's Station south of Gilroy, optimistic reports of their value have never been fully realized. Courtesy, Sourisseau Academy

for commercial use. But in October 1879, a well drilled only 100 feet from Boyer's first well came in. The promoters quickly laid a two-inch pipeline from the drilling site to a 250-barrel tank at Alma Station, more than a mile away. Expecting a boom in the oil fields above Alma, the South Pacific Coast Railroad constructed a 400-foot siding to better serve the new venture.

With the establishment of a real oil well the San Jose, newspapers were again filled with talk of an oil boom. By December, however, the once-glowing reports became moderate, as the well, once producing sixty barrels a day, slowed to between eight and fourteen barrels a day.

Rather than giving up, the promoters took heart as the oil was of a finer grade than other California crude oils. Boyer decided to buy another 765 acres of oil leases. In addition, the promoter looked at a forty-acre site in Alma for an oil refinery. Up to this junction the Santa Clara Petroleum Company shipped its crude oil 400 miles south to the nearest refinery. Fortunately for the investors, Boyer decided on a more centrally located site at Alameda Point and abandoned the Alma refinery site in 1880.

During 1880 Boyer's company drilled eight more wells, but only four came in. The largest well produced 100 barrels a day, but by 1884 production diminished and the company abandoned the wells. After four years the Moody Gulch site produced only 24,000 barrels of crude oil, a seven-to-ten-week supply for the Alameda refinery.

Even with this failure the last chapter in the history of oil exploration at Moody Gulch was not yet closed. In 1886 and again in this century the area was discussed, but not reopened.

While the promise of oil did not mate-rialize, the mountain farmers experienced considerable success in growing fruit. In Lyman Burrell's memoirs, the pioneer wrote:

It soon became generally understood that the Santa Cruz Mountains were especially adapted to fruit-growing. Families came flocking in and settling in every direction. In a short time other orchards and vineyards were set out. Farming families such as the Burrells, the Schultheis, the Morrells, the Wrights, and many others moved into the mountains. Farming in the Santa Cruz Mountains consisted of dry farming as it would be impossible to irrigate on the hillsides and rolling terrain. Although the farmers produced smaller fruit than that of the irrigated Santa Clara Valley the orchardists reaped better prices because their product was sweeter than the irrigated valley fruit. Growers shipped French prunes, silver prunes, grapes and wines to the East Coast and on to Europe once the South Pacific Coast Railroad reached the foothills above Los Gatos and pushed into the mountain at Wrights in 1877.

These early orchardists and vinticulturists formed the Fruit Growers Association of the Santa Cruz Mountains in the 1870s. Called "the model Fruit Growers Association of the state" by the *Pacific Rural Press,* the association's members won gold, silver, and bronze medals at various fairs and expositions throughout California. The group remained active until 1885, when the Association's members joined the local branch of the Grange, or Patrons of Husbandry. After the local Grange disbanded, some of the local farmers joined Local Number 137 of the Farmers Union. Finally, in the early twentieth century many local farmers joined the Farm Bureau.

The primary function of these farming societies centered around the day-to-day and season-to-season problems facing farmers. However, the secondary function of the agricultural groups was to serve as social centers for the mountain residents who eagerly sought out social activities. In the late 1800s and early 1900s the little community of Burrell on the county line boasted a store, a blacksmith shop, the Wright's Presbyterian Church, several hotels, the Santa Cruz Mountain Telephone Company, and across the road in Santa Cruz County, the Burrell School. Although the original community no longer exists, the school still remains and is now a private residence. The only remaining hotel, the Bohemia, once a favorite spot for San Francisco's literary establishment, is now abandoned. A commercial establishment consisting of a general store, beauty shop, real estate office, and a video rental store exists 100 yards east of the old town in a converted fruit-packing shed.

The little burg of Wrights, located 1.25 miles down the hill from Burrell along the Los Gatos Creek, began as a railroad con-

struction site for the South Pacific Coast Railroad. The railroad was the dream of Senator James G. Fair and Alfred E. "Hog" Davis. The entrepreneurs incorporated the railroad on March 29, 1876, with the intention of building a narrow-gauge railroad from Alameda to Santa Cruz via San Jose, Los Gatos, and through the Santa Cruz Mountains.

Costing $110,000 per mile in the mountains, the South Pacific Coast Railroad became the most expensive narrow-gauge rail line of the era to complete. The twelve miles from Wrights Station to Santa Cruz took two years to build. This section consisted of six tunnels totaling 12,000 feet. The longest tunnel, from Wrights in Santa Clara County, through the summit area, and daylighting in Santa Cruz County near Laurel, was 6,115 feet long, one of the longest tunnels in the world.

When the railroad construction crew reached Wrights in 1877 the men found only an abandoned woodcutter's shack at the site of the future town. Within a few

The Fourth of July requires a parade. This parade along First Street took place in 1890. Only St. James Park remains from this scene. Courtesy, San Jose Historical Museum

weeks the crew built a small town consisting of bunkhouses, a cookhouse, and tool sheds for 2,500 workers. The construction site became a major operation for the railroad as the construction supervisors realized that the crews would be living in the area for some time.

At 10 a.m. on April 11, 1880, the construction crews connected the last track on the line to Santa Cruz. Two years later Wrights was the most important shipping center in the Santa Cruz Mountains. Lumber, fruit, grapes, wine, and other provisions were all shipped to and from the small station. The town, located on the east side of the Los Gatos Creek, consisted of a store and post office, operated by Judge S.P. Hall, a hotel and saloon run by Charles Grant, and a blacksmith's shop, owned by a Mr. Woodruff. The community built a school in the 1880s that operated until the close of the 1928 school year. In addition, Wrights boasted a hotel for the tourist trade. In 1914 the Santa Clara County Library system was organized and Wrights School became one of the first branch libraries in the county.

The Southern Pacific Railroad turned Wrights into a well-frequented tourist attraction after the company bought out the South Pacific Railroad and established

Sunset Park there in the 1890s. As many as 5,000 tourists came up the mountain on picnic trains each weekend. The park featured picnic tables, barbecue pits, cabins, and hiking trails with electric Japanese lanterns strung through the trees. The tourists included fraternal organizations and social clubs from throughout the state.

The 1906 earthquake severely damaged the entire railroad throughout the Bay Area. Tracks twisted, bridges collapsed, almost all the tunnels through the Santa Cruz Mountains caved in, slides blocked the entrances to the tunnels, and the Wrights tunnel shifted five feet at the point the bore crossed the San Andreas Fault.

Over the next two years, as the Southern Pacific Railroad rebuilt the line from Los Gatos to Santa Cruz, passengers and freight traveled via Gilroy and Watsonville and on into Santa Cruz. During the repair period Sunset Park did not operate, and Southern Pacific officials decided to open a new tourist park to handle the demand for a summer resort. The old Seale and Flynn Quarry, along the Alamitos Creek at Seale Station in Santa Clara County, became the site of a new park. The park featured several buildings to accommodate tourists traveling from as far away as San Francisco during the weekends. The resort operated until 1909 when the original Sunset Park at Wrights Station reopened. After the Southern Pacific Railroad abandoned the temporary park, crews removed the buildings in February 1910 and the company sold the land to farmers.

In addition to weekend tourists, the mountains above Los Gatos and Saratoga seemed to be full of campers during the summers. From the 1880s to the early 1900s campers going into the mountains or to Santa Cruz blocked the roads with horse-drawn buggies and wagons. At the height of the season as many as seventy-

Father Riker's Holy City, pictured here in about 1922, was located near the summit of the Santa Cruz Mountains on the old Santa Cruz Highway. Courtesy, William A. Wulf Collection

five teams waited in Los Gatos, Lexington, and Alma to travel up the mountain on the Santa Cruz Highway, with a similar number waiting to travel up Congress Springs Road out of Saratoga.

Families spending the entire summer in the mountains arrived in Wrights on the Saturday train where they were picked up by waiting buggies from the various Santa Cruz Mountain resorts. After helping their families settle in at the mountain hotels, the men of the households returned on the Sunday evening train to the Bay Area to their jobs during the week. On the following weekend the men again traveled by train up to Wrights to join their families for the weekend. The cost for the vacationing family was seven dollars per week for room and board.

With the advent of reliable automobile travel after the turn of the twentieth century, the resorts in the Santa Cruz Mountains no longer drew large crowds during the tourist season. In 1910 the Southern Pacific Railroad closed Sunset Park; other resorts and hotels throughout the mountains quickly followed suit. Vacationing tourists began traveling outside of the greater San Francisco Bay Area.

In 1936 San Jose Water Works bought Wrights and tore down the buildings. Today the only remnants are the concrete tunnel face, the old concrete railroad bridge abutments, and the automobile bridge, built in 1917, that crosses the Los Gatos Creek. The United States Army Corps of Engineers blasted the tunnel shut in 1942 as part of war exercises.

The only vestiges of resort days in the Santa Cruz Mountains are the summer cabins built by families who spent their summers and weekends in the hills above Los Gatos. During 1927 and 1928 S.D. "Dean" Balch and James A. Case subdivided a section of the summit area above the Santa Cruz Highway that they named Redwood Estates. Featuring a combination of resort and vacation homesites, Redwood Estates consisted of a store, community center, swimming pool, and tennis courts.

The entrance sign to Father William E. Riker's Holy City on the old Santa Cruz highway announced one of Riker's gubernatorial slogans. Courtesy, William A. Wulf Collection

Below Redwood Estates along the Santa Cruz Highway stood one of the most interesting cities in the mountains above Los Gatos—Holy City. It was established in 1918 by "Father" William E. Riker, founder of the Perfect Christian Divine Way (PCDW) of San Francisco. Riker, who was also known as "The Comforter," was born in Oakdale, California, in 1873 and grew up in Oroville before moving to San Francisco at the age of nineteen.

Living in the city by the bay, Riker worked at various jobs until he developed a new religion in 1907. Claiming he received messages from God through his nerves, Riker declared that his teachings were "100 percent brand new, all-wise and strictly up-to-date." Although Riker taught celibacy, the preacher left the state after the San Francisco district attorney learned that Riker was married to two women. After being on the road for five years Riker returned with yet a third wife, Lucille Jensen, or Mother Jensen as she was known, and in 1918 began preaching to all who would listen. To further spread his beliefs Riker ran for governor of California four times, starting in 1937. His campaigns and sermons were extremely racist. Among other beliefs the self-styled preacher argued that orientals and blacks should not be allowed in business, a notion that was not unpopular in turn-of-the-century California.

In 1918 Riker purchased property near the summit of the Santa Cruz Mountains along the Santa Cruz Highway. The Comforter's followers built homes and a commercial center consisting of a complete service station, a grocery store, a restaurant, a printing shop, and radio station KFQU. Brightly colored racist slogans and biblical paintings covered the false fronts of the commercial buildings and stone retaining walls. To protect his enterprise Riker incorporated the Perfect Christian Divine

Way in 1922.

Over the next three decades Riker was constantly in the newspapers. Reporters could always count on a good story for a slow news day if they looked into Riker's colorful life. He was constantly in the courts for alleged misdeeds, including reckless driving, fraud, evasion of taxes, breach of promise, sedition, and murder.

No matter how colorful Riker was, he could not battle the effect of the state's decision to build a new highway over the Santa Cruz Mountains in the late 1930s. With the completion of Highway 17 Riker's various businesses slowly faded into memories. Although as popular as ever in the late 1940s and early 1950s—he received almost 15,000 votes in the 1950 gubernatorial primary—Riker's followers dwindled to twelve by 1952. Five years later The Comforter sold Holy City.

While no longer as controversial as he had been, Riker's conversion to Catholicism in 1966, when he was ninety-three, drew some ink in Bay Area newspapers. During his last years Riker proved difficult to get along with. Although his health was failing, nursing home operators refused to keep him as Riker could not get along with other patients. Riker died on December 3, 1969, in Agnew State Hospital.

Much of Holy City burned in various arson fires during the late 1950s and 1960s. Although a modern establishment replaced some of the burned and dilapidated businesses, the bar at one end of the building never drew enough clientele to stay open, and in 1982 the U.S. post office in the middle of the structure closed due to lack of patrons. The only business in the town in the mid-1980s was a stained-glass studio.

While all but a few remnants of Riker's Holy City are long gone, his home, sitting on a small knoll overlooking the desolate townsite, remains. Riker's life and vision continues to draw the interest of local reporters. Once every few years an article on Holy City appears in a Bay Area newspaper.

Due east, across the valley floor from the Santa Cruz Mountains, stands the Diablo Range. Together with the Santa Cruz Mountains the two ranges define the Santa Clara Valley. The Diablos were not explored much during the Spanish and Mexican rule and did not offer much to earlier inhabitants of the valley. Later, during the early American rule settlers repeated the patterns found in the Santa Cruz Mountains, although without the lumbering phase. Ranches in the area consisted primarily of cattle. Several pioneering families moved into the Diablo Range. The best known is the Joseph D. Grant family. Better known to valley residents is the James Lick Observatory sitting high atop of Mount Hamilton. The observatory was a gift from James Lick to the newly established University of California.

James Lick was born on August 25, 1796, in Fredericksburg, Pennsylvania. When he was a teenager Lick learned carpentry and became a piano maker by his mid-twenties. When he turned twenty-five he decided that opportunites for riches were to be found outside of the United States. The young man found a sea captain who agreed to give Lick passage to Buenos Aires in return for a piano.

Although he did not speak Spanish, upon his arrival Lick soon became a success with his piano business. Over the next two decades, Lick moved from Buenos Aires to Valpariso, Chile, and finally to Lima, Peru. Upon learning that the United States took control of California from Mexico in 1846, Lick decided to try his fortunes once again. With $30,000 worth of gold and 600 pounds of chocolate for

James Lick was a native of Pennsylvania who came to California in 1848, where he made his fortune in real estate. He also was involved in flour milling and fruit growing in the county. His great interest in science led him to bequeath the bulk of his large estate to the University of California and the Academy of Science for the construction of Lick Observatory atop Mount Hamilton. Courtesy, San Jose Historical Museum

trading, Lick set out for San Francisco in November 1847.

The California of 1848 offered little business for piano makers, and Lick decided that his opportunites were best met in real estate. In the first few months of 1848 Lick purchased land in San Francisco and after exploring the Santa Clara Valley he decided to expand into the San Jose area as well. In May, Lick, like most other settlers, came down with gold fever, as John Marshall's discovery on the American River leaked out to the world. However, the piano maker quickly realized that bending over a gold pan in a freezing river was not for him, and after one week he returned to the Bay Area and his investments.

During the inital phase of the gold rush Lick purchased almost $10,000 in real estate. This investment soared to a worth of about two million dollars by December 1848.

One of the properties Lick purchased was a flour mill site on the Guadalupe River from Manuel Diaz Miranda near the present-day site of the Montague Expressway, Agnew State Hospital, and the Lick Mill Road. The flour mill became the center for Lick's growing real estate empire. With flour selling for forty dollars a barrel in San Francisco, Lick planted wheat on his property, located only three miles from the port of Alviso, and quickly prospered.

In the mid-1850s Lick constructed a larger mill and a unique circular brick granary on his growing farm. The millionaire experimented with new varieties of fruit and methods of cultivation. Lick became one of the valley's pioneer orchardists with the planting of apples, peaches, quince, cherries, plums, pears, and apricots on his farm.

In 1860 Lick attended a lecture in San Jose given by George Maderia. Lick became fascinated with astronomy and invited Maderia to stay at his San Jose home. Over the course of the visit Maderia taught Lick to use a telescope and some basic knowledge in astronomy. As the two men talked, a vision of building the largest telescope in the world began to take hold of the real estate tycoon.

In the early 1870s, due to failing health and family problems, Lick gave his mill to the Thomas Paine Society of Boston and moved to the Lick House, his San Francisco hotel. At the Lick House, in the summer of 1872, Lick became aquainted with Joseph Henry, the secretary of the Smithsonian Institute, and one of the United States' leading scientific figures. During the course of their discussions Henry explained to Lick how James Smithsonian used his vast fortune to establish the Institute. Lick decided that he too should leave something to science and donated some of his real estate to the California Academy of Sciences the following year.

George Davidson, the president of the California Academy of Sciences, visited

with Lick to express the Academy's appreciation for the donation. Through the next few months Davidson, an astronomer, convinced Lick that the millionaire should build an observatory to house the most powerful telescope in the world.

Although Davidson wanted the observatory built in the Sierra Nevadas, other astronomers pointed out the disadvantages of the Sierra Nevada winters. Lick's advisors urged him to pick a spot in the San Francisco Bay area, near the state's scientific community.

During the summer of 1875 Lick asked Thomas E. Fraser, an employee, to look at four possible sites: Mount Diablo, in Contra Costa County, Mt. St. Helena in Napa County, as well as Loma Prieta and Mount Hamilton in Santa Clara County. Late in the summer Fraser and Mayor Bernard D. Murphy of San Jose rode horses up to the top of Mount Hamilton. The mountain's access was easy and the view superb—this was the site.

Before he agreed to place the new observatory on Mount Hamilton, Lick proposed that Santa Clara County build a year-around access road to the observatory site. Mayor Murphy used his influence, and in September 1875 the Board of Supervisors approved Lick's proposal.

In February 1876 the surveying crew, headed by A.T. Herman, completed their survey, and construction on the road commenced. However easy it was to approve the road, the supervisors quickly learned that the mere fact that the county was going to have the best astronomical observatory in the world was not enough to quell politics. On February 17, 1876, the *San Jose Weekly Mercury* published an article condemning the supervisors and the road contractor they hired for allowing Chinese laborers to construct the new road. By April the Chinese workers were a minority of the workforce.

On June 7, 1876, the United States Congress granted the trustees of the Lick Observatory 1,350 acres on top of Mount Hamilton for the road and buildings. Earlier in June, the Board of Supervisors appointed a committee to oversee construction of the road. What they found made the front page of the *San Jose Weekly Mercury*. Derby announced that he could not complete the road to the standards of the contract. The road stood incomplete and unable to withstand the coming winter's storms.

The supervisors hired Drinkwater and Swall, road contractors, to finish the road before the rains hit. In December the road to Mount Hamilton, which had cost the county $73,455.81, was ready.

Over the next three years both engineers and scientists developed plans for the buildings and the instruments. In addition, litigation concerning the Lick Trust took time in the court in San Francisco. Finally, on July 23, 1880, work on the James Lick Observatory began.

To speed up the construction process and avoid more than twenty miles of roads, the men built a brick kiln in order to use the clay in a depository near the summit to make the bricks used in the observatory buildings. Teamsters and their horses and wagons hauled everything else up the hill from San Jose.

In October 1887, twelve years after the Board of Supervisors approved James Lick's plan, the contractors completed the complex. Millions of bricks went into the construction of the two buildings at the observatory.

The observatory had been working, however, since October 1881 when the Lick astronomers installed a twelve-inch telescope purchased from the firm of Avan Clark and Sons of Cambridgeport, Massa-chusetts. This firm also won the contract to build Lick Observatory's main telescope, which was the largest instrument in the world. The Parisian glass firm of Feil and Company, the manufacturers of the lenses in the twelve-inch telescope, cast the glass for the thirty-six-inch refractor. Alvan Clark and Sons took one year to finish the lens. The mounting for the telescope took another year for Warner and Swazey, a Cleveland firm to build. In January 1888 the largest telescope in the world stood complete and James Lick's dream was a reality.

Lick never had the pleasure of looking at the heavens from his observatory. Due to ill health he was not able to visit the site of the future observatory before his death at the Lick House in San Francisco on October 1, 1876. However, in observing his wishes the contractors sealed his remains in a vault in the foundations of the giant telescope on January 8, 1887.

A break for tea and rice during the building of Mount Hamilton road is pictured here. In order to transport building materials to the Lick Observatory site atop Mount Hamilton, the county supervisors approved the building of the twenty-eight-mile road to the summit, completed in December 1876 at a cost of $78,000. Courtesy, Sourisseau Academy

The thirty-six-inch Refractor Telescope was the largest telescope in the world when it was installed at Lick Observatory atop Mount Hamilton in 1888. As the first mountaintop observatory, Lick Observatory was a major tourist attraction for many years. Courtesy, San Jose Public Library, California Room

The Mount Hamilton Stage Company operated excursions from San Jose to Lick Observatory. The stable pictured at Smith Creek was a normal stop to change horses. Standing second from the right is Charles Miller, owner of the stage line. Courtesy, San Jose Historical Museum

This group paused to capture the spirit of their excursion to Mount Hamilton before the turn of the century. The trip to the observatory is a popular outing for both visitors and natives. Today the paved road follows the same route laid out in 1876. Courtesy, San Jose Historical Museum

SEEDS
OF
CHANGE

In the 100 years after the Santa Clara Valley became a California county, a great number of people planted seeds in the valley's fertile soil. These seeds included those of government, newspapers, education, culture, and industry. The men and women who nurtured these enterprises helped to develop Santa Clara County from a frontier society into a modern one.

This change that inevitably occurs in Santa Clara County has carried a price, and often this price came at the expense of those pioneers who planted the seeds of change. One such change occurred during the formation of California into a state.

The most hotly debated issue at the California Constitutional Convention of 1849 was where to locate the new state capital. Rodman Price, a San Francisco delegate, urged the convention to adopt San Francisco, California's economic hub, as the state capital. This suggestion was opposed by most delegates from other areas who feared the continued dominance of what was already California's fastest-growing city.

Henry H. Halleck, a delegate from Monterey, wanted Monterey, to host the first session, after which the government could be transferred permanently to San Jose. But Kimball H. Dimmick of San Jose reported that Monterey was not centrally located and that the former capital of Spanish and Mexican California had been the seat of government for too long. Dimmick then campaigned for San Jose as the best location and reported that the people of San Jose would provide a building free of charge to house the new state

California's first state capitol building was an adobe, located on Market Plaza near San Antonio Street. Originally built in 1849 as a hotel, it was the only building in San Jose of sufficient size to house the first California State Legislature. It burned in 1853 and this replica was built in 1899 to commemorate California's fiftieth anniversary. Courtesy, San Jose Historical Museum

government.

Jacob Hoppe, another San Jose delegate, told the delegates that San Jose was ready to give more than thirty acres to the new government and that the nearly complete Pierre (Pedro) Sainsevain house, a two-story building measuring seventy feet by thirty-five feet and located in the 100 block of South Market Street, would be available for both the House and Senate.

A delegate from Benicia urged a compromise that would make Benicia the capital, although he favored San Jose for the seat of government. Other delegates pushed for their towns of Stockton and Santa Barbara, as well as other favorite locations in California.

Finally, Rodman M. Price of San Francisco backed San Jose, and Joseph Aram of San Jose pointed out to the delegates that the state of Ohio had suffered problems until the capital was moved to a geographically central location. For this reason, San Jose was more secure than either San Francisco or Monterey in case of a foreign invasion. When Aram finished speaking, Robert B. Semple, the president of the convention, called for a vote on Halleck's amendment to hold the first session in Monterey. The amendment was defeated twenty-three to fifteen. The delegates then voted twenty-three to fourteen to place the capital at San Jose.

After the delegates voted on the other provisions of the Constitution, the document was sent to Washington, D.C., for congressional approval. The people of California voted for the Constitution on November 13, 1849. The proposal easily passed, with 12,064 votes for statehood and 811 against.

On December 12, 1849, the military governor of California, Brigadier General Bennett Riley, declared the Constitution valid and, on December 20, Riley surren-dered his authority to Peter H. Burnett, who became California's first governor.

The first legislature met on December 15 in San Jose at the still unfinished Sainsevain home. The first legislature accomplished enough to be praised by most historians, although some labeled the session "the legislature of a thousand drinks," citing State Senator Thomas Jefferson Green of Sacramento, who asked for several adjournments during the proceedings so the legislators could partake of some refreshment. While the candidates for United States senator, Charles Fremont and William M. Gwin, did give away free drinks in the evenings, the official record does not show adjournment for the purpose of drinking.

That the legislators might have reason to drink was evident by the conditions they found in San Jose. Between October 28 and March 22, thirty-six inches of rain fell on San Jose, leaving the road between San Jose and the Embarcadero at Alviso a muddy quagmire. On December 15, the opening day of the legislative session, only six senators managed to struggle into the new capital of California.

In the ensuing days, as the rest of the members of the first legislature reached San Jose, they found that their promised capitol building was still unfinished. For the first few weeks the senators met at the home of Isaac Branham on the southwest corner of the Plaza. Once the Senate was seated in the building with the lower house, William Kelley, an Englishman, wrote a description of the capitol and both houses in his book, *An Excursion to California,* published in London in 1851:

. . . the Senate, or Upper House, occupy the lower apartment, which is a large, ill-lit, badly ventilated room, with a low ceiling, and a rough railing a little inside the door, beyond which none but the elect may

California's first state governor, Judge Peter H. Burnett, arrived from Oregon in 1849, settling in San Jose. In addition to conducting a successful law practice, he also speculated in the development of Alviso. Courtesy, San Jose Historical Museum

pass. Each member had a rush-bottomed arm-chair, and a small desk with stationery, that was not in much requisition. At the further end the Speaker was perched in a species of pulpit; the floor was covered with a number of little carpets, of various shapes and patterns, looking as if every member contributed a patch to make up the robe, which had quite a mosaic appearance, the idea of antiquity being assisted by the threadbare state of the whole. A slip of paper was stuck with wafers on the door as you entered, labeled "wait for a pause," reminding me of the familiar inscriptions on those of the billiard-rooms at home, "wait for the stroke," which, from the turmoil inside, would be the more opposite of the two, from the great probability of its ending in blows. The other apartment is precisely the same size, but has the advantage of greater loftiness, and exhibits at once the difference of grade betwixt the two bodies in the style of furniture—plain common chairs, flat deal tables, and a strip of matting thrown where the feet are erroneously supposed to rest, being the extent of accommodation, a paltry difference at best, and as it appeared to me, at variance with the republican doctrine of equality, and the "genius of free institutions." A similar notice was struck on this door; but were I to wait at the threshold of either house for a pause, I should wait for the daily adjournment, for the noise of jabbering was as incessant as the twittering of a flock of swallows chatting over their intended migration.

Kelly's description of the legislators left no doubt that they fit into their rough chambers:

Nothing can be more remote from the regularity, decency, or decorum of deliberative assemblies, than the proceedings of these bodies; there was no order of debate or

*system of discussion, but a turbulent din-
ning colloquy, made up of motions, inter-
ruptions, assertions, and contradictions; several members generally on their legs at the
same time, and those with legs on the tables, adding to the tumult by the music of
their heels. I never could catch the faintest
idea of the subject under consideration, nor
is it possible that the merits of any measure can be sifted under such a species of
discussion. They meet at ten o'clock A.M.,
and are let loose for dinner at one o'clock,
when they come out with a rush, like so
many overgrown school boys. It is unneces-
sary to add, that smoking, chewing, and
whittling, do not constitute an infraction of
the rules of either house, privileges that are
accorded also to a squad of slip-shod
clerks or messengers who loll about the
stores, making a tout ensemble really
unique, and entirely characteristic.*

If the State House was seen and described
in less than lofty terms, the legislators also
faced bleak housing accommodations. Between Market and First streets downtown,
San Jose was virtually a tent city. Living
costs soared. Dinners, consisting of mostly
potatoes, cost at least two dollars, and
boiled eggs for breakfast cost the amazed
legislators fifty cents each. Furthermore, although the elected officials were paid sixteen dollars per day, the payment was
given to them in state scrip—and only San
Jose merchants would redeem scrip at face
value. In other cities, scrip dollars brought
only forty cents.

Other than sitting in front of the fire-
place at the Mansion House, the legislators
had little to occupy their spare time. Although the officials took a three-day recess
for Christmas, the road conditions were so
bad that no one could go home. To com-
pensate the beleaguered men, the citizens
of San Jose gave the first State Ball on

December 27 in the Assembly. Women,
however, were few and reports of them
coming from as far as Benicia by steam-
boat, braving a drenching rain to attend
the social event of the year, demonstrate
the difficulty in securing dance partners.

The officials were treated to a bull and
bear fight in the old pueblo ring on February 3, 1850. On March 3 the entire legislature adjourned—senators, assemblymen,
clerks, and loafers left downtown for the
Coyote Creek with pickaxes and pans on
a short-lived "gold rush." The following
month the legislators and their assistants
celebrated April Fools' Day by watching a
$10,000 horse race.

On the afternoon of October 18, 1850,
the sailing ship *Oregon* docked in San
Francisco with news that sent the city's
citizens into a frenzy of celebration in
Portsmouth Square: California had been
admitted to the Union as the thirty-first
state on September 9, 1850. Governor Peter Burnett rode to San Jose the next
morning beside Jarad Crandall as the
famed "whip" raced another stagecoach
driver to be the first to give the news to
the citizens of the new state capital. Crandall, with the Governor at his side, made
the run in record time and the afternoon
and evening was full of the noisy celebration.

These diversions, interesting though
they may be, could not totally satisfy the
legislators and, after some debate, both the
Assembly and Senate voted to move the
capital to General Manuel Vallejo's property in the North Bay. The capital briefly
returned to San Jose during the period
when it traveled from Vallejo to San Jose,
then back to Vallejo for a month, before
moving on to Sacramento, and then to
Benicia after Sacramento flooded. Finally,
on February 5, 1854, the capital was permanently located in Sacramento.

Santa Clara County was a small agricultural area of 6,764 people in 1852, when the capital was finally lost. By the beginning of the next decade, however, the county boasted 2,295 families and a population of 11,912. San Jose grew from about 2,500 people in 1852 to 3,430 in 1860. The county's commerce consisted of small businesses, banking, and newspapers, while the biggest businesses in the county were cattle and grain.

In 1861 a war of sorts occurred in Santa Clara County by squatters claiming land that was part of Rancho Yerba Buena, located between Coyote Creek, Tully Road, and Metcalf Road. Land titles in the Santa Clara Valley were in a state of uncertainty during the 1850s and early 1860s, as residents waited to see the outcome of the United States Land Commission's decisions concerning ownership of the county's ranchos.

Due to the less-than-perfect descriptions and legal titles to the ranchos found after the American takeover, the United States government decided that the claimants would have to prove that they were entitled to their land. This process took many years and cost the claimants a fortune in lawyers' fees. The claimants, most of whom were Californios, did not speak English or understand American law, and were at a disadvantage during the lengthy process that often ended in the United States Supreme Court.

This process was also harmful to the newly arriving settlers, who were unable to determine which land was private and which was public land that could be homesteaded. Due to this confusion, many immigrants settled on lands they erroneously thought were public.

In 1860, when Antonio Chabolla was awarded his Yerba Buena Rancho, many American immigrants who had lived there for ten years—paying taxes on what they thought was government land—became outraged. Many of the settlers felt that Chabolla's grant was fraudulent, even though it had been upheld by the government.

In 1861 Chabolla asked the Americans to leave. The settlers, or squatters, as they were called, refused to leave and armed themselves. Chabolla's legal council, William Matthews, obtained writs of eviction from Judge Sam Bell McKee of the Third Judicial Court of Santa Clara County and presented them to Sheriff John Murphy for execution.

Sheriff Murphy gathered a posse of 600 men to help evict the thirteen families named in the writs. When the posse gathered at the courthouse they were unarmed, and when the sheriff asked them to arm themselves the men refused. Murphy had no option other than to excuse the men from duty. That afternoon, before Sheriff Murphy could come up with an alternate plan, 1,000 well-armed settlers came into San Jose from their homes with a small cannon donated by some citizens of Saratoga. Sheriff Murphy could do little but watch. However, the protesters did no damage. They wanted only to let the sheriff and court know that they would not allow the families on Rancho Yerba Buena to be forcibly evicted.

Sheriff Murphy then sent a petition to Governor John Downey and the California State Legislature requesting that the state militia be brought in, at a cost of $100,000. Governor Downey realized that bloodshed would be the result of sending the militia to San Jose and decided to see if the parties would get together once the situation calmed down. Judge McKee refused to allow the court to open the following month unless law and order were returned to the county. His action and the governor's plan worked, as Chabolla and the settlers managed to reach a compromise that allowed the squatters to keep the land at a reasonable price.

The most important event for the nation during the decade of the 1860s was the Civil War. Hundreds of young men joined the Union Army where most served in the Indian Country, Arizona, New Mexico, and Texas. There was some sympathy in the county for the Confederacy, but the only local event that could be traced to the ongoing war occurred in 1864 in The Battle of Almaden Road.

In an attempt to raise money for the South, a secret group of Confederate sympathizers led by "Captain" Ralph Henry, who was also known as R. Henry Ingraham, held up the Virginia City to Placerville Wells Fargo stage in May and June. Captain Henry gave a voucher to the driver as a receipt for the eight sacks of silver bullion his men took. The following day the band killed Deputy Sheriff Staples of El Dorado County, who had unwisely tried to capture the gang by himself. One of the highwaymen, Thomas B. Poole, was wounded before he could be captured.

Three members of Henry's gang then traveled to the Santa Clara Valley, where they intended to rob the New Almaden Quicksilver Mine payroll aboard the stage from San Jose to the mines. On the evening of July 14, the men stopped at a farmer's house on the New Almaden Road about 2.5 miles from San Jose. The trio told the farmer, a man named Hill, that they were waiting for some friends. Hill allowed the men to sleep in a shed, but the following morning, after the men stayed indoors, Hill became suspicious and alerted Sheriff John H. Adams. After gathering a posse consisting of deputy sheriffs G.W. Reynolds, Fred Morris, and J.M. Brownlee, and six other men, the sheriff rode out to Hill's ranch.

After surrounding the small building,

Sheriff Adams called for the three men to come out. In the pitched battle that followed, Sheriff Adams was hit, but his watch deflected the bullet, and he only received a minor wound. John Clendennin, who was also wounded, escaped, and was later found near Willow Glen, dying from a bullet wound. Another robber, John Creal Bouldware, was also killed. Abraham Gillespie (or Glasby) was captured alive after his pistol was shot away. One of Sheriff Adams' men suffered two small wounds in his leg. Over the next few months the remaining secessionists were arrested and tried in Placerville for their crimes. Thomas B. Poole was hung for the death of the deputy in El Dorado County, while Preston Hodges, a resident of Santa Clara County, was sentenced to twenty years in San Quentin Prison.

John Grant, who had broken away from the Captain Henry gang, was later captured at the home of a female friend in Los Gatos. Although he was taken by surprise, Grant managed to break free and grab Sheriff Hall's gun, but was unable to use the pistol before he was shot with both barrels of a shotgun. Severely wounded, he was nevertheless brought to San Jose and jailed.

In another Civil War-related incident, the Methodist Church at Berryessa was burned to the ground. Although no one was captured, most people in the valley attributed the burning to members of Dick Baker's band of Confederate sympathizers. The Civil War divided the Methodist Church into two factions—North and South. The church remained split for more than a century after the war.

During the Civil War a small group of citizens actively supported the Confederacy. George O'Doherty, editor of the *San Jose Tribune,* a pro-Southern newspaper, was silenced when the commanding general of

Artesian water was discovered in San Jose in 1854. The availability of this abundant water source had a great impact on the economic development of the Santa Clara Valley. This well, photgraphed in 1895, was one of five artesian wells located on the north San Jose ranch of Coleman Younger. Courtesy, San Jose Historical Museum

the Western States, George Wright, revoked the privileges of pro-Confederate newspapers to use the United States mail. Most of the county's citizens, however, remained pro-Union.

One of the most pressing problems facing both the farmers of the nineteenth century and the developers of the twentieth century has centered around the need for an abundant supply of water. By the early 1850s the citizens of San Jose realized that the old Mexican Acequia could no longer supply enough water to the former pueblo, and in 1851 the city council decided to lay water pipes for the city. Three years later, in January 1854, the Merritt Brothers drilled a six-inch-by-eighty-foot well on

their property at Fifth Street and hit an artesian well. Later that month, three miles east of town, J.S. Shepherd hit the second artesian well at eighty feet. Shepherd's well rose in a pipe sixteen feet above the ground. The following month T. Meyers hit yet another artesian well. Thinking that he could solve the fresh water problems for the city's inhabitants, William Campbell drilled for water at First and Santa Clara streets downtown. The resulting gusher flooded the downtown area to Market Street until it was diverted into a ditch known as Fountain Alley.

In August 1854, G.A. Dabney hit an artesian well at sixty feet near San Fernando Street. Dabney found that he could not control the gusher, and it, too, flooded the area. The city council declared the well a nuisance and ordered Dabney to pay a fine of fifty dollars a day until he capped the well. Unfortunately, the water continued to pour out of the ground for six weeks, producing a four-foot-wide by six-inch-deep stream downtown. In an effort to cap the well, Dabney hired 100 workers to bring two huge redwood logs out of the Santa Cruz Mountains. The pressure of the water, however, was too strong to be tamed. Finally, after several other wells were sunk in the area, Dabney managed to cap the water.

Artesian wells continued to come in for the rest of the century, as more than 2,000 wells supplied the valley's towns and farms. By 1914, however, most of the wells were abandoned, as the valley's farmers drew more water from the underground supply than could be returned by natural percolation. Farmers began to rely on their own wells and irrigation projects.

As early as 1859, Theopholus and Socrates Kirk organized one of the valley's first irrigation projects. The Kirk Ditch Company took water from the Los Gatos Creek and supplied water to local farmers. Clarence H. Kirk, a grandson of Socrates Kirk, ran this system until the late 1960s.

In 1889 George W. Page developed two irrigation ditches on the west side of Los Gatos Creek to supply Campbell's farmers. Two other projects included the Masson Ditch on the east side of Los Capitancillos (Guadalupe Creek) and the Auzerais Ditch on the Penitencia Creek.

During the late 1890s and early 1900s, farmers began drilling more wells, due to several dry years, and by 1915 farmers were taking more than eight billion gallons of water out of the ground per year. In 1920 farmers, businessmen, trade union members, and the Board of Supervisors formed the Santa Clara Valley Water Conservation Committee. This group became increasingly concerned that the county's natural yearly rain water was not being utilized properly. The committee hired engineer Fred H. Tibbetts of Campbell and his associate, Stephen E. Keiffer, to conduct a survey of the county's water resources.

Eight months after they started, the two engineers presented a report to the Santa Clara Valley Water Conservation Committee. Their report concluded that more water was being pumped from the ground in the valley than could be naturally recharged. Furthermore, about 1,700 new wells were being dug each year to irrigate almost 68 percent of the valley floor. Tibbetts and Keiffer wrote that seventeen reservoirs, costing a total of $10,947,495, needed to be built in order to hold the winter rain and get the water to the valley's farmers. The Tibbetts and Keiffer report was the beginning of several decades of effort to preserve winter runoff in order to recharge the valley's groundwater supply.

In order to get voter approval, the legal counsel for the Water Conservation Committee, former State Assemblyman L.D. Bohnett, drew up a bill to organize a water district, and State Senator Herbert C. Jones pushed the bill through Sacramento. The Jones Act became law in June 1921 and provided that the cost of construction for the reservoirs would be borne by those who used the water, provided the citizens voted for a water district.

While farmers, business groups, and trade unions generally favored the creation of a water district, there was enough opposition to the overall cost of the project to defeat the measure on September 17, 1921. The district failed in a second vote on the issue in 1924. This time the plan met opposition from the County Board of

During the early years of this century, water conservation became a serious local issue, and in the 1920s the Santa Clara Valley Water Conservation District was formed. By 1950 the district had built nine large dams across streams flowing into the valley, effectively raising the underground water level. Here is a scene of the construction of Almaden Dam in 1936. Courtesy, Sourisseau Academy

Supervisors and other government bodies. With this second defeat and growing opposition from local government, the Santa Clara Valley Water Conservation Committee soon disbanded.

Two years later, on December 1, 1926, the Santa Clara Valley Water Conservation Association incorporated and began to fight for water conservation. This organization had the support of farmers and the Chamber of Commerce. The farmers were concerned with having enough water available to irrigate their crops, while the Chamber of Commerce was concerned with providing enough water to expand industry in San Jose.

Again Senator Jones was called on to push legislation through Sacramento legalizing the establishment of water conservation districts, and in 1929 he managed to gain enough support for the Water Conservation Act. As was the case in the past, however, the voters would have to approve the creation of local districts.

In addition to the lowering of the water table, a new issue was brought to light when San Jose City Engineer J.R. Byxbee wrote a letter to the County Board of Supervisors advising them that saltwater seepage from the San Francisco Bay was beginning to intrude into the shrinking water table. Byxbee urged the supervisors to require all brackish wells to be sealed. The Board concurred and Supervisor Joseph McKinnor reported that Gus Hunter was the county's official "well plugger."

On November 5, 1929, the county's citizens finally approved the creation of a water conservation district and elected seven directors. The new Board of Directors elected Leroy Anderson as president, R.P. Van Orden as secretary, State Senator Jones as district counsel, and Tibbetts as chief engineer.

Although the voters approved the cre-ation of the water conservation district in 1931, when they were in the grip of the Depression these same taxpayers decided not to support the six-million-dollar construction project that was needed to build a series of dams and reservoirs. The Board of Directors turned to the new Public Works Administration for 30 percent of the necessary funding on November 7, 1932. With assurances that the federal government would help finance the mammoth water project, the voters approved a two-million-dollar bond fund on June 19, 1934. By the following year the Almaden, Calero, Guadalupe, Stevens Creek, and Vasona projects were complete.

The completion of the Coyote Dam was delayed until 1936, due to the discovery of the Hayward Earthquake Fault. This discovery mandated new engineering studies. In addition, the construction took longer than anticipated when the crews were forced to bring in rock for the dam from a quarry located more than one mile away from the site.

The Anderson and Lexington projects were completed in 1950 and 1952, respectively. Although the Lexington Dam project had been planned since 1931, delays were caused by the failure of the State Highway Department to locate Highway 17 in relationship to the dam. This forced the Water Conservation District to look for another site in 1948. The result was the Leroy Anderson Dam and Reservoir.

After several years of delays, Santa Clara County assemblymen John F. Thompson and Robert Kirkwood managed to successfully guide through the California State Legislature their $2.5 million appropriation bill to relocate Highway 17 in 1947. After more years of delay by the State Highway Department, work was finally begun to move the highway in 1950, and it was completed in 1951. The actual

The Enright Straw-Burning Threshing Engine was used by hundreds of farmers in areas where wood was scarce. This one is shown being repaired in 1910 at the Enright Foundry on the south side of Pierce Street, near Market Street. The foundry was originally established in 1864 by Irish inventor, Joseph Enright. Courtesy, Sourisseau Academy

construction of Lexington Dam took less than a year from start to finish.

The farsighted wisdom of constructing the Santa Clara County water system was evident to both farmers seeking to replenish the groundwater system, and planners seeking to diversify the economy of the county. Although the Chamber of Commerce supported the creation of the county's water conservation dams and percolation ponds for future industrial growth, some industries had already been established in the area.

One of the Pueblo de San José's early blacksmiths was Peter Lassen, a Danish immigrant, who arrived during the winter of 1840-1841. After moving to Santa Cruz

he built the first lumber mill in the region for Isaac Graham. Other blacksmiths began building mills throughout the redwoods.

After the American takeover a German wagonmaker, John Balback, came to San Jose in December 1849 and established the Pioneer Carriage Factory. In 1852 he built perhaps the first commercially manufactured plow on the Pacific Coast and the following year produced about fifty plows.

Another horse-drawn farm equipment manufacturer was the San Jose Foundry, established in 1852. This firm built harrows, windmills, gang plows, and the Pilton Six-Fold Horse-Power Threshing Machine, which was purchased by many local grain farmers.

John Bean settled in Los Gatos in 1883 on a small almond ranch. Finding the spraying equipment inadequate, he invented the continuous spray pump, a device that helped establish the fledgling company as one of the premier pump suppliers in California. Shown here, Bean demonstrates one of the original sprayers in his own orchard. Courtesy, FMC Corporation

As Santa Clara County's grain farmers expanded more agricultural manufacturers arrived in San Jose. In 1864 Joseph Enright established his foundry manufacturing the Patent Wood and Straw-Burning Portable Engine. This steam engine used the stubble byproduct of threshing to power the machine and found acceptance all over the state. It was used into the early 1920s.

Other early agricultural firms included J. and J. Ingham, builders of the Sulky Gang Plow. The Inghams advertised that their plow was sold at "Prices twenty-five percent lower than any other plow made in the State." The Knapp Plow Works was located on the 400 block of First Street in San Jose. This firm, established by H. G. Knapp and his son, built sidehill plows used in the Santa Cruz Mountains. By 1900 the Knapps had two plants in the city and employed forty-five workers. They shipped agricultural implements all over the western states as well as to Hawaii and the Philippines.

By 1875 San Jose boasted fifty-two blacksmiths and seventeen carriage and wagon manufacturers. Many of these businessmen were prominent citizens, For example, Clark S. Crydenwise, a buggy manufacturer, served two terms on the Common Council. The oldest such company in the county, the Pacific Carriage Factory was founded in 1874 by David Hatman and Amable Normandin. The firm was the predecessor to today's Normandin Chrysler and Plymouth.

Other county manufacturers, such as J. S. Smith and Son on Stockton Avenue, built machines for fruit growers, canners, and dried fruit packers. The American Can Company, in addition to manufacturing cans, produced torches used to light

The Joshua Hendy Iron Works (later Westinghouse) was established in Sunnyvale in 1907. For many years, the company was the largest foundry on the Pacific Coast. In 1912 the City of San Jose con- tracted with the Iron Works to manufacture the ornate electroliers, some of which are pictured here, that were to grace the city's streets. Courtesy, San Jose Historical Museum

smudge pots. American Can, a New Jersey company, opened operations in San Jose during 1912. By 1919 the plant, located on one block of Martha Street, produced ten million cans annually and had the capacity to store thirty-two million cans. The plant employed 450 workers during the canning season.

Several early inventors developed canning machines that are still used by packers. At the California Packing Corporation Joseph Amori developed a machine to cut and pit apricots. This machine remains one of only two types still in use. Amori also developed a machine to pit Italian plums. Joseph Perrelli, a partner of the Filice and Perrelli Company (F & P Brand) developed a machine that pitted

cling peaches without wasting the fruit. The "Filper" is also still used by canneries.

One of the most important agricultural manufacturers was John Bean, who moved to Los Gatos in 1883 from Ohio. Bean, who invented the double-acting water well pump in the 1850s, used his pump principles to manufacture the first successful high-pressure spray pump for agricultural use when his almond orchard developed San Jose Scale and he was unable to find a suitable method of applying caustic oil on his trees.

After successfully exhibiting the new pump at several California fairs in 1884, Bean started his new manufacturing concern in Los Gatos. Bean's son-in-law, D. C. Crummey, became the company's

John Bean (standing) was the inventor of the Continuous Pressure Spray Pump in 1883 and the founder of the Bean Spray Pump Company in Los Gatos. This company absorbed many small, agriculturally oriented manufacturing companies in the area. In 1915 the company moved to San Jose and merged with the Anderson-Barngrover Mfg. Co. in 1928, changing its name to Food Machinery Corporation. Courtesy, Sourisseau Academy

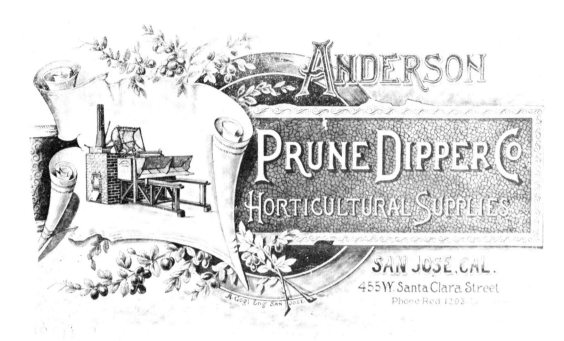

president in 1888. In 1903 the company moved to a larger building in San Jose and by 1908, the year of Bean's death, the Julian Street was the largest spray pump company in the world. In 1909 the company built a factory in Berea, Ohio. Five years later the eastern branch moved to Lansing, Michigan.

During this period the John Bean Company purchased the rights to Alf Johnson's track-layer crawler tractor. The Johnson Tractor Company first developed a three-wheeled tractor in Woodland near Sacramento before moving to Sunnyvale in 1907. In 1912 the Joshua Hendy Iron Works bought the rights to Johnson's tractor. This factory, located in Sunnyvale, built the three-wheeled tractor used by orchardists. Hendy eventually sold the rights to Rumely Products Company of Indiana. In the meantime, Alf Johnson developed a crawler tractor, which was better for orchard work. The track-layer design allowed crawler-type tractors to be used in damp conditions whereas wheel tractors would dig into the ground. Johnson sold the design to the John Bean Company. The new product was popular during

World War I; however, Bean could not compete with the new Caterpillar tractor developed in Stockton. Johnson continued to do tractor design work for the Bean Company until the late 1940s.

In the same time period, Luther Cunningham invented the prune dipping machine. Prunes were dipped in lye to make the skins crack, allowing moisture to escape and the prune to dehydrate quickly without fermenting. Cunningham was a partner in the Cunningham and Barngrower Company. At the turn of the century the firm consolidated as Barngrower, Hill and Cunningham. In 1902 W. C. Anderson joined the firm as the president and the company was renamed Anderson-Barngrower Manufacturing Company. Anderson began his manufacturing career in 1897 and established the Anderson Prune Dipping Company a few years later.

In 1910 Anderson-Barngrower moved from Santa Clara Street to a five-parcel lot near the Southern Pacific rail yard on Julian Street. Between 1912 and 1920 Albert Thompson, an engineer for Anderson-Barngrower, developed the continuous can sterilizer which sterilized, cooked, and

The San Jose Ostrich Company farm was located at Alum Rock Avenue and King Road from 1904 to 1909. The farm was established by Colwell Leitch when ostrich plumes were a high-fashion item. Visitors were attracted to the farm and arrived in a steady stream by buggy and trolley car. Plumes were plucked every eight months and, after special processing, retailed from six to eight dollars each. Courtesy, San Jose Historical Museum

cooled cans in one process, thus eliminating hand labor. The company manufactured canning machinery for canners of fruit, vegetables, and fish throughout California and as far away as Australia.

In 1928 the Bean Spray Pump Company, under the leadership of John D. Crummey, the son of D. C. Crummey, merged with Anderson-Barngrower and the Smith Manufacturing Company. The new firm was named Food Machinery Company (FMC). During the 1930s the company's engineers developed a pear machine that cored, halved, and peeled pears. Between 1946 and 1950 they developed an orange juicer machine that won an award from the American Society of Mechanical Engineers.

One of the smallest but best-known of Santa Clara County's industries is the Macabee, Gopher Trap Company. The company was started by Zepf Macabee who arrived in Los Gatos when he was seven years old. He lived on his family's ranch before his father began operating first the Coleman Hotel and later the El Monte Hotel in Los Gatos. Zepf worked for his father as a clerk, handyman, and bus boy

before branching out on his own as a barber at the Royal Shaving Parlor.

Zepf Macabee was well-known as a handyman and in 1900 his cousin asked him to develop a workable gopher trap to save his orchard. On October 22, 1900, Macabee obtained a patent for his trap and began manufacturing the devices in his house at 110 Loma Alta Avenue in Los Gatos. The company, under the management of Ron Fink, is still operating in the same house, which is now a historic landmark.

One of Santa Clara County's most unique manufacturing enterprises was introduced by Louis Prevost, who brought silkworms and the silk industry to California in 1865. Prevost built a factory and planted a thirty-acre mulberry tree plantation in the county. A.F. Sauffrignon and Company operated the Pacific Silk Company at Delmas Avenue and San Salvador in San Jose. Unfortunately for Prevost and his followers, the silk industry did not catch on in the valley.

The Garden City Manufactory was established in 1919 by S.C. Kimball at the corner of Willard and San Carlos. The thirty female workers manufactured women's and children's clothing.

The State Foundry and Pattern Works was also established in 1919 on the Alameda. This firm built oil burning equipment for heating homes, cook stoves, and prune dipping and evaporator heaters.

By 1920 the Chamber of Commerce reported that the seventy- three industrial companies in the county produced twenty-five million dollars worth of manufactured goods. While this amount was five times greater than in 1910, it was only half the annual income of the county's canners.

The county's industrial concerns continued to expand during the 1920s. In 1920 the National Axle Corporation built a $68,000 manufacturing plant on twelve acres. The business, located on Berryessa Road, employed fifteen mechanics. That same year A. L. Solon, the president of the S. & S. Tile Company, established a tile plant on Fourth and Lewis streets in San Jose. This was the only handmade tile business in the United States during that time. The company's potters made mosaic tiles in the Moorish style.

Before the Great Depression slowed expansion to a crawl the county's manufacturing concerns included potteries, broom factories, box factories, refineries, book binderies, creameries, sheet metal factories, wagon makers, mattress factories, water pump manufactories, rug works, macaroni makers, a violin maker, paste makers, and coffee and spice mills.

Santa Clara County also became a center of higher education in California throughout the nineteenth century. On July 10, 1851, the new state government granted the first charter of higher education to Reverend Isaac Owen, who established California Wesleyan University. Owen changed the name to the University of the Pacific a month later. In 1911 the name was changed to College of the Pacific;

however, it is now once again called the University of the Pacific. The college was located in Santa Clara until 1870 when it was moved to San Jose in the area still known as College Park. In 1924 the college sold the grounds to the University of Santa Clara, and moved to Stockton. The old College Park campus is now the home of Bellarmine College Preparatory School.

In 1851 two nuns of the order of Sisters of Notre Dame de Namur, Sister Mary Catherine and Sister Loyola, arrived in Santa Clara County from Oregon. With the help of their parents, the two women established a school on West Santa Clara Street later that year. The College of Notre Dame received a charter in 1855 as the first women's college in California. In 1888 the campus stretched along West Santa Clara Street to Santa Teresa and Notre Dame streets and back to San Augustine (St. John) Street. By 1923 the downtown business district expansion forced the sisters to move the college to Belmont where the campus is located on the historic William Ralston estate.

On March 19, 1851, two Jesuits, Michael Accolti and John Nobili, established Santa Clara College in the old Mission Santa Clara buildings. The college was a preparatory school during the first few years until the state granted the college a charter in 1855. The college fathers changed the name to the University of Santa Clara in 1912 and in the 1980s changed the name to Santa Clara University. The university quickly became established as one of the best Catholic schools in the west and many Santa Clara County business, legal, and political leaders graduated from the institution. In 1971 the university became the first Catholic co-educational college in California. Currently about 7,500 men and women attend the university in its undergraduate, graduate,

and professional schools.

The oldest publicly-funded institution of higher education in California is San Jose State University. George W. Minns established Minns' Evening School in 1857 to ensure that San Francisco's teachers were kept up-to-date. The teachers, most of whom were women, attended classes once a month and the school graduated two classes of fifty-four women before moving to San Jose in 1870. The Normal School, as the university was then called, held classes at the local high school during the first session in 1871 before moving into a $285,000 building at Washington Square.

The school attracted students from all over California and the state funded more buildings. However, fires and the earthquake of 1906 caused the school to be rebuilt several times. The university's current landmark, Tower Hall, was built in 1910. In 1921 the state granted a name change to San Jose Teachers College. The school's name was changed again in 1935 to San Jose State College. In 1971 the school was awarded university status as California State University, San Jose, but, while the students and faculty appreciated the change in status, no one liked the name and two years later, in 1974, the name became San Jose State University. The university now educates about 25,000 students a year.

The last university to be established in Santa Clara County was the Leland Stanford Junior University, founded in 1886 on 8,800 acres of Senator Leland Stanford's Palo Alto farm. Senator Stanford was the governor of California during the Civil War and one of the founding "Big Four" of the Central Pacific Railroad, which became the Southern Pacific Railroad. Stanford and his wife established the university as a memorial to their sixteen-

year-old son, who died of typhoid fever while vacationing in Venice, Italy.

In addition to acreage, the Stanfords gave the university a thirty-million-dollar endowment fund. The campus opened in 1891 under the leadership of President William Starr Jordan, one of the nation's most respected ichthyologists; about 1,100 students showed up to attend the new university, twice as many as expected. The original buildings, designed in a Mediterranean Moorish style and made of locally quarried limestone, were severely damaged during the 1906 earthquake. The sandstone gates fell straight down, leaving a pile of rubble. The top portion of the arch at the entrance to the main quadrangle was removed, and Memorial Library lay in ruins.

Through the years, Stanford graduates have been among the nation's top leaders in law, medicine, business, and academics. Herbert Hoover, a member of the first granduating class, was a respected engineer

before entering public service during World War I and becoming President of the United States. In the 1980s Stanford University has averaged 13,000 students in its undergraduate and graduate programs and is ranked as one of the best universities in the United States.

The seeds of change that the valley's early pioneers planted can be seen as blooms today. Although the county lost the state capital, Santa Clara County is one of the most influential counties in California. State legislators from the county hold key positions in Sacramento.

While the Settler's War is but a distant memory, its effects linger on. By the turn of the century, there were no great ranchos left in the valley. Little is left to remind us of the Civil War, but the State of California, which was a remote outpost of the Union, is today the most populated state and the most influential in the nation politically and socially.

Many of the buildings at Stanford University were seriously damaged during the 1906 earthquake. This photograph of the statue of geologist Louis Agassiz is often labeled by pundits as "Louis taking a closer look at the cause of the earthquake." Courtesy, Hoover Institute Archives

CHAPTER SEVEN

GOVERNING SANTA CLARA COUNTY

This photograph of the Santa Clara depot, taken in 1901 from the Santa Clara Water Works tower, captures the San Francisco-bound commute train. This depot was built in 1864 for the original San Francisco & San Jose Railroad and presently serves as a Railroad Museum. Courtesy, Sourisseau Academy

Santa Clara County is one of California's original twenty-eight counties, created on February 18, 1850, by a state legislature that, interestingly, was not admitted to the United States for another five months. On April 11, a Court of Sessions was created to run the new county. That same afternoon the local Ayuntamiento, the town council that had governed San Jose and hence much of the Santa Clara Valley since the Mexican revolution, met for the last time.

California counties are unique in at least one respect; they were conceived as an arm of state government to deliver ser-vices difficult to administer from a central location in a state as large as California. Their purview thus included areas such as child welfare, jail and court administration, hospitals, schools, and road maintenance and construction, giving them far more authority than is found with most counties in the United States.

Under guidelines from the state, each county had a judge and each township two justices of the peace. In the first Court of Sessions, County Judge J.W. Redman sat as president while justices of the peace Caswell Davis and H.C. Smith served as associate justices. The county's judicial system was actually in place a month before

In 1887 Samuel A. Bishop obtained a franchise to electrify his horsecar line on Santa Clara Street. Underground construction, which began in October of that year, is seen here being inspected by railroad officials near Second Street. The electric railroad encountered problems and public criticism because of its unreliability. Underground electrification was replaced by overhead wires in 1890. Courtesy, Sourisseau Academy

the county was created—law and order were more important than governing bodies at the time.

The first Court of Sessions opened on April 23, 1850. Among its first acts was the division of the county into five townships: San Jose, Santa Clara, Washington, Redwood, and Gilroy, which served as polling places, with an additional polling place located in Alviso. During the next thirty years five more townships— Almaden, Alviso, Burnett, Fremont, and Milpitas—were added. Washington Township was removed from Santa Clara County in 1853 with the creation of Alameda County. New voting districts were added as the population grew. By 1872 there were eighteen such districts.

On June 3, 1852, the county went through the first of several reorganizations. Voters elected Isaac N. Senter, Fred E. Whitney, William E. Taylor, and Jacob Gruwell to the Board of Supervisors. Senter became the board's first chairman. Within six months a new five-member board was elected; they served one year before a new board was elected at the end of 1853. On April 7, 1854, the Court of Sessions again took control of the county government, with Judge Richard B. Buckner serving as president and Caswell Davis and Thomas Vermeule as associate justices. Buckner went on to become mayor of San Jose in 1860.

Less than a year passed before Santa Clara County again came under the control of the Board of Supervisors, this time with three members. On April 9, 1855, Samuel Henderson, W.R. Bassham, and Daniel Murphy were elected to the board. In 1864 the board was expanded to five members, and in 1874 two more were added. The board remained at seven members until March 1885, when it was reduced permanently to five.

Like most California counties, Santa Clara was administered under the general laws of the state. By 1879 the legislature, continually bogged down by special legislation needed to run the loosely regulated county governments, began a series of actions giving each county an elected Board of Supervisors, sheriff, district attorney, tax collector, treasurer, coroner, auditor, surveyor, along with a superintendent of schools and a Board of Education. Under the new legislation, counties could establish their own charters, allowing the assumption of additional responsibilities and often reducing the total number of elected officials. Santa Clara County, however, would not take the opportunity for some seventy years.

The county courthouse doubled as the seat of county government, the first being the old adobe jail on Market Street, near El Dorado Street (now Post Street), owned by the City of San Jose. Over the next few years the county government moved several times. From the jail the Court of Sessions moved to a building on First Street across from Fountain Alley late in 1850. This building was also inadequate for the government's needs, so the court moved to the Bella Union Building (and saloon) on Market Plaza. The Bella Union was a popular place, so much so that its visitors sometimes disturbed government meetings and forced the sheriff to issue orders that no dances or balls were to be held in the building while the court was in session.

The old State House was used until a new building on the southeast corner of Second and San Fernando streets was ready in December 1853. The new building was used for sixteen years before county government and the business of the court grew too large. The court was the first to leave, and in 1860 the county

"Billy the Masher" was built by the Enright Iron Works for the care of San Jose streets, then only macadamized. Joseph Enright stands on the front, waiting for its first demonstration run before the San Jose City Council in front of the old City Hall on Market Street. Courtesy, Sourisseau Academy

leased the second story of San Jose City Hall to use as a courtroom. Two years later the court again relocated, this time to the Martin Murphy building on Market Street, which later became Hart's Department Store.

On September 25, 1865, the Board of Supervisors approved the construction of a permanent facility for both the court and county government between St. John and Julian streets facing St. James Square. The brick building was designed by Levi Goodrich, a respected local architect who had served as a supervisor in 1852. Goodrich personally directed construction of the building. The state authorized the county to issue bonds for the new building on

March 1, 1866; it was completed on January 1, 1868. Eleven years later the courthouse was expanded, adding a new wing for the Board of Supervisors and three new courtrooms. The finished Roman-Corinthian domed structure was one of the finest courthouses in California, at least in the eyes of the supervisors, who offered the building to the state—if the government would relocate again to San Jose.

On May 18, 1931, the courthouse was gutted by fire. Although the structure was rebuilt and ready by September 17, 1932, the familiar dome was replaced by a much-needed third story. The court continues to operate from that building, while the supervisors and the remainder of the county's government moved to First and Hedding streets in the 1950s.

In addition to finding places to house the government, the justices and supervisors were responsible for the creation and upkeep of the county jail. The county's first jail was erected in 1849, next to the old State House on Market Street. The Court of Sessions moved the jail in 1852, and had a new one built by Marcus Williams on the southeast corner of Second and San Fernando streets. The $15,000 structure was built under the supervision of Judge Buckner and completed on January 2, 1855; it was used until the court moved to St. James Square. In 1869 the supervisors approved construction of a new jail, again designed by Levi Goodrich. The new jail was completed in 1870, using brick from the 1855 building.

The supervisors were also responsible for a system of public health. So in 1854 they created a Board of Health and the following year established a board of directors for a County Infirmary. The board appointed a county physician and arranged to purchase the Sutter House in northeast San Jose as the first county hospital. The house was used between November 1855 and February 1856. The supervisors then hired Dr. G.B. Crane for $4,600 annually to take care of the sick. Lacking a real hospital, Crane arranged for his patients to be housed in a variety of places. The arrangement was less than perfect, and the board soon saw the need for a central facility. Thus from 1860 to 1871 the County Hospital and Pest House was located on South Street (now Park Avenue) in farm buildings renovated for the purpose.

Realizing the need for still better facilities, the supervisors authorized the purchase of a 114-acre site southwest of San Jose on the San Jose-Los Gatos Road (now Bascom Avenue) in 1871. Construc-

tion of a new hospital was approved in 1875 and the county's hospital has remained there ever since. In 1967 Santa Clara County Hospital was renamed Santa Clara Valley Medical Center.

The Board of Supervisors voted to construct a county almshouse in 1884, as they were also responsible for the indigent. The board then appropriated money to the Ladies Benevolent Society for the care of destitute children.

In addition to the creation and maintenance of public buildings, the board's most pressing business was the granting of franchises for toll roads throughout the county in the 1850s. In 1852, when the first supervisors were elected, the wheat farmers of Saratoga petitioned for a new road by which to deliver their harvest to the flour mills and port of Alviso. The board agreed, but the farmers balked at the tax hike necessary to complete the venture. Exercising a little psychology, the supervisors offered to hire any farmer willing to work on the project after the harvest, thus earning back their tax dollars. That road became the Lawrence Expressway, connecting Sunnyvale and Santa Clara to San Jose and Saratoga.

The often muddy Alameda was improved under a common franchise scheme whereby the toll road operator would agree to construct and maintain the road for a fee. The county guaranteed the operator's investment and a given rate of income during the period of the franchise. When the franchise ended, the county bought the road for the cost of construction. The Santa Cruz and Pacheco Pass roads were originally completed under similar agreements.

While the creation of turnpike companies for the construction and maintenance of roads was the most expedient thing to do in the first years of county government, numerous citizen complaints of excessive charges or poor maintenance caused the supervisors to reconsider the situation. By the end of the 1870s the county bought all of the toll roads. Pacheco Pass Road was the last to be taken over in 1879.

The supervisors were also interested, then as now, in other means of transportation, and in 1861 authorized a bond sale for a subscription to $200,000 worth of stock in the San Francisco & San Jose Railroad. Three years later, the first train arrived from San Francisco; the fare for the trip was three dollars. In 1869 the county sold the stock for $100,000 plus a commitment for the construction of a railroad between San Jose and Gilroy. The supervisors also purchased $150,000 worth of stock in the Niles to San Jose Railroad

in 1865; that stock was sold in 1872 at a $39,000 loss. While the railroad ventures seldom made money for the county, they did open the valley up to the rest of the state and nation.

In addition to helping fund intercity railroad ventures, the Board of Supervisors and the San Jose City Council joined together to authorize the franchise of several horse railroad companies in the 1870s. These early railroads opened the city to expansion and provided easier access to other cities and towns within the county.

Santa Clara County's interurban railroads thrived for seventy years, falling victim, finally, to the growing popularity of the automobile and a remarkable, if not entirely ethical, scheme by the General Motors Corporation. By 1920 there were

San Jose Railroad's electric streetcar #17 stops to pick up passengers at the Southern Pacific passenger depot on Bassett Street near First Street in about 1895. Seen in the background are railroad passenger-oriented businesses, a "fast food" restaurant, the Broad Gauge livery stable, and several turreted hotels. Courtesy, Sourisseau Academy

The Peninsular Railroad Company established an interurban route to Cupertino in 1907. Seen here in about 1914, eastbound car 108 leaves Cupertino on the high-speed Stevens Creek line. Courtesy, San Jose Historical Museum

The earliest rail service to Alum Rock Park was provided by a steam dummy shown here at the Alum Rock Park station about 1900. This line was completed by Hugh Center in 1896 and electrified in 1902. Courtesy, Sourisseau Academy

more than 120 miles of rail lines running from Los Gatos and Congress Springs resort west of Saratoga to Alum Rock Park in the east foothills, and to Palo Alto and Stanford University.

In 1925, however, executives at General Motors began to see the nation's hundreds of small inner city railroads as competition for its products, so the giant auto maker acquired Yellow Coach, then the nation's largest maker of buses. In 1932 GM began a systematic campaign to replace electric streetcars with its buses. Through a variety of partnerships and holding companies, GM acquired and shut down streetcar lines around the United States, including those in Santa Clara County.

The buses, however, were inherently more expensive to operate and maintain, in addition to creating more noise and pol-

lution than the streetcars. People flocked to the automobile dealers—which also proved to be a benefit to GM, especially as the population began expanding.

From the 1880s through the end of the 1930s Santa Clara County experienced moderate growth. Political influence rested largely with landowners, a few merchants, and the competing political machines of attorneys Louis O'Neill and Jim Rea, foundry operator John McKenzie, and Charlie Bigley, a beer distributor and ambulance company owner.

Farming concerns—roads and water—occupied county government much of the time; Santa Clara was, after all, a basically agricultural county through World War II. But the need for war material brought manufacturers of aircraft, missiles, and defense electronics to the valley. With the expansion of business, workers and their families poured into the county. Following the war, the transistor and fledgling electronics industry began changing the face of Santa Clara County, and, indirectly, the nature of county government.

Orchards were subdivided and developed to provide needed housing and schools. In the thirty years from 1950 to 1980, the county more than quadrupled in population. Many small unincorporated towns run under the general laws of the state disappeared. Communities like Edenvale, Evergreen, Linden, Wright's Station, Mayfield, Linda Vista, and others disappeared.

Campbell and Milpitas incorporated to protect themselves from voracious annexations by San Jose, Santa Clara, and Sunnyvale. Others, like Willow Glen, had earlier been convinced that merging with the larger community held some advantage.

Developers intent on subdividing farmland south of Sunnyvale sought to incorporate an area known as the Crossroads so it could be developed without interference from farmers wishing to preserve the orchards. But in a twist of fate the farmers themselves led efforts to incorporate the land around a feedlot owned by the Cali brothers. Thus, Cupertino became a city in 1955 to protect farmland coveted by those developers. Three decades later the old, small Cupertino business district has been torn down. The Cali brothers feedlot is about to make way for an office complex and luxury hotel. The farmers left long ago.

The supervisors, who had allowed development outside the cities as a matter of course, were now confronted with suburban tracts requiring fire, police, road repair, and sewage disposal services. The county government was ill-prepared to provide these services. Builders found land cheaper outside the cities, and frequently

On March 7, 1938, the Railroad Commission approved the final abandonment of South Bay electric traction. This poster announced the last day of service for the Berryessa Street line. Commemorating seventy years of streetcar service, the towns of Santa Clara and San Jose celebrated with a colorful festival where people of all ages who loved the trolleys came to join in the farewell service. Courtesy, William A. Wulf Collection

Since 1944 First Street has been a one-way street. The bank tower remains visible on the downtown skyline, although it is dwarfed by the increasing number of high-rise buildings. Courtesy, San Jose Historical Museum

pitched "country living" to those who bought their new homes. San Martin, Burbank, Cambrian Park, and Rancho Rinconada are among the unincorporated areas developed under this system.

In 1951 voters approved the county's first charter. This move gave the county government authority to take on new responsibilities, and changed the way the government itself was run. Howard Campen, an attorney and member of the citizens committee that wrote the charter, became the County Counsel after its approval. In 1957 Campen was appointed county executive, serving for nearly twenty years and setting up the county's civil service system.

Although revised and streamlined in 1976, the charter had, at its adoption, forced a radical change in the way the county was run. For years the five members of the Board of Supervisors had divided the government's basic functions—land use, public works, health services, and tax collection—among themselves. They nearly ran the departments under a spoils system; knowing the right people counted for much. During one supervisor's years in

office those who were in a position to know said that if one of his friends did not ordinarily qualify for free medical help from the county hospital, a simple phone call could quickly clear the way. Each supervisor was also a road commissioner, thus influencing road construction and repair contracts.

The 1951 charter mandated hiring a professional administrator, the county executive, to run the bureaucracy. Members of the board would exercise authority over policy only, while the day-to-day administration was left to department heads. The supervisors became true part-time representatives, with markedly diminished influence.

With the 1960s other changes came to the board. The decade of the civil rights movement had begun, and reform in representation was among its goals. Since the 1880s the county's five districts were drawn according to no real formula. Thus in 1960 District 1 contained only 3 percent of the voters, but a distinctly larger portion of the county's more than 1,300 square miles.

Public pressure forced supervisors to consent to redistricting as early as 1963, but new boundaries drawn in early 1965 still gave District 1 Supervisor Sig Sanchez only 12 percent of the county's population. A lawsuit filed in October 1963 on behalf of the San Jose Jaycees, led by lawyer John T. Ball and businessman Robert Miller, forced another attempt at drawing the districts to assure equal representation. Ball was the executive director of San Jose's Junior Chamber of Commerce, and Miller was its president. Both were thought to harbor political ambitions. The suit had the desired effect; supervisorial districts were again redrawn in December 1965, using the one-man-one-vote rule.

Miller went on to win a seat in 1968 on the San Jose City Council, eventually

In 1931 President Herbert Hoover signed a bill approving construction of the five-million-dollar United States Naval Air Station located in Sunnyvale. Seen here in 1932 is construction of the large dirigible hangar that continues to be the dominant feature of the air station, which had its name changed to Moffett Field in 1933. Courtesy, San Jose Historical Museum

The Tidal Wave ride provides thrills and chills at Great America Amusement Park in Santa Clara. Courtesy, San Jose Convention & Visitor's Bureau

serving as the city's vice-mayor. Ball refused repeated entreaties to run for office, preferring instead to stick with a lucrative law practice, but later became a municipal court judge. The supervisorial districts were redrawn again on the basis of the censuses in 1971, 1975, and 1981.

While the supervisors attempted to settle disputes over district boundaries, transportation began to loom again as a major regional problem. Three freeways were built in the decades after World War II, connecting the valley to the East Bay and San Francisco, but the roads still were loading up during rush hours. Industry had concentrated in the north, along the Bayshore Freeway from Palo Alto to northern San Jose, while the majority of the valley's new homes were being built to the south and east. The county's mass transportation system had consisted of privately operated bus lines during the thirty years since the demise of the interurban railroads. Southern Pacific commuter rail service to San Francisco deteriorated as the railroad downgraded service to favor more profit-

able freight business.

Santa Clara County never really had a chance to join the Bay Area Rapid Transit District (BART) in the 1960s; there was little interest in the South Bay after BART had been turned down by San Mateo County to the north. Both county and city governments feared the financial burden BART presented. The issue never came before the county's voters.

Work began during the mid-1960s to establish a countywide transit district funded by a one-half cent sales tax. Legislation by State Senator Alfred Alquist to create a district was turned down by Santa Clara County voters in 1968 and 1970. A year later Alquist found a way around voter antipathy toward a new tax to fund transit efforts, and pushed through a bill offering one-quarter cent of the state's sales tax to counties establishing transit districts.

In June 1972 voters approved the idea and the supervisors began convening as the board of the Santa Clara County Transit District in January 1973. County Executive Campen persuaded the board to elevate James Pott, then heading the Public Works Department, to the directorship of the Transportation Agency. Pott had ably led the development of the county's expressway system, but had little knowledge of mass transit.

The Santa Clara County Transit District bought out the existing local bus lines, obtaining seventy-eight aged GM coaches, and leased eighteen World War II vintage buses from Alameda-Contra Costa (AC) Transit to serve the new system's main routes. Money was scarce despite the one-quarter cent from the Transportation Development Act funds.

In the search for funding to build a transit network, Pott persuaded the board that an on-call transit system would show the initiative needed to convince the federal government to grant the county enough cash to buy newer equipment. Spending $4.5 million in federal dollars and another $200,000 in county money, the County Transit District began offering "Dial-a-Ride" service on November 24, 1974.

The system immediately was swamped with 80,000 calls per day. Dial-a-Ride buses proved costly to operate compared to those running on standard routes and, during the nation's first gasoline shortage, demand for Dial-a-Ride continued to be heavier than expected. Buses frequently ran without scheduled maintenance. The propane coaches presented their own special mechanical problems: their engines sometimes burst into flames while running. Lacking needed capacity and suffering frequent breakdowns, the experiment lasted less than six months. The 134 small Dial-a-Ride coaches joined County Transit's other dilapidated rolling stock in rudimentary route service in August 1975. Despite its many problems and inauspicious start, the transit system carried 12,000 passengers per day that month.

Meanwhile the supervisors sought other means to cover the cost of building an effective system. Although voters had twice refused to tax themselves an additional one-half cent for transit development, frequent traffic jams and pollution problems convinced many that more money was necessary if the county was to avoid gridlock. Efforts headed by newly elected Supervisor Rod Diridon began to put a local measure on the ballot. On March 2, 1976, during a school board election that drew only 30 percent of the county's registered voters, the tax passed with just more than 55 percent in favor.

Moves were already afoot to use some of the new money to develop a transit system less dependent on already clogged roads. The Rapid Transit Development Project study began in 1973, concluding two years later that Santa Clara County needed, along with a decent bus system, 140 miles of Medium Capacity Rapid Transit. In modern terms, light rail, in more antiquated speech, trolley cars.

Studies began immediately to identify the best routes for a rail system, and finally the board chose a north-south corridor stretching from South San Jose to Santa Clara's Great America amusement park. A joint powers board chaired by Diridon worked its way through numerous federally required studies, and construction began in 1984 on the twenty-mile system. The $372-million light rail line, called the Guadalupe Corridor Project, was expected to go into revenue service in the north county in 1987, and along its full length in 1989. Combined with costs for an expressway which will parallel the system, the more than $500 million project is the largest public works effort the county has yet seen.

Voters in 1984 also approved a ten-year, one-half cent tax to complete three local highway projects neglected or cancelled by the state. Under a county traffic authority chaired by Supervisor Zoe Lofgren, highways 237 and 101 were to be upgraded or widened, and the long-planned Highway 85 was to be completed.

Under the direction of County Executive Sally Reed and Transportation Director James Reading, County Transit today operates a modern 550-bus fleet carrying more than 130,000 passengers each day. Future plans call for the addition of 150 buses, expansion of the light rail system, and upgrades of CalTrain (the old Southern Pacific commute) service to San Francisco. A possible BART connection to San Jose from its terminus in Fremont is being considered by the Fremont-South Bay Corridor Joint Powers Board.

The beauty of Calaveras Reservoir is captured in this John Elk III photograph.

worked full-time; the board thus began to wield an influence not felt since the 1940s.

Steinberg was not alone in breaking new ground for women in Santa Clara County. Janet Gray-Hayes was elected mayor of San Jose in 1974—the first woman mayor of a major city in the United States. Numerous other women won seats on city councils throughout Santa Clara County during the 1970s, quickly bringing it a reputation as a "feminist capital."

The 1980 election of supervisors Zoe Lofgren and Rebecca Morgan, along with the election two years earlier to the board of Susanne Wilson, brought county government its first female majority. Morgan has since moved on to the State Senate, but the majority continued with the 1984 election of Dianne McKenna, a former councilmember and mayor of Sunnyvale.

Veering from its history of *laissez faire* policy toward growth, the board passed a number of ordinances aimed at guiding development. McCorquodale, Steinberg, and Diridon eventually voted to impose a two-year moratorium on all subdivision requests for unincorporated land, allowing time for a new general plan to be completed. Future plans to protect the valley's remaining open space and hillsides were assigned to the county's Preservation 2020 project, led by Supervisor Dianne McKenna.

The board also began expanding what was once a nearly nonexistent parks system. In 1972 voters approved a charter amendment requiring that ten cents of the tax rate go to parks acquisition and development. With this mandate, the board adopted an aggressive expansion policy, buying available acreage and building sixteen regional parks ranging from the 10,000 acre J.D. Grant Ranch to the near wilderness of Sanborn Park and Uvas Canyon. Santa Clara County now owns

Transportation is only one area that demonstrated a shift in the nature of county government starting in the late 1960s. As managing growth became the county's biggest challenge, the closed network that had for so long characterized local politics began to break down. Many of the county's newcomers had their own ideas about how things should be run.

Often coming from farm or ranch backgrounds, and representing an agricultural community, board members were generally conservative, as were many of the valley's other leaders. The 1970s brought a change in leadership and philosophy. Dan McCorquodale, a special education teacher and former Marine, won a supervisor's seat in 1972. Two years later, Planning Commissioner Geraldine Steinberg was appointed to the board, later becoming the first female to be elected supervisor. Unlike their predecessors, McCorquodale, Steinberg, and Diridon

45,000 acres of parks, connecting them with San Francisco Bay through a series of streamside trail projects. The county also cooperates with the Mid-Peninsula Regional Open Space District in purchasing tracts of hillside land to be preserved as undeveloped, permanent open space.

Through the 1970s and early 1980s, the supervisors continued to move toward an agenda marked by "quality of life" issues. The civil rights and free speech movements of the 1960s spawned the county's Human Relations Commission in 1972. Charged with eliminating prejudice and discrimination in the community, the commission has built a reputation as a forum and mediator of public disputes, helping resolve tense public issues through open proceedings and investigation. In 1973 the board established the county's Commission on The Status of Women to monitor and aid in the reform of laws and discriminatory practices as part of a countywide affirmative action program.

Where members of the board once divided the running of county departments, they now divide issues. Thus while all of the supervisors are expected to understand the wide variety of issues concerning county government, specific assignments allow each to gain expertise in particular areas. For example, Susanne Wilson, 1986 Board of Supervisors chair, worked a great deal on issues of water quality, hazardous materials, and Valley Medical Center, while Supervisor Lofgren specialized in highways, the justice system, and public health. Supervisor Thomas Legan paid particular attention to county business and capital expenditures, and Transit District chair Diridon spent much of his time on mass transportation and air quality. Supervisor McKenna made special efforts on parks and land use planning as well as related environmental issues.

The sharing of direction and administration of projects among governmental organizations is also a recent phenomenon. Joint powers boards, usually made up of representatives of the county, cities, and other involved jurisdictions, control a number of important public projects in a task force approach used throughout the state. Such boards exist while a project is under planning and construction, usually disbanding upon completion. The Guadalupe and Fremont-South Bay Corridor joint powers boards and Santa Clara County Highway Authority examples of such systems, as were the boards responsible for completion of San Jose's Transit Mall and studies to determine the ultimate fate of the CalTrain commute line to San Francisco.

As local governments have chosen to share power in pursuing large goals, regional government has become second nature to much of California. The county, cities, and special districts of the Santa Clara Valley deal locally with such issues as water conservation, child welfare, housing, business development, public health, and justice, but regional bodies have evolved to deal with issues that know few borders. Members of the Board of Supervisors today serve on the boards and committees of the Bay Area Air Quality Management District, Metropolitan Transportation Commission, Bay Conservation and Development Commission, Association of Bay Area Governments, County Supervisors Association of California, and National Association of Counties, among others.

The changes in county government structure and the ability of county and city governments to work together would prove invaluable as the county population grew from 1,300,200 in 1980 to 1,808,056 by 2007 and is projected to top 2 million by 2020.

CHAPTER EIGHT

HARVEST OF CHANGE

During World War II, Joshua Hendy's iron works manufactured ship engines for the military. Seen here in 1944 are the employees of the plant sitting for a photograph celebrating the completion of the 500th engine. Courtesy, San Jose Historical Museum

The harvest of change that the early pioneers looked forward to was completely different than the small egalitarian model that the independent farmers envisioned when they settled in the Santa Clara Valley. Instead of planting seeds on yeoman farms, the seeds of change bore subdivisions, streets, and industrial parks. Furthermore, during the transition phase there was essentially no unified planning. Each city went its own way with no thought to the overall impact on the county or region. When this change occurred is hard to pinpoint; however, that it centered around the nation's defense industry is certain.

With the beginning of the Great Depression in the 1930s the Chamber of Commerce reported that thousands of workers found employment only during the active farming and canning season. However, with wartime recovery, the county's industries began a surge of growth that continued into the next four decades.

In 1930 the United States Navy was looking for a West Coast base to house the Navy's lighter-than-air-ships. Citizens in Santa Clara County joined together and purchased the land that was once part of the main village of the Posolmi, a local Ohlone tribe. In 1931 the Navy purchased the land from the citizen group for one dollar and quickly began building the five-million-dollar Naval Air Station at Sunnyvale. Hanger One, designed for the USS *Macon* is 1,138 feet long, 308 feet wide, and 198 feet high, which left just enough room for the giant dirigible to fit inside.

After the *Macon's* sister ship, the

167

Blooming orchards are a lovely site in Santa Clara County. Photo by John Elk III

Akron, crashed, killing Rear Admiral William A. Moffett off the New Jersey coast, the base was renamed in his honor. Unfortunately, the giant air ships were prone to disaster and the *Macon* crashed off Point Sur while on military maneuvers in 1935.

The base was used as an Army air station until 1940, then became a training center. In 1942 the Navy again used the base, this time to house a squadron of blimps. The blimps were much smaller than the dirigibles and were used to scout the coastline during the war years.

During the Korean War, Moffett Station was the largest Naval air transport base on the West Coast. From 1950 until 1961 fighters were based at Moffett. The jets were moved, however, as the area became too populated and local residents complained about the noise and potential safety problems. The base is presently used to house seven squadrons of the Navy's P-3 Orion antisubmarine airplanes.

During World War II, East Coast manufacturing areas converted their existing factories to wartime production. In California, however, there were very few existing factories to convert, so Californians built new facilities. During the war, government and industry invested an estimated

$800 million into defense plants. Between 1943 and 1947 about seventy new industrial plants were built in the county. In San Jose alone, the federal government invested $8,496,000 in new plants for the production of magnesium, ferro-silicon, and plastics, and more than thirty-one million dollars was spent for defense contracts in Santa Clara County during the war years.

The Food Machinery and Chemical Corporation (FMC) of San Jose began making tanks for the army. In 1943 the International Business Machine Corporation (IBM) decided to locate a plant in San Jose. Sunnyvale's Joshua Hendy Iron Works employed 7,500 workers and built naval landing boat engines for the war effort. Hendy was the largest manufacturer in the county and one of only four industries in Sunnyvale. A decade later, however, Hendy's was bought out by the Westinghouse Corporation and by 1956 Sunnyvale boasted forty-four industries. Between 1945 and 1965 more than 550 new industries moved into Santa Clara County. The industrial capital investment improvements were worth more than $600 million.

With the end of the war, county leaders braced themselves for severe cutbacks. However, in the years between 1946 and 1949 the federal government spent about 60 percent of the United States budget on defense industries, the military, veterans benefits, and on the wartime debt.

Thousands of servicemen and defense workers came to California during the war years. After the war ended, many people decided to remain or return to California. The postwar period saw a building boom in California as private enterprise, catering to pent-up demands from the Depression and war years, built new homes and shopping centers while the federal, state, and local governments began construction on highways and streets. In addition, the state

This circa 1940 aerial view of Moffett Field shows dirigible hanger Number 1. From 1935 to 1942 Moffett was under Army control and was the headquarters of the Air Corps 82nd Observation Squadron. Photo By U.S. Army-Air Corps, courtesy, San Jose Historical Museum

On October 15, 1933, the dirigible *Macon,* seen here approaching its mooring dock, arrived with orders to establish its permanent base at Moffett Field. The *Macon* crashed into the Pacific Ocean near Point Sur on February 12, 1935. Courtesy, San Jose Historical Museum

received about 15.5 percent of the nation's defense spending. By the late 1940s, California was becoming the dominant state in defense industries and Santa Clara County was a major factor in this development.

In addition to the growth of the defense industry, by 1945 Santa Clara County was also the tenth largest county in the nation in agricultural income, with an annual value of more than sixty-five million dollars. In the late 1940s the city directory labeled San Jose as an "agricultural community." Downtown San Jose was the shopping hub of the county. Almost 70 percent of the county's retail business was conducted there. The population of the city was 80,734 people living in an area of 15.58 square miles. In 1946 the city's bonded indebtedness was only $2,454,000 while the school district's indebtedness was only $430,000. The problems facing the city were parking for downtown businesses and expansion of bus

service. San Jose was a typical small town in a typical rural county.

In 1944, with the end of the war in sight, 100 of the most prominent men of the city formed the Progress Committee. The members included merchants, attorneys, industrialists, and major property owners. They banded together in hope that postwar San Jose would expand and that they could initiate progress.

Earlier that year, in March, the Owen-Corning Fiberglass Corporation bought forty-three acres in Santa Clara and began construction on a seven-million-dollar plant that would employ between 800 and 1,000 workers with an annual payroll of $1.5 million. If Santa Clara could attract industrial growth, the leaders of San Jose felt that they too could do more toward progress.

In an effort to diversify the county's manufacturing base, the Santa Clara County Board of Supervisors and the San

Jose City Council each gave $35,000 to the County Chamber of Commerce in 1944. The chamber hired a public relations representative to visit industrial leaders interested in expanding into California. The public relations director's job was to tell the manufacturers about the virtues of Santa Clara County. The Chamber of Commerce promotion campaign ended in 1965, after costing the county and city about one million dollars. The success of the campaign is legendary; people learned the way to San Jose.

The natural amenities of the county helped the public relations director's marketing efforts. Santa Clara County offered a good climate, the county's cities offered low taxes, plenty of land for new industry, and the area had few unions—all of which nurtured the growth of an infant industry that had its start at Stanford University before World War I.

In 1909 Cyrus Elwell, a Stanford graduate, established the Federal Telegraph Company in Palo Alto. Financed by university officials and faculty, the new company was able to conduct research and in the 1920s one of Federal Telegraph's engineers, Lee de Forest, developed the vacuum tube. In 1931 the company moved to New Jersey while several engineers remained in the county and later established Litton Industries and Magnavox.

In the 1930s Frederick Terman, Jr., became an engineering professor at Stanford. Under Terman's guidance the university became one of the leaders in the field of electronics. Two of Terman's students, William Hewlett and David Packard became close friends during their senior year at Stanford. Graduating in 1934, Packard went to Schenectady, New York, to work for General Electric's vacuum tube department, while Hewlett finished a master's degree at the Massachusetts Institute of

Valley View Packing Company used this mixed fruit label on their product. Courtesy, William A. Wulf

Technology. In 1937 both Hewlett and Packard returned to do graduate work at Stanford with Terman and graduated two years later. The pair began making electronic test equipment in a one-car garage on Addison Avenue in Palo Alto and built eight 200A audio oscillators for the stereophonic sound in Walt Disney's *Fantasia*. In 1940 the young men moved their operations to Page Mill Road and hired four employees. During the World War II the company obtained government contracts and although Hewlett joined the Army, Packard managed the business and production for the company. In 1947 Hewlett-Packard incorporated, and by 1950 the firm had a new building, 200 employees, and sold seventy different products with an annual income of two million dollars.

In November 1946 Stanford University established the Stanford Research Institute (SRI). The university appointed R. William F. Talbot as the director of SRI. Talbot was the president and technical director of the Fine Chemicals Division of Sun Chemical Corporation. In addition to SRI, Stanford officials leased land to Varian Associates, established in 1948 by Russell and Sigurd Varian, brothers who worked on developing radar during the 1930s and, like Hewlett and Packard, were Stanford graduates. In 1952 the University leased land to Hewlett-Packard.

By 1954 Terman, then the dean of the Engineering School, developed and pushed for the concept of a Stanford Industrial

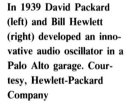

In 1939 David Packard (left) and Bill Hewlett (right) developed an innovative audio oscillator in a Palo Alto garage. Courtesy, Hewlett-Packard Company

Park. The university's trustees agreed with Terman and established a high technology industrial park on university property. This development led to further expansion by Sylvania (GT&E), Philco-Ford, General Electric, Lockheed's Research Laboratory, and Hewlett-Packard.

In 1954 Ames Aerospace Laboratories began construction valued at almost thirty-nine million dollars, in addition to the thirty-seven million dollars already spent at the facility, located on 365 acres of Moffett Field. By the 1980s, Ames had grown into thirty-four laboratories and seventeen wind tunnels for testing new aircraft designs. Furthermore, Lockheed liked the area and the amenities surrounding the Stanford Industrial Park well enough to invest ninety-one million dollars on its own 700 acre Missiles and Space Division at Palo Alto in 1957.

In 1955 William Shockley, one of the three scientists who invented the transistor at Bell Laboratory in 1947, formed the Shockley Transistor Corporation in Palo Alto. By the late 1950s and early 1960s, Fairchild, Raytheon, Signetics, National Semiconductor, Intel, and many other firms were established in what was to become Silicon Valley.

In addition to the electronics and defense manufacturers, other companies such as the Kaiser Corporation built facilities in the county. Henry J. Kaiser built Kaiser Permanente Cement Corporation on 3,400 acres in the Cupertino Hills. The plant was built in six months during 1939 at a cost of four million dollars. Kaiser was the largest cement plant in the world, producing 1.6 million tons of cement annually, which was used in the building of Shasta, Hoover, and Bonneville dams, and the San Francisco Bay Bridge. By the 1980s, one-third of the cement for Northern California

Below the Stanford foothills at the north end of Silicon Valley lies Hewlett-Packard's world headquarters and central research labs. Courtesy, Hewlett-Packard Company

Kaiser Permanente established a cement plant in the hills above Cupertino in 1939. It was the largest cement plant in the world, providing cement for many large construction projects. Courtesy, San Jose Historical Museum

construction came from Kaiser's Santa Clara County plant. In 1981 the company was forced to rebuild the plant, at a cost of $112 million, to limit air pollution associated with the manufacture of cement.

In 1946 Chicago's International Minerals and Chemical Corporation opened an Accent plant in San Jose. In 1953 the Ford Motor Company built a $60.5-million factory in Milpitas. During the 1950s General Electric built its first plant for the production of nuclear power in San Jose.

While the county saw continuous construction of new businesses, the county's established companies were expanding their operations in the valley. International Business Machines (IBM) built a thirty-two-million-dollar plant in south San Jose in 1953. The directors of Food Machinery Corporation, one of the county's oldest firms, expanded their main plant as well as building other facilities throughout the valley. By 1958 Santa Clara County's industrial buildings were worth $671,982,000. Two years later, in 1960, there were 807 industrial plants in the county.

By the 1960s Santa Clara County's economic base was clearly dependent upon its industries, most of which were defense oriented. In 1950 only 13 percent of the county's manufacturing was in durable goods—electronics and ordnance; however, by 1969 this figure rose to 60 percent. Between 1955 and 1963, nearly 80 percent of all new manufacturing jobs in the valley were in the electronics or ordnance fields.

The defense-related industrial base of the county meant more jobs and more money for Santa Clara County residents. In 1952 defense-related companies paid their workers thirty million dollars; however, ten years later this figure jumped to $384 million. In Palo Alto alone, the county's four largest companies—

Lockheed, Philco-Ford, Varian, and Hewlett-Packard—paid their workers $104 million annually. Lockheed was clearly the largest employer in the valley employing one out of every fifteen workers.

Although Palo Alto dominated the new industrial base, by the mid-1960s Mountain View and Sunnyvale had more than 130 companies, most in the electronic fields. This phenomenal growth in Santa Clara County was tied to the fact that by the 1960s California was receiving more federal defense money (electronics, communications, aircraft, and space) than any other state. By 1965 50 percent of California's jobs were related, either directly or indirectly, to the defense and space industries; more than one million Californians were employed by the federal government or its contractors.

As early as 1960 the Santa Clara County Planning Department estimated that each industrial job brought eight to ten new residents into the county while providing another 1.5 non-manufacturing jobs. Furthermore, another study reported that for every 100 factory jobs created, four new retail stores opened to serve the 112 new households. These new jobs resulted in $360,000 worth of new retail sales and an additional $270,000 more deposited annually in local banks.

When local public officials realized that the valley was almost totally dependent upon defense spending, they began to fear that the area would suffer a depression if the federal government cut back on military spending. Furthermore, in 1965 the *Wall Street Journal* predicted that an economic slowdown in California would spread to the entire nation.

This fear was shared by the defense industries and by the late 1960s many local firms were entering non-defense fields. Lockheed's Missiles and Space Division di-

Radio pioneer Charles David Herrold founded the world's first broadcasting station in 1909 in San Jose. His first broadcasts consisted of music, weather reports, and farm tips. The original call letters were FN, changed to KQW in 1921, and KCBS in 1949. Herrold and his assistant are seen here in the KQW equipment room on the corner of South Second and San Antonio streets in about 1926. Courtesy, San Jose Historical Museum

versified its interests into petroleum, education, hospitals, and law enforcement. Philco-Ford began looking into sewage treatment, water systems, and rapid transit. Sylvania opened research into highway planning and water resources. United Technology opted for new divisions in garbage disposal and oil pipelines. Varian reduced its military operations from 80 percent of its income in 1963 to 40 percent by 1968.

In 1983 the valley's defense contractors produced four billion dollars worth of government projects constituting 3.2 percent of all defense department contracts.

The diversification of the electronics industry received a shot-in-the-arm with the introduction of Apple computers in the mid-1970s. Apple was the creation of two young entrepreneurs Steven Wozniak and Steven Jobs. The two met in high school where they developed a passion for high-technology electronics. In the early 1970s, while attending the University of California in Berkeley, Wozniak and Jobs built and sold to students about 200 *Blueboxes* which were used to bypass long-distance telephone charges. Wozniak also worked for various computer firms, including Hewlett-Packard, where he designed calculator chips.

In 1970 Wozniak built a simple computer operated by a toggle switch computer and five years later, after joining the Homebrew Computer Club, decided to build a microcomputer out of available low-cost components. Wozniak tried to sell Hewlett-Packard on the idea, but they were not interested.

Not dissuaded, Wozniak enlisted the help of his old friend Jobs and started making computers on a contract basis for the Byte Shop in Sunnyvale. The Byte Shop ordered twenty computers to be delivered in thirty days.

Jobs obtained $320 worth of capital to purchase the needed components and Wozniak built the computers in Jobs' garage. The Apple One was a success and soon other computer people were interested in the new concept. Wozniak quickly designed, at Jobs' insistence, a "user friendly" computer, the Apple II. The pair moved from the garage in 1976 to a $200 million facility in Cupertino. In six short years they had completely revolutionized the personal computer industry.

Apple rose to become the second largest company in the world in micro-computers with revenues in 1984 of $1,897,900. Hewlett-Packard was ranked as the fourth largest microcomputer manufacturer with $510 million in revenues. The world's largest computer manufacturer was IBM.

The phenomenal industrial growth in Santa Clara County meant a staggering population change for the county. In 1940 the county claimed 101,666 acres in farmlands. Thirty-three years later, however, only 23,511 acres remained. One of the contributing factors was the growth of the county between 1950, when there were 290,547 residents, and 1970, when the

The Apple I Computer, the product from which the Fortune 500 Apple Computer, Inc., traces its beginnings, was developed by Stephen Wozniak. This computer was little more than a printed circuit board stuffed with chips, about the size of a portable typewriter, but it had a profound impact on the personal computer industry. Courtesy, Apple Computer, Inc.

In 1884 Charles M. Shortridge gained control of the *San Jose Mercury*. The *Mercury* office, shown here in about 1886, was located at 171-173 West Santa Clara Street, where it shared an office with the Santa Clara Land Agency. Courtesy, Sourisseau Academy

population jumped to 1,064,714. Ten years later the population had jumped to 1,289,600. By 1986 the county's population was 1,403,100. Seventy-six percent of this increase came from new residents moving into the county.

These newcomers came for jobs. In 1960 there were 224,810 jobs in the county. By 1978 the number jumped to 609,900. Between 1975 and 1980 the county saw 39,000 jobs added per year and by 1986 792,300 people were employed in Santa Clara County. Much of this increase came from manufacturing and trade positions. The rate of job increase per annum was greater than the rest of California or the nation.

In addition to adding new jobs to the county's base, these jobs were high paying positions. By 1963 the average family income in the county was $7,417; the state

average was $6,726, while the national average was only $5,660. In Santa Clara County the average household income, after taxes, rose to $27,001 by 1979 and jumped to $40,841 by 1984.

As new families moved into Santa Clara County, they were offered a ready supply of homes to purchase. In 1966 the *San Jose Mercury* reported that the most frequently-seen vehicles on city streets, other than automobiles, were moving vans. Throughout the central and northern portion of the county, acres of orchard land continually gave way to vast communities of tract homes.

During the late 1940s and 1950s, California's farm acreage increased by 5 percent. However, in Santa Clara County the farm acreage decreased by 27 percent as the county shifted from an agrarian to a manufacturing economy. In 1978 more

than 30 percent of all jobs were manufacturing, while agriculture accounted for only one percent of the jobs.

Much of the development of the county can be attributed to the pro-growth spirit surrounding the Progress Committee of 1944 and the choice of Anthony P. "Dutch" Hamann as San Jose's city manager in 1950. The new city manager formally served as the business manager and alumni director at the University of Santa Clara which was, and continues to be, the training ground for many local civic leaders. Hamann served from 1950 until he retired in 1969.

Two years after Hamann's appointment, in 1952, the *San Jose Mercury and News* was sold to the Ridder Group. The new publisher, Joseph B. Ridder, was an advocate of development and his support, manifested in editorials and general reporting, provided free publicity.

Another important figure to the growth of San Jose was Russell Pettit, manager of the San Jose Chamber of Commerce. The *Mercury* praised Pettit as being responsible for the "transformation of San Jose from an agricultural community to a leading electronics and aerospace metropolis."

The friendly local government and business environment, with help from both the state and federal governments, allowed the new residents to settle in the Santa Clara Valley. The federal government made owning a home possible with low-interest rates through VA and FHA loans, as well as providing tax benefits. While federal and state government cooperated with water, sewage, and airport development funds, the biggest boost to development was highway construction. Highways 101, 17, 280, and 680 opened up new areas in the county.

Development and annexation became the bywords of San Jose's boomers who looked unabashedly at Los Angeles for

A.P. "Dutch" Hamann became San Jose's city manager in 1950. Before his retirement in 1969, he saw the population of San Jose skyrocket from 95,000 to 400,000. Hamann directed the rapid geographical spread of the city in all directions with his vigorous annexation policies. Courtesy, Santa Clara University Archives

their model of growth. City growth by annexation spelled the end of agriculture and the "Valley of Heart's Delight." Between 1950 and 1960, 491 annexations occurred, and in the next decade there were more than 900 annexations.

Other cities and towns in the county soon followed San Jose's lead and either began the annexation process themselves or incorporated in order to maintain their industrial and commercial tax base. In 1940 the county's nine incorporated cities included Palo Alto, Mountain View, Sunnyvale, Alviso, Santa Clara, San Jose, Los Gatos, Morgan Hill, and Gilroy. By 1960 there were seven new jurisdictions—Los Altos Hills, Los Altos, Cupertino, Milpitas, Saratoga, Campbell, and Monte Sereno. Eight years later, after a lengthy fight, San Jose annexed Alviso, which was the first incorporated city in Santa Clara County.

As early as 1953, Santa Clara, Sunnyvale, Mountain View, and Los Altos were involved in bitter annexation wars with San Jose. The county government attempted to develop a county sewage and storm drainage system so that the entire valley would be more attractive for development. San Jose, however, reacted to the annexations and incorporation of other areas within the county and blocked the proposal. Instead, San Jose, which had the largest sewage treatment plant, refused to allow new connections from areas not annexed to the city.

The City Planning Department also resorted to strip annexation and leapfrogging in an effort to block annexation by other cities. Further, when San Jose officials met resistance in an area they simply annexed all the property around a small pocket, realizing that eventually that area would be forced into the fold. Hamann's philosophy was that the area should have one large city rather than several smaller competitive cities.

Santa Clara and San Jose became involved in costly legal actions and decided to engage in "peace talks" over the expansion and annexation of industrial lands. During the early 1950s all the county's cities were isolated from one another and from the county government as well. A total of seventeen different zoning ordinances and building codes existed in the county.

To further complicate the problem and alienate the different parties, the representatives from the cities pointed out that although the County Board of Supervisors was elected by both rural and urban voters throughout the county, three of the five districts had a total combined population of only 148,299 while the other two districts had at least 200,000 each. This meant that only 23 percent of the county's population controlled the board. The Board of Supervisors responded to their rural farming constituents by establishing greenbelts between the cities in 1954. The cities accused the Board of Supervisors of being "hicks" who stood in the way of progress.

In an effort to get all sides talking to one another Mayor W. J. Nickolson of Santa Clara invited elected officials from throughout the county to a meeting in Santa Clara to discuss mutual problems on June 25, 1953. Out of this meeting the cities and county governments agreed to form an Inter-City Council of Santa Clara County.

During the third meeting of the Inter-City Council San Jose's planning director, Michael Antonacci, reported that none of the incorporated areas within the county had any real planning and that the cities needed to take an unselfish attitude about planning and design. Karl Belser, county planning director from 1950 to 1967, wanted the council to work out "fundamental points" of planning for the county's future.

As the Santa Clara County Charter Review Commission prepared the 1960 charter, several commission members suggested the creation of regional guidelines to regulate uncontrolled growth. The idea was to create a super-zoning commission that would oversee all zoning in the county.

While this idea did not receive much support from the county's elected city and town leaders, the concept resurfaced in the early 1970s by a new County Charter Commission. This time resistance was overcome by the fact that the new planning body, the Inter-Governmental Council (IGC) had no statute authority to enforce the council's decisions. The programs and recommendations developed by the members were carried back to each of the county's municipalities by their representatives on the council and the municipal city and town councils were free to accept or reject the proposals.

In the ten years after the creation of the Inter-Governmental Council and before the acceptance of the Inter-Governmental Council, little of organized planning was actually accomplished. New cities were created and older municipalities continued to expand into the orchard lands of the county. Finally, in 1963 the California State Legislature passed a law creating a Local Agency Formation Commission (LAFCO) in each county in an effort to control urban sprawl and encourage local agencies to control growth. The LAFCOs had the responsibility to approve or reject the formation of new cities or special districts and any annexation of territory by a city.

The commissions were made up of two members appointed by the local County Board of Supervisors, two members appointed by the county's cities, and the fifth member appointed by the first four members. In Santa Clara County,

this meant a shift in power. The governments in the smaller rural cities and the county government would dominate the commission. Therefore, in an effort to expand before LAFCO came into existence, San Jose, in the twelve months between October 1963 and 1964, annexed 3,765 acres in ninety-four different annexations, chiefly in the Morgan Hill area. By 1964, when the Santa Clara County LAFCO came into existence, San Jose was the third largest city in land area in California.

During the growth period of the 1950s and throughout the first half of the 1960s, San Jose did not have an official policy to manage the expansion of the city. Although the state mandated a general plan for all cities and counties in 1960, San Jose's plan was only a collection of documents showing streets and sewers.

In 1960 Chamber of Commerce Manager Pettit and San Jose City Manager Hamann managed to have San Jose designated as an "All American City." In a classic example of urban development during this time, a developer pitted the City

Located in the center of Market Street Plaza, San Jose's 1887 City Hall was designed by architect Theodore Lenzen. The first meeting was held in the new building on April 17, 1889. It stood until municipal government moved to the new City Hall on Mission Street in 1958. Courtesy, San Jose Chamber of Commerce

of Milpitas against the City of San Jose by demanding that Milpitas grant a lot size variance on the McGinty Ranch, which was within the city's sphere of influence. When Milpitas refused to grant the change, the developer annexed to the City of San Jose even though San Jose had to annex a three-mile strip of roadway to reach the development. However, once there the city could not provide the needed urban services. San Jose had to truck drinking water into the development while trucking the development's waste out. Eventually, permanent utilities were installed at a cost to San Jose taxpayers of $3.5 million.

Finally, in 1966 a General Plan was adopted, but developers soon found that it was easier to change the city's zoning than to submit their plans for a variance. The result was strip-zoning and uncontrolled zoning. One of the few portions of the General Plan that did prevail was the small lot sizes of 5,000 square feet.

New growth meant new streets, new storm drains, an improved sewer system, a municipal airport, a new City Hall, and a deep water port, but voters rejected initial attempts to place them further in debt. However, by holding elections on off-years when there was little voter interest, the boosters generally got their way on most of these issues with the exception of the century-old fight for a deep water port at Alviso.

Interestingly, developers did not pay for the new services they needed to build new tracts. Instead, under an ingenious plan, the current taxpayers paid the bill for the new development. The new residents did not have to pay for their own sewer expansion, streets, or other public works.

The most serious obstacle to San Jose's growth was posed by rural school districts in the county's unincorporated areas. California school districts were re-

quired by law to be in the same boundaries as the city they were in. Therefore, due to the rapid uneven expansion, the San Jose School District was faced with an impossible problem; they simply could not support San Jose's rapid and haphazard growth. The rural school districts sued the city to stop the annexation of their tax base.

Since schools were not important to the city's annexation plans, San Jose's representatives in Sacramento gathered the votes necessary to separate school districts from city boundaries in the mid-1950s. This move placated rural school districts and the San Jose School District. However, by 1980, this resulted in twenty-four different school districts for San Jose's students.

Although the boomers of San Jose seemed to have their own way throughout the 1960s, change was occurring within the city's power structure. In 1962 three new council members were elected on a platform designed to provide basic city services such as police, fire, streets, and schools. Furthermore, the city taxpayers saw their bonded indebtedness skyrocket. In the late 1960s the city's voters elected a majority council that had a different view toward development and Hamann resigned.

The new change from unlimited development to restricted development did not occur without a fight, and in the late 1970s the power within the city council changed again, this time in favor of pro-development. But the switch was short-lived because one of the new majority resigned and another one was replaced in the November 1978 election.

A change in the philosophy of growth was not limited to the cities. By 1972 the County Board of Supervisors decided to get the county out of the development business. Within three years they ruled out any urban development in unincorporated areas; development henceforth was to be within city limits. However, the subdivision applications continued to flow into the Planning Department and in 1977, in an effort to stem the tide of continuous development, the supervisors declared a two-year moratorium on such requests. This time was needed to develop a new comprehensive general plan for the county.

The new plan, as adopted in 1980, incorporated several innovations, such as a formula that takes into consideration the size, slope, and geological stability of the land at the time decisions are made. Should the conditions on a given property not meet the standards, then development is curtailed. The county's planners have utilized this new concept in development to effectively block development in the rugged mountains surrounding the valley floor and in other unstable areas.

In order to help counties save their remaining agricultural lands, the California State Legislature passed the California Land Conservation Act, better known as the Williamson Act, in 1965. Santa Clara County was thus able to set aside 150,000 acres of land for agriculture. Unfortunately, little of this was prime agricultural land.

The rapid growth by the incorporated areas forced the county to develop a planning department in 1950. In the early 1970s the staff of the County Planning Department formulated a guideline for "Urban Development Policies for Santa Clara County" which was adopted by the county and the cities. This plan called for future development to occur only in urban areas, with no high-density development of the unincorporated areas. The plan also required that cities provide urban services on the land they annexed. Furthermore, in 1973, the county adopted an Urban Development Open Space Plan. This strengthened the decision made in 1967 by the Board of Supervisors to refuse county ser-

At the time of its construction, Eastridge was the largest enclosed shopping center in the nation and the largest regional retail development in the West. The development entails more than 1.75 million square feet of retail shopping area and the interior features large-scale sculptures, pools, and garden landscaping. Courtesy, San Jose Convention & Visitor's Bureau

vices to developments in the unincorporated urban areas.

One result of this period of rampant growth was massive traffic congestion. This was aggravated in the late 1970s when the California Department of Transportation ran out of money to build new freeways.

In the 1970s the federal government created the Urban Mass Transit Administration to provide transportation planning, but it was too late for Santa Clara County.

Another discovery after the fact was the truth about the so-called clean industries of the Silicon Valley. For instance, in 1982, Mountain View discovered high levels of cancer-causing chemicals in the aquifer that supplied the city's drinking water. Tricholoroethylene, an industrial cleaning solvent known to cause cancer, was found as deep as 500 feet near the Intel Corporation, Fairchild Semiconductor, Raytheon, Siltec Corporation, and Nippon Electronics Corporation (NEC). Fairchild, Raytheon, and Intel announced that they would pay for the cleanup costs and would continue to monitor the area for future leaks. Unfortunately, the Mountain View case was not isolated and in 1984 tricholorethylene and Freon 113 was found in drinking water wells near IBM's South San Jose facility. Although the California Water Resources Control Board did not seem to be overly concerned, local political officials and the public were skeptical about the state's assurances that the situation was under control.

In 1984, due to pressure placed on the federal government to intervene in the groundwater dispute in Santa Clara County, the Federal Environmental Protection Agency established a pilot project, the Integrated Environmental Management Project. Santa Clara County is one of only three counties in the nation that participated in the project. The concept was to bring together all phases of governmental pollution management to effectively deal with the administration and local enforcement of federal and state pollution regulations. Supervisor Susanne Wilson's district, the south county, was facing problems with both industrial and agricultural pollutants. Because of her concerns over the issue of safe water, Wilson was selected by the Board of Supervisors to chair the Drinking Water Subcommittee.

Ironically, the groundwater pollution of the 1980s was created by the turn of the century concern that a falling water table would mean the end of agriculture in Santa Clara County. The completion of the massive water project came in time to aid in the county's transformation from an agricultural center to a high technology center. By the mid-1980s, governmental agencies began cleaning the water under the valley floor.

By the mid-1980s, most of the remaining agricultural lands in the county were located in south county near Morgan Hill and Gilroy. Only a small portion of the valley floor, once recognized as one of the richest agricultural areas in the world, remained in production. Much of the Valley of Heart's Delight was covered with blacktop, homes, business parks, and shopping centers. The millions of rows of orchard trees were simply a memory to those who lived here before the harvest of change.

In 1945 Santa Clara County was the tenth largest county in the United States in agricultural income. Agriculture remained the key economic industry through 1960 when the county was a world center for fruit and vegetable processing with 215 canneries and packing plants. By 2005 the county ranked as only the thirtieth county in California in terms of annual agricultural value, yet remnants of the past remain evident in scattered orchards, vineyards, and cattle ranches. Photos by Kevin Sterling Payne

In 1776 Fray Tomás de la Peña established Mission Santa Clara de Thamien along the Guadalupe Creek near the Indian village of So-co-is-u-ka. The local Ohlone, the Taris, called the mission area Thamien or Tamien. The first baptism was held on July 31. Three years later the Guadalupe Creek escaped its banks and destroyed the mission. This is a view of the fifth and current mission from the rose garden. It was rebuilt in 1929 after a fire in 1926. Photo by Kevin Sterling Payne

Right: Although the valley has been transformed into an urban center over the decades, and is the world center for high technology, traces of the past and the wildlife that once inhabited the valley are still evident. Photo by Kevin Sterling Payne

Above: Water from the Santa Cruz Mountains collects in Lexington Reservoir before flowing down the Los Gatos Creek and into several holding and percolation ponds designed to recharge water in the valley floor. Mount Umunhum, the former site of an early-warning radar station, the Almaden Air Force Station, and the Santa Cruz Mountains are in the background. Much of the mountains are part of the Sierra Azul Open Space Preserve. Photo by Kevin Sterling Payne

Right:
Designed by William H. Weeks, whose architectural firm Weeks and Day, was responsible for the Mark Hopkins and Saint Francis hotels in San Francisco, as well as numerous schools along the Peninsula and in Santa Clara County, the Saint Claire opened in 1926 as the center of San Jose's social scene. The Spanish-Italian Renaissance-style hotel underwent a $12.5 million renovation in 1991 and is listed on the National Register of Historic Places. The hotel and its classic Italian restaurant, Il Fornaio Cucina Italiana, have helped to transform the image of downtown San Jose evening life. Photo by Kevin Sterling Payne

Below:
Although called the Galindo/Leigh House, J.D Guerraz was likely the builder of the early 1850s portion of this Campbell residence. In 1874 Guerraz sold the house and 180 acres to Hugh Alexander Leigh, an English seaman, for whom Leigh Avenue is named. Leigh married in 1881 and in the 1890s he had the Queen Anne style wing added to the original home as the couple had three daughters and a son. The house remains an excellent example of an early Santa Clara County wood frame construction and is on the National Register of Historic Places. Photo by Kevin Sterling Payne

The development of Silicon Valley led to dramatic growth. As the population of the county grew from 642,315 in 1960, to 1,731,281 in 2006, more and more farmland was subdivided for homes. Initially the growth was felt in the heart of the valley but by 2000 it expanded southward into Morgan Hill and Gilroy. Photo by Kevin Sterling Payne

The San Francisco Bay National
Wildlife Refuge was established
in 1973 as the first urban
wildlife refuge in America. The
refuge covers 30,000 acres in the
south San Francisco Bay,
providing a natural habitat for
migratory birds as well as
threatened and endangered
species, while also providing an
outdoor laboratory for the study
of wetlands. It was renamed in
1995 the Don Edwards San
Francisco Bay National Wildlife
Refuge after South Bay
Congressman Don Edwards for
his efforts in preserving
wetlands. Photo by Kevin
Sterling Payne

In 1990, after a major
restoration, the historic
Saint Joseph Church was
dedicated as a cathedral.
The original structure,
built in 1803 from adobe
bricks, served as the first
parish in California. After
several earthquakes dam-
aged earlier structures,
this, the fifth structure was
consecrated on April 22,
1877. Photo by Kevin
Sterling Payne

This portion of el Camino Real still has the distinctive road signs first introduced in 1906. The bell signifies that the 600-mile long road was built to connect the missions of Alta California and the support pipe is bent in the shape of a walking stick of the type used by the Franciscan padres as they traveled from Mission San Diego de Alcalá to Mission San Francisco Solano. Across the street in front of the weather-beaten building was the zero-mile marker for the stagecoach route between San Jose and New Almaden. The building, located on First and Margaret Streets was built in 1884 and once housed a saloon called "Benjamin's Corner" operated by Nuncy Benjamin, along with a plumbing and blacksmith shop, until Prohibition forced the saloon to close in 1920. The following year, Jake Faber moved his nine-year old bicycle business, Faber's Cyclery into the building and in 1978, Paul LaRiviere bought the business and ran it until his son, Alexander, took the business over. When it closed, in August 2007, it was the oldest bicycle shop in the United States. Photo by Kevin Sterling Payne

Left:
Julius Wesnitzer built this building, located at 399 S. First Street, San Jose, in 1908. Wesnitzer moved his family into the upstairs apartments and operated the "San Jose Plumbing and Sheet-Metal Works" downstairs. The building has also housed the Fair McQuoid tire store, the Moorhead Flemming Drug Company, Garrucio Drugs, the Three Star Tavern, Marsugi's (a punk rock club), and currently, the Agenda Lounge. Photo by Kevin Sterling Payne

Above:
The 1936 Civic Center is reflected in the entrance to the 1989 McEnery Convention Center. The Convention Center, renamed the McEnery Convention Center for former Mayor Tom McEnery (1983–1990), was the centerpiece of the thirty-year redevelopment effort. Photo by Kevin Sterling Payne

Left:
Constructed in 1905 as the City Hall for Gilroy, this is the most famous landmark in the South County. The 1989 earthquake damaged the Frank Delos Wolfe eclectic "Flemish" or "Baroque" designed structure. The city restored the National Register of Historic Places building at a cost of $1.25-million and reopened it in 1998 as the New Renaissance Center to serve the city as a social services and business center. Photo by Charlene Duval

In 1993 the San Jose City Council renamed the old pueblo plaza, Plaza de César Chávez, in honor of the famed civil rights and farm workers organizer who started his career in Santa Clara County in the 1960s. The Hispanic heritage of the county was further recognized in 1999 with the opening of Mexican Heritage Plaza San Jose. The cultural center sponsors numerous events, including the annual International Mariachi Festival and Conference. In addition, the City of San Jose hosts the annual *Cinco de Mayo* Festival and Parade that draws over 300,000 people into downtown. Photo by Kevin Sterling Payne

Standing twenty stories above downtown and the old San Jose Post Office are two Knight Ridder signs, one on each side of the building thirteen feet tall and ninety-four feet wide, each weighing 57,000 pounds. The signs were erected in 1998 when the newspaper giant moved its headquarters from Miami to San Jose to locate in Silicon Valley. Eight years later, in March 2006, the McClatchy Corporation purchased Knight Ridder and by the end of April 2006, sold the *Mercury News* to the MediaNews Group and while the Knight Ridder signs still overlook Plaza de César Chávez they are dark at night. The post office, constructed in 1892, served as the main post office until 1933. Willoughby Edbrooke, who designed the main post office in Washington, DC, designed the Richardson Romanesque style building. The building has also served as the city library from 1937 until 1969 when the building was converted into the San Jose Museum of Art. Photo by Kevin Sterling Payne

A kinetic marble sculpture welcomes visitors to the Tech Museum. Photo by Kevin Sterling Payne

Opened in 1993, the 20,000-seat $150-million arena, now named the HP Pavilion, is the home of the Sharks of the National Hockey League, the SaberCats of the Arena Football League, the Sybase Open tennis tournament, and the San Jose Stealth of the National Lacrosse League, as well as providing a venue for musical performances. Photo by Kevin Sterling Payne

Tech Museum of Innovation began in a temporary facility in 1990. The permanent three-story museum has 132,000 square foot of exhibit space, gift shop and cafe, and Hackworth IMAX Dome Theater opened in 1998. The Tech has permanent educational exhibits that demonstrate how technology influences day-to-day life as well as special exhibits. Photo by Kevin Sterling Payne

The keystone of the renovation of downtown San Jose was the opening of the new San Jose City Hall on the corner of East Santa Clara and Fourth Streets in 2005. The architects, Richard Meier & Partners, based in New York, have a worldwide reputation having designed the Getty Museum in Los Angeles, the Hans Arp Museum in Rolandseck, Germany, the Ara Pacis Museum in Rome, the Beach House condominiums in Miami, and numerous other civic and private buildings. The high-tech building, seen here through the glass domed rotunda, was able to house services that were scattered in eleven different locations. Photo by Kevin Sterling Payne

Cupertino native James Reber established the San Jose Repertory Company in 1980. For its first seventeen years, the company called the 1926 Montgomery Theatre, a Spanish Revival Moderne style theater attached to the Civic Auditorium, home. In 1997 the company moved into the new Rep that was funded by the Fine Arts Commission, the William and Flora Hewlett Foundation, and other community leaders. Actor and director Timothy Near became the artistic director in 1987. Her goal was to produce works that would take the theater in new directions. Photo by Kevin Sterling Payne

The Jain Temple in Milpitas serves many of the Indian technology engineers who have immigrated into the county over the past two decades and have helped transform the county into one of the most diverse places in the world. Completed in 2000, the temple is adorned with marble and granite carved by hand and shipped from India. It is one of two such temples in California and serves about 4,000 Jains living in Northern California. Photo by Kevin Sterling Payne

In its third year, the Amgen Tour of California has proven to be a flourishing addition to professional bicycle racing. Stage 3, a 102.7 mile route between Modesto and San Jose wound over Mount Hamilton Road and into the Santa Clara Valley, was won by the Dutch racer Robert Gesink of Team Robobank, shown here in the lead (below), followed by American born Levi Leipheimer of Team Astana on the Category 1 Sierra Road climb. Leipheimer had enough of an overall lead to claim the yellow jersey in San Jose and went on to repeat his win of the Tour of California. Photos by Kevin Sterling Payne

The inaugural race of the San Jose Grand Prix Champ Car World Series, featuring open wheeled race cars, was run with a $4 million subsidy from the city. Almost 156,000 fans came downtown to see the race events run on a 1.443 mile, seven-turn downtown street circuit. Dutch rookie driver Robert Doornbos of Minardi Team USA, driving a Panoz Cosworth, won the 2007 race, which proved to be the last time San Jose was host to the event, as the series merged with the Indy racing league for 2008. Photos by Kevin Sterling Payne

Adobe, better known for its desktop publishing software, was the first corporation to win three awards from the U.S. Green Building Council for retrofits to its East and Almaden Towers, pictured here, which serve as its headquarters. John Warnock and Charles Geschke left Xerox PARK in Palo Alto in 1982, to start the software company. In 1985 Apple Computer began using Adobe PostScript for its LaserWriter printers and began the desktop publishing industry. By 1994 the company had earnings of $676 million and in 2007 it reported $3.158 billion in revenue and employed about 2,700 people in San Jose and approximately 4,000 more worldwide. *Forbes* magazine has consistently ranked Adobe as one of the best places to work since 1995. Photo by Kevin Sterling Payne

CHAPTER NINE

SECOND HARVEST

During the last decades of the twentieth century the world economy moved from the Industrial Age to the Information Age, with Santa Clara County at the center of this transformation. In the mid-1980s the microprocessor and computer manufacturing industries reached their zenith in terms of jobs in Silicon Valley. The county's connection with chip manufacturing remained so strong, that many people outside Santa Clara County only knew the area as "Silicon Valley" a name coined by Don C. Hoelfer, the publisher of the weekly *Microelectronics News*, in 1971. By the 1990s most manufacturing jobs had been outsourced to other states or countries; but valley firms were still designing ever-faster chips and computers. At the same time, new technology firms began developing software to be used on the computers designed in the valley. The ability of the valley's businesses to adapt led to the county's second harvest of change. With this change, the county and its cities and towns completed a metamorphosis to the cyberspace future of Silicon Valley, a future with a vastly different economic, physical, and cultural face than was evident in the agrarian past of the Valley of Heart's Delight.

In the late 1980s the technology industries based in Silicon Valley remained dependent upon the nation's defense initiatives. The demise of the Soviet Union on December 25, 1991 led to the "peace dividend" and military spending plummeted by 17 percent between 1989 and 1993. In the seven months between November 1989 and June 1990 the valley's electronic industry laid off 9,500 employees. By December 1990 the county's unemployment rate hit 4.8 percent and throughout the following year unemployment hovered at 5.7 percent. The news did not improve the following year. From August to September 1991, 3,100 county electronic workers lost their jobs and in 1992, the unemployment situation was worse.

Throughout the county service industries and suppliers filled fewer orders and business owners were forced to lay off employees. Potential customers continued driving their older automobiles and auto dealers let sales and service staffs go and spent less on advertising. The price gains seen in the county's real estate market during the 1980s quickly eroded. Besides permanent layoffs, tens of thousands of workers throughout the electronics industry faced furloughs during the last two weeks of the year, resulting in slumping sales at stores during the holiday season.

Many Silicon Valley executives claimed that high tax rates and stringent pollution laws in California acted as a deterrent to growth and were a cause of the recession. Industry leaders contrasted the business climate in Santa Clara County with other states that promised low or no real estate taxes, rebates on business taxes, and low-paid non-union employees. Silicon Valley was an extremely expensive environment in which to operate a business as its unskilled, clerical, and skilled electronics workers were among the highest-paid in the nation. Furthermore, during the recession, the state legislature did little to combat the increasing layoffs. Legislators,

already facing reduced tax revenues due to the recession, were extremely reluctant to diminish the state's income through the granting of special dispensations to businesses already located in California. Silicon Valley, the hub of technology and the birthplace of the personal computer revolution, was in danger of being replaced.

With state government officials hesitant to act, local government and business leaders realized that the welfare of the county could not be left to others. In March 1992 a group of business executives and public officials established Joint Venture: Silicon Valley, to look into ways to get the economy out of the deepening recession. Joint Venture included the San Jose Metropolitan Chamber of Commerce, nearly 800 Santa Clara County business leaders, and over twenty public officials, as well as county labor leaders and valley educators. The new organization quickly established itself as a major force in revitalizing the economy.

As expected, the focus of the 1992 presidential election campaign was on the economy with California and Silicon Valley at the center of the debate. Democrat Bill Clinton wooed Silicon Valley employers and employees with his campaign slogan, "It's the economy, stupid!" and by election day, key Silicon Valley business leaders became "Friends of Bill" and county voters endorsed him over incumbent George H. W. Bush.

In July 1993 President Clinton's commerce secretary, Ron Brown, visited the county with the message that federal government and private business would work together to create jobs. That September, President Clinton and Vice President Al Gore came to the county to discuss their vision of "reinventing government" and Clinton announced the creation of a

Joint Venture Silicon Valley recently relocated to this modern office building at 60 S. Market Street, San Jose, next to the 1910 Pacific States Telephone and Telegraph Building. Photo by Kevin Sterling Payne

federal task force to create jobs in California. Along with gaining federal support, business leaders won local tax and policy concessions. In November 1993, for the first time in the decade, the jobless rate began falling. The recession ebbed and Silicon Valley firms began hiring workers and building new facilities. While Joint Venture: Silicon Valley did not end the recession, the consortium did bring about the possibility of divergent groups working together and the jobs that were created were centered squarely in the region's technology industry.

Although the nickname of the valley remained tied to its recent past, during the 1990s, Silicon Valley gained a new reputation in the nation and the globe due to the rise in importance of a new form of communication—the Internet. Created over a period of thirty years, the Internet was the product of the Department of Defense and computer scientists at various companies and universities. The initial goal of those working on computer-to-computer communication was to enable defense work to be conducted on supercomputers at research universities. However, the introduction of small computers in the mid-1970s, as well as the utilization of the disc operating system

(DOS) by IBM in its line of personal computers, and the Apple Macintosh, with its revolutionary operating interface in the early 1980s, coupled with the business applications that personal computers brought about, dramatically altered the direction of the blossoming Internet.

In 1985 the National Science Foundation formed the National Science Foundation Network and in 1991 it allowed the commercialization of the Internet. By 1995, the Internet was a self-supporting industry. Although many valley firms helped in this transformation, four were at the center of this change: Intel Corporation, Netscape Communications, *Yahoo!*, and Google.

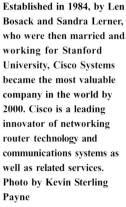

Established in 1984, by Len Bosack and Sandra Lerner, who were then married and working for Stanford University, Cisco Systems became the most valuable company in the world by 2000. Cisco is a leading innovator of networking router technology and communications systems as well as related services. Photo by Kevin Sterling Payne

In 1997 Stanford graduate students Larry Page and Sergey Brin built an Internet search engine that used PageRank algorithms to find and list pages based on the number of times the page had been accessed by others. After testing their concept on the Stanford website, they registered the name Google.com and incorporated in 1998. The new search engine quickly outpaced *Yahoo!* in terms of users and by 2007, 48 percent of the US Internet searches occurred on Google.

When IBM entered the personal computer market in 1981, and began using Intel Corporation microprocessors, Intel was still a relatively small firm. By 1997 three-quarters of the personal computers in the world featured Intel microprocessors. A major factor to buyers seeking out and paying for computers featuring Intel's microprocessors was the birth of the Internet, and the key to the Internet was Netscape.

In 1992 Marc Andreessen and Eric Bina, then students at the University of Illinois, wrote a software program that provided easier access to Internet sites. After graduating, Andreessen worked as a software writer in Palo Alto before establishing Mosaic Communications, later renamed Netscape, early in 1994, with Jim Clark, the former chairperson of Silicon Graphics.

The success of Netscape was based on its ability to run on computers with different operating systems such as Macintosh, Windows, and UNIX. Within seven months of its development, 6 million of approximately 9 million Internet consumers used Netscape Navigator to browse the Internet. The small Mountain View company grew to over 200 people in 1995, and expanded to over 1,250 people the following year. Netscape was the path to cyberspace, a path that by 1995 was followed by 30 to 40 million people in over 160 countries. America Online, now AOL, purchased the company in 1998. After a legal settlement with Microsoft giving AOL the right to use the Internet Explorer browser for seven years, work on new versions of Netscape slowed and by the end of December 2007, AOL decided to stop all further development on Netscape. The remaining remnant of Netscape is Mozilla Firefox, a free browser controlled by the Mozilla Corporation in Mountain View.

With thousands of new sites spouting up across the globe, users became increasingly frustrated with the growing labyrinth of the Internet. They found themselves lost in a virtual city, built overnight, with no street names. In April 1994, the same month that Netscape incorporated, two Stanford University electrical engineering doctoral students, Chih-Yuan "Jerry" Yang, and David Filo, developed a search engine to help users find information on the Internet. *Yahoo!* allowed users to search the Internet, by topic or keyword, and connect to thousands of sites. By December 1995 the directory included almost 100,000 sites and the following year the pair incorporated *Yahoo!* in Sunnyvale.

Two years later, in 1997, another pair of Stanford graduate students, Larry Page and Sergey Brin, built a new search engine. After testing their concept on the Stanford website, they incorporated the new business in 1998 under the name Google. The new search engine quickly outpaced *Yahoo!* in terms of users and by 2007, 48 percent of the U.S. internet searches occurred on Google.

The new virtual city now had a navigation devices in Netscape and Explorer and directories in *Yahoo!* and Google.

Throughout the valley entrepreneurs began establishing e-commerce companies such as eBay in San Jose and Netflix in Los Gatos to take advantage of the commercial opportunities that the Internet offered.

In August 1995 Netscape began selling shares on the NASDAQ stock exchange. Overnight, the value of the firm reached $2 billion. By December 1995 the stock value of the infant company was greater than that of established companies such as Delta Airlines, General Dynamics, and Bethlehem Steel. The initial public offering of *Yahoo!* in 1996 brought in $33,800,000. Although the stock price fell from $13 to $4.50 a share early in January 1997, it rebounded to $25.38 a few months

Created in 1999 by Reed Hastings in Los Gatos, Netflix brought the DVD rental store into private homes via the Internet, allowing users to rent a movie that arrived and was returned via the postal service. In 2007 the company expanded its business by renting movies or television shows on the web. Photo by Kevin Sterling Payne

later, with the news that the company reported an unexpected profit.

In only a few decades, the technology companies of Silicon Valley became so important to the national economy that the success of both the NASDAQ and older New York Stock Exchange became linked directly to what occurred in Silicon Valley. The influence of Silicon Valley was also reflected in the national media. Where once Santa Clara County received an occasional line in national newspapers and newsmagazines, by the 1990s articles describing the emergence of Silicon Valley onto the economic arena were read worldwide. As Santa Clara County became known for its electronics and technology based products, stock market investors and advisors began to purchase stocks in Silicon Valley's new crop. Like other "boom to bust" cycles in history, the dot-com bubble of the mid to late-1990s developed overnight though unrealistic speculation by investors who were lured by the belief that they could strike it rich without much effort. While established companies felt the need for a "Web presence" to publicize their goods and services, during the dot-

com boom new businesses were created with little capital and no real business plan. The dot-com business model offered the potential of future gains, not the reality of current productivity.

The explosion in Internet users helped persuade venture capitalists to fund the new businesses. Soon, they began investing in almost any idea with a dot-com name. Unlike the expectations with more traditional business, investors were not initially concerned about the immediate return on investment in the new technology

In April 1994, Chih-Yuan "Jerry" Yang and David Filo, then graduate students at Stanford University, developed a software classification system that allowed searches on the Internet by topic or keyword. Their company, Yahoo!, became one of the major search engines on the Web. Courtesy, *Yahoo!*

Empty phone booths appeared as cell phones, first envisioned in the mid-1940s, became a staple of every-day life by the 1990s. With the release of the Apple iPhone on June 29, 2007, cell phones threatened to make obsolete the usefulness of landline phones, which were first tested on March 10, 1876, by Alexander Graham Bell. The iPhone includes a camera, iPod player, and internet services, allowing users to connect to the web and receive and send e-mail from almost anywhere. Photo by Kevin Sterling Payne

Right:
eBay, established in 1995, has revolutionized the way people bought and sold items. Now an international auction powerhouse, the first item sold was a broken laser printer. Today, the company has helped sellers auction everything from automobiles, to collectables, to a small town. Photo by Kevin Sterling Payne

start-up companies; rather they looked at how quickly the business could build up market share in products or services. Branding became more important than quarterly returns, and once a company established its name, it turned to the stock market and an initial public offering (IPO) to bring in additional capital to continue to grow. Stock market investors, large and small, saw IPOs as their chance to get a stake in the new world of e-commerce. The phenomenon was not limited to Silicon Valley. Because of the power and reach of the Internet, dot-coms began sprouting up throughout the United States as well as Europe and Asia, all based on the same model.

As was the case with other such economic cycles, from railroads, mining, and land rushes of the nineteenth century, to the stock market crash of 1929, and the time-share vacation homes of the 1980s, the dot-com bubble finally burst. On Monday, March 13, 2000, several large sell orders of technology stocks were processed and they triggered even more sell orders via automatic computer programs. By Wednesday, March 15, the value of the NASDAQ was down by 9 percent and continued falling before losing 69 percent of its value by the end of September 2002. During the ensuing months, e-commerce companies, as well as companies that supplied everything from computers, software, chips, and fiber optic cable, began to furlough employees or simply closed their doors after finding that venture funding was no longer available. Yet, Silicon Valley did not disappear.

In 2005, after five years of a fairly stagnate economy, companies specializing in the Internet began to see some growth and earnings as Internet advertising sales began to climb and companies began posting profits. Employment in the valley picked

up once again, and Internet related businesses, led by Google, outpaced the older valley microchip industry in stock valuation. By the end of April 2006, the surging Internet dot-com industry peaked, once again, in terms of stock price. However, rather than a continued devaluation such as had occurred during the first dot-com decline of 2000 to 2002, values sagged slightly before leveling out and beginning a slow rise as new technology start-ups focused on medical and environmental concerns and, like the dot-coms of the 1990s, began attracting venture funding to unproven potential.

The dot-com bubble was not limited to the high-tech industry. In the 1990s, the housing market experienced a boom period that continued into the new century. Both of these events were fueled by the seemingly limitless wealth that was manufactured in Silicon Valley.

The resurgence of the technology industry, coupled with falling mortgage interest rates, woke up the real estate industry for the first time since late 1989. More Silicon Valley workers purchased homes and technology executives sold stock options and moved to the higher priced neighborhoods in west valley cities. The median price of single-family homes in Santa Clara County began to climb. In 1997 Congress gave home sellers a capital gains tax relief of between $250,000 and $500,000 on profits made on the sale of a principal residence. Home ownership became more than shelter, it became an investment, and the median price of a single family home in the county rose from $355,000 in 1998, to $525,000 by 2000. Price increases were further exacerbated from 2000 through 2004, as interest rates on 30-year fixed mortgages began a decline from 8.14 percent to a low of 5.37 percent and adjustable interest rates began considerably lower. Soon, lenders also began offering subprime adjustable rate loans with starting rates as low as 1 percent, with 100 percent financing. Between 2004 and 2006, 21 percent of loans occurred in the subprime market. These factors resulted in a frenzy of speculative home purchases and "house flipping" (buying a home in need of repair, living in it for two years while remodeling it, and then selling it for a huge profit) became a new industry.

In June 2005 homes remained on the market for an average of two weeks before selling. The median sales price in the county reached approximately $739,000, and bidding wars were common. In June 2006 the median sales price peaked at about $820,000. By November the frenzied buying was over and the median sales price for single-family homes plummeted to $734,500 and continued to fall through 2007. In August 2007, the rates for adjustable mortgages climbed above what some homeowners could afford and defaults on subprime loans began to climb. The median price for a single-family home fell to $692,000 in January 2008, with no end in sight. During the same period, prices for condominiums fell from $513,000 to $458,000.

By mid-February 2008 there was an 8 1/2-month inventory of unsold homes on the market. Although the resulting shock wave was felt throughout the county and, indeed, throughout the nation, the hardest hit areas in Santa Clara County were in the lowest priced housing and increasingly first-time homeowners faced the prospect of losing their homes.

Another significant problem in Santa Clara County real estate was the rental market. With the demand for new homes rising and the prices soaring, home builders moved their energies to the single-family market and away from the multi-family market and the vacancy rates hovered between 1 and 3 percent from the mid-1990s to 2006. San Jose became the least affordable place to rent in the nation by 2003. By 2006 the average rent for an apartment was $1,450 per month, a cost that required an income of over $50,000 per year, and it became common for workers to commute from Hollister or even the Central Valley.

During the last three decades of the twentieth century, an influx of new resi-

Designed by William H. Weeks, one of California's most prolific school architects, the Campbell Union Grammar School first opened in 1923 and was finally completed in 1929. It closed its doors to elementary school students in 1964, but that fall it reopened as the first campus of West Valley College and remained a school until 1976 when the new college campus opened in Saratoga. In 1979 the property was sold and was remodeled as Heritage Village. The executive business complex and residential condominium development and cornerstone of the redevelopment of downtown Campbell is on the National Register of Historic Places. Photo by Kevin Sterling Payne

In an election that would prove historic no matter the outcome, Dolores Carr became the county's first female district attorney in 2006 when voters elected her over Karyn Sinunu. District Attorney Dolores Carr is sitting at the head of the table with her staff: Chief Assistant District Attorney Marc Buller, Assistant District Attorney Rolanda Pierre-Dixon, and Supervising Deputy District Attorney JoAnne McCracken. Courtesy, Office of Clara County District Attorney

dents, drawn into the valley to fill the new jobs, dramatically changed the demographic makeup of the county, giving it the most ethnically diverse population in the Bay Area. Joint Venture: Silicon Valley reported that 55 percent of the technology workers in the county were born outside of the United States. County residents spoke over forty languages enabling valley firms to establish close contacts with other high-tech centers of the world from Asia to Europe.

The diversification of the population led to a new political structure in the county. This was first apparent with the successful elections of ethnic minorities and women to county and national political offices. In 1967 Norman Mineta became the first Asian American to serve on the San Jose City Council, and in 1971, he was the first Asian American to be elected mayor of an American city. After his election to Congress in 1975, where he served until 1995, Mineta became the first Asian American to serve as a cabinet member when President Bill Clinton appointed him secretary of commerce in 2000. In 2001 President George W. Bush appointed Mineta secre-

tary of transportation where he served until 2006. In 2000, Mike Honda, a former Assembly member and first Asian American to serve as county supervisor, became the second Asian American from Santa Clara County elected to Congress.

Hispanics have also played significant roles in county politics for several decades. Segundo "Sig" Sanchez represented the South County and part of the Santa Cruz Mountains as a supervisor from 1963 until 1979. Ron Gonzales began his political career as mayor and Sunnyvale city councilmember from 1979 through 1987, and was elected to the County Board of Supervisors serving from 1989 until 1996, before becoming mayor of San Jose from 1998 to 2006. In 1980 Blanco Alvarado entered elected politics as a San Jose City Councilmember and in 1996, became the first Latina to serve on the County Board of Supervisors and later, was the first Latina chairperson of the Board

In addition to ethnic groups rising to prominence in the county, women moved into key roles in county politics. When Janet Gray-Hayes became the mayor of San Jose in 1974, she also became the first woman to head a city in the United States with a population of over 500,000. That year, Geraldine Steinberg was appointed to the Board of Supervisors and in 1976, became the first woman elected to the Board. Three decades later, two of the five county supervisors were women, Liz Kniss and Blanco Alvarado, and three women represented the county in Sacramento, Ellen Corbett and Elaine Alquist in the State Senate, and Sally J. Lieber in the Assembly. In addition, two of the three elected county administrative officers are women. Sheriff Laurie Smith was elected the first female sheriff in 1998, and Dolores Carr won an election against

Karyn Sinunu to become the county's first female district attorney in 2006. Finally, in 2007, Governor Arnold Schwarzenegger appointed the first Vietnamese woman, My-Le Jacqueline Duong, to a seat on the Santa Clara County Superior Court. Duong joined Judge Thang Barrett, who was appointed to the bench in 1997, as the first Vietnamese judge to preside over a Santa Clara County Superior Court.

With all the success of more recent immigrant groups, the struggle for recognition continues for the valley's Native American community. In 1906 the United States government maintained a "Trust" relationship with three "Costanoan" or Ohlone tribal groups. However, in 1927, the Muwekma Ohlone tribe was administratively terminated from its status. In 1998 the Bureau of Indian Affairs agreed to review the case but required additional documentation from the tribe. In 2006, after decades of legal struggle, a U.S. District Court ruled that the Department of the Interior had to explain the Bureau's decision to require the Muwekma Ohlone to complete a procedure that other tribes bypassed in gaining federal status. At the end of February 2008, tribal leaders were hopeful that they would win tribal status; however, by mid-April 2008 they were still awaiting a final determination.

The development of Silicon Valley's technology industries and the resulting affluence in Santa Clara County in the last decades of the twentieth century allowed for an examination into quality of life issues throughout the county. Local, state, and federal government agencies halted decades of unchecked environmental abuse under the valley's floor and began massive environmental cleanup efforts.

On January 20, 1982 *San Jose Mercury News* reporter Susan Yoachum published a story that changed the way Silicon Valley residents thought about their "smokeless" technology industry. Yoachum described how underground storage tanks located at the South San Jose Fairchild Semiconductor plant were leaking 1,1,1-trichloroethane, a toxic carcinogen, into the drinking water supply. Ten years later, with the majority of the cleanup complete, at a cost of $40 million, the *Mercury News* reported that the Fairchild plant sat abandoned, "a scar on the placid suburban landscape . . . the place where Silicon Valley lost its innocence." Finally, in 1998, the San Jose City Council allowed a shopping center to be built on the location.

Investigations and reports for the next two decades continued to show increasing pollution throughout Silicon Valley, not just in South San Jose and not just by technology industries. By the mid-1980s, Santa Clara County had the dubious distinction of having the highest number of Superfund sites of any county in the nation. County and private inspectors identified 1,930 sites with leaking tanks and twenty-nine of the nation's 1,250 Superfund sites. Environmental specialists working in Mountain View, labeled the nation's number one Superfund site, reported that the cleanup efforts of the toxic plume under that city's industrial district might take as much as 160 years to decontaminate.

In 2000, at the other end of the county, the Santa Clara Valley Water District found that a ten-mile long underground plume of perchlorate, originating at the site of the former Olin Corporation flare plant, had contaminated well water from Morgan Hill to Gilroy. The Regional Water Quality Control Board ordered Olin to provide free bottled water to homeowners and to clean the underground contamination, which they accomplished by August 2006. The project received an Engineering

The pristine appearance of the Almaden Quicksilver County Park belies the toxic residue from over 100 years of mining activity. Although active mining ended in 1975 when Santa Clara County purchased the mines, methylmercury from the mine tailings have slowly worked downstream to the Guadalupe River and into sloughs at Alviso in the southern portion of the San Francisco Bay. The Santa Clara Valley Water District and the San Francisco Bay Regional Water Quality Control Board are working to reduce additional mercury deposits with an aim of making the bay to the point where fishing will again be feasible by 2020. Photo by Kevin Sterling Payne

Excellence State Award by the American Council of Engineering Companies.

Throughout the 1980s and continuing into the new century, massive cleanup efforts and toxic emission controls were underway or being planned throughout the county. By 1996, 735 sites were cleaned at a cost of $110 million. In 2006 Santa Clara County industries were markedly cleaner than they were in the 1980s. While in 1988 valley industries accounted for 2,850 tons of toxic chemicals dumped into the valley's air, water, and soil, by 1994 Silicon Valley industries reduced emissions by more than 80 percent. Besides the decreased amount of industrial pollutants, county businesses and employees developed environmental programs ranging from recycling to ride-sharing to environmental fairs held at companies throughout the valley.

In addition to manmade disasters, natural disasters seemed to plague the county in the 1980s. In 1984, a 6.2 magnitude earthquake originating on the Calaveras Fault hit Morgan Hill. The quake injured 24 people and caused $10 million worth of damage to structures throughout the area. However, that was just a prelude to what occurred five years

later. At 5:04 p.m. on October 17, 1989, as commuters hurried home to watch the first game of the Bay-Bridge World Series between the San Francisco Giants and the Oakland Athletics, a 15-second earthquake measuring 7.1 on the Richter Scale hit. The earthquake, named the Loma Prieta Earthquake, collapsed over fifty feet of the Oakland Bay Bridge, as well as a long stretch of an elevated portion of the Nimitz Freeway. In addition, fires burned portions of San Francisco and to the south, the downtown areas of Watsonville and Santa Cruz lay in ruins.

On the Santa Clara valley floor, damage ranged from cracks in chimneys to major structural damage to homes, public buildings, churches, and schools. Downtown Los Gatos was especially hard hit and in the Santa Cruz Mountains, large portions of Highway 17, the main artery between Santa Clara and Santa Cruz Counties, lay under tons of dirt from landslides, while hundreds of mountain residents had homes damaged or destroyed.

Local and state agencies began assessing the damage and the United States Congress stepped in with $4 billion to assist the rebuilding of private homes and public buildings as well as bridge and road repairs throughout the quake-damaged area. All totaled, the massive repair costs came to well over $10 billion. The Federal Emergency Management Agency brought in teams of caseworkers to handle over 10,000 disaster claims and over 400 inspectors to assess damage to property. Other federal aid came from the Small Business Administration, which set up offices to process disaster loans amounting to millions of dollars, and the National Endowment of the Arts, which, with the assistance of Northern California Grantmakers, established a $2.2 million Arts Recovery Fund. Assistance also came from private aid organizations ranging from the American Red Cross, which was the first on the scene in many communities, to the Mennonite Disaster Service volunteers, who helped hundreds rebuild their homes and lives.

Unlike unpredictable events such as earthquakes, some disasters can be mitigated. From the Pueblo days to the end of the twentieth century, the Guadalupe River has been a threat to San Jose. In March 1995 the Guadalupe River escaped its banks and devastated parts of downtown San Jose. A decade later, in 2005, a massive flood control project with a 2.6-mile long park, the Guadalupe River Park, was complete.

Beginning in the late 1970s and continuing through the 1990s, county supervisors as well as city and town councils began providing the county's citizenry with a better transportation network, revitalized cities and towns, increased cultural and convention opportunities, as well as more parks on the valley floor, and large open spaces in the surrounding mountains.

During the last decades of the twentieth century, the highway system throughout the valley was completed. State Route or Highway 237 opened in 1997, Highway 85 in 2004, and Highway 87 (the old Guadalupe Parkway) in 2005. Nonetheless, transportation planners realized that the freeway system of the twentieth century would not meet the needs of the twentieth-first century as the population of the county was expected to increase by 25 percent, to 2.27 million people.

In 2004 the California Legislature authorized the establishment of toll lanes on Interstate 680 from Pleasanton to Milpitas, as well as on highways 101 and 85.

Construction on the combination toll and carpool lanes will begin in 2010 and eventually circle the bay from Alameda County to San Francisco. Yet the planned freeway improvements were expected to increase capacity by only 5.6 percent and many city and county politicians and planners realized that the continued reliance on freeways could not continue to serve the population of the county in the twenty-first century.

Without the ability to build more freeways, transportation planners looked to the past for an answer to congestion. Light rail, a system that was abandoned in 1938, became fashionable once again and in 1987, the Valley Transit Authority Light Rail opened. Since then, the system has expanded to three lines: the Alum Rock

The view from Sierra Road, Milpitas looking across the width of Santa Clara County, an area once filled with wheat fields and orchards, to the Santa Cruz Mountains in the distance. Photo by Kevin Sterling Payne

Santa Clara County had horse drawn trolley cars in the 1870s, and by 1920 had an electric powered inter-urban trolley system of 120 miles of line spanning the valley from Los Gatos and Saratoga to Alum Rock Park in the east foothills, and from San Jose up the Peninsula to Palo Alto and Stanford University. Unfortunately, by 1938 the trolley was abandoned as passengers switched to automobile or bus service for the next five decades until 1987 when the Valley Transit Authority Light Rail system opened. The system currently consists of 42.2 miles of tracks with sixty-two stops, serving cities of San Jose, Santa Clara, Sunnyvale, Campbell, Mountain View, and the Mineta International Airport. Photo by Kevin Sterling Payne

Roughly parallel with El Camino Real, the old Spanish route between Los Angeles and San Francisco, Highway 101 runs from Washington to the Mexican border. Here in Mountain View, with the Moffitt Field blimp hangers on the east side of 101, Highway 85, the West Valley Freeway, skirts around the valley and rejoins 101 in South San Jose between the old settlements of Edenvale and Coyote. The 23.7 miles of Highway 85, built between 1965 and 1995, have helped to alleviate the traffic along the west side of Santa Clara County. Photo by Kevin Sterling Payne

to Santa Teresa line, the Mountain View to Winchester (Campbell) line, and the Ohlone/Chynoweth to Almaden line serving South San Jose, downtown San Jose, Campbell, Santa Clara, Milpitas, Sunnyvale, and Mountain View, as well as the Mineta International Airport.

The light rail was seen as a solution that could be acted upon at a local level, but it only provided an alternative to the Bay Area's freeway system within Santa Clara County. The real solution, many politicians, planners, and environmentalists believed, was the extension of the San Francisco Bay Area Rapid Transit, BART, system into the valley. However, after more than fifty years, the long-awaited link to BART remains an unresolved issue. Although county voters were generally inclined to favor BART, political and financial factors have delayed the decision to fund and build the system from Warm Springs to downtown San Jose. In June 2006 voters narrowly defeated a half-cent sales tax by a vote of 58 percent to 42 percent. Not dissuaded, in December 2006, the Valley Transit Authority Board of Directors allocated $185 million to complete the engineering and environmental clearance work for the project and to bring the issue to the voters in 2008.

In addition to automotive and rail transportation, the county also has the

Norman Y. Mineta San José International Airport, named after Norman Yoshio Mineta a native of San Jose, former councilmember, mayor, congressional representative, and United States Secretary of Transportation. The airport has expanded from providing access to regional carriers on a 4,500 foot-runway servicing DC-3 propeller driven aircraft in 1949, to an international destination with two runways of 11,000 feet capable of serving Boeing 777 jet aircraft and a 4,599-foot long runway serving general aviation. In 2005 the International Terminal opened and the airport commission authorized an expansion project to include a new terminal to replace Terminal C, a North Concourse, and additional work on Terminal A. Scheduled for completion by 2010, the airport project is expected to ease travel into and out of the capital of Silicon Valley.

Although the title of "Capital of Silicon Valley" is claimed by the City of San Jose, most of the developments associated with transforming a once agrarian economy into a technological based economy occurred in Palo Alto, Mountain View, Sunnyvale, and Cupertino. Nonetheless, San Jose is the county seat and by virtue of being the third largest city in California and the tenth largest city in the nation, it is *de facto* the capital of Silicon Valley.

That San Jose became a major city, was the result of the foresight and determination of civic leaders, elected and voluntary, city workers, and the efforts of the San José Redevelopment Agency. They took a city that in the 1960s and 1970s resembled anything but a capital and transformed it into a flourishing metropolis. The first evidence of a reborn downtown was the opening of the Pavilion Shops, the Fairmont Hotel, and One Fairmont Plaza in 1987. Two years later, in 1989, Market Plaza and the San José Convention Center, the centerpiece to the redevelopment effort, opened. The Convention Center was renamed the McEnery Convention Center in honor of former Mayor Tom McEnery (1983–1990) who was instrumental in the redevelopment of downtown. The Convention Center was matched with the opening of the 20,000 seat, $150 million indoor arena in 1993. The HP Pavilion is home to the Sharks of the National Hockey League, as well as the SaberCats of the Arena Football League, the Sybase Open tennis tournament, and the San José Stealth of the National Lacrosse League. In addition to sporting events, musical artists including Barbra Streisand, Simon and Garfunkel, and the late Luciano Pavarotti have performed at the HP Pavilion. The success of the Convention Center and the Pavilion led to the building and remodeling of hotels for convention attendees and arena events.

Redevelopment also benefited San Jose's cultural assets: the Children's Discovery Museum, a new wing to the San José Museum of Art, the new San José Repertory Theater, and a new home for Symphony Silicon Valley and Opera San José. The city also commissioned four "gateway" sculptures along Santa Clara and Market Streets. The Catholic Diocese of San José rebuilt the historic St. Joseph's Church and consecrated the structure as a cathedral in 1990. The rebirth of downtown fostered more development and in 1994 Adobe Systems became the first Silicon Valley firm to move its headquarters downtown.

Part of the success of the Redevelopment Agency was a willingness to try new approaches. In 1998 the City of San Jose and San José State University joined in a unique partnership. The downtown city library and university library merged and built a new facility to house both collections on the site of the old Wahlquist Library at San José State University. The new facility, dedicated to the memory of Martin Luther King, Jr., opened in 2003. It is the largest library west of the Mississippi and the first cooperative venture between a major city and state university in the United States.

Across Fourth Street from the King Library, a series of townhouses sprung up, changing the character of the once seedy area. The rebuilt downtown brought new businesses and tourists downtown and, with the various evening-based cultural activities such as the opera, ballet, civic light opera, and repertory theatre, created a vibrant nightlife in San Jose for the first time in decades. The capstone of the renovation of downtown occurred in 2005, when the San José City Hall moved back downtown to the corner of East Santa Clara and Fourth Streets.

Successful redevelopment efforts were also underway in other valley cities and towns. In the late 1980s, the real estate boom coupled with a lack of available building lots confined redevelopment in Palo Alto. Developers and home builders either remodeled older commercial buildings and homes, or, after obtaining planning department approval, purchased existing houses, tore them down, and rebuilt much larger homes.

In contrast to Palo Alto, Mountain View civic authorities built a new city hall and renovated the downtown during the 1980s. Mountain View, like Palo Alto, began its redevelopment process with a lack of vacant land, but as city planners embarked on their rebuilding efforts they sought to establish a new identity by promoting larger modern office buildings and research facilities. The Tasman Corridor of the light-rail system reached Mountain View in 1999, after the city's business district received $11 million renovation and pledged $15 million toward the project.

Cupertino tore down the last vestige of its agricultural past, the Cali Brother's grain silos, and built office buildings and a hotel. Milpitas built the Great Mall of the Bay Area, the third-largest shopping center in the nation at the abandoned Ford Motor Company assembly plant in 1994.

At the other end of the county, Gilroy, once known for its auto row, became known for its new designer outlet shopping center when the Pacific West Outlet Center (renamed Gilroy Premium Outlets) opened with 60 stores in 1990. By 2000 the complex expanded to 145 stores bringing in customers from San Benito, Monterey, and Santa Cruz Counties. Gilroy also attracted a unique theme park in 2001, when Michael Bonfante opened Bonfante Gardens, renamed Gilroy Gardens in 2007.

Gilroy Gardens was not the only theme park in the county. In 1976 the Marriott hotel chain opened Marriott's Great America in Santa Clara. Although the park was financially successful, it did not produce the expected revenues and in 1985 the city purchased the park and Kings Entertainment stepped in to manage it. In 1989 the city sold the business to Kings, but retained ownership of the land and leased it back to the park. Paramount Communications acquired Kings Entertainment in 1992, and ran the park as Paramount's Great America. Fourteen years later, in 2006, Paramount sold Great America to Cedar Fair Entertainment Company along with the operating rights to Gilroy Gardens.

In addition to Great America, the City of Santa Clara opened a Convention Center near Great America in 1986, and sought to attract a professional sports team to complement the amusement park and convention facility. In 1988 the owners of the San Francisco 49ers made Santa Clara their headquarters and training center and in 2003 moved their summer pre-season camp to the city. In late 2006 the city and the team began negotiations to build a new sports stadium near Great America.

By the mid-1990s the expanding technology industry in the county helped to renew the downtowns along the western edge of the valley. Saratoga boasted outdoor cafes, boutiques, wine tasting rooms, and restaurants featuring California cuisine. Los Gatos built a $4 million parking garage to attract more shoppers and restaurant patrons. Neighboring Campbell brought in several new discount warehouse facilities to increase its tax revenue and began transforming its antiquated downtown.

During the last decades of the twentieth century farming continued to shrink in economic importance. The few remaining

farms on the valley floor were subdivided for homes or technology parks. The agricultural supply and service industries and the valley canneries moved to San Benito and Monterey Counties or to the San Joaquin Valley. In the 1980s, however, wine making, one of the first farm industries in the county, experienced a renaissance as the Santa Cruz Mountains remained an attractive option for those who chose to remain in the industry.

In the 1980s, only a handful of wineries remained in the area, but by 2007 the Santa Cruz Mountains Winegrowers Association noted sixty wineries from the mountains above Half Moon Bay, to the Chaine d'Or region above Cupertino, and the hillsides above Gilroy. In addition to the wineries, dozens of new vineyards were planted in the mountains, from small family owned one-acre boutiques specializing in one grape, to large commercial establishments with plantings of chardonnay, cabernet, pinot noir, and over twenty other varietals.

The second harvest of change affected not only the economy, but also changed the face of Santa Clara County. Throughout the 1950s and into the new century, valley cities spread into the surrounding orchards creating countless subdivisions and suburban shopping centers while also renewing their city centers. During the last decades of the twentieth century, Santa Clara County shed its agricultural heritage and rebuilt on the stage of the future. Yet traces of the past are found each spring as fruit trees, once part of vast orchards, blossom and brighten countless backyards, and those who lived in the county before it became known as Silicon Valley are reminded why this area was once known as, and still may be thought of, as the Valley of Heart's Delight.

Completed in 1986, with financing from the City of Santa Clara Redevelopment Agency, the Santa Clara Convention Center has 45,600 square feet of meeting space that connects to the 500 room Hyatt Regency Hotel and boasts an 18-hole Golf and Tennis Club. Photo by Kevin Sterling Payne

CHAPTER TEN

CHRONICLES OF LEADERSHIP

The 1905 bicycle race between the Garden City Wheelmen (left) and the Sacramento Capitol City Wheelmen (right) took place at the Agricultural Park. Bicycling was a popular sport and a big business in San Jose. In 1894 there were twenty-eight agencies selling more than 1,000 bicyles a year. Teams from all over the state came to compete on San Jose's one-third mile cement track. Courtesy, San Jose Historical Museum

A common theme running through these stories of local enterprise is opportunity. No matter when a company was founded—and the businesses represented in this chapter range from the simplest agricultural beginnings to the highest of high-tech—they give a nod to the area itself in the story of its success.

Originally, of course, the opportunity was in land and climate. San Jose was California's first town, established to raise food for the mission and presidio settlements of the Spanish conquerors. Following the Civil War came experiments in prune and apricot growing, to the extent that The Valley of Hearts Delight eventually became the largest canning and dried-fruit-packing center in the world. Many locals can describe summer jobs picking orchard fruit, and even young residents recall the acres and acres of fruit trees in bloom.

After World War II came a different type of opportunity as the open spaces of the valley drew both population and industry. It was a good time to start or enlarge a business, and many people did, crediting their success in part to good luck in timing. The postwar expansions saw big and little enterprises of all kinds, from consumer shops in the new shopping malls to divisions of industrial giants such as Lockheed.

Even the focus of agribusiness changed, as farmers turned to more profitable row and flower crops instead of orchards. But the agrarian era was definitely over, and the electronics age was about to begin. With the advent of the computer chip came another enormous opportunity—and a change of nickname as well. The term Silicon Valley was used by a local journalist named Don Hoeffler in 1971; virturally the whole world knows Santa Clara Valley by that name today.

There are a wealth of commercial enterprises here, and on the following pages you will meet some of them and find out how they moved from their generally humble beginnings to what they are today. Proud of their pasts, and with an eye to the future, they reflect the area's great diversity, and its myriad opportunities.

AC PHOTONICS INC

AC Photonics develops and manufactures both passive and active fiber optic components for the telecommunications market, which in turn provides fiber optic products to individual customers. The company, located in Santa Clara, was founded in 1995 and markets to telecommunications companies worldwide. Arthur Wang, founder of the firm with his wife Christina, humbly considers himself to be a "reluctant entrepreneur." With a background weighty in American literature and educational studies, Wang would not have guessed that a business in Photonics would be his "road less traveled by."

Mr. Yongjian "Arthur" Wang was born in China and grew up in the tumultuous era of the Cultural Revolution. His father, Wang Sr., was from a well-educated intellectual family. At a time when intellectual pursuits were frowned upon and, in some cases, punished, Wang Sr. encouraged and supported Arthur to pursue his academic studies at Shanghai Foreign Language Studies Unviersity. Arthur attended the university until 1985 and excelled in his American literature studies. In addition to falling in love with American drama, he also fell in love with

Arthur Wang in ECOC, Cannes, France, 2006

a fellow classmate, Christina (Zuhong Qu), who would soon become his wife. Upon completion of his master's degree in art, Wang was asked to stay on at the university to teach American literature to Chinese students. He stayed at the university until 1990.

As a professor, Arthur Wang eloquently shared his deep passion for American Literature with his students. He was well-read in his favorite authors: William Faulkner, Tennessee Williams, Ernest Hemingway, and Arthur Miller. Wang had previously completed his dissertation on Arthur Miller's *Death of a Salesman* and had such respect for the author, he borrowed his name to use when he moved to the United States in 1990.

Clearly possessing a gift and a love for education, Wang continued to gain respect for his teaching skills. In 1990 Wang was given a scholarship to continue his teaching education and was offered an assistant teaching position at Delta State University in Cleveland, Mississippi. He accepted the position, moved to the United States and continued on the path of what he believed would be a lifelong career in education.

Despite the vast cultural differences between the metropolitan city of Shanghai and the small town of Cleveland, Mississippi, the experience at Delta was a positive one for Wang. However, finances were a bit of a struggle. Even though he was given an additional scholarship from Lee's Foundation in Singapore, he had to take a second job serving food in the University's cafeteria.

In 1992, Wang's wife, Christina, was offered a job in San Francisco after her completion of a master's degree in education. Not wanting to be away from her, Wang took a summer job in the bay area at a fiber optics company. Around this time, Wang learned that he was accepted at the University of Texas in Austin where he had hoped to complete a Ph.D. in education with the goal of returning to China to teach American literature to Chinese students.

The end of summer came and the fiber optics company, impressed with his hard work, offered Wang a full-time position in the sales and marketing division. He was faced with a crossroads decision. "The road diverged in front of

Arthur Wang and family

me and I had to choose a path," states Wang. Wanting to remain in the same city with his wife and seeing the financial possibilities in fiber optics, Wang chose to detour from the path of education, and remained at the fiber optics company.

Soon after, the company went through some internal changes which resulted in its dissolution. Wang, however, was now intrigued by the potential growing demand for fiber optics and felt a desire to remain in the industry. In the year 1995, with the full support of his wife, and putting all of his family savings into his business, he started AC Photonics Inc.

Wang spent most of his time at the company, almost sixteen hours a day, seven days a week, both managing the company and learning the technology of fiberoptics. Together with his team, Wang's company provided high quality fiberoptic components and excellent services to telecommunication companies in need of product. In 1997, compelled by customers' needs for better and less expensive products as well as custom designed components made to order, AC Photonics began a research and production arm of the company in Santa Clara. Any new product created by the research team would, over time, be sent to overseas OEM factories for mass production.

"We had an advantage over other companies from the beginning," explains Wang. "Other companies started doing mass production in the United States and then later decided to move their production arm overseas. After the telecom bubble—that move became too expensive and a little too late," states Wang.

In fact, when other fiber optic companies were hit hard by the crash of the stock market following 9/11 and the plummeting telecommunications market, AC Photonics remained strong. Revenue did decrease, but it later recovered and has grown steadily ever since. AC Photonics brought in approximately a half million in its first year of operations and grew to $10 million in 2001. During the crisis of the market crash, revenue dropped to $3 million. Now it has surpassed all its earlier numbers and brings in average annual revenue of $20 million.

AC Photonics began with Wang's savings and two employees. Now, the company has close to thirty employees who specialize in research, sales, production, or administration. The annual revenue is $20 million and growing steadily. Wang believes 'the customer is king,' and credits his employees for their expert research and product development

Arthur Wang (third from the right, second row) and Christina (fifth from the left, first row) with company staff (March 2008).

in the technology of mastering light for those customers. The company creates both passive and active fiber optic components such as switches, DWDM, CWDM, isolators, hybrid, couplers/WDMS, attenuators, collimators, pigtails, and other related products. In addition, AC Photonics also offers custom-made optical components such as lenses, prisms, mirrors, achromats, and cylindrical lenses.

Wang believes he will return to teaching some day. "I will go back to teach American literature when AC goes IPO. My favorite authors should include Arthur Miller with his *Death of a Salesman*. Now I know that sales isn't just selling product, it's selling yourself—your integrity, honesty, and credibility—in addition to product quality and service. Now I'll be able to teach that from actual experiences," states Wang. But for now, he is happy with the path that he is on. Wang quips, "Two roads diverged in front of me and I had to choose a path. I chose the real world of commerce and a future in the fiber optics industry, and that has made all the difference."

Dear Dr Smith,
you saved my life!
Thank You.
Paul Hulme

ALAIN PINEL REALTORS

Alain Pinel Realtors is truly an original Saratoga treasure, established here in 1990. Sales volume of $7.2 billion in 2007 eclipses that first year's total by about 40,000 percent. Alain Pinel Realtors is the largest privately owned independent in California ranked by volume, second largest in the nation, and seventh among all residential real estate companies. The company has over 1,300 sales professionals in twenty-seven offices surrounding the Bay Area.

The company dominated the industry in the development of state-of-the-art software, technology, and broad use of computer applications in real estate that immediately attracted national media attention. Combining this with high-end marketing expertise and award-winning advertising and marketing, the firm attracted superstar managers and agents.

Paul Hulme is the sole owner of the firm founded with original partners, Alain Pinel and Helen Pastorino. The first office opened in Saratoga on August 27, 1990 and Pinel resigned less than two months later to return to his native France. Pastorino subsequently resigned as well.

Being an entrepreneur in Silicon Valley doesn't distinguish one business person from another. It's a common designation. Starting your first enterprise at age eight and not looking back, however, does make you different. While most list

The first APR office, Saratoga.

Paul Hulme, founder, owner & CEO of Alain Pinel Realtors. In a day when real estate firms proliferate, merge, morph and disappear, Alain Pinel Realtors thrives.

makers jot down things to do at work or home, Paul Hulme keeps lists of businesses to start. The founder, chairman and CEO of Alain Pinel Realtors could write the book on running a business. He earned his first income delivering both the morning and evening newspapers for eight years in southern Utah—sometimes by bicycle, sometimes on horseback.

Paul Hulme was born on a 250-acre farm near Panguitch, Utah. He was one of six children in a Mormon family. The family house was a simple country home with two bedrooms; it did not have plumbing, water or electricity. The paper route was the beginning of a career that now enables Hulme to live in a beautiful, big home and own a large real estate portfolio.

Even as a child, the rigors of horseback and bike riding made him strong. A high school

teacher recognized Hulme's toughness, and recruited him for the wrestling team. Besides, the teacher and part-time coach needed a 160-pound boy to fill an empty slot. Despite his inexperience, Hulme lost only one match that year—in the Utah state finals.

By the time he was twenty-four years of age he had earned a bachelor of arts degree from the University of Utah, completed his tour of active duty as a Captain in the U.S. Air Force, served a two-and-a-half-year mission in Germany for his church, and was accepted into medical school at the University of Utah, founded and operated a successful chain link fence contracting business and established himself as a full-time licensed life insurance agent. By age twenty-eight he was the district manager in San Jose for Massachusetts Mutual Life Insurance Co.

Hulme chose a business career rather than proceeding with his original plan of medical school, continuing on in securities sales, estate planning, agency development and management, and property development and management. As a life-long entrepreneur he has usually had several businesses going simultaneously, including chemicals, equipment, products, sales, mortgage businesses, and service companies.

He currently has over 1,500 employees in more than thirty states. "I find a niche for services and hire good people to run the business," says Hulme. While day-to-day operations are managed by others, he consults to his own companies. All of his companies are service or investment oriented.

"Paul is the best salesman in the company, and he does not "control" people or push them around," said Barry Baltor, vice president of Alain Pinel Realtors.

Some of his businesses almost start themselves. In the 1960s, for example, he accepted some commercial cleaning equipment and materials in lieu of payment on a debt. Just about the time his wife, Helga, resolved herself to the idea, Hulme had started a janitorial business. Professional Maintenance Co. in San Jose is one of over fifteen companies started by Hulme. One of his early accounts was Mervyn's Department Stores. Professional Maintenance got the cleaning contract in 1968 for Mervyn's when the fledgling department store had just three outlets. I've never met a man of greater integrity or a better human being," says Mervyn Morris, founder of the retailing chain, of Mr. Hulme. "My experience with him could not have been better." Messrs. Hulme and Morris maintained a professional relationship until 1979, when Mr. Morris sold the retail chain he founded. They still talk occasionally, of investment opportunities and their personal lives.

Paul Hulme still sees plenty of business opportunities. He seems almost frustrated when he says today, "There are just *so* many things to make a business of." Since 1972 he has been heavily involved in various real estate activities as well as ownership of farms; orchards; shopping centers; office, apartment and medical buildings; single family residences; etc. He says he likes real estate because of the interaction of working with people. "It seems like it's all I've ever done. It's one of the reasons I agreed to start this company [Alain Pinel]," says Hulme.

Unlike a lot of captains of industry, Paul's not an enigma. "What you see is what you get," said Ron Huber, a former executive at Medallion Mortgage in San Jose. He's always taken a low-profile approach.

Part of his inclination toward privacy has to do with a personal tragedy he and his wife, Helga, endured in 1974. One of their daughters, Kelly, was murdered

while on her way home from school. She was ten. The Hulmes lived in San Jose at the time. "The man is still in jail . . . I check at the beginning of every year," said Hulme. The convicted assailant is serving three consecutive life sentences in a California state penitentiary. The Hulmes moved to Saratoga and have lived there since 1974.

Hulme speaking at the APR kickoff in 2007.

In every industry there is a group of people distinguished by a passion for excellence and an eagerness for new ideas. In residential real estate, Alain Pinel Realtors are those people.

Busy days a year after opening in 1991.

ARBORWELL PROFESSIONAL TREE MANAGEMENT

Arborwell Professional Tree Management has been recognized by publications such as *Inc.* magazine and the *San Francisco Business Times* as one of the fastest growing companies in the Bay Area while its president and founder Peter Sortwell was recently awarded the Service Entrepreneur of the Year Award by the *East Bay Business Times*. These accolades are impressive, but not surprising, given the company's gold star management and top-tier services, which include pruning, tree preservation and tree removals. Yet the company may never have come to be had it not been for a very inauspicious event.

After leading the tree division of one of the largest horticulture companies in the nation for over fifteen years, Sortwell was let go after a new company president restructured operations. This left Sortwell in a quandary; in the small horticulture industry, there were very few companies that his specialized skills would mesh with. "I began to soul search to try to decide what I wanted to do," Sortwell remembers. When he broached the subject of possibly relocating to another state with his wife, she kindly made known her intention to remain in the Bay Area, telling him: "The kids and I will come and visit you often."

Arborwell safety training

Certified arborist

Still weighing his options, Sortwell attended a seminar in Walnut Creek put together by an executive recruiting firm. The all-day event focused on whether or not attendees had entrepreneurial aptitude. It was the perfect opportunity for Sortwell to explore the idea he had been dwelling on for months: opening his own company. At day's end, attendees were given one hour to compose a business plan, which they then pitched. Sortwell's presentation received a standing ovation and a resounding response. "Everyone in the class said they would hire me, and said 'Why haven't you started?'" says Sortwell.

So he went home and laid out his proposal for his wife, Anne. Despite the gravity of the personal and financial risk involved, Sortwell recalls her response well: "She said, 'Let's

do it.'" With no small-business financing options, mortgaging their home was the only way to turn the idea into a reality. "It was a big risk," Sortwell acknowledges. "The house was 75 percent paid for, so it was a step back."

With this in mind, Sortwell put his business plan on a fast track. Knowing that starting a business from scratch would take valuable time and money, he located a small mom-and-pop tree service in the East Bay and worked out a deal to purchase the company. Though the company was very small with only a short roster of residential clients, the infrastructure was invaluable. With a contractor license in place, office space, phone number, computers, two trucks and six employees, Sortwell had the perfect springboard to hit the ground running.

He utilized his contacts in the industry to build an impressive and productive sales team. Paired with a crew of top-notch arborists, the formula was a success. By the first year, after the purchase of the business, Sortwell had taken Arborwell from a \$.5 million-a-year operation to a \$2 million-a-year venture.

In six years the company has continued its exponential growth with a staff more than ten times as large as its initial workforce of just six. The company now employs seventy-eight people, from front-line laborers who man thirty-two service vehicles in the field, to a sizable middle management force, two full-time mechanics, account managers that see projects through from beginning to end, as well as administrative staff. Major projects include the posh and polished Stanford Shopping Center as well as pristine tech headquarters for Apple Computer, Oracle, and Google.

However, even with the company's success, Sortwell keeps Arborwell meticulously focused on quality service and safety, starting from the top, down. Sortwell himself holds a degree from the University of Maine in plants and soil sciences and is a certified arborist. This certification, which is held by nine other employees, is administered by the International Society of Arboriculture and involves a rigorous, seven-step process that includes tree biology, tree species identification, safety, care and maintenance, among other technical topics. "It is a pretty intensive study program and test to prove your knowledge to earn the certification," Sortwell notes.

To maintain excellence, Arborwell sticks to a smaller spectrum of specialized services. "Our services will be strictly related to trees," Sortwell says emphatically. "If it's not related to trees, we're not doing it." This helps keep the business focused and also avoids competition with some of Arborwell's own clients—landscape contractors.

Safety is also of the utmost importance. "This is a very high-risk industry," Sortwell explains. "These guys are working in trees 100 feet in the air, hanging from ropes and handling chainsaws. You just don't go out there without training, knowledge and professionalism." To that end, Sortwell institutes a "culture of safety" at Arborwell. Four Arborwell employees are now certified by the Tree Care Industry Association (TCIA) in

Arborwell headquarters, Hayward. In addition, the companyy has three other locations: San Jose, Redwood City and Sacramento.

Peter Sortwell

professional tree care safety, far beyond the one or two certified employees at many other national companies.

While Sortwell's leadership has propelled the company to success, he is quick to give credit to his staff. He points to the enthusiasm and buzz around the business as helping attract the best talent for his team. A collaborative environment is always cultivated; its successes are celebrated with events like the company's end-of-summer picnic, an annual party with soccer, food, entertainment, and plenty of camaraderie and fun for employees and their families.

Looking back, Sortwell has no regrets about losing his job and risking everything to launch Arborwell. "I don't know what I would have been doing if I hadn't done this, but I know I would have been miserable." Not that the process was simple: "The first two years I didn't sleep," he says. "It was very, very stressful." But with Arborwell's growth and continued ascent as one of the Bay Area's leading service companies, Sortwell knows it was well worth the sacrifices to build the team he has today, noting, "It was the best thing I've ever done."

BUTLER-JOHNSON CORPORATION

"Butler-Johnson Means Service" has been more than a motto for this San Jose based company. From the very beginning, Butler-Johnson (BJC) has made customer service for the products that they bring to market a top priority. It is a part of a business formula that has produced more than forty-seven successful years.

When Rolston Johnson and Dan Ford formed their partnership that became BJC, their vision was a wholesale distribution company that would provide innovative, brand name products to the construction industry. While their competitors were selling typical commodity-type products with little or no service, Rolston and Ford recognized that a new business environment was evolving. Customers were becoming more service-minded in a highly competitive market. Butler-Johnson differentiated itself by offering distinctive new products, marketing support and customer delivery. It was a winning combination.

As Butler-Johnson looked to expand their product offering, non-traditional building products, specifically products made with innovative plastics, presented an emerging opportunity. On the strength of their marketing efforts and customer service reputation, BJC began to receive calls from such manufacturers as Formica and DuPont™. In 1971 Butler-Johnson

An experienced management team provides solid leadership.

would become the first DuPont™ distributor west of the Mississippi and, thirty-six years later is recognized as one of the leading DuPont Surfaces distributors in the country. BJC would continue to expand into the surfacing arena adding flooring products such as Mannington and Johnsonite. In 1995 Steve Johnson, Rolston's son, joined the company and soon after created their Tile Division. This included Butler-Johnson's own imported tile, along with Crossville Inc®, Casa Dolce Casa®, Florem®, Dorset by Questech® and Mapei. As the Premium Surfacing Solutions Distributor in Northern California and western Nevada, Butler-Johnson is one of the largest distributors on the west coast of interior surfacing products, representing more than twenty estab-

lished flooring, tile, and surfacing brands. BJC expanded its offering once again in 2005 with the addition of natural stone products including granite slab, pre-fabricated modular granite and Benissimo Systems® Granite Solutions. In 2007 BJC added to its fire and safety component offering with Lumonall™, an innovative, photoluminescent (PLM) product, featuring exit signs and Safety Way Guidance Systems (SWGS).

The focus for BJC has been to provide its customers with world class service. Today, the company maintains an inventory of more than $11 million, housed in its 120,000 square foot distribution center; located at their corporate headquarters in San Jose and at its regional distribution facility in Sacramento. In operation twenty-four hours a day, Butler-Johnson night crews load twenty-five trucks for next-day deliveries while BJC drivers arrive at 2:00 a.m. to prepare for their delivery routes. At the same time, unloading teams arrive to unpack product in waiting trailers, to replenish inventory in time for the arrival of the day crew, which begins a new twenty-four-hour business-day cycle.

Since the purchase of their first delivery truck in 1960, BJC has provided customers with next-day delivery service.

Butler-Johnson corporate headquarters in San Jose, California.

An extensive inventory ensures that BJC has the products their customers need.

Today, its fleet of company-owned and operated trucks delivers product five days a week, to all major cities in northern California, plus the Tahoe and Reno, Nevada areas several times per week. A unique service offered by BJC is "before 8:00 a.m. delivery." More than 500 customers demonstrate their trust and respect for Butler-Johnson by taking advantage of this service. They provide BJC with keys and security codes to their facilities. With this access, BJC drivers can deliver products directly into customer warehouses during off business hours, ensuring that the material they require is "just in time" for the approaching business day. To accommodate deliveries to the Sacramento area, including Stockton and Fresno, ten to twelve trailers are transferred from San Jose to the BJC Sacramento facility each night for Sacramento's next-day delivery or will-call services.

In the late 1970s with their customer base rapidly expanding and sales volume growing, the need for automated services and operating efficiencies became apparent and in 1981 BJC computerized all operations. Rolston Johnson, the company's forty-seven-year CEO, is a proponent of technology, and continues to explore new ways for the company to increase its menu of online services. "Customers are looking for faster, more efficient ways to do business," says Rolston, "and this is one way to meet that need." In response, BJC implemented eCustomer, an e-commerce site that allows customers to check inventory, place orders, confirm pricing and review order status and payment history, online 24/7. In addition, BJC has an extensive corporate website, www.butler-johnson.com, which caters to the industry professional, as well as a retail website, www.homesurfacing.com, which provides homeowners with the information they need when building or remodeling a home.

In recent years, Rolston and Dan have dedicated time and effort into the growth

Company owned and operated trucks provide next day delivery.

and development of a management team capable of leading the corporation into the future. This team includes Steve Johnson, VP Business Development; John Cherry, VP Premium Surfaces Division; Clay Covington, VP Flooring Division; Jennifer Patrick, VP Operations; and Gary Knoll, Controller. Each of them has fifteen to twenty years of professional experience in their respective fields. This team is complemented by an infusion of a new generation of "young tigers," including Rolston's grandson, Jon Johnson, who are being groomed and developed to handle BJC's continued growth and increasing professional demands. As BJC continues to expand, emphasis is placed on training and maintaining an already low turnover rate of key employees. In 1997, as the company moved into the second generation of corporate ownership, BJC initiated an Employee Stock Ownership Plan (ESOP). ESOPs encourage maximum employee loyalty, stability and conscientiousness since every employee learns to appreciate the lessons of becoming an "owner."

The strength of a company lies in the quality of its people. Throughout its nearly fifty years, BJC's concept has been to hire the best person for each position. That philosophy still guides the company today. Approximately 1,800 times per day, 150 Butler-Johnson associates interface with customers. Those daily calls are referred to as "1,800 moments of truth." Happy and conscientious employees create satisfied customers. BJC associates live this and believe this. These values and beliefs, together with the "Hallmark of Service" that Rolston Johnson and Dan Ford infused into the company forty-seven years ago, is what will allow Butler-Johnson to continue to grow and prosper as it reaches its half-century mark and beyond.

CALIFORNIA MONUMENTAL CO.

When people envision monuments, they often think of the large-scale tributes erected to celebrate great leaders or commemorate wars. In the Bay Area there is a place that people can go to get an equally beautiful, handcrafted memorial to the life of single loved one, famous or anonymous, but no less loved and remembered. This place is California Monumental, a family company that has been creating these personal remembrances for generations, following a belief that a monument is not to memorialize death, but is rather created "because someone lived."

Throughout its long history, California Monumental has always had its own strong family connections. The father of founder George Demicheli owned several memorial shops and Demicheli ultimately continued in this family business. He began California Monumental in 1930, hiring stone cutters and letterers to craft the monuments while he managed all of the business aspects.

Just a few years later, another young man got his start in the memorial business. Andy Brunetti was still in

Andrew Brunetti at eighty-seven still cutting stone.

high school in 1936 when he began working part-time at Oak Hill Monument Company. After graduating from school, Brunetti began a full-fledged apprenticeship, learning the trade from Oak Hill owner Francis O'Brien. The apprenticeship blossomed into a full career, and Brunetti stayed with Oak Hill for twenty years. After his time there, Brunetti left Oak Hill and began his tenure at California Monumental in 1956.

George Demicheli managed the successful business until his retirement in 1969. At that time, he sold California Monumental to then longtime employee Brunetti, who enlisted his wife, Eleanor, to take over management duties. Andy continued to create monuments, a craft he thoroughly enjoyed. Eventually, Andy and Eleanor's son, Michael, joined in the family business, working part-time while still in high school, just as his father had years before. After graduation, however, Michael did not join California Monumental full-time; instead, he chose to take some time to learn more about the funeral and cemetery business, which gave him a great deal of insight into all aspects of the industry. After four years, Michael returned to California Monumental, where he has been ever since.

The family connection built by the Brunettis at California Monumental continued long after Michael took over the duties upon his father's 1983 official retirement. (The elder Brunetti would still report to the office every day well after retiring to help make monuments. He continues to remain involved with research and development as well as general consulting.) In 1988 Eleanor likewise passed the torch in managing the office to her daughter, Geralyn Brunetti-Hall, while Geralyn's husband, Greg, also joined the team, changing careers to learn the craft of monument making. The other two members of the California Monumental team, Tony Linares and Pracilla Truong, are not related by blood or marriage, but Michael Brunetti says that these longtime employees "are just like family," as well as being essential members of the close-knit operation. This level of professional closeness and affinity speaks volumes about the values embodied by those at California Monumental.

In addition to the unique lineage of California Monu-

Original location in Santa Clara, established in 1930.

The California Monumental Co. family in 2008.

mental, its services are also distinct in the industry. The company is the last in the Bay Area to build its monuments from raw materials to polished memorial. Where most other monument companies buy pre-cut polished granite from quarries and merely add the requested lettering, California Monumental has a team of highly skilled artisans who blend modern technology with the time-tested methods of craftsmanship that produce the finest results. "We start with a raw piece of stone, which we cut to size and polish," Michael Brunetti explains. "Then the lettering process is primarily—and has been since the early 1940s—a sand blast process, cutting the stone with sand under enormous pressure." The company has distinct specialties as well, offering a wide range of languages for their monuments, such as Spanish, as well as Chinese and Vietnamese characters.

While some individuals come in to pre-select their own monuments, most of California Monumental's customers come in after losing a loved one. Brunetti notes that everyone at the company does their best to make this time as easy as possible for customers who are grieving. "We don't do high-pressure sales," he says adamantly. "We want people to work with us because they want to and because it is the right choice for them."

Once California Monumental's services are commissioned, the process becomes all about quality. "The quality of the job far outweighs how fast something gets done," says Bruneti. "Our products are going to be there a long, long time. When it is all said and done, the time and effort invested in each monument is well worth it. It needs to stand up to the test of time because it invokes the memory of a loved one."

Brunetti says that there is nothing more satisfying than a customer later remarking that they were happy that they had given the California Monumental craftsman the right amount of time to perfect their work as the finished product was a beautiful testament to their loved one even after the weathering effects of time had passed.

While its Santa Clara office was recently consolidated, California Monumental is located in San Jose and the company still primarily serves the Bay Area from Gilroy on the south to South San Francisco.

Like the monuments they create, California Monumental has also stood up to the test of time. This has been accomplished by a true love of the art form and a commitment to delivering the best quality products on the market. Yet the company is more than willing to take the time to put this extra care into each and every monument, with the belief that this is all necessary in order to best render memorials that reflect the joy and memory of lives that were lived.

CHILDREN'S DISCOVERY MUSEUM OF SAN JOSE

Back in the 1980s Children's Discovery Museum (CDM) of San Jose, California existed only as an educational outreach program and a $10 million capital campaign. Apple Computer's co-founder Steve Wozniak recognized the importance of the venture and came forward with an $800,000 donation. "His gift came early on in the campaign," says Marilee Jennings, CDM's executive director, "and it really got us going."

The city of San Jose came on board as the Museum's public partner, and many high-tech luminaries like David and Lucile Packard made very generous donations. Jennings stresses that founding executive director Sally Osberg nurtured relationships with established San Jose philanthropists including real estate developers Barry and Molly Swenson and communications icon Allen Gilliland and his wife, Gloria, allowing the Museum to secure the $10 million it needed to break ground in 1988.

The unique, 52,000 square-foot purple building on the banks of the Guadalupe River on the edge of downtown San Jose has been a welcoming landmark since its opening in June 1990. Today the river figures prominently in CDM's culture and programs. "In our BioSITE (Students Investigating Their Environment) program," says Jennings, "children put on rubber boots and go into the river to take water samples and monitor other conditions for scientists who determine the health of the river. And an upcoming exhibit will feature Lupe, the 14,000 year-old mammoth discovered along the Guadalupe."

This kind of hands-on experience speaks to the core of CDM's philosophy, which is that children learn best by doing. "We're strongly committed to providing experiences that recognize that children have different learning styles and need to be physically active in the learning process," says Jennings. "It's not possible for schools to meet every child's learning needs, so we provide a range of opportunities that help to fill this need."

Many such experiences are available

Children's Discovery Museum of San Jose, designed by architect Ricardo Legoretta.

in thirteen semi-permanent exhibits which encourage touching, exploring, manipulating and experimenting. The popular Bubbalogna exhibit, for instance, allows children to joyfully learn about physics by making and interacting with bubbles of all sizes, discovering how light changes their appearance, how they can be stretched into different shapes, and how unpredictable they are.

Don't assume, however, that CDM is a science museum. The Museum's exhibits and programs revolve around the ideas of Community, Creativity, and Connections and cover a broad educational swath, including science, math, and the humanities—all set in a rich multicultural milieu. Role-playing activities include Pizza, Please, a pizza parlor where kids explore healthy choices as they cook and serve a pizza to their parents; and, the Post Office, housed in an original wooden structure donated by a nearby community.

To get the biggest educational bang, CDM has formed a partnership with the developmental psychology department at the University of California, Santa Cruz. "Researchers come into the Museum and study the learning that is actually

taking place at each exhibit," explains Jennings. "They videotape interactions between parents and kids and code the conversations for very specific behaviors." The staff then uses the information to improve the Museum experience. They learned, for instance, that adults were four times as likely to discuss the science content of a particular energy exhibit with boys, than with girls. To reverse this, staff created a graphic character named Power Girl who invites interaction at a number of the energy exhibits. "We also installed a dollhouse in which you can power the lights with energy that you generate in the exhibits," says Jennings. "We were able to turn it around so that parents were engaging in discussions about science equally with daughters and sons."

Local culture and history are highlighted throughout the Museum. The Kids' Garden is an outdoor space that reflects the region's rich agricultural tradition—Silicon Valley was originally known as the Valley of Heart's Delight. "Kids help cultivate the land, water the plants and harvest," says Jennings. Soon a farmer's market with local vegetables and low-fat cheese will be added to the Pizza, Please exhibit to promote healthy nutrition.

In addition, specific events are designed to address cultural traditions. The annual Three Kings celebration from Latin America takes place twelve days after Christmas. CDM also celebrates *Lunadas* six times a year with stories, poetry and music. "Many cultures participate in this Mexican tradition," says Jennings, "reflecting the Museum's highly diverse neighborhood. We may see Chinese dragons, hip-hop performers and *folklorico* music in the same evening!"

Performing arts are a big draw for families, according to Linda Fischetti, CDM's education and programs manager. "We have a forty by forty foot theater, which is the perfect size for young visitors," says Fischetti. "Children are so close that they feel very connected to the performers, making the experience a powerful one, even for very young children. And kids need to be physically comfortable and able to leave when they're ready," says Fischetti, who also offers workshops that put the children themselves on stage. In addition, the Lee and Diane Brandenburg Theatre, as well as the Museum's outdoor Cadence Amphitheatre space, provide venues for performances by local community groups and schools.

Fundraising at CDM is ongoing. The Museum's Annual Fund consists of about 500 donors who contribute anywhere from $100 to $10,000 each. The Museum aggressively raises money to cover daily operating expenses and subsidized admission through the Museum's Open-Door policy and for the creation of new offerings.

Replacing exhibits also requires a constant flow of capital. Due to the hands-on approach, most of CDM's exhibits have a five-to-six year lifespan before they must be retired. "With 300,000 visitors a year the wear and tear

Children's Discovery Museum highlights local cultures with experiences for all ages. Here, a young visitor explores the Vietnamese Fire Dragon.

takes its toll," says Jennings. Fundraising for new exhibits includes securing major grants from organizations like the National Science Foundation.

Volunteerism is welcome and encouraged. High school students can fulfill their community service requirement at CDM, and the Museum has developed a unique program through which families can volunteer together and facilitate a hands-on activity or experiment on the floor.

CDM has become a welcome resource for the area's schools. According to Jennings, over 50,000 children visit the Museum every year on school field trips. At the same time, the Museum staff creates programs that travel to local schools. "Among others, we offer Family Science Nights where the whole student body and their families can participate, and a performing arts workshop that gets an entire class involved in rewriting and performing a familiar fairy tale."

Exploring physics is fun when you dive right in, as this budding scientist in the Waterways exhibit will discover when the balls begin flying.

The Museum's innovative exhibits and educational programs have garnered national recognition, including being ranked in the Top Ten children's museums by *Child Magazine* and in the Top Five science centers in the world by *The London Observer.* CDM is also the proud recipient of the National Award for Museum Service, bestowed by First Lady Laura Bush, the highest honor a museum can receive for its commitment to extraordinary community service. Two CDM exhibits, Alice's Wonderland and The Wonder Cabinet, received the coveted Excellence in Exhibits award from the American Association of Museums.

What does the future hold for Children's Discovery Museum of San Jose? "We're in the throes of thinking through the third decade of our existence," says Jennings. "We're looking forward to using the beautiful park around us to help families further explore, understand and appreciate the Guadalupe River with activities based on the educational opportunities that the outdoors naturally provides."

CSL, INC.

An innovator in plating technologies and service systems, CSL, Inc. was established in 1986 and has developed alongside a number of world-renowned technological corporations in Silicon Valley. Co-owners Naishadh Saraiya and Shirish Desai founded the company in response to a need in the plating industry for more technologically advanced and environmentally friendly processes. Today, CSL offers an unparalleled selection of plating and support services for customers in the semiconductor, electronics, medical, communications, aerospace, and data storage industries. The company's cutting-edge technologies and proactive environmental stance have earned it a reputation among clients and competitors alike as a model twenty-first-century business.

Saraiya and Desai founded CSL after both had spent almost two decades in the engineering industry. The partners have much in common: both came to the United States from India during the early emigration surges of the 1960s; both already had bachelor's degrees and went on to earn degrees in engineering; both proceeded after graduation to work in the field, while nurturing a strong tendency towards entrepreneurship.

Desai earned an M.S. from the University of Illinois at Urbana and an M.B.A. from Santa Clara University; he then pursued a career in operations management. Saraiya earned a second bachelor's and an M.S. in chemical engineering from the University of Missouri at Colombia and went on to work for Honeywell as a chemical engineer.

Saraiya spent only two and a half years at Honeywell before his entrepreneurial spirit led him to found Integrated Memories, a company that engineered magnetic plating for memory disks. Unfortunately, Saraiya says, despite the fact that he and his partners "did everything we could do," the company folded three years later. Saraiya returned to the corporate world, spending one year with Control Data Corporation in Omaha, Nebraska, before applying for and

CSL twentieth anniversary celebration.

receiving a job at Caelus Memories in 1974.

Saraiya and Desai met at Caelus. While Saraiya continued to work on the technical side, Desai had become successful in the field of operations management. Caelus Memories was later acquired by Information Storage Systems (ISS), which became part of Sperry Univac, where Saraiya rose through the ranks to become a group manager for Advanced Recording Technology. Both left Sperry to pursue individual dreams; Desai became part of a growing startup company, while Saraiya joined a group of three to start MegaStor, a thin film magnetic media company.

During this time, significant developments were taking place in the Santa Clara Valley. First termed "Silicon Valley USA" by entrepreneur Ralph Vaerst in 1971, the region has been a major center for technological innovation since the early twentieth century. It boasted the United States' first radio station in 1909 and, during World War II, became a premiere site for defense technology companies who wanted to supply Moffett Field, a naval air station in Sunnyvale. After the war, Stanford University began

leasing its lands to highly technological companies for use as an office park, thereby drawing dozens more such companies to the area.

By the time Saraiya and Desai were working for Caelus, the Santa Clara Valley was fast living up to its new name. Venture capitalists spurred growth, pouring capital into the area's economy and encouraging technological entrepreneurship. Many of the region's best-known companies—including Hewlett-Packard, National Semiconductor, Apple (formerly Apple Computer), Oracle, and Xerox—were already well established by 1980 and were making their technologies available to a variety of industries around the world.

Ironically, however, this high-tech revolution had not extended to the electroplating industry—the very industry that was plating and packaging components of increasingly delicate microcomputer and semiconductor machinery. According to Saraiya, typical plating shops of the time had two common characteristics: They were low-tech, and they tended not to concern themselves with cleanliness. Cyanide was a common ingredient used in some plating processes; industry workers inevitably ingested the chemical and were occasionally poisoned.

Such was the state of the plating industry during the years that Saraiya and Desai were considering starting a business together. When AA Plating in Santa Clara, California became available in 1986, they purchased the business with the goal of offering innovative, technology-driven plating and plating-related services to the Silicon Valley's booming high-tech industry.

At the time of sale, AA Plating had been operating in Santa Clara for more than a decade. The company had a number of loyal clients, to whom CSL would continue to provide services, offering two plating processes, zinc plating and anodizing. Zinc plating was considered harmful both to employees and to the environment because of its use of cyanide.

"We couldn't sleep," Saraiya said, knowing that this hazardous process was one of only two that they had to offer.

Twentieth anniversary group picture

Only two years after opening the business, they closed the zinc plating process and cleaned out the area. They replaced the process with electroless nickel plating, a chemical reduction process that provides exceptional corrosion resistance and a high level of hardness, and can therefore be used to extend the service life of components exposed to harsh conditions. Critical to producers of oil machinery and defense technology, this process therefore provided CSL with a wealth of potential clients.

Meanwhile, Saraiya says, he and Desai noticed the Santa Clara area becoming "cleaner and cleaner"—in other words, more and more devoted to health and environmental safety. A number of medical companies moved into the region, bringing with them a need for immaculately clean machine components. In response to this growing need, in 1990 CSL constructed a class-100 clean room, where newly plated products could be cleaned and packaged with almost no risk of contamination.

As in the case with the clean room, a number of CSL's major innovations occurred in response to some evident need in the industry—sometimes even in response to a customer's direct request. Such was also the case with TTH, a process invented by CSL engineers and then exclusively used by Icore International. At the time of its invention, cadmium was one of the most commonly used plating metals. It was considered an occupational hazard because of its capacity to cause

Nickel line set up.

chemical pneumonitis, pulmonary edema, and even death, but because there was no comparable substitute, most plating shops continued to use it.

According to Saraiya, Icore originally came to CSL to request a non-cadmium plating with cadmium-level performance. "We took it as a challenge," he says. Two years of research and experimentation resulted in the first and only cadmium replacement that met all the performance criteria of the original metal, with a 1,500-hour salt spray life, electrical conductivity, high voltage dissipation, and self-lubricating, low-friction properties. Upon utilizing the substance, Icore liked it so much that they bought the rights to its name, TTH, which stands for Tougher Than Hell.

Some time after TTH was developed and successfully employed in 1997, the U.S. Joint Striker Fighter (JSF) program introduced new specifications for submarine components. The nature of submarines requires that their parts be exposed to extremely corrosive conditions which, under normal conditions, would ravage metal within a matter of days. According to the new specifications, plated parts had to withstand immersion in sulfur dioxide for at least two weeks as a test of their ability to continue functioning in marine environment. CSL continued to experiment with TTH after receiving the new specifications and eventually developed a series of coatings called the JCP series—the first and, to this day, only process in the industry that meets the new requirement. While developing the JCP series, CSL engineers also introduced a new process called the "nano-coat," a superbly hydrophobic topcoat for which, along with the JCP series, the company has since filed patent protections.

These processes exemplify one of the primary characteristics that set CSL apart from its competitors: its capacity for innovation. CSL is one of only a handful of plating companies in the country that perform research in-house and develop unique processes. The results are cutting-

Dicronite show

edge technology; increased efficiency; and, ultimately, satisfied clients. Companies as diverse as Space Systems/Loral, Icore, and Multichip have expressed great appreciation for CSL's ability to develop processes that specifically meet their companies' needs as the needs arise.

Today, CSL offers the most extensive line of plating, cleaning, packaging, and labeling services available throughout the industry. They provide plating services with every available metal, including nickel for the medical, semiconductor, and computer industries; silver for automotive, electronics, and jewelry undercoats; gold for microwaves, electronics, and semiconductor equipment; and tin for lead frame and semiconductor applications. In addition, they provide anodizing, passivative, and chemical film plating, along with bead blast, strip plating, and ultrasonic finish. Their specialized processes include Dicronite, TTH, JCP, Ni-Lube, and exotic metals plating, which uses a unique electroless deposition technique to plate passive substances.

The entire facility is monitored by the AIMS software (Advanced Integrated Manufacturing Software), implemented by Desai. This is enterprise software,

whereby the plating process is tracked through each major step via barcode, providing interactive COC (Certificate of Compliance), total quality assurance, financial performance, and an overall facility maintenance system. Because the AIMS is based on a relational database, it allows CSL to collect historical data continuously, in addition to maintaining traceability of all process parameters.

"Our objective is to make a system independent of people who run it so that there will be no mistakes," says Saraiya. His company appears well on its way to realizing that goal. In addition to the AIMS system, CSL also employs a fully integrated parts tracking system. Invoices are presented on a computerized screen much like that used by UPS. Once a satisfied client signs the screen, a printed copy is automatically generated for the client, while the order information is transmitted to the accounting system.

CSL's efficiency does not just apply to its accounting practices, however: company leaders have applied the same principles they use in operations to revolutionize the interactions between a plating company and the environment.

When Saraiya and Desai purchased the company in 1986, it used 20,000 gallons of water a day. In 2000 the company was granted the Industry of the Year Award by the California Water Environment Association for cutting its water use to less than 5,000 gallons a day—while increasing production eightfold. The company has also remained dedicated to finding new, safer ways to achieve the same results their clients desire, true to the decisions they made twenty years ago.

"Taking care of the environment is part of the business," Saraiya says, adding that the company spent $300,000 in 2006 to bring in new, more environmentally sound technology. As the head of CSL's earth-friendly programs, Saraiya has been invited to participate in the Santa Clara County Pollution Prevention program as an "eco-mentor," teaching other business leaders how to make their companies as efficient and safe as CSL. Thus CSL has become a leader in the search for sustainable industry, in addition to continuing to excel in the field of metal plating.

"We got lucky," Saraiya says when asked how CSL has become such a success. "When we started, we had eight people and two lousy processes." He laughs. "Now we have forty different processes, most unique, and about fifty employees. A lot of things we did came out right in the end." He adds, however, that such an achievement would only have been possible in a country such as the United States, where the business mindset of the citizens encourages and rewards people like him and Desai— people who have a desire to explore, to take risks, and to dream. Luck aside, Saraiya says, it was thanks to the American appreciation for enterprise that he and Desai have been able to accomplish what they have.

The truth of this statement can be seen by CSL's success and the variety and quality of services they offer today. From pre-cleaning to post-cleaning, plating to packing, special orders to nano-coding, CSL offers a combination of processes

unavailable anywhere else in the country. A leader in both metal plating and sustainable industry, CSL, Inc. is a model twenty-first century corporation: extraordinarily skilled at adapting the environment to suit the needs of humankind while ensuring that their processes foster a better environment for the future.

CSL employees

Clean room

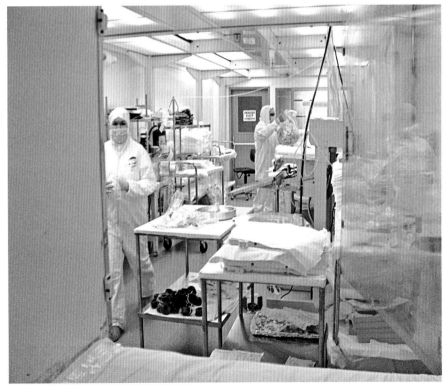

DATA PHYSICS

When one thinks of the Santa Clara Valley, visions of cutting-edge tech companies definitely come to mind. Yet looking beyond the silicon and the left-brain stereotype will reveal a host of brilliant inventors whose creativity and imagination underscore their technological advancements.

Such is the case with Data Physics Corporation. What began as a two-man operation helmed by Sri Welaratna and Dave Snyder has now evolved into an international technology firm that sets the industry standard as a manufacturer of test and measurement solutions, including dynamic signal analyzers, vibration controllers, shakers and power amplifiers.

Data Physics was founded in 1984 by Welaratna and Snyder, two alumni of tech giant Hewlett Packard (HP). The road to the creation of Data Physics was paved with hard work, inspired intellects, and some well-timed serendipity. Welaratna originally trained as an engineer in his native Sri Lanka (then Ceylon) before continuing his education at the University of Bradford in Yorkshire, England. It was there that he began research on Fourier transforms, in which he utilized a Hewlett Packard analyzer to test some of his theories for his thesis. This research impressed HP and Welaratna was invited to join the HP team. "In a way, it was a dream come true, because if anyone had asked me where I wanted to work, HP

Dr. Sri Welaratna, co-founder, president and chief executive officer

One of the important factors in Data Physics ongoing success in delivering breakthrough technology is its dedicated team of software and hardware engineers (2007).

would have been my number one choice," recalls Welaratna. "I was delighted to be asked to join them."

After a few years working in the UK office, and much to the chagrin of his superiors there, Welaratna was transferred to Santa Clara, what he describes as "the mecca of signal processing." The Santa Clara division was working in the field of Fourier analysis, Welaratna's specialty, and his talents were needed there.

Within a short time frame, however, HP began comprehensive corporate restructuring. The signal analysis groups of the Santa Clara, California and Loveland, Colorado divisions would eventually be combined into one office in Everett, Washington, just outside of Seattle. This upheaval displaced a great number of people, and Welaratna struggled between staying at HP in the

Santa Clara area by moving to the field of computers or leaving HP to pursue his chosen field of science. His passion for signal analysis won and Welaratna decided to shift into consulting work for large companies such as IBM for the next few years. An accidental meeting with another HP alumnus, Dave Snyder, also working as a consultant in the bay area, was the catalyst to look to bigger and better options. "We started off with the slogan: solutions for signal processing, as our original mission statement," Welaratna recalls.

David Snyder, co-founder, chairman & chief technical officer

Welaratna credits their HP pedigrees with instilling strong values in the overall approach to their work. Snyder, who had designed hardware and software for the Fourier analyzers developed at the Santa Clara division of HP, and Welaratna had instant synergy. The first project they collaborated on in 1983 was the design of the UD 400AT vibration controller, the first such instrument to use a PC as the host computer and the very first DSP-based signal processing peripheral, which was built with the Texas Instruments TMS32010. It was their success on this undertaking that allowed them to begin building their Data Physics team.

At Data Physics, invention for invention's sake is never the aim. The company strives for high performance above all else; at Data Physics, there is always room to innovate. "We carried the idea that HP lived by," he explains, "that it was never very useful to make a product unless you made a strong contribution to the technology: pushing technological frontiers, or streamlining the size, the cost, and so on."

"HP was very good at both, very brave in their research," Welaratna continues. "Behind invention, there was a second wave in the company into miniaturization, and one could see how this could bring about a dramatic change in the size and price of the product. This was a strong cultural influence that stayed with us—the idea of high performance of the product and a strong contribution to the user."

The composition of the company is another important element of Data Physics' success. What began with just Snyder and Welaratna has now blossomed into a sizable enterprise; the Data Physics team now consists of eighty-plus employees, most of them professional engineers. Many others play important roles in management and research. Welaratna takes great pride in the synergy of his team as well as its unique global complexion. "It is almost like the U.N. when you come to work," says Welaratna, noting that the

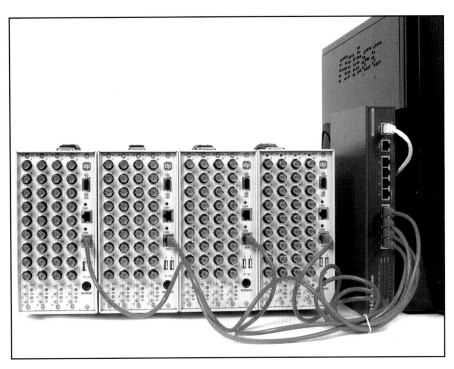

Above: Abacus, a DSPcentric hardware platform (2003)

Below: Quattro, an ultra-portable DSPEngine (2005)

employees represent a wide number of different countries, from his own Sri Lanka, to the United Kingdom, France, Italy, Sweden, Russia, Rumania, Iran, India, and China. He and Snyder endeavor to create a comfortable and pleasant work environment that mirrors the comforts of home. "We want to provide a nice place to work, a gracious treatment of employees," he explains.

Data Physics also has a factory in Corona, California where large shakers used in the testing of heavier products are manufactured. Building shakers is a more recent activity at Data Physics and the company's drive for groundbreaking technological advancement has already given rise to higher performing new products.

"Fourier transform is the cornerstone of this area of work," says Welaratna, giving some insight to Data Physics' area of expertise. "It gives a perspective of frequency domain, meaning you understand the behavior of something, through its natural frequencies of vibration." It is the properties of things in motion, and the effects of sound and vibration on those components, that occupy the minds of the Data Physics team. "What we discovered is that the preponderance of applications came from aerospace and automotive industries, engineers are constantly looking for solutions for resisting vibration—whether building a longer lasting car, a quieter airplane or electronic instruments that can withstand the rigors of air travel."

Welaratna explains that the applications of this technology accounts for the vast improvement in car performance in the past few decades. "A related area where vibration is damaging to products is from transportation, whether by road, rail or air, so we look to build better mechanical things that can withstand vibration and shock."

While Data Physics is at the very top of its field with this specific type of testing, the company has expanded its range of products in recent years to create a more complete solution for its clients. Welaratna points to an example of one area of work: satellite testing. "A satellite is fragile, is built to have minimum weight, and it is hugely expensive. It has to be tested to verify that it will not fail during launch and passage into space but

A thousand channel system based on Abacus (2006)

very carefully, so that testing itself is not damaging to the satellite." This is precisely the work that is performed by customers of Data Physics, who not only test to verify the integrity of their test objects, but also to uncover just what frequencies and vibration will be problematic for the devices being tested. Simulating the vibration environment during ascent into space and testing a satellite, makes use of the entire range of hardware and software products provided by Data Physics. "The motion is produced by the shakers, the type of vibration and shock is carefully simulated by the vibration controllers and the behavior of the satellite is studied using the dynamic signal analyzers, all three types of test instruments manufactured by the company," Welaratna explains, noting that in recent years, Data Physics has actively sought to create complete solutions such as this for its clients. "One other UK company has similar range," says Welaratna, "But we are the only supplier in the US that has all of those products."

Both Welaratna and Snyder also conduct training seminars with their clients, which gives them the opportunity to connect with their customers and share their detailed knowledge of the complex systems they create. "Typically, users need some tech-

nical background to make use of the products because the applications are highly technical," Welaratna says of the training sessions. "Usually the user is knowledgeable because that is the field they are in, but even then, it is often very beneficial to spend a week learning the finer points of the measurements and the visualization of data with the specific instrumentation, so they can realize the highest potential from their investment."

"It is very satisfying to teach, it gives you a chance to see in the eyes of the student that there is something wonderful about the discovery that you've made," says Welaratna. "It is also a chance to leave someone else with the ability to improve their work," says Welaratna, whose own passion for the products and services offered by Data Physics is evident in his voice.

"There are other competing companies," Welaratna notes, "but our products are the best in the industry," he says simply. "We continuously innovate; there have been a number of major discoveries that have been made in our twenty-five-year history." While the company has a list of impressive inventions, Welaratna notes that they eschew patents. "You can patent an invention and expect others to pay you," says Welaratna, explaining that the patenting process and subsequent legal enforcement is a great strain on resources for companies that are not conglomerate-sized. "Or," he continues, "you can use the invention yourself and let others compete." It is this philosophy that keeps Data Physics one step ahead of the curve with its innovations.

Yet innovation alone has not been the secret to the company's success. The most important element, human ingenuity, has elevated Data Physics. "We have evolved," says Welaratna, "to become a complete solution supplier." This is the plan for Data Physics in the future as well. "We plan to continue to innovate and to spread the breadth of solutions that are offered, so the user looking for several products can find all those compatible solutions together."

SignalForce 50,000 lb. water cooled shaker with monobase, head expander and amplifier, the latest addition to engineering developments (2007).

CISCO SYSTEMS, INC.

A multinational corporation headquartered in San Jose, Cisco Systems, Inc. designs and sells networking and communications technology and services. Husband and wife team Len Bosack and Sandy Lerner, who worked in computer operations at Stanford University, founded Cisco Systems in 1984. Bosack adapted multiple-protocol router software originally written by William Yeager, another staff employee who had begun the work years before.

Cisco was not the first company to develop and sell a router (a device that forwards computer traffic between two or more networks), but it was one of the first to sell commercially successful multi-protocol routers, to allow previously incompatible computers to communicate using different network protocols. Cisco hardware, software, and service offerings are used to create the Internet solutions that make networks possible, providing easy access to information anywhere, at any time.

Since 1986 Cisco has been helping companies increase productivity and profits with Internet Protocol (IP) communications. Today, with more than 63,050 employees worldwide, the firm's tradition of innovation continues with industry-leading products and solutions in the company's core development areas of routing (the process of selecting paths in a network along which to send data) and switching (a communications paradigm in which discrete blocks of data are routed between nodes over data links shared with other traffic), as well as in advanced technologies. Currently, millions of Cisco access routers help businesses of all sizes around the world extend their networks to all divisions of their organizations.

Initially manufacturing only routers for businesses, Cisco later decided to move into the home-user market with the purchase of the brand Linksys, while expanding its offering for corporate customers.

In 1990, when the firm was listed on the NASDAQ stock exchange, Bosack

World of Solutions, Networkers Conference 2005

and Lerner left the company. During the Internet boom in 1999 the company purchased Cerent Corp., a start-up company in Petaluma, California, for about $7 billion. Since then, only Cisco's acquisition of Scientific-Atlanta has been bigger. In late March 2000, at the height of the dot-com boom, Cisco was named the most valuable company in the world, with a market capitalization of more than $500 billion.

The company was a 2002–2003 recipient of the Ron Brown Award, a presidential honor awarded to companies for the exemplary quality of their relationships with employees and communities. Cisco supports Networking Academy programs in more than 160 countries, with approximately 10,000 academies. More than 430,000 students—in high schools, technical schools, colleges, and community organizations—learn hands-on networking skills to prepare for the workforce of today and the future. The Jordan Education Initiative, a partnership between Cisco, the World Economic Forum and several other organizations, continues to expand its interactive e-curriculum-based education programs into new geographic areas such as Egypt and India. The education initiatives in the Mississippi and Louisiana school systems after Hurricane Katrina are rebuilding schools for the twenty-first century.

Cisco has put a major effort into its move into virtualization technologies. Some of Cisco's advances include the emergence of the network at the center of innovation as it is expected that as many as 14 billion devices will be connected to the Internet by 2010. This explosion of devices will be increased by more and more services and tasks that will be handled online—from phone calls to personalized searches to downloading videos, games and other forms of entertainment. Now known worldwide, Cisco's stated vision is "Changing the Way We Work, Live, Play and Learn." That rings true as we learn that users soon will be able to communicate from any device and in whatever mode they choose—at home, at work and in the world.

GARDNER FAMILY HEALTH NETWORK/ GARDNER FAMILY CARE CORPORATION

More than forty years ago, a small clinic was created to meet the healthcare needs of the migrant and agricultural workers in Silicon Valley. Many of the workers, predominantly Spanish-speaking and of Mexican descent, lived in the community of Alviso, an unincorporated area of Santa Clara County at the southern tip of San Francisco Bay that became a large migrant labor camp during the harvest season.

In 1968 members of the Alviso community, with help from Stanford Medical School and the U.S. Office of Economic Opportunity, started a community clinic to address the critical need for medical services that were non-existent for the people of Alviso. This community project was first known as the Alviso CSO Health Foundation, which then grew into the Family Health Foundation of Alviso. When services were expanded from Alviso into the city of San Jose, as a result of the needs of its growing patient base, the organization's name was changed to the Family Health Foundation.

In 1971 Stanford Medical School students and Sacred Heart Church worked with community members in the Gardner neighborhood of San Jose to organize another community clinic for a local population working in the canneries in that part of San Jose. This population worked in the local fruit packing plants and shared the same demographics—race, culture and language—and also

Woman in front of Gardner Clinic on Willow Street in 1971.

suffered from the same lack of medical care as the Alviso workers who picked fruit. This clinic was called the Gardner Health Center.

During the time that this clinic was changing and growing, so was Gardner Health Center's current CEO Reymundo Espinoza, who was still in school. Having grown up as a migrant-worker child, Reymundo's path to his current work began with a traumatized family life: a sister who passed away at age twenty from toxemia, a sister at age twenty-eight who committed suicide, another brother and his father who both passed away at an early age.

In the early 1970s, at age twenty-one, Reymundo married. On his honeymoon in Guaymas, Mexico, a friend of his wife, Beatriz, suggested that he apply for a master's program, at Berkeley in health. "I was a high-risk youth," Reymundo admits. "I worked between two worlds, one with smart kids, and another with kids who didn't have the same opportunities. I liked school and athletics and had a strong desire to compete. If someone said I couldn't do something, like go to college, all I wanted was to prove them wrong." He credits his aunt Dolores Barns Espinoza with pulling him in the right

Dr. Fernando Mendoza as a child with parents, Aurelio and Delia, in the Gardner community. Dr. Mendoza is the chief of general pediatrics at Lucile Packard Children's Hospital at Stanford. In the summer prior to entering Stanford Medical School, Dr. Mendoza helped to start the Gardner Health Center .

direction. She helped with his application and set up a meeting for him in 1969 with Riverside County's Congressman John Tunney, who nominated him for Annapolis. "My eyesight is poor, so I failed the physical," says Gardner's CEO. His response to it all is, "I'm a blessed child. Growing up, I didn't know what I wanted to do. I was in the right place at the right time."

When he was accepted at Stanford University at age eighteen, he claims that he didn't understand the value of his acceptance. "Until that time, my family's greatest excitement was traveling to Compton from the desert. Stanford was bigger than my hometown."

After Stanford, Reymundo received his master's degree in public health from Berkeley and worked for Boswell Memorial Hospital, a variety of health system agencies in Arizona and Ventura, California, then for the Hospital Association of Central Valley for three years in

St. James Health Center in downtown San Jose

Fresno, followed by a for-profit hospital corporation in Riverside County. When David Correa, director of Gardner Health Center invited him to apply for the position of executive director of Gardner in June 1986, he accepted and worked there from 1986 to 1990. From 1990 to 1994 he worked for the larger Family Foundation of Alviso, then left briefly to do some private consulting. Invited by board members to return to Gardner, Reymundo came back in 1995.

In 1997 Gardner Health Center and the Family Health Foundation merged. They became Gardner Family Health Network, which provides primary medical care, and Gardner Family Care Corporation, which offers behavioral care/substance abuse services. The Gardner corporations continue to be directed, focused and staffed by the local community and governed by one board of directors, one management team and one vision. As Reymundo puts it, "We have two corporations—one is the parent, and the other is a subsidiary. The parent handles primary care, and the subsidiary handles behavioral care. There are two separate boards, but both organizations' board members are the same people."

Together, the Gardner corporations provide comprehensive healthcare services dedicated to improving the health status of low- and moderate-income communities in Santa Clara County, especially the disenfranchised, poor and most vulnerable members.

As the population grows, so does the community's need. Gardner applies for grants on an ongoing basis. The organization's focus is always on covering the uninsured and underinsured. "Of the 50,000 individuals Gardner serves, 45,000 are at the 200 percent of the poverty level or below, which is an

average family of four earning $40,000 per year, or less, and more than 15,000 are uninsured. We try to fundraise," says Espinoza. "We've received many grants and worked hard to maintain the organization. We received a New Start grant that gave us the base funding to start a health center in Gilroy." That grant for South County Health Center in Gilroy generated more resources, including help from Medicare, Medi-Cal and other insurances. "We leveraged the money we received through all insurers," he says.

Gardner's hard work has lead to its current status. "Historically we've been dealing with uninsured populations," says Reymundo. "Unlike other organizations that advertise, our success has been word-of-mouth. It's not a matter of people not being able to get care elsewhere, it's a matter of their wanting to get it from us. More healthcare providers have been coming into our arena as well." Some of the programs Gardner offers are, no doubt, why the organization stands apart from others. For example, Gardner is developing a program to assist people with chronic diseases, which can be expensive if they aren't managed properly. They can result in

Brand new 14,000-square-foot health center in downtown Gilroy

hospitalization and/or long-term care. Gardner Family Health Network teams are working on implementing a chronic disease collaborative to help the community with diabetes and other chronic diseases. They started this program by setting up population-based practices for patients with diabetes. Team members are developing a database on patient diabetics, and establishing benchmarks to see how their diabetes population is progressing. They're also developing a case management component wherein the individual must have a treatment plan—for exercise, medication, daily steps they can do themselves. "We're not there yet," says Reymundo, "but we're developing the plan."

Their next step is to integrate patient information they acquire and individuals in the community who can help these patients. If a particular diabetic needs to exercise, a *promotora*—a community health promoter—helps that person by organizing an exercise program, perhaps something as simple as a daily walk. "We are limited at Gardner by our four walls," says Reymundo. "To be completely successful, Gardner must work with the community at large." Gardner hopes to organize more such communities in the future.

Gardner has offered such programs as free mammograms for low-income

Entertainment at a health fair

Noe Pablo Lozano Ph.d., Gardner board chairman

women for more than ten years. They afford this by getting about 50 percent of their operating budget from grants and contracts, and the other 50 percent from services they provide.

In the late 1960s and early 1970s, when Alviso and the Gardner communities were predominantly Latino, the individuals in these areas organized storefront operations—the Alviso and Gardner Health Centers. Their primary goal was simply to get people to be seen and medically helped. Over time, the transition has been that of a contractor partnering with many agencies in the county. The County of Santa Clara is aware that if Gardner Family Network and Gardner Family Care Corporation were to go out of business, the County would suffer consequences. Gardner has been at the table when major decisions were made, such as developing health insurance plans that deal with Medicare, Medi-Cal, Healthy Family and Healthy Kids. "We were the first county to develop the Healthy Kids health insurance program, now being duplicated throughout the state. Gardner has also advocated at state and federal levels—the National Association of Community Health Centers is one example, as is the local Commu-

nity Health Partnership of Santa Clara County. Gardner advocates to enhance patient healthcare access by improving reimbursement; securing financing for infrastructure development, such as Information Technology systems; and continuing to be at the table when crucial healthcare policy and decisions are made.

An original member of California Primary Care Association, which represents more than 600 not-for-profit community clinics and health centers that provide comprehensive, quality healthcare services, particularly for low-income, uninsured and underserved Californians who might not otherwise have access to healthcare, Reymundo acknowledges that CEOs can make a difference. But he claims that Gardner has qualities that are far more important than a single CEO—a team called the User Majority Board, which consists of concerned patients; a knowledgeable and hard-working board of directors such as Dolly Ares, Esq; an outstanding team of care professionals; and a local community of caring constituents. These, he says, are the people who make a difference.

Gardner's mission has always been to provide high quality, primary medical, behavioral and social care that includes education, prevention, treatment, intervention, and advocacy services that are affordable, respectful, and culturally, linguistically, and age appropriate. Languages spoken at Gardner include English, Spanish, Vietnamese, Tagalog, French, and Russian.

"One of our greatest successes," says Gardner's longtime CEO, "are the results of a combination of dedicated, long-term employees, new employees who are young, energetic and knowledgeable, a visionary and dedicated Board of Directors, and local, county, state, and federal partners who believe in us. More than anything else, they are our success. Also, the County environment is such that we try to work *with* each other rather than *against* each other. There's so much needed that we're always working together to help people improve their lives."

INTEL CORPORATION

On April 19, 1965 co-founder of Intel Corporation, Gordon E. Moore predicted in *Electronics* magazine that the number of components the semiconductor industry would be able to place on a computer chip would double every year. In 1975 he updated his prediction to once every two years. Now known as Moore's Law, his prediction has become shorthand for rapid technological change. His law has become the guiding principle for the semiconductor business to deliver ever-more-powerful chips while decreasing the cost of electronics.

The corporation that today is the largest semiconductor company and inventor of processors found in most personal computers started when Gordon E. Moore and Bob Noyce left Fairchild Semiconductor and incorporated a new venture, NM Electronics, in 1968. Along with venture capitalist Arthur Rock, they pooled resources and rented a space in Mountain View, California. They purchased the right to call their company Intel (INTegrated ELectronics) by paying $15,000 to a company called Intelco.

Pursuing the "next leap ahead," in 1969, its year of inception, Intel an-

Children visiting the Intel Museum try on "bunny suits."

Intel Museum in Santa Clara, California

nounced its first product, the 3101 bipolar random access memory (RAM); launched the world's first metal oxide semiconductor (MOS); received its first customer order from Hamilton Electric; opened its first outside-U.S. sales office in Geneva, Switzerland; and established sales and marketing functions in Japan. Intel was distinguished by its ability to make semiconductors—its primary products, and static random access memory (SRAM) chips. Business grew during the 1970s as it expanded and improved its manufacturing processes and products, still dominated by various memory devices. It was a time when computers were getting personal.

By the early 1980s Intel's business, dominated by dynamic random access memory chips, faced increased competition from Japanese semiconductor manufacturers. The sudden success of the IBM personal computer convinced then-CEO Andy Grove to shift the company's focus to microprocessors. By the end of the 1980s this decision had proven successful, and Intel embarked on a ten-year period of unprecedented growth as the primary hardware supplier to the

PC industry. In 1983 Bob Noyce was inducted into the National Inventors Hall of Fame.

Intel's successful advertising campaign of the 1990s made it and its Pentium processor household names, becoming the largest semiconductor supplier in the world. Developing the firm's outreach, the company started the Intel Foundation to expand Intel's contributions to local communities, awarding minority fellowships and graduate fellowships to local recipients.

In 2000 the company focus on wireless computing expanded, along with Intel's Teach to the Future program, providing technology training to thousands of teachers. Its Museum of Science was opened to help children in underserved communities work with adult mentors to develop technology skills. In 2003 Paul Otellini, Craig Barrett, and Andy Grove were running the company as Intel celebrated its thirty-fifth anniversary and shipped its billionth processor, while introducing a microchip that combines key components of cellular phones and handheld computers on a single piece of silicon.

Every year of its existence, the company has continued to create great leaps in technology that have led to positive change. In 2008 Intel announced it would purchase more than 1.3 billion kilowatt hours per year of renewable energy certificates as part of a multi-faceted approach to reduce its impact on the environment, making Intel the single largest corporate purchaser of green power in the USA visit to the company website shows this accomplishment as well as its ongoing pursuit of new research, technology, and work with the community. Intel co-founder Robert Noyce's words clearly continue to inspire employees today: "Don't be encumbered by history. Go off and do something wonderful."

KRYTAR INC.

Krytar Inc., located in Sunnyvale, is a long-established and respected name in the technology industry. The company was founded in 1975 by Thomas J. Russell, a veteran design engineer who had worked for Bendix Corporation, McDonnell Douglas, and Alfred Electronics. From his years of experience, Russell knew that he was uniquely suited to design and develop a far superior range of ultra broadband microwave components than what was then available. From this was born Krytar, a privately owned corporation serving both the commercial and military markets.

When launched in April 1975 at its original Palo Alto office, Krytar employed just two people: Russell and co-founder Marion Molley, a team that would remain the cornerstone of Krytar through its first decade. By 1978 Krytar added its third team member, Don Yoshii, and shortly thereafter, sales manager Carol Gentile, a very important element in Krytar's early growth and success. The company also began the first of its many long-term alliances with leading test and measurement companies, becoming a strategic supplier of passive microwave components in test and measurement systems found worldwide.

Over the course of its decades as an industry leader, the Krytar team has worked to research and refine their product line, which includes a number of complex components suited for microwave instrument use as well as system manufacturers. The products include directional couplers, directional detectors, three dB hybrids, MLDD power dividers/combiners, detectors, terminations, coaxial adapters and a power meter, covering the DC to 67.0 GHz frequency range. As might be expected of a frontrunner in the technology field, Krytar holds several patents for unique designs in the broadband arena. With an eye toward innovating and streamlining processes, Krytar gives customers the most technologically advanced, durable products at the most cost-effective price.

Krytar headquarters

While its products may be intricate, the company's secret to success has been simple: "I think we were successful through all these years," muses Yoshii, "because we stuck to our basic philosophy of offering superior products with high quality standards and exceptional customer service." Yoshii emphatically credits the Krytar staff, now having grown significantly from the early days, as the driving force behind bringing this vision to life.

The year 1988 proved to be an important one in Krytar's evolution, as the company shifted gears to become a global player. That year, co-founder Marion Molley retired, and those at the company began to seriously assess the future. "We evaluated the overall operation of our company," Yoshii says, "and came to the conclusion that to compete not only in the domestic market, but the global market, we had to improve our productivity and become more effective and efficient." This resulted in a comprehensive retooling of every aspect of Krytar's inner workings. The product line was wholly redesigned, the company's machine shop was phased out, and a lineup of top-notch suppliers was culti-

vated before putting a brand new marketing strategy in place to propel Krytar to success into the twenty-first century.

This change helped Krytar adapt and prepare for challenges ahead. In 1994 Krytar founder Thomas Russell passed away. This loss was deeply felt by all of those at Krytar, a company so imbued with Russell's expertise and leadership.

"Tom was brilliant, a very gifted engineer," his wife, Nancy Russell, remembers. With a master's degree in electrical engineering, and another in mathematics, Russell was experimenting and innovating on the computer long before programs or applications had ever been invented. This "really put him in the forefront of this field," Nancy Russell notes. "He was way ahead of his time."

Reeling from the unexpected loss, there was some uncertainty about how best to proceed. Nancy Russell was herself a successful executive at a Fortune 500 company. She grappled with whether or not to sell the company or leave her own career to lead Krytar. Tom Russell

Some of the Krytar team in a 2006 picture. Center front row is Nancy Russell with Don Yoshii next to her.

had managed both the technical and business sides of the company, leaving very large shoes to fill. However, when Don Yoshii stepped in to manage business operations as the new company president, taking on all of the technical aspects of the business, it seemed a logical progression for Nancy Russell to take the reigns on the non-technical end, becoming the company's new CEO. Yoshii notes that though this time was extremely difficult, the success in transitioning the company and continuing on after the loss of Thomas Russell is a moment in Krytar's history that he and Nancy are especially proud of.

In the subsequent years, Krytar remained well known for its outstanding products and service. The corporation now possesses all the electronic test equipment necessary for testing its products from DC up to 67 GHz. Included in the test equipment is a Hewlett Packard 8510C Automatic Network Analyzer with 8515A (45 MHz - 26.5 GHz) and

8517A (45 MHz - 50.0 GHz) S-Parameter Test Sets and Agilent Technologies E8361A PNA Series Network Analyzer (10 MHz - 67 GHz).

Krytar also maintains the very highest standards in making sure its products are top-notch, with its Quality Assurance Program designed in accordance with military-level protocol MIL-I-45208, which includes a calibration system per MIL-STD-45662, the standard approved by the United States government for use by all departments and agencies of the Department of Defense.

The new millennium has been exciting and challenging for the company. But the focus, insight, and leadership it gained from both Molley and Russell remains with the company to this day, and is a legacy continued on by the company's current leaders.

"I'm very excited about Krytar," says Nancy Russell, who points to both veteran staff and an emerging new generation as keeping the company focused

yet dynamic. "We have employees who have been with us for a long time, people who believe in what they are doing and are committed to top quality products because they know it was something Tom was committed to," she says. "We also have some new, young employees who are very enthusiastic . . . . My son is coming in and he is learning the business, too. So I can see the next generation coming in and it is very exciting."

With rapid growth in global communications, wireless, satellite and radar, the future is bright for Krytar, which remains committed to consistently delivering the best products for its customers. "We are constantly engaging in development of new products as well as improvements on present products to drive our growth into the future," says Yoshii. It is this steady approach that has earned Krytar its stellar reputation in the industry.

LIN ENGINEERING

Lin Engineering was founded by Ted Lin, engineer, ideologist, educator and the "father of new step motor technology." It is Mr. Lin's vision and enthusiasm which drives his solution-oriented company and encourages creativity and top performance from his loyal employees. He is a recognized technology leader in the field of step motors, spindle motors, voice coil actuators and control devices. Lin's extensive knowledge in step motors, in particular, was born of his own initiative. Seeing the market void of step motor expertise, he began to specialize in the technology and in doing so, carved out a niche in the marketplace.

From grad student to the leader in step motor technology, Lin paved his path with innovation and entrepreneurial sensibilities. "The American dream means opportunity," states Lin who capitalized on his innate skills and good fortune to attain his dream. His journey began in Taiwan, his birthplace, where he learned first hand about motor technology. "My brother owned a motor manufacturing company, so I learned the basics about motors at a young age," explains Lin. Out of his interest and practicality, Lin attended Tsing Hua University in Taiwan.

Ted Lin, president and CEO

After receiving a B.S. degree in physics, he was granted a scholarship in the states and earned an M.S. degree in physics from Northern Illinois University. He graduated in 1973.

Upon graduation, Lin found it difficult to find a job utilizing his degrees in physics. He saw an opening for a motor engineer at a company called McGraw-Edison located near Chicago, applied for the job and was hired because of his experience gained working for his brother's company when he was in Taiwan. Lin was given the title of development engineer and learned quickly about the various types of motors the company manufactured. He advanced with the company and when McGraw-Edison made a move to Columbia, Missouri, Lin moved with them. From there he worked for two more motor manufacturing companies offering better positions with each move. His knowledge grew with each company. "Every company had a different line of motors and I had to learn everything about each one. After working for several different companies, I knew almost everything I could know about different kinds of motors. I knew a lot," quips Lin.

In 1981 a new opportunity presented itself at a company called Warner Electric. The company was looking for a step motor engineer. By now Lin had learned about various motors but did not have experience with step motors. He applied for the job anyway. As it turned out, Lin was one of the few who applied for the job because step motor technology was so new at that time. Because of his wide range of experience in various motor technologies, he was hired. Lin quickly advanced at the company and learned through hands-on experience about step motor technology. Within six months, Lin was the company's step motor expert. He rapidly transitioned from student to teacher of the new technology.

Lin was fascinated with step motors and began to explore new applications for the systems he developed. He began to create step motors for various uses, advancing the company's line of motors in the marketplace. "I kept thinking, how come nobody ever thought about this before," remembers Lin. By the time he left the company, multiple new step motors were included in Warner Electric's retail line. Lin was sent off with a grand party and an impressive title of being the "father of the new step motor technology."

Ted Lin at work

In 1984 Lin moved to California to begin a partnership with a company who wanted to capitalize on his expertise in step motors. Lin was more than able to use his engineering skills to provide innovation in product, but his entrepreneurial sensibilities were stifled. He had ideas about how to grow the company and expand the customer base, but he was not called upon for those ideas. After a few years Lin realized he was limited in his responsibilities at the company and felt he could be more productive on his own. It was at this time that he started his own business.

Lin Engineering began in 1987 as a consulting entity specializing in step motor applications. Gradually, Lin brought on an engineering staff and began to produce prototypes and develop product. By 1992 the company had expanded its capabilities in the areas of design engineering, manufacturing, and customer service. The step motor still remains at the center of Lin's business.

The step motor is essentially a digital device which follows and processes digital instructions with the result of

Lin's dedicated engineering team

controlled motion. The most common applications of these types of motors are for surveillance cameras found in casinos, department stores and supermarkets; they are used in food wrapping machines, medical equipment, eye surgery equipment and other motion controlled products. Lin's step motor can even be found in the B-2 Stealth Bomber.

Lin Engineering is a solution-oriented company known for creating motors which can "maximize torque at the customer's desired speed." This eliminates guess work for motor selection, one of the most common problems when

Lin Engineering headquarters, Santa Clara, California

choosing a step motor. Customers use Lin Engineering for a number of reasons, but most commonly to avoid the following problems: selection of a motor for an application is time consuming—Lin Engineering specialists guide the customer quickly and efficiently making the selection process easier; the design margin of the motor being selected is unknown—Lin's engineers give clear explanations and take away the guess work. One such example is of a California based company who had been unsuccessfully trying to select the right motor for a medical pump application for five months. Engineers at Lin were able to solve the problem over the phone within one hour without seeing the device. The motor was successfully tested and verified by the prospect a couple of days later. Overjoyed after seeing the revitalization of their project, the customer praised Lin by declaring "You are a genius!"

Another challenging issue that faces customers in need of this type of motor is finding one that runs with smooth motion. This problem is eliminated with a properly working motor with technology that Lin's engineers have perfected. Finally, the price of competitors' motors from China is inexpensive, but there are concerns about quality. Lin Engineering has spent years perfecting step motors so the quality is top of the line. The price, however, is still competitive as prototypes and smaller volume motors are manufactured at the company's headquarters in Santa Clara while higher volume motors are manufactured at Lin Engineering owned entity, Linex, in China.

The product line for the company has expanded over the years with several new products at the forefront of the industry's current market. The 0.9° Modular motor is one of the more recent devices. It is unique because of its diminutive size and shape. Not only can it provide better than industry standard step accuracy and resolution, it is also ideal for custom made housings. Developing high quality and customizable motors like the Modular series has propelled Lin Engineering to become the highest volume manufacturer of 0.9° motors.

A line of motors called the SilverPak Series is unique as it combines all the crucial components needed to effectively operate a step motor into one compact package. This product line integrates a

Specialized modular motors

step motor with a driver and controller enabling users to experience the notion of "plug and play." Not only is the SilverPak Series smaller in size and easier to use, it is more cost effective as well.

Lin is most proud of his engineering staff for their ability to custom design motors on an individual basis. Following Lin's example, his engineers appreciate the challenge of creating specialty motors for specific needs. Instead of the usual month or more lead time that this kind of specialty would normally take, Lin's engineer specialists can turn around a product within a week.

Lin's employees are unique in that most were not engineers in the motor manufacturing industry when they first came to work for Lin. The technology was so new when he formed the company; Lin personally trained his employees in the fundamentals of step motors. "I had to find people with good attitudes, good character and a great desire to learn and I had to train them," says Lin. He has a continuing education program so employees can discover their interests in the industry and by doing so move into a specialty. Lin not only offers ongoing training for his employees, he has also created a Leadership Handbook and a published pamphlet of his business philosophy called Core Ideologies which he uses to encourage and train his employees.

In the Leadership Handbook, Lin lists seven secrets of effective leadership. The first is as follows: "Inspire by example—don't ask people to do anything you wouldn't do yourself. Share your vision of the goals and ask for their ideas on how to achieve them. Get commitment to "the plan" and be honest at all times. Give constant encouragement and feedback and share the rewards."

Lin's business philosophy stated in his Core Ideologies is equally inspiring:

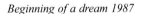

Beginning of a dream 1987

"Strive for the best—at a minimum, everyone must become an expert in the company at his or her job. At the next level, people become experts in their marketplace and then in their industry. The ultimate goal is to become an expert in the world."

At Lin Engineering, the retention rate of employees is extremely high. Monthly production meetings are held that all employees attend and are encouraged to have a voice in how to improve their specific areas of operation. Employees are informed about how production is going and about the financial status of the company.

It is evident that Lin practices his seven secrets of effective leadership. The second secret in the leadership handbook states: "Share information widely and deeply so that employees understand the firm's goals, values and operating performance. Set high standards for yourself, as well as for others. Take responsibility for your decisions and take prompt action when things don't go right. When delegating to others, encourage wise risk-taking. Support a broad-based ownership culture that rewards integrity, loyalty, and accountability."

Employees are rewarded for their consistent performance and loyalty to the company. At the end of each year, 20 percent of the profits are distributed as a bonus among all employees. With the hard work and dedication of everyone at Lin Engineering, the company was recently honored as the 2007 Leader in Engineering for the Motion Control Industry by *Design World Magazine*.

In addition to his tenacious work for his company, Lin reaches out to the community. He stays involved with the educational world by giving seminars at San Jose State University, Northern Illinois University, and donating motors for various student projects to local universities. His desire is to inspire the next generation to pursue their dreams and learn the value of leadership. "Lead by example and exhibit passion," states Lin in his Leadership Handbook.

Ted T. Lin is the president and CEO of Lin Engineering. He is one of the foremost step motor designers in the industry holding eight patents in motor engineering. He is the author of twelve publications. His company has grown from just three employees in 1987 to 120 employees at present. The annual revenue is $19 million and growing. Lin Engineering is the highest volume manufacturer for several of the most highly used motors in the industry.

Lin remains a perfect dichotomy: a great student, always curious and active in new discovery and a great teacher, always eager to impart new ideas. At

Top: Manufacturing facility 2008

Below: Product line greatly expanded over the years

the core of his business philosophy, it is clear he is committed to excellence, "If there is a single precept to which we dedicate ourselves, it is that of excellence; excellence in attitude, excellence in performance, excellence in our relationship with each other and our customers."

MACSA-MEXICAN AMERICAN COMMUNITY SERVICES AGENCY, INC.

In 1964, Lino Lopez, who lived in the Santa Clara community, decided to take action to combat the police brutality he saw. He pulled together community activists to identify ways to help the emerging Latino community respond to discrimination, racism, poverty, police brutality, educational inequity, and inadequate access to public services. Mr. Lopez explained that, "behind the banks and the supermarkets and behind the landscaped arterial ways there are slums, hovels, and hungry people—the discards of society. Those most affected are Mexican Americans."

Forty-four years later, the Mexican American Community Services Agency (MACSA), the small community organization that Lopez began, has grown into an extraordinary complex of buildings, programs and members who remain steadfast and committed to improving the quality of life for youth, families and seniors. Today, the Latino community, affected by the major economic shift that transformed the Valley of the Heart's Delight into Silicon Valley, is substantially better organized than thirty-five years ago. It no longer has to engage in shouting protests outside local establishments, because it has become an establishment itself—one that serves its community well. Important advances

Housing project, San Jose

have been made in education, employment, and political empowerment. However, despite these advances, a walk through any barrio reveals that many old difficulties persist and new ones have emerged. It is precisely these challenges that inspire MACSA to continue its tradition of providing quality and innovative services.

More than forty years after its inception, it's hard to believe that an organization such as MACSA, now with several sites and programs in East and Central San José, Morgan Hill and Gilroy, started as a small "project." In the early 1960s, the Mexican-American Community Services Project was sponsored by the Community Council of Central Santa Clara County, the planning arm of United Way of Santa Clara County, and funded by the Rosenberg Foundation as a demonstration project. Al Piñon and Manuel Martinez incorporated the Mexican-American Community Services Agency (MACSA) as an independent, tax-exempt nonprofit corporation. Lino Lopez was appointed its first executive director.

MACSA received an $18,330 grant from United Way and raised another $9,000 to begin operations. Continually seeking ways to help its community, MACSA is always finding ways to raise money. During the 1960s, MACSA led an aggressive civil rights campaign against the State Department of Motor Vehicles and Employment Development Department, resulting in the hiring of twenty-seven Mexican-Americans to provide bilingual services at those agencies. A statewide Mexican-American Leadership Conference was awarded funding and attended by more than 100 representatives.

Working closely with United Way, MACSA received a $95,000 grant to continue its work. It was also granted $27,000 to implement a college work-study program for the community's youth. Participants provided tutors, mentoring, recreation programs and citizenship classes. As a result of this work, the Mexican-American Youth Organization (MAYO) was established to offer high school and college-age youth train-

Youth at after school summer day camp, Gilroy

ing and mentoring opportunities. More than 250 students attended the first annual MAYO Leadership Conference. Five years later, attendance rose to 1,000 youth, representing thirteen Santa Clara County high school MAYO chapters.

When Lino Lopez retired, Pete Silva became the second executive director. He proposed expanding services to address educational inequities. As a result, college students were hired by MACSA to mentor and tutor school children. MACSA also hosted educational community forums to increase political activism and participation in the electoral process.

Under the leadership of José Villa and Jack Brito, services continued to focus on the needs of the Latino community. Funds were secured to provide childcare, legal and prison aftercare/recovery services. Through its advocacy efforts in 1970, MACSA's successful campaign against racially motivated police brutality by the City of San José Police Department, resulted in the replacement of both the police chief and city manager, and the hiring of Latino officers. A law clinic was established to provide free and subsidized legal services to the low-income community. Moreover, MACSA opened Casa Libra, a transitional housing program allowing male inmates to complete their sentences in a community setting.

Even Start program family, Gilroy

100 Most Influential Latinos, Red Carpet Gala, 2007, San Jose

Seeing the need for services in other areas, MACSA expanded to Gilroy and South Santa Clara County, offering family and youth programs at Luchessa Migrant Camp. The organization also started assisting seniors in the community; it organized the San José Seven Trees area residents in a successful petition to the City of San José for construction of a community gathering place, the Solari Center.

By the early 1980s, funding for MACSA started to evaporate. The activists and leaders, whom MACSA had groomed, commissioned an independent study which determined that the agency should remain open and continue to offer its essential community services. When United Way withheld funds pending proof of the organization's stability, the community responded. The board identified Esther Medina, a respected and recognized activist, to take the helm and was charged with rejuvenating the wavering organization. With two employees and no budget, Medina was ready for the challenge. "Plant the seed, nurture it and watch it grow," was her response. Serving as MACSA's executive director for the next twenty-two years, Medina returned the

community organization from the brink of financial disaster in 1982 to the powerhouse that it continues to be.

"Esther," says Olivia Soza-Mendiola, who became chief executive officer after Medina retired twenty-two years later, "was my mentor. I grew up in her footsteps and watched closely and learned."

It was under Medina's twenty-two years at the helm that MACSA flourished. Today the legacy continues, the new leadership continues to forge and nurture partnerships with individuals, political leaders, other nonprofits and private industry to address the most urgent needs of Santa Clara County residents and to educate tomorrow's workforce. The agency has created a model human-service business with a proven high return on its investment.

Like Medina, who came from a migrant background, Olivia Soza-Mendiola draws from her passion, her own personal life and a vigilant unrest with the disparity between the haves and the have-nots. Her family of thirteen children settled in Santa Clara County after migrating throughout the Southwest in the early 1960s. Her nine brothers and three sisters were raised in Gilroy by their parents. With her family, she picked the fruits and vegetables that brought fame to this area of California. She was accepted at San José and San Diego Universities when she graduated from high school but made the decision to go to the local junior college and continue to help her family financially.

In 1984 Olivia heard about a job-training program at the San José YWCA. The program was designed to help divorced women learn how to identify their strengths and personal qualities, improve interviewing skills, and enter the workforce. MACSA was seeking bilingual staff to work with young children in after-school programs. "Little did I know," she says, "that this was my destiny and my road to higher learning. I never finished my formal education, but got entrenched instead in serving people," an education she says she would not trade today.

MACSA's commitment to progressive community change and development is demonstrated in its numerous youth development programs offered at three youth centers, thirteen schools, numerous libraries and community center sites throughout Santa Clara County. MACSA has earned local, state and national acclaim for its cutting edge youth programs such as its Male Involvement Teen Pregnancy Prevention Program. To date, MACSA operates licensed after-school latchkey childcare sites, licensed senior services, charter high schools, nationally recognized soccer leagues, and continues to develop and operate senior housing and community centers in the lowest income areas of the county.

Through city, county, state and federal grants, MACSA expands and enhances existing programs and starts new programs designed to meet a very specific need in the community. In 2001 a three-year grant from the John S. and James L. Knight Foundation helped implement a gang intervention service model in East San José. This grant supported an aggressive effort to purchase a facility and expand services designed to specifically meet the needs of young men in the community. The concept was so well received that MACSA was awarded a three-year

Mariposas affordable housing first-time home buyer project, San Jose

grant from the state Office of Family Planning to implement their Male Involvement Program, a teen pregnancy prevention program focusing on male youth. MACSA has mentored other organizations on how to start a program for community men. This innovative program received honors from First Lady Hillary Rodham Clinton and Vice President Al Gore in 1998 through the National Campaign to Prevent Teen Pregnancy. Additionally, these services continue to be offered at Santa Clara County Elmwood Correctional Facility and Juvenile Hall. Uniquely, MACSA Intervention Services also offer an aftercare component to support inmates after release from incarceration.

Continually fighting the 1999 Census Bureau's report that Hispanics nationwide are less likely to have a high school diploma, more likely to be unemployed and three times more likely to live in poverty than non-Hispanic Whites, in the summer of 2001, MACSA became the first organization to receive approval from two school districts, Eastside Union High School District and Gilroy Unified School District, to open *El Portal* Leadership Academy, a charter high school in Gilroy; and *Académia Calmecac*, a charter high school in East San Jose. In 2004, 100 percent of high schools seniors who graduated have pursued post-secondary education. Many students have been ac-

cepted at San Jose State University, San Francisco State University and San José's very own National Hispanic University. Some students opt to go to local junior colleges in order to help their family, or are not ready to leave home. The most important fact is that they have a choice.

"All classes," Olivia says, "are college prep. The kids know they are going directly into college prep classes—there are no other options. We have approximately 200 students per school annually and fifteen to twenty in each class. This allows teachers to teach," she says. "We're getting students who thought they would never graduate high school and who have a long way to go to compete with their peers applying for the same schools. The course work is rigorous and focused. We work through the first year on assessing where they are and bring them up to grade level and most importantly work on getting them to believe they are gifted learners who have purpose and a responsibility to their families and community. Some of them get scared and try to leave the school; we hunt them down and bring them back. Others cause trouble to divert us from what they fear the most—failure. We help them see in themselves what we see in them. Through a lot of hard work with students and families, by the end of the year, they realize we're not going to give up on them, and they buy in."

True to its mission of serving the entire family, MACSA also serves its elderly, operating one of only two Adult Day Health Care Senior Centers in the county to ensure that the aging population in the community grows old with dignity. In the early 1990s MACSA was awarded the first of three grants from the U.S. Department of Housing and Urban Development (HUD). In total, the three grants provided $13 million to develop three affordable senior housing apartment complexes. In 1995 MACSA completed construction of Jardines Palma Blanca, followed by Girasol in 1998, and Las Golondrinas in 2004. In 2005, MACSA, through its subsidiary Ketzal Community Development Corporation, completed a sixty-six-unit condominium and townhouse development for first-time home homeowners. In 1990 MACSA developed its headquarters along with a day health center for seniors in East San José. And in 1995, MACSA developed a 24,500-square-foot full- service youth center in East San José. In early 2008 MACSA will complete construction of a charter school campus and a 9,000-square-foot multi-service complex in Gilroy.

With services continuing, developing and growing, the MACSA programs surpassed a $7.5 million operating budget in 2005. Today, MACSA's operating budget exceeds $10 million, and its payroll has grown to 126 employees. Consistent with its commitment to foster professional development and nurture leadership, 90 percent of MACSA's management staff have been promoted from within the agency. Many continue to serve the community by assuming political office or move on to management and decision-making positions throughout the city and state of California. "We call them Macsistas," says Olivia.

Seniors exercising, adult day healthcare, San Jose

"We retain passionate, mission-driven leaders," says Olivia. "I've been here twenty-four years, Xavier Campos our chief operations officer nineteen, Maria Elena De La Garza our deputy director fifteen, Aurora Cepeda our human resources director eighteen, and Enrique Arreola our deputy director of Intervention and Education is on his fourteenth year. Many of our people come straight out of college and want to make a difference. They fall in love with the organization's culture and commitment to service, and they stay.

"The magic of MACSA," says Olivia, "is that a lot of us who work here *are* the people we serve. I *am* the child whose mother was ill and on Medi-Cal, and the young single mother with limited skills. These life experiences keep us true to our purpose and help us be mindful of how

we serve people and how we treat them. When kids and families go to a place where they can identify with themselves, relate to people serving them, and speak the same language, the most difficult barriers are broken. We have learned," says the hardworking CEO, "that we have to work with an entire family. Regardless of which member is at this point of entry, we make sure we strengthen the entire family because we are all a part of a bigger network."

In 2007 MACSA initiated an awards ceremony that recognized local Latinos. The community identified 100 leaders to be honored, plus the top 10 of those 100. The event ended up becoming Silicon Valley's Latino gala of the century with more than 900 attendees. MACSA received press attention from this event that helped promote its influence in the community. MACSA is working on developing a Latino Hall of Fame—to immortalize legendary leaders. "Through this venue our young people can research Latino leaders in Silicon Valley and be inspired to reach for the stars. The ultimate vision for me" says Olivia, "is that someday a youth who was once a client will become the future leader of this incredible organization."

Charter High School graduating class, San Jose

WAYNE MASCIA ASSOCIATES

The tradition of technology in the Santa Clara Valley dates to the early part of the century when Charles Herrold started the first radio station in the United States in San Jose. It flowered in the decades following World War II, spurred by support from Stanford University and funded by military research contracts from the concentration of aerospace firms around Moffett Field, but the modern age of technology in the area can be traced to the early 1970s. About the time that journalist Don Hoefler first coined the term "Silicon Valley" to describe both the area and the phenomenon, Wayne Mascia, fresh from several years as a commercial real estate broker in the more metropolitan San Francisco to the north, was setting up shop in Sunnyvale not far from NASA's Moffett Field and the electronics and aerospace firms like Lockheed that it spawned.

Begun in 1973, Wayne Mascia Associates grew as the Silicon Valley mushroomed, by specializing in the representation of the high technology firms attracted and nurtured by Stanford and other nearby universities, the critical mass of like-minded innovators, and

Redback Networks leased this 300,000 square-foot building in San Jose through Wayne Mascia Associates. The broadband network leader employs more than 1,100 people in the Silicon Valley.

the emergence of the venture capital industry on Sand Hill Road, beginning with Kleiner Perkins in 1972. Working in close support of these engines of growth and the pioneering real estate developers who converted the Valley's historic orchards into countless industrial buildings and massive campuses, Wayne Mascia Associates was increasingly recognized as an authoritative and responsive part of the booming growth.

To track the new developments and whirlwind of commercial real estate activity, Wayne Mascia began hiring brokers in 1977. Further, creatively harnessing the technology of the electronics industry it served, Wayne Mascia Associates was among the first to develop and refine the new information technology of the computer age to assure that its clients' real estate decision

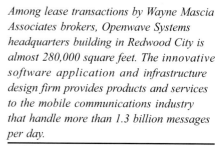

Among lease transactions by Wayne Mascia Associates brokers, Openwave Systems headquarters building in Redwood City is almost 280,000 square feet. The innovative software application and infrastructure design firm provides products and services to the mobile communications industry that handle more than 1.3 billion messages per day.

making process was the most informed possible. With a core of five brokers, several of whom not only remain with the firm and are among the commercial industry leaders to this day, Wayne Mascia Associates in 1979 undertook the first of several moves to both accommodate ongoing growth and reflect the Silicon Valley's expansive migration south from its original cradle surrounding Stanford University toward metropolitan San Jose, today's heart of the Silicon Valley. Paralleling its high technology clientele, the firm occupied a new, two-story building in Sunnyvale developed by, and in partnership with the McCandless Companies, one of those pioneering real estate entrepreneurs with whom Wayne Mascia Associates has maintained more than three decades of mutual support. That building was expanded and the brokerage team had grown to an even dozen as the best and brightest professionals, along with energetic recent graduates from the area's universities, were attracted to a corporate culture that encouraged and rewarded dedication, hard work and innovation.

As it was growing in size and stature, the firm continued to adapt to the evolving nature of the ever-changing technology industries it served. Through the decades since the early 1970s, the high technology engine that drives the Silicon Valley has morphed through many incarnations as hardware becomes more sophisticated and the application uses of that hardware more imaginative. Beginning with early defense contracting, to the semiconductor that gave the region its name, to computers from Apples to PCs, software from Adobe to Z, connectivity as computers learned to talk to each other, the internet revolution, biotechnology, green technology, nanotechnology and whatever new wave is still only a spark in the mind of today's and tomorrow's Silicon Valley entrepreneur or Stanford grad student, Silicon Valley is perhaps the most dynamic environment on the face of the earth.

Along the way, Wayne Mascia Associates has participated in some of the most massive and trend-setting real estate transactions for both industry leaders and innovative start-up entrepreneurs. Mirroring the evolution of the industry, the firm has represented chip makers and chip handling equipment manufacturers such as Fujitsu and Applied Materials on properties exceeding a million square feet in San Jose and Santa Clara, Software leaders such as Infomix, McAfee, Software Publishing, Edify and Magma Design, connectivity luminaries like Anda Networks, Bay Networks and Redback Associates, as well as today's internet and new media stars like Openwave.

Through the typical boom and bust cycles that characterize the rise, then maturing and replacement of each technology with the next newest phenomenon, Wayne Mascia Associates continued to grow, innovate and prosper. In 1984, challenged to keep up with its growing position in the industry, the firm purchased an office condominium on Scott Boulevard in Santa Clara,

allowing expansion to sixteen brokers.

Again crowded by its very success, the firm moved in 1989 to larger 12,000 square-foot quarters on Mission College Boulevard, adjacent to Marriott's Great America, a vestige of a less high-tech, less urban Santa Clara County. The Sobrato Company-built multi-story structure was a reflection of the evolving architecture of the Silicon Valley. Increasing numbers of technology companies were shifting from industrial manufacturing space to office buildings to house the employment shift from hardware to software, from things to ideas that would eventually evolve to today's internet-driven industry. To place the dynamic nature of the evolving Silicon Valley landscape in perspective, of the more that 275 transactions Wayne Mascia Associates handled last year, fully 75 percent were for internet and new media companies.

In 1994 the firm moved again, this time around the corner to the commanding McCandless Towers, a taller still office building looming over the main artery of Silicon Valley, reflective of the Valley's continuing pattern of growth and evolution. In 2000 the firm moved vertically from the third to the ninth floor of McCandless Towers to its present 13,000

Wayne Mascia founder (center) is flanked by long-time associates, Craig Leiker on the left who started with the company in 1981, and Jim Maggi on the right who started in 1978.

square feet of space and expanded the sales force to thirty-one brokers.

As the nature of the communities of the Santa Clara Valley continue to evolve—from historically agricultural to high technology employment centers to sophisticated urban centers—so too has Wayne Mascia Associates changed and grown. Originally focused primarily on tenant representation, helping technology companies identify and acquire space, today the firm is also providing investment sales and retail sales and leasing. The recent decade has, like its predecessors, witnessed notorious booms and busts as Silicon Valley rode each new wave of technology, most recently the internet bubble which dramatically impacted employment and commercial occupancy. Today, led by a variety of industries, including clean energy, biotechnology and new media, and stimulated by new urban initiatives, Silicon Valley is poised for resurgence and Wayne Mascia Associates is positioned to lead and support that reality.

MONTGOMERY PROFESSIONAL SERVICES CORPORATION

A pioneer in the field of outsourcing and innovative staffing solutions, Montgomery Professional Services Corporation (MPSC) represents a stronghold in the rapidly changing corporate history of Silicon Valley. Henry C. Montgomery III co-founded the company in 1986 under the name of Private Financial Services, later renaming it Montgomery Financial Services. Throughout the explosive growth period of the late 1980s and early 1990s, two economic recessions, and the dot-com disaster of 2001, the company has continued to expand and grow. Its true history, however, begins long before its inception in the story of current company President/CEO Rick Giorgetti, a key figure in helping make the company what it is today.

Rick is a second-generation American of Italian heritage and the son of Leo Giorgetti, co-founder of the legendary Iron Horse restaurant in San Francisco. He learned much about business and entrepreneurship from his father. But it was due to the bravery and perseverance of his grandparents, however, that Rick and his father were given the opportunity to

Rick, his brother Bob, and grandparents in front of Saints Peter and Paul Church in San Francisco in 1968 celebrating Enrico's and Maria's fiftieth wedding anniversary.

pursue their passion for commerce in beautiful Northern California.

In 1912 Frederico Giorgetti and his young sweetheart, Maria, agreed that they would leave Italy and go to America to find a better life. Federico would go first, find work, save money, and set up a homestead, and then he would send for Maria.

Frederico arrived in the United States and settled in Half Moon Bay, California, a small town south of San Francisco. He found work as a foreman and labored for several years in the green hills off Old San Mateo Road (which would later become Highway 92). Six years later, he was finally able to send for Maria. She endured a battering, month-long ocean voyage and a two-week cross-country train ride to meet him in San Francisco. The two were married at last on Easter Sunday in 1918.

On December 11, 1920, Maria gave birth to her first and only child, Leo Giorgetti. Leo learned English as a second language, worked in the fields picking brussels sprouts and artichokes after school, and shot birds that his father would then sell for fifty cents at the market.

After serving several years as a cook in the Coast Guard during World War II, he returned home and went into the bakery business. When an old war buddy Sam Marconi invited Leo to join him in the industrial cafeteria business, he accepted. By 1950 the two were running eighteen establishments throughout the Bay Area— one of which was at the main branch of Bank of America in San Francisco.

They came to know Carl Wente, who at that time was serving as president of the bank. When an ideal location became available just up the street from Wente's bank, Leo and Sam asked him for

Enrico plowing in a Half Moon Bay field circa 1916.

help. Wente accompanied them to the property and returned to give his employee the following instruction: "Take care of my two Italian boys here. Give them what they want and send the paperwork up to me."

On April 6, 1954, Leo and Sam opened the Iron Horse. The restaurant soon became a favorite hangout of numerous celebrities, including Joe DiMaggio, Maria Callas, Liberace, and Pete Rozelle. According to Rick Giorgetti, the Horse's success was due in large part to his father's extraordinary partnership with Sam Marconi.

"Sam Marconi worked well behind the scenes," Rick explains. "He was a terrific businessman. My dad, on the other hand, was great up front. As a kid, I remember watching him and thinking, 'Wow, I could never be like that. That guy is awesome. He knows everyone in San Francisco.'"

Leo Giorgetti's connection with other people went far beyond the walls of the Iron Horse. He was a member of a service club through which he contributed to a number of community-building projects. In addition, he was very active in the Giorgetti's church congregation, where he provided and served food for many events over the years. "He gave back his entire life," Rick says, citing one of the greatest lessons he learned from his dad.

He had ample opportunity to learn. At age 13 he began working for his father under the direction of a Filipino chef named George Valenzuela who, on Rick's first day of work, pointed out a fifty-pound sack of potatoes and said, "Start peeling." He learned the value of hard work during his years at the restaurant; more importantly, however, he had the opportunity to watch his father in action, to learn everything about small business—from how to save a dollar to the importance of knowing people's names.

Meanwhile, Rick was attending St. Ignatius College Preparatory, a Jesuit school founded in San Francisco in 1855. The Jesuits, also known as the Society

Rick and Terry in 2007.

of Jesus, are a religious order of the Catholic Church dedicated to lifelong service to the Church and the community. Rick graduated from San Ignatius in 1966 and went on to Santa Clara University, another Jesuit institution where he continued to build on the principles of generosity he'd learned initially from his father.

After graduating from Santa Clara in 1970, Rick moved on from the family business, never forgetting what he learned there. He went into the Navy and, shortly thereafter, married Terry Tarantino, with whom he would have

three children—Jason, Tracy, and Alison. The couple had much in common: Terry, like her husband, is a second-generation Italian; her grandfather and his brothers founded A.Tarantino & Sons, a wholesale fish and poultry company still in operation today. Additionally, both seemed to be drawn to a life of service. In 1974 the couple settled in San Jose and joined a Jesuit parish, in which they have been active ever since.

Rick spent the first fifteen years of his business career in what he calls "basic training": the practical field of accounting. He earned an M.B.A. from Pepperdine University and spent four years at Price Waterhouse, where he attained his CPA certificate. Over the next twelve years, he served as an internal auditor, corporate controller, and CFO of various companies.

In 1987, while Henry Montgomery was just getting his company off the ground, Richard Williams contacted Rick through a mutual friend and invited him to be a part of his new staffing company. Rick had been longing for an opportunity to live up to his father's example of entrepreneurship, so he readily agreed.

"Best decision I ever made," he says. The staffing company, Management Solutions, was an admirable success, as was Rich and Rick's business relationship. Though Rick started out as a recruiter, by the early 1990s, he and Williams were able to join forces to buy out the other three partners. They acted like a partnership, Rick says—very much, in fact, like the partnership between his father Leo and Sam Marconi.

"Rich was the man driving the company," he says. "I was out front with people, selling and being the face of Management Solutions. When I walked down the street in San Jose, I started realizing I knew lots of people—just like my dad did in San Francisco."

Over the next decade and a half, the two men focused on developing their company. The concept of staffing solutions was not new at the time, but Management Solutions innovated the field by providing professional level employees. By 2001 they had built the company from an idea to a $50 million business. Monster.com offered to buy; on March 29, 2001, just before the final bit of dot-com bubble blew, they sold.

Rick and Terry discussed retirement, but they were only in their early 50s— what Terry called "the age of mastery"— so they decided to stay in the Bay Area. Rick spent the rest of the year relaxing

Rick, Kyle Krajewski and Monty Montgomery (son of Henry) at San Mateo office in early 2003.

and thinking about his next career move. By New Year's, he had decided that he wanted to return to his roots: to run another small company, like his father's.

In early January 2002, Rick had breakfast with his old friend Mike Patterson of Price Waterhouse. "I'm going back to work," Rick told him. "I'd like to run a small business." Later, Rick drove home and walked up to his study, intending to start his jobs search, but he was interrupted by a telephone call. On the line was Henry Montgomery, who had just gotten off the phone with Mike. "Stop looking," Henry said. "Come and run my company."

Rick and Henry had crossed paths several times over the years as members of the Silicon Valley finance community. Like Rick, Henry had left a background of working for large companies— Fairchild Camera and Instrument Corporation, Memorex Corporation, Pinnacle Micro, and Theta Microelectronics, among others—to focus on a smaller business. The two shared a passion for finance, a genius for business, and a wry sense of humor. It was a perfect fit.

Henry's company, which provided financial outsourcing solutions under the name Montgomery Financial Services, had overcome a number of obstacles since he had founded it. Most of these obstacles were due to the fact that the company was ahead of its time. As Henry explains, "Outsourcing wasn't as accepted or understood as it is today. We didn't have the ability to go to lower-cost environments because we couldn't communicate securely."

But by the time he invited Rick to run Montgomery Financial Services, Henry says, the Internet had "blasted all that away." It had grown to a $2 million enterprise and was ripe for expansion into a market that now understood the value of its services. This was the atmosphere into which Rick stepped after that January 15 phone call, and he took full advantage of its potential.

Within months of speaking with Henry, Rick had devised a business plan that would expand Montgomery Financial Services from its current size to a $20 million business. The plan involved keeping the outsourcing unit intact and

Rick Giorgetti (left) and Rich Williams (seated) at Holiday party with Management Solutions executive team and spouses in late 1990s.

adding marketing, human resources, information technology, and eventually staffing. The two made a financial deal, and Rick became co-owner of what would thenceforth be known as Montgomery Professional Services Corporation.

Rick started putting his plan into action right away. By July 2003 he was able to add the staffing division. That staffing division ended 2007 at $6 million in revenue. Total combined revenue for the company was approximately $9 million for the year. With confidence, he says, "We'll reach $20 million in 2009."

Rick's passion for the business, how-

ever, has little to do with money. It comes instead from the joy of entrepreneurship he learned from his father, the pleasure in hard work he inherited from his grandfather—possibly even the native enthusiasm of his Italian progenitors. And it shows in the outpouring of generous spirit that has made him a friend, associate, and neighbor to many in the San Jose area.

Over the years Rick and Terry have served their community in a number of ways. Active in the church, they have also co-chaired many fundraising activities for their children's schools. Rick has been a member of the San Jose Rotary, the Santa Clara University Bronco Bench Foundation, and a number of other organizations. "My dad and the Jesuits taught me to give back," he explains, "so that is what I do."

Today, Rick spends much of his time working for MPSC, striving to realize his

vision for the company. Henry, who now serves as chairman of the board, runs MontPac Outsourcing in Honolulu, Hawaii. There he is not just realizing, but living the vision he had for the company he started twenty years ago. "My dream was to bring big-company financial management and operational support to smaller enterprises at a cost incentive," he explains. "Believe it or not, the dream is now here."

Perhaps the dream of Frederico and Maria Giorgetti—the dream of giving their family a chance to lead a good life—has also been realized. Rick Giorgetti's story demonstrates what entrepreneurship can achieve in a country that allows it to grow. In essence, MPSC and MontPac Outsourcing continue to foster that spirit today by providing service to small companies once only available to large companies, thereby helping them to grow.

NVIDIA CORPORATION

When Jen-Hsun Huang worked at LSI Logic, and Chris Malachowsky and Curtis Priem were at Sun Microsystems in the early 1990s, the three met and engaged in ongoing brainstorming sessions at a San Jose, California Denny's restaurant. What evolved from these sessions and from a single PC in the living room of Curtis' condominium in Fremont, California, is NVIDIA, a multinational corporation, currently based in Santa Clara. Today, over fifteen years later, the company has achieved notable success in providing graphics-processor technologies for workstations, desktop computers, and handheld devices. NVIDIA products power the displays of most modern mainstream professional and personal computers including cell phones and game consoles.

Since its inception, NVIDIA has demonstrated its founders' passion for graphics. Its entrepreneurial leaders sensed that the 3D graphics industry

Inset-An early prototype of NVIDIA's groundbreaking PC graphics processors.

NVIDIA has achieved notable success in providing graphics-processor technologies for workstations, desktop computers, and handheld devices.

A collage of all NVIDIA employees taken in 2006.

GLOBAL COMPANY. ONE CULTURE.

was ripe for innovation and, as CEO Jen-Hsun Huang said, "The technology it required had nearly infinite headroom." The founders saw an opportunity to adopt techniques that were initially developed for flight simulators and scientific computing and make them available to consumers.

The three creative minds went to work, first, on naming their company. Says cofounder Chris Malachowsky, "We wanted to come up with a name that could represent us, was catchy, and easy to remember." Jen-Hsun added the requirement that the name itself should not say what they do, just identify who they were. When Curtis weighed in

Chris Malachowsky

with his desire to exploit a homonym for the word "envy" in naming the new company's products, the root of the name (NV) was chosen. After some searching, ultimately the name NVIDIA emerged. It is derived from real words in multiple languages meaning "envious" yet, with its current spelling, is not a real word.

NVIDIA was officially founded in January 1993 and incorporated in California in April of that year. NVIDIA's first product, the NV1, was released in the fall of 1995. It was an ambitious attempt to bring a rich set of multimedia functionality (2D/3D graphics, video, and sound) to the Windows based PC. This occurred at a time when PCs were primarily focused on office tasks such as spreadsheets and word processing. While the ground-breaking NV1 did not achieve much market success, the process of developing NV1 formed the genetic makeup from which NVIDIA's reputation took root. NVIDIA established itself then and continues to be known for its innovations, technical prowess, relentless execution, and its ability to transform the markets in which it competes.

On the heels of NV1, the company remained relatively low-key until it refocused its attention on the emerging 2D and 3D graphics accelerator market. With the introduction of Microsoft's Window's 95 operating system, consumer interest was rapidly moving to graphically rich visual experiences on their PCs. This trend was fueled by the introduction of numerous games and applications with stunning interactive imagery. From that point forward, NVIDIA's principal product focus was set.

In 1997 NVIDIA introduced its breakout product, the RIVA 128—an industry breakthrough. This accelerator, also known internally as NV3, was one of the first graphics chips to integrate 3D acceleration in addition to traditional 2D and video acceleration, and did so at a price point and performance level that appealed to consumers. It became NVIDIA's first commercial success and set new standards for PC-based graphics all the while transforming the world of 3D gaming, which was the first popular application of graphics on the PC.

In 1999 NVIDIA went public, also launching its GeForce 256, the world's

Jen-Hsun Huang

Curtis Priem in 1993

first GPU (Graphics Processing Unit). The GPU represented a new class of processor (as opposed to a traditional CPU) in a computer, one capable of doing all the complex math and algorithmic computation to render graphical objects on its own. This far exceeded the capabilities of the RIVA family of graphic accelerators and launched the company on a growth trajectory that has been unmatched in the semiconductor industry. Starting with the GeForce 256, the GeForce brand of GPUs has continued to evolve to this day shipping in even higher volumes and with an unmatched worldwide reputation for performance, value, and quality.

In 2000 NVIDIA acquired the intellectual assets of its one-time rival 3dfx, one of the largest and successful graphics companies of the mid to late 1990s. The company then set out to woo the engineers of 3dfx to join the NVIDIA team. "We had to recruit from, what the day before, had been our biggest competitor," says Malachowsky. In one day 120 engineers showed up. The two teams integrated well, acknowledging that each had something to contribute to the techniques of the other. This influx of experienced talent, combined with the resources NVIDIA already had, created what was destined to be one of the world's largest R&D teams dedicated to advancing graphics technologies.

Things went well until 2002, when NVIDIA found itself at a competitive disadvantage. Having pushed themselves to enable their processors to be more user-programmable, the advancement, though welcome, hampered performance in some critical markets and inflated the product's cost. "We had stayed on top of our world for a long time," Malachowsky recalls. "Then, we found ourselves no longer number one." Whereas a challenging time like this might knock some companies off kilter, the situation became a rallying cry for NVIDIA. Within one product cycle (about twelve months) the company was able to reinvigorate itself by thoroughly scrubbing and optimizing how it did everything from product definition and design through improvements in how it analyzed its designs prior to actually building them. The results have been spectacular with the company regaining its product leadership position in 2003 and it being able to continually improve on its market and business competitiveness ever since.

Over the next few years NVIDIA's team of inventors pushed the original GPU and its early attempts to add user programmability a step further with the notion of "real-time programmable shading." This put the processing power of the GPU squarely into the hands of 3D content developers around the world, providing them with an infinite palette of capabilities to create better, more realistic imagery. Today, NVIDIA products utilizing this innovation, power the visual experience on a variety of progressive, market-leading platforms, from the Sony PlayStation 3 game console to sophisticated workstations tasked with solving the world's most difficult problems.

As a notable point of comparison, the first NVIDIA GPU contained 4 million transistors. Today's GPU has already exceeded 1 billion. At its core,

In 1994 co-founder Chris Malachowsky works from his office as the company remained relatively low-key until 1997–1998.

NVIDIA is driven by a culture of innovation and a desire to build products that transform industries. As Jen-Hsun Huang says, "At NVIDIA, we never set out to build things that our competitors are building; we build things we truly think people need. I absolutely believe that this passion for innovation and relevance will ensure our long-term success."

Today, with nearly 5,000 dedicated employees worldwide, NVIDIA has become the consummate supplier of computer graphics technologies. "One of management's most important jobs is to hire the best people," says Malachowsky, who has overseen much of NVIDIA's engineering and operations over the years. "We are always looking to raise the intellectual horsepower of our employee base and find folks who are bold and courageous enough to thrive in our competitive market segment. Some people are afraid of being under a near-constant competitive threat; others thrive on it. I liken it to trying to find the Michael Jordans of our industry—the folks who want the ball during the last two min-

utes of a close game. They simply want the chance to make a difference in the game, especially when the pressure is on." Matching people's personalities as well as their skills to the work environment is one reason NVIDIA has enjoyed phenomenal employee retention and was recognized in *Fortune* magazine's 2004 list of the "100 Best Companies to Work For."

As a testament to the products and innovations that NVIDIA's employees have created, NVIDIA has been recognized as the fastest semiconductor company in history to reach $1 billion in revenue (achieved in 2001) and then the first to reach $2 billion just a few years later. The company's devices have powered the graphical capabilities of such recognizable products as Microsoft's XBox, Sony's Playstation 3, and Motorola's Razr cell phones. It also sells its products to most every major computer manufacturer for integration into their computer systems whether it be a workstation, a personal computer, a laptop, a server, or a personal portable device. NVIDIA even received an Emmy award in 2007 for its contribution to the visual arts. All this has culminated in one of the company's more recent and most prestigious awards, *Forbes* magazine's coveted "Company of the Year" selection, which came out in their January 2008 issue singling out NVIDIA from America's 400 Best Big Companies.

The cover of the *Forbes* issue that honored NVIDIA featured a laser gun-touting picture of NVIDIA's CEO locked in battle with an unseen foe. Stanford-trained engineer Jen-Hsun Huang, co-founder, president and CEO of NVIDIA, is exactly that kind of brilliant and competitive person the company treasures. In addition to his innovative contributions at NVIDIA, in 2004 the Fabless Semiconductor Association honored Mr. Huang with the prestigious Dr. Morris Chang Exemplary Leadership Award, which recognizes a leader who has made exceptional contributions to driving the development, innovation, growth, and long-term opportunities of the fabless semiconductor industry. Additionally, Mr. Huang is a recipient of the Daniel J. Epstein Engineering Management Award from the University of Southern California and was named an Alumni Fellow by Oregon State University. He is also on the Board of Trustees of the RAND Corporation, an internationally renowned nonprofit research institution, and has been honored extensively for his corporate, industry, and philanthropic leadership.

Chris Malachowsky, the enterprising co-founder, senior executive, and NVIDIA Fellow, who has authored close to forty patents, believes that a successful company's attitude, behavior, work ethic, and sense of business and community responsibility all stem from the right leadership. These elements set a tone, what he calls a professional compass. "We feel responsible to our families, employees, and shareholders to not be a fly-by-night operation, and instead to build a company that gives us all a sense of pride and delivers lasting value. Since it's not our style to let anyone one-up us in the marketplace, it's also not our style to be victims of our own success within the company. The ingenuity and creativity required to keep our products flying off the shelves does not allow us time to sit back on any accomplishments or to do anything that isn't straightforward and honest."

Long-term, NVIDIA's leaders believe that its place in history is yet to come. "We are at a point," says the University of Florida and Santa Clara University graduate Malachowsky, "where today's dominant computing platforms are not likely to be the dominant ones in the future. The personal computer is going to be something you carry with you." At a recent Mobile World Congress gathering, NVIDIA featured a new concept handset that showed off a user-interface powered by the company's new APX 2500

mobile applications processor. "This device has the potential to be another home run for the company," says Malachowsky. "It will spur the development of new products, encourage new business, and it will improve people's lives."

The whole story behind NVIDIA is not easily summed up by simply looking at the balance sheet or its design successes. NVIDIA has made it a point to make charity and philanthropy a key part of its corporate culture. Examples of how this manifests itself are evident throughout the company. For example, instead of holiday parties, NVIDA sponsors charitable events involving its employees and their families. The firm has helped renovate schools, worked in shelters, furnished food and supplies for the needy, built for and donated computers to the underprivileged, and donated generously to aid in world disasters. It also has set up and funded a multi-million dollar Corporate Foundation that provides for totally employee-directed grants and donations.

NVIDIA is a company at the top of its game. It is well positioned for the future and it has a good sense of the type of impact, both commercially and at the personal level, that it can have on the markets and communities its

serves. Its strength clearly lies in its talented and dedicated employees. Jen-Hsun has often been heard referring to NVIDIA's employees as the company's only real asset. He backs the statement up with the admission that they represent an asset that has to be excited, encouraged and re-recruited to come back to work each and every morning. Malachowsky sums it up by saying, "There is a special breed of people who work in this graphics world. They gracefully operate where science and art intersect. They have a certain love for competition and for being in the 'game.' When you win in this industry, you don't win for long. You always need something better, bigger, faster, glitzier … significantly more competitive in some manner. The bar must always be raised. We get it. We thrive on having to be at our best to beat the best. It's in our blood. It's who we are and it's what makes NVIDIA work."

CEO, Jen-Hsun Huang, has often been heard referring to NVIDIA's employees as the company's only real asset. He backs the statement up with the admission that they represent an asset that has to be excited, encouraged, and re-recruited to come back to work each and every morning.

O'CONNOR HOSPITAL

In the tradition of its founding organization, the Daughters of Charity, San Jose's O'Connor Hospital carries on its mission of excellent healthcare and tending to the sick poor. The 358-bed, not-for-profit tertiary healthcare facility was the very first hospital in Santa Clara County when it opened in 1889. Today, it remains the only Catholic hospital operating in the region. With its state-of-the-art medical capabilities and talented, compassionate staff, O'Connor Hospital fulfills a distinct and vital role in the community, healing patients in body, mind, and spirit.

The Daughters of Charity is a religious order that originally hailed from France, part of a long tradition begun by priest Vincent de Paul in 1663. Under St. Vincent's leadership, a group of peasant women committed themselves to the care and aid of the sick and the poor. The sisters were empowered to minister outside of the walls of their convent, and they sought out the members of society most in need of care and solace. The Daughters of Charity flourished throughout Europe, bringing aid to people both on

In January of 1954, O'Connor Hospital welcomed its first baby. Several years later, the O'Connor Hospital would register more patients than any other hospital in the U.S. Courtesy, Mines to Medicine, *by Daniel Ilruby, 1965*

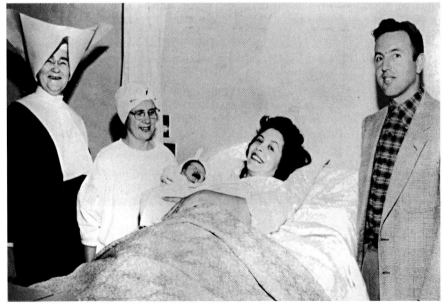

the streets as well as in their homes. Eventually, the organization united with another like minded convent in Maryland run by St. Elizabeth Ann Seton to bring the Daughters' mission across the Atlantic.

On a distant coast, a young Santa Clara couple was also on a path of service to others. Having made a fortune in the California Gold Rush, Judge Myles P. O'Connor and his wife, Amanda, sought to use their wealth to help build and enrich their community. In

The entire enrollment of the O'Connor Sanitarium Nursing School in 1910. The O'Connor School of Nursing was founded in 1898 and was the first Catholic nursing school in California.

the summer of 1884 the couple bought an 8.395-acre lot in San Jose on which they planned to build a sanitarium and home for the aged infirm. Amanda O'Connor, who had recently converted to Catholicism while residing in Baltimore, requested that the Daughters of Charity at the Maryland convent assist in the management of the facility. It was thus that the O'Connors united with the Daughters of Charity to begin the hospital that remains an integral part of the San Jose community to this day.

At the outset, the sisters were the direct providers of care, gently tending to the sick while wearing distinctive winged veils that extended a foot in either direction. Over time, the role of the sisters evolved. Now, they manage O'Connor Hospital under the larger Daughters of Charity Health System, which also includes five other healthcare facilities throughout California.

In addition to bringing healthcare services to all in the Santa Clara Valley, O'Connor Hospital serves the community in a variety of other ways. The hospital

is a major employer, providing over 1,800 jobs to a highly skilled workforce, which includes an experienced team of 650 physicians, 485 nurses and many other clinical and support staff who provide the highest quality healthcare to all patients, regardless of financial circumstances.

It is this accessibility that is at the core of O'Connor's philosophy of care, which hospital president Robert H. Curry brings to the fore in his leadership of the organization. "I'm a strong believer that

In a 2007 national patient satisfaction survey, patients who received treatment in O'Connor Hospital's Radiation Therapy Department rated the skilled staff with a score of 99 out of 100.

healthcare should be not only excellent in its outcomes, meaning its quality, but we need to treat the whole person," he explains. "People come in with more than a diagnosis," he continues. "They have needs in body, mind, and spirit. And we should treat all of that."

It is this foundation upon which all of O'Connor Hospital's services and programs are based. In conjunction with a deep commitment to the highest level of safety and service, the hospital has built a reputation as a top-tier facility, as evidenced by many awards and accolades, including a recent HealthGrades Distinguished Hospital Award for Patient Safety that placed O'Connor in the top 3 percent of a nationwide assessment of more than 4,200 hospitals.

Excellent service delivery comes into play in every one of the hospital's thirty-two individual departments. The recently expanded state-of-the-art Emergency Department is one of the hospital's busiest areas. Over 40,000 patients are seen each year in the twenty-one-bed unit. In order to serve those with acute-care needs, the Emergency Department is

equipped with a chest pain room where doctors can diagnose myocardial infarctions (heart attacks) within moments, and an automated, paperless prescription system that ensures accuracy in both medication dispensing and dosage instruction.

The hospital also has a highly active obstetrics department, which welcomes over 3,500 new babies to Santa Clara County every year. Children can be treated at the hospital's satellite Pediatric Center for Life, which offers a full spectrum of medical care for the youngest patients. "The Center for Life takes care of over 12,000 children each year that have trouble getting into the mainstream of medicine because they have a tough time accessing healthcare," says Curry, who stresses that the program is therefore a priority for the hospital. This is vitally important given that California places last in terms of MediCal reimbursement. From preventative care to full pediatric treatment through age eighteen, the Pediatric Center for Life is dedicated to ensuring that children grow up happy and healthy regardless of their families' means.

The hospital also offers a wide variety of specialized care. O'Connor has been designated by the Joint Commission as a Primary Stroke Center, and is the first hospital in Northern California to receive Joint Commission designation as a center of excellence in hip and knee replacement. The hospital's Cancer Care Center is well respected throughout the region as a focal point for education, support, and a complete range of treatment options to treat any type of cancer. O'Connor also has a comprehensive cardiology program, and was one of the very first facilities in the Santa Clara Valley to perform open-heart surgery. The cardiovascular specialists there have made dramatic advances in cardiovascular surgery and electrophysiology.

O'Connor Hospital is committed to passing knowledge and skill down to the next generation of physicians. The hospital has recently incorporated a family medicine residency program that teaches top medical students from around the country. Eight residents are enrolled for each year of three years of study in what is known as the "8-8-8" program, which is accredited by nearby Stanford University. These students not only benefit from this practical experience, but also contribute significantly, with at least one faculty physician on hand at all times to assist with precipitous deliveries or other rapid response emergencies. Under the supervision of twelve faculty physicians, the O'Connor Family Health Center (the primary outpatient teaching site for the residency program) sees almost 13,000 visits a year. Curry says that the whole hospital staff learns and grows from the eager, young physicians. "It improves the overall service," he says of the pro-

In the summer of 1884, Miles and Amanda O'Connor returned to San Jose and purchased an 8.395-acre plot upon which they intended to construct a two-story hospital. The hospital—located south of Stevens Creek Road between Meridian and Race Street—in Mr. O'Connor's words, was to be used as a "sanitarium for the sick, a home for the aged, an asylum for orphans and a school for children."

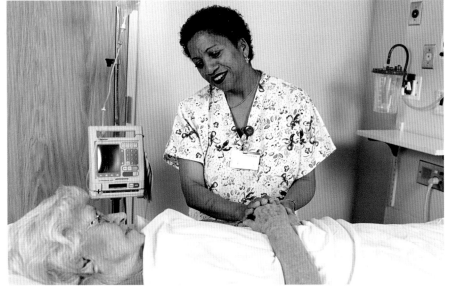

gram. "The students are always learning, asking . . . it elevates the whole team."

The hospital encourages members of the community to participate as well, which over 400 volunteers gladly do, enthusiastically contributing their time. Since the volunteer program began in 1952, volunteers have contributed over 2 million hours of service, doing everything from running the hospital gift shop and staff information desk to acting as part of the hospital's Pastoral Care program. This particular program offers members of the community the opportunity to serve the sick poor through personal visiting and offering the Eucharist, just one way that the hospital endeavors to serve its patients in body, mind and spirit.

Like most large hospitals, O'Connor Hospital offers a wealth of support services for the community, such as free health and wellness and a wide variety of support groups. But one support service that is unique to O'Connor Hospital is its Parish Nursing program. Through parish nursing, the hospital carries forth its Catholic heritage and ministry. Parish nurses are registered nurses on staff in local churches, performing independent, professional nursing practice in the provision of faith-based, whole-person-focused, community health nursing services. Parish nurses assist in the

Today, O'Connor Hospital has an experienced team of 650 physicians, 485 nurses and many other clinical and support staff who provide quality healthcare to the community, accepting all patients regardless of financial circumstances.

provision of health and wellness education through the implementation and evaluation of health ministry activities, which include group education; home visits; health screenings for blood pressure, blood glucose, and cholesterol; flu immunization clinics; support groups; and the training of volunteers to give safe and effective respite care services. This hands-on approach to serving the health needs of the community directly descends from the tradition of the Daughters of Charity, with parish nurses acting as counselors, resources, spiritual supporters and advocates for parishioners throughout the San Jose community.

Just like when it was founded, O'Connor Hospital continues to live the values established by St. Vincent de Paul with a special emphasis on advocacy for the poor. "We welcome those who are less fortunate, uninsured, and marginalized," says Robert H. Curry. Though this is a challenging mission, it is one that the hospital staff, much like the original Daughters of Charity before them, meets every day with enthusiasm, skill, and faith.

R.C. BENSON & SONS

R.C. Benson & Sons is a family-owned construction company founded in the American way. Started by an individual, built by the family, grown by virtue of quality service and customer loyalty, R.C. Benson & Sons represents the kind of success that can be attained by any American who is willing to work hard for the people he serves. As the company celebrates its fortieth anniversary in 2008, the Bensons maintain their commitment to family and community that has made the company what it is today.

R.C. Benson & Sons was founded in 1968 as R.C. Benson Construction in Cupertino, California and a few years later moved north to Mountain View. Mountain View is, in a sense, a contractor's town. Though the city was founded in the 1850s around a stage coach stop, it became very much a planned city in the mid-1860s when Cristiano Castro, a prominent Mountain View resident, granted permission to the San Francisco-San Jose Railroad Company to lay tracks over his property. After inviting the railroad to come through town, Castro huddled up with his lawyer S.O. Houghton and designed plans to construct a new Mountain View, which would eventually become the city's downtown. The city's first period of major growth came during that time, just after 1860, as Castro's plans began to be brought to life.

The city's second major growth period came almost 100 years later when, after World War II, many military

servicemen returned to the Bay Area in search of a comfortable home. Mountain View began to expand and develop from a town of 3,000 nestled among farmlands to a modern city, complete with apartment complexes and shopping malls.

It was during this period of intense development in Mountain View that Robert Benson decided to found his company, initially called R.C. Benson Construction. Having worked several years as a construction manager for a contractor at Lockheed, managing around 100 carpenters, Benson decided that he had learned enough to set out on his own. He did so, founding R.C. Benson Construction in 1968 and getting started by doing house remodels, mostly for people he knew.

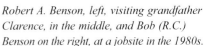

Robert A. Benson, left, visiting grandfather Clarence, in the middle, and Bob (R.C.) Benson on the right, at a jobsite in the 1980s.

The transition from construction manager to contractor was not a difficult one for Benson, as his son Bob explains, because carpenters often supervise the work of other trades. "Our carpenters can do framing, drywall, concrete, doors, and ceiling work," he says. But the trades are so specialized that contractors often subcontract the work, except on smaller projects, and become the project manager of all the specialized contractors. To run his own company, therefore, Benson had only to begin to apply what he knew on a regular basis.

Nevertheless, running a business wasn't always easy for the family. Because growth depended largely on connections and word-of-mouth, it took some time for Benson to start bringing in steady contracts. Meanwhile his wife Jean took care of the accounting from an office the family had set up in a bedroom of their house. She continued to work side by side with her husband for many years as the company grew. Benson's sons did their part to help out, too—both Bob and Richard Benson worked holidays and summers doing basic projects,

First real office in Mountain View is next door to the current office.

such as digging and demolition for several years.

The boys didn't seem to mind. Today, nearly four decades later, Bob describes his early experiences working with his father with a sense of amusement. "We were involved from day one," he explains, "digging trenches, doing demo…I had a Lockheed badge at age thirteen." The Lockheed badge would allow him access to the work sites at the company where his father had once worked for another contractor and was now running his own projects.

Despite the various hardships, Benson and his family enjoyed the work they did, and their enjoyment soon led to positive results. Business increased steadily, thanks in part to the outstanding work R.C. Benson provided and in part to the outstanding service. According to Bob, who has been promoted over the years from a thirteen-year-old with a Lockheed badge to company president, "Customer service is number one. If it's not right, we're going to make it right." Benson started off doing housing projects, and within a decade, his reputation as an excellent contractor was bringing in jobs from Hewlett Packard—a sign not only of his company's capacity to grow, but also of its capacity to evolve with the changing times.

Meanwhile, Bob had left the family business to attend college at California Polytechnic State University ("Cal Poly"), hoping to earn a bachelor's degree in architectural design. He remained at Cal Poly for about three years, returning home during the summers to work at the family business. At first, Bob says, the physical labor offered him a way to clear his mind and relieve his frustrations. Soon, however, he realized that it was what he really wanted to do. He left Cal Poly just before earning his degree and began a carpentry apprenticeship instead, soon to rejoin his father's construction company.

Bob's brother Richard, who serves today as the company's vice president, had decided a little sooner that he wanted

Bob and Jean Benson

to stay with the business. During high school Richard took a half-day of classes and a half-day apprenticeship, with the result that he completed his apprenticeship shortly after graduating high school. By 1975 he and Bob were both on the company payroll and were ready to take on business in the field.

The sons' full involvement in the business helped R.C. Benson grow considerably. Within five years the company was able to move into a new location at 1959 Leghorn Street, the building from which they still operate today. (The company

had already made its first move, from the bedroom office to a small office building on Leghorn, around 1973.) Revenues grew from about $1 million per year in 1968 to $6 million around 1975, and on up to $30 million in 2007.

Though Benson built his company's foundation on housing and remodel projects, R.C. Benson & Sons went on to provide for Silicon Valley's changing needs over the decades. "As the Valley grows and the different companies grow," Bob explains, "we have been able to adapt to what's there."

From its origins as a housing contractor, R.C. Benson & Sons has moved on to complete projects for the space industry, the electronics industry, and the biotechnology sector. Some of the company's best known clients over the years have included Lockheed, NASA, National Semiconductor, Hewlett Packard, and Stanford Medical Center. They've gone from doing mostly "plans and specs" jobs, in which an engineer decides how most of the work will be done, to doing more design-build jobs

R.C. Benson crew in the 1980s; Bob Benson is second from the end on the right, Rich Benson is on the far left.

in which they help make the decisions with a team.

Bob Benson cites two primary reasons for their success. The first—perhaps surprisingly in a region known for speculation—is temperance. The Bensons have found that by keeping business small, they maintain the ability to oversee each project personally—a fact their customers greatly appreciate.

"We could have gotten a lot bigger a long time ago," Bob says, "but we wanted to stay in control. As soon as you start passing too many things off onto someone else, the client starts to feel unimportant." To make sure each client feels like the most important client, therefore, the Bensons choose only those projects which at least one of the brothers will be able to follow from survey to completion.

The second reason for the Bensons' success is the very philosophy on which their company was founded: the importance of family. To the Bensons, family includes not only their relatives, but also their employees. "We consider our whole company a family," Bob says, adding that his father had made the company's "golden rule" never to lay anyone off before Christmas. Such loyalty on the part of the Bensons begets loyalty in their employees, and the Bensons count on that. "Our superintendents are extensions

R.C. Benson's and Sons current office, built by R.C. Benson and designed by Robert A. Benson.

of our family, and our success depends on what they do in the field."

Robert Benson retired in 1994, but his sons have gone on to provide the same quality, family-oriented service upon which he founded the business in 1968. Despite the advent of telecommunications technologies such as the fax and the Internet that make everything run faster, Bob and Richard Benson still take the time to meet with their clients face-to-face and to finish their meetings with a handshake. Today they are teaching Richard's sons Ryan and Rick to do the same. "It's the American way," Bob says. His company's commitment to maintaining this American small-business tradition ensures that it will continue to thrive in Santa Clara County for years to come.

Other projects

Stanford project for its centennial celebration, restoring fountain, precast benches with laser etched names of all donors in excess of $100,000.

RAE SYSTEMS

RAE Systems is a company that's in the right place with the right products at the right time. Founded in 1991, the San Jose-based company is living up to its motto: protection through detection. That may mean protection from terrorism in public venues or protection from invisible toxins in industrial or urban confined spaces that could turn deadly. Either way, RAE Systems offers a myriad of solutions to meet the ever-changing security and safety threat landscape.

RAE Systems develops and manufactures rapidly deployable sensor networks that enable its customers to identify safety and security threats in real time. Using proprietary sensing technology, RAE Systems' advanced products deliver information that helps people making life-critical decisions. RAE Systems also offers a full line of personal, portable, wireless and fixed atmospheric monitors, photo-ionization detectors as well as gamma and neutron radiation detectors that detect and offer early warnings of the presence of hazardous materials.

RAE Systems' products are sold in over eighty-five countries and are used by many of the world's leading corpora-

San Jose Mayor Ron Gonzales admires RAE System's array of detection products.

tions, as well as the U.S. military and government agencies. The company offers solutions for many different industries including mining, energy production, petrochemical, plastics, metals, food processing, and homeland security. The firm has built on its core strengths to continually expand into new verticals and new geographies over its almost twenty-year history.

"Even though we are fundamentally a sensor company, we have found that people are especially interested in the life critical information we provide," says

San Jose City Councilman Chuck Reed celebrates the opening of Rae System's new headquarters.

Robert Chen, president and CEO of RAE Systems, Inc. "We are proud of the fact that we can provide people with information quickly enough so decision-makers can move to protect life and property."

Robert Chen and Peter Hsi founded RAE Systems in 1991. Chen worked his way through entrepreneurial and corporate ranks, selling a company called Applied Optoelectronic Technology Corporation, an automatic test equipment producer, to Fortune 500 high-tech firm Hewlett-Packard in 1990. Chen migrated to HP with the acquisition, but was soon stirred to launch another company.

"One of Bob's employees at AOT confronted him about the equipment his company was selling —it was for destructive purposes," Bob Durstenfeld, director of public relations, says. "That employee compelled him to use technology in a way that would benefit society." Those words rumbled in Chen's head, so he went back to Harvard University, where he participated in the Harvard Business School Owner/President Management Program, and discussed some of the day's current issues.

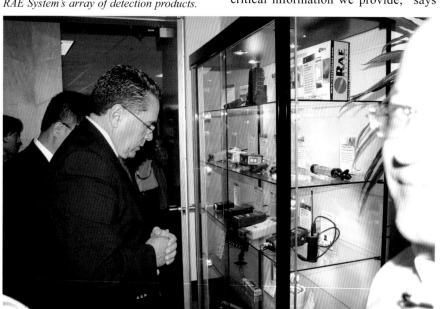

Chen's research lead him to draft a business plan for a new company to solve one of the most pressing issues he identified: cleaning up Environmental Protection Agency, or EPA, Superfund sites. Superfund is the federal government's program to clean up the nation's uncontrolled hazardous waste sites. Chen discovered one of the major issues were a class of chemicals called volatile organic compounds, or VOCs, the hydrocarbon derivative of oil that include fuels, solvents, resins, plastics, lubricants, and fertilizers. The process was lengthy, requiring officials to send a bag of dirt to a lab for testing. Two weeks later, the results would come in and determine whether a project could move forward.

"Bob Chen and Peter Hsi invented a way to miniaturize the technology used to measure these samples and developed a handheld device," Durstenfeld says. "They used a technology called photo-

AreaRAE was deployed in the restoration facility for the Teracotta Warriors in China.

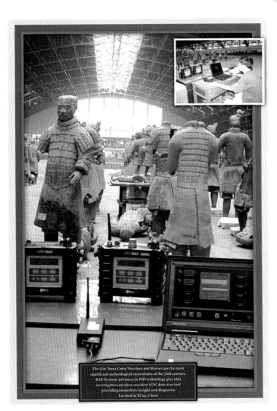

ionization that relies on high energy ultra violet light to excite the chemical in the air and in real time. Once it's charged, you can actually measure the concentration down to the individual molecules."

That handheld device is called a MiniRAE. It was Rae Systems' first product. Today the company is on the third iteration of its founding platform, dubbed the MiniRAE 3000. Chen and Hsi, however, didn't rest on its laurels. The duo continued to develop additional detection products for different applications. The next innovation was discovered in the late 1990s. The founders learned that its technology could also be used to measure jet fuel. After jetliners struck the World Trade Center towers and the Pentagon on September 11, 2001, RAE Systems' technology was brought in to accelerate the investigation.

After moderate growth for about a decade, 2002 turned out to be a banner year for RAE Systems. The company went public and continued innovating new products based on its breakthrough technology. In April 2002 the company introduced the world's first portable indoor-air-quality, or IAQ, monitor to include both a photo-ionization detector for the direct measurement of VOCs and a proprietary, non-dispersive infrared sensor for direct detection of Carbon Dioxide (CO_2), all in the same compact design.

Continuing its product development roll, September saw RAE Systems introduce two new personal gas detectors, the BadgeRAE Hydrogen Sulfide and the BadgeRAE Carbon Monoxide personal gas detectors for worker safety, with built-in vibration alarms. And in November, the company

AreaRAE wireless toxic gas monitors are often deployed at large public events to detect unseen threats.

launched a global positioning satellite option for its existing AreaRAE wireless gas detectors, offering hazardous material response teams a marked advantage in defining a perimeter as well as protecting personnel and communities. The company inked a contract to provide AreaRAE monitors to the U.S. Coast Guard and the State of Iowa and set its sites on the next need. Of course, there were challenges along the way.

"Trying to figure out how to make our products, particularly our wireless products, what's called intrinsically safe, was our biggest obstacle," Durstenfeld says. Intrinsic safety is a protection technique that ensures electronic equipment will perform safely in explosive atmospheres. That status was critical to the company's ability to move into industries like oil and gas and steel mills. RAE Systems, for example, manufactures fourteen different flavors of Single Gas Personal Protection units that are about the size of a flip cell phone. Steel mill workers clip them onto their coveralls or hardhats and are alerted when the toxic gases approach unsafe levels. Individual devices can detect ammonia, chlorine, carbon monoxide, hydrogen sulfide and ten other toxins.

With a growing line of products and growing opportunities that lead to a tipping point, RAE Systems set its sites on global expansion. The company opened a new office in Denmark in October 2002. "There was a strong need to provide service and sales support in local languages and in similar time zones," Chen explains. In 1995, RAE Systems also established a strong presence in China, with localized sales and support and broad coverage.

In 2003 New York State chose RAE Systems for hazardous incident response and has become the de facto standard for hazmat teams, large public events, and government agencies, Durstenfeld says. "Terrorism has really opened up a big piece of business for us because we can

Pictured is an AreaRAE product, the Steel Wireless Toxic Gas and radiation detector.

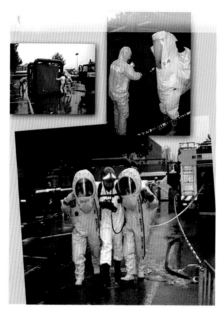

Toxic gas monitors are used for a decontamination drill.

detect the unseen threat and that's our real business," he explains. While the company continued winning patents, RAE Systems also pushed deeper into the homeland defense market.

The company launched two new personal radiation sensors for homeland defense in 2003 and demonstrated breakthrough technology use at the TOPOFF II terrorism drill in Seattle. TOPOFF is the result of a Congressional mandate passed in 1998 that called for practice operations for a terrorist attack. RAE Systems proved that technologies now exist to move gas threat detection from a traditional "one-man-one-monitor" model to a wireless age "situational awareness" model that includes not only the local incident commander, but can include remote high level coordinators and experts anywhere in the world.

The realization that RAE Systems products have industrial applications was yet another growth driver. The company develops monitors that help organizations comply with Occupational Health and Safety Administration (OSHA) regulations. Products like the QRAE, the MultiRAE Plus, the VRAE and the SentryRAE are designed to monitor gases

in confined spaces and in environments where the power is shut down. "When you turn power off to make a repair in an industrial environment, you take down the built-in sensor systems. So, using our equipment as the first layer of protection when you are working on a large industrial site, such as a chemical plant, makes a lot of sense. Global industrialization has helped our growth in the last three years.'"

Additional growth came from yet another revelation: the company's products could be used to detect danger in public venues. In February 2006 over forty of the company's AreaRAE atmospheric monitoring systems were used at Ford Field and at key strategic locations in and around Detroit to monitor for possible chemical or radiation threats before, during and after the Superbowl. RAE Systems' AreaRAE is a rugged chemical-only detector that's no bigger than a lunchbox.

AreaRAE networks have been deployed at prior Super Bowl games in Tampa and Houston, as well as many other similar events around the country.

An employee is checking for leaks at a chemical storage facility.

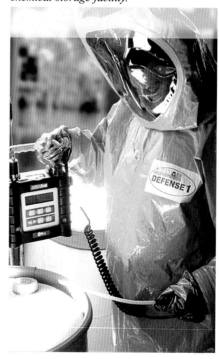

It has also been deployed at McAfee Stadium in Oakland, during the Kentucky Derby at Churchill Downs and at architectural digs. It's even been used to test pollutants affecting the Terracotta Warriors and Horses, a collection of thousands of life-sized figures in China.

With so many growth engines revving, it's no wonder that in 2006 RAE Systems made its way on to Deloitte's prestigious Technology Fast 50 Program for Silicon Valley, a ranking of the fastest growing technology, media, telecommunications and life sciences companies in its region. Rankings are based on percentage revenue growth over five years from 2001 to 2005. Over that period RAE Systems revenue grew from $19 million to $90.3 million, or 27.1 percent.

"Sustaining high revenue growth over five years is an exceptional accomplishment," says Mark Jensen, National Director of the Venture Capital Services Group for Deloitte & Touche LLP, one of the nation's leading professional ser-

Firefighters rely on toxic gas monitors to know when to don breathing protection.

RAESystems MiniRAE 2000 featured on TV Show "CSI Miami."

vices organizations. "We commend RAE Systems for making the commitment to technology and delivering on the promise of market longevity."

Chen credits eighteen patents in product and technology, innovation in sensors and wireless monitors, being a pioneer in developing solutions to meet the needs of the convergence of safety and security, as well as global reach into Europe and China, with RAE Systems' sustained growth. The company now has 1,400 employees worldwide, and it's still growing strong. In January 2007 the company announced the addition of nine regional sales managers and two senior area managers to meet the global demand for toxic gas and radiation products. New managers are in the United States, Europe, the Middle East and North Africa, India and Japan. "By restructuring our worldwide sales organization and hiring several new regional sales managers," Chen says, "we will strengthen our overall global sales team to better serve our global customers."

The company has also continued launching new products steadily over the past six years, and has no plans to stop innovating. The drive to innovate is one of the only things that hasn't changed at RAE Systems since 1991. "We started working in the environmental space and that was our focus for years, but our business has evolved now to become what we call protection through detection," Durstenfeld says. "That's really the philosophy of the company now: to provide protection through the sensor technology that we have innovated and continue to innovate."

Chen, Hsi, Durstenfeld and the company's employees have plenty to be proud of. Chen and Hsi answered the challenge to use technology in a way that helps people. The company has the potential of saving thousands and thousands of lives. Chen is most proud of the ongoing development of sensor technology to deal with the threats of today and will continue developing new technologies as the threats change and grow. "We are bullish," Durstenfeld says. "This is a technology that won't go out of style regardless of the economic boom and bust cycles. People have to be protected."

REGIONAL MEDICAL CENTER OF SAN JOSE

A healthcare leader for more than four decades, Regional Medical Center of San Jose was first built in 1965, when Silicon Valley consisted of mostly fruit orchards and a handful of young, visionary entrepreneurs. Built on property donated by Mildred Overfelt, the hospital was originally established by a religious order.

In 1999 Regional was acquired by Nashville, Tennessee-based Hospital Corporation of America (HCA), the largest healthcare organization in the U.S., adding a 35.7 acre campus to HCA's local holdings. Hospital leadership took on a huge challenge—closing an aging San Jose Medical Center and relocating its tertiary services into the larger Regional campus.

That same year, William L. Gilbert was named chief executive officer. He served as CEO for both San Jose Medical Center as well as Regional from 1999 to 2001. With a degree in healthcare administration and a master's in business administration, he served several hospitals before relocating to San Jose. His experience most likely helped when, in 2004, the San Jose Medical Center closure was announced—a move that triggered many challenges.

High-tech diagnostic epuipment such as MRI (pictured below) and 64-slice CT Scan help physicians make the proper decisions about patient care.

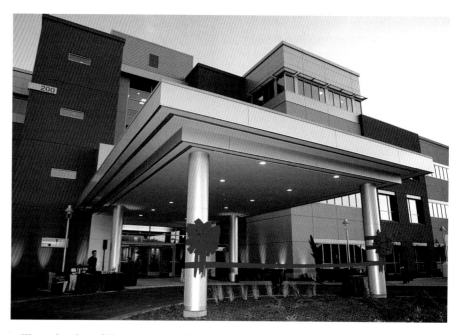

"It took a lot of listening and a lot of understanding of the needs of community, staff, independent doctors and the employees of our two hospitals," recalls Gilbert. "We were open about our goals and we asked key stakeholders to participate in the plan for bringing the two hospitals together. What resulted is the best of both worlds as far as acute-care hospitals are concerned. While we hadn't addressed some of the culture clashes that can happen between organizations, once we got together under one roof, we established a new culture for the organization that made quality patient care our first priority while working together as a team to understand and work through our differences."

Some doctors had offices located near the old hospital. They had to decide whether to relocate to the new Regional campus, or stay where they were and work with another hospital. "The majority," says Gilbert, "adapted quite nicely and have become strong members of the Regional Medical Center staff. At

A new three-story Medical office building opened on campus in late 2007.

the end of the day, they are more pleased than they've ever been because we are able to provide far more resources to care for their patients.

"When you're looking down from the 50,000-foot level making a plan," says Gilbert, "it's one thing to see the right thing to do. It's another thing to implement what has to be done."

What they've achieved is remarkable. In one year, in addition to merging one hospital into another, Regional's leadership built a trauma center, opened a cardiovascular surgery unit, started a neurosurgery program, added wound care, and expanded advanced imaging capabilities.

In October 2005 Regional broke ground on a $160 million capital expansion project that adds a new patient wing of sixty-six beds, expanded ICU, enhanced emergency department, new helipad, and a central plant.

That same year Regional opened its neurosurgery program with a highly qualified team of surgeons and was approved as one of three trauma centers in Santa Clara County. A helipad was constructed to accommodate trauma patients.

California Emergency Physicians named Regional the Emergency Department of the Year. The hospital launched a partnership with Stanford University Medical Center to create the Stanford Cardiothoracic Surgery Program at Regional, offering patients greater access to care.

In late 2007 Regional opened a new medical office building on campus to provide easy access for physicians and their patients. More medical offices are planned for future construction.

A second wing for inpatient care is planned to meet the State seismic code requirements. Parking areas are being redesigned to accommodate the hospital's new additions along with other changes that will benefit local residents and affiliated physicians. Regional has its own helipad for emergency care, but is building a new elevated one closer to the emergency department.

Another clinical improvement has been the hospital's approach to reducing medication errors for patients by using bar code scanners at each patient's bedside. The new electronic Medical Administration Record (eMar) & Bar Coding system adapts Meditech, HCA's Clinical Patient Care software, for use via wireless computer networks, portable computers and scanners.

Cardio scan

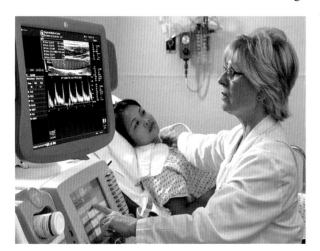

Board chairman Roger Knopf and Bill Gilbert, chief executive officer

Among many methods of measuring and evaluating its clinical quality, Regional participates in the clinical care outcome performance measurement system called the Comprehensive Health Outcomes Information System (CHOIS), which compares the clinical outcomes of patients with expected outcomes for such patients across HCA hospitals and other hospitals in the U.S. Safety brochures for the hospital are available in several languages. Regional cares deeply about patient care, safety and care outcome and works continually to improve its procedures.

Regional is one of 277 hospitals in the U.S. recognized in a 2007 issue of *U.S. News & World Report* by the American Heart Association/American Stroke Association's Get with the Guidelines (GWTG) program. It also received the designation of Primary Stroke Center from the Joint Commission on Accreditation of Healthcare Organizations.

Interested in building a healthier and stronger Santa Clara Valley community, Regional partners with local organizations to build awareness of health issues to improve people's lives. There are community and corporate health fairs, an annual Regional Golf for Health charity tournament that benefits School Health Clinics of Santa Clara County, and speakers for community outreach.

In an issue of Regional's community magazine, *Silicon Valley Health Source*, CEO Gilbert wrote about the hospital's Sunshine Club, holiday celebrations, donations to Family Giving Tree and the HCA Hope Fund, a nonprofit organization that helps employees who have experienced extreme tragedy or hardship.

"We focus on customer satisfaction almost as much as we do on clinical excellence," says Gilbert. "People may not be aware of the training and equipment that serve them when they're patients here, but they're going to remember and judge us on how good the food tastes. We want all of it—clinically and environmentally—judged well. Is the room clean? Did the nurse answer your call light promptly? Patient care for us includes all of that." Regional Medical Center of San Jose brings new meaning to the word "hospitable."

SANTA CLARA COUNTY FAIRGROUNDS

Before civic centers, industrial parks and tracts of suburban homes covered much of the land that wraps around the southwesterly end of San Francisco Bay, and before that same area had transformed itself into the global high-tech capital of the world, much of what is now commonly called Silicon Valley was referred to as the "Valley of Heart's Delight." That name was given to the region because of the cherry, apple, plum, and apricot orchards and fields of strawberries, garlic, and flowers that dominated the landscape between Palo Alto and Gilroy. Many who now live in the Valley are distant offspring of families who settled the area, and they recall a time when the region's fertile soil and temperate climate sustained a local economy that was based around crops rather than computer chips.

Agriculture was the thriving base of the Santa Clara County economy from the early 1800s to 1950s. By the mid-1800s, the proliferation of naturally grown products had encouraged local farmers, businessmen and politicians to begin celebrating each year's harvest

County Fair, 1950.

with a festival. The gathering, which would become the Santa Clara County Fair, featured music, food, fireworks, children's games and dancing, along with some of the finest exhibits of locally grown produce and livestock that could be found at any fair in the nation.

During its early years, Valley residents celebrated their annual harvests at a variety of different sites in the South Bay, including on a piece of vacant property that ran along Race Street in San Jose. That street is now lined by businesses, but quarter horse races delighted patrons when an unpaved Race Street hosted the Valley's first fair in 1856. Other locations were thereafter used to host the fair, and after decades of moving the event to different sites, its popularity generated growing sentiment for finding it a permanent home. By the 1930s, that sentiment in turn led the Santa Clara County Board of Supervisors and local Chamber of Commerce to explore options for acquiring property that could be permanently dedicated to a fairground. In 1939 the Board allocated $35,000 to purchase the 97-acre Macomber Ranch for that purpose. Later acquisitions of contiguous land would expand the fairgrounds to in

Expo Hall in the 1960s.

excess of 200 acres, although later development would cause the complex to shrink to its present size of 150 acres. The property, which in 1939 sat in the middle of a farming area on the southern outskirts of San Jose, now is situated in the geographical heart of America's tenth largest city.

The first major improvement to the old Macomber Ranch was a mile-long dirt track, which attracted patrons to harness races on the property beginning in 1939. The ranch would not host its first official fair until the late summer of 1941. That fair, which was held in canvas tents, was attended by an estimated 55,000 people. Japan shortly thereafter bombed Pearl Harbor, and the annual fair was postponed until the war ended in 1945. But the development boom that followed the war would soon transform the makeup of the Santa Clara County Fairgrounds.

Between 1944 and 1950 San Jose Technical High School students built the Sheep & Swine Building and helped with carpentry work throughout the Fairgrounds. In 1950 the State Capitol Replica Building was built, which now is used primarily for board meetings. By 1952, a 4,500 seat grandstand was erected to support harness racing, and a 45,000-square-foot exposition building also was erected on the site. The most visible and signature piece at the entrance of the fairgrounds, the Main Arch, was constructed in 1956 and it continues to this day to span the main entrance to the complex on Tully Road.

By the early 1960s, the fairgrounds was being transformed from a complex that simply hosted the annual fair to a location that would be used for various events throughout the year. The demand for space to host home arts, quilting, stamp and coin collections, antiques, preserves and flowers for the annual fair would lead to the addition of a second exposition building at the fairgrounds in 1960. Pavilion Hall, a 35,000-square-foot building, was erected in 1962 at a cost of $593,000. A small

Cinco de Mayo on the Fairgrounds.

administrative building was added to the complex that same year, along with a cafeteria, an equestrian arena, boarding stalls for horses and several other live stock facilities to host the growing fair. Expo and Pavilion Hall continue to be used for general exhibits throughout the year, including pet and hobby shows and trade and consumer exhibits. By 1965, a 20,000-square-foot facility called Gateway Hall was added to the fairgrounds, and a 10,000-square-foot building called Fiesta Hall would be constructed shortly thereafter. Currently, private businesses and nonprofit groups rent the latter halls throughout the year for different events. The grounds and these same halls also are used as venues for cultural festivals every year, including Cinco de Mayo, Fiesta del Sol, the Vietnamese Tet Festival, a Puerto Rican Festival and an Islamic gathering to celebrate Ramadan.

From the late 1950s to the early 1980s the fairgrounds drew its biggest crowds

with average annual attendance exceeding 1.5 million people. The fair itself had grown during this period to average more than 300,000 patrons per year. By the late 1960s the complex's grandstand had become a major destination point in the Bay Area, not just for motorized racing, which had supplanted harness racing in popularity, but also for outdoor rock and roll concerts. Headliner bands of the period like The Beach Boys, The Doors, Jefferson Airplane, Grateful Dead, Big Brother, and The Doobie Brothers performed at the fairgrounds during this period and the venue continued to be popular for these kind of events throughout the ensuing decade. By the early 1980s, however, Shoreline Amphitheatre had been built roughly ten miles north of the fairgrounds and the run of popularity for major music performances at the complex had ended. Motorized racing also would be discontinued at the fairgrounds by the late 1990s.

The scope of activity at the fairgrounds has changed dramatically during the past forty years, along with Santa Clara County's demographic. Like many urban areas in the United States, the county's population and economy is drastically different now than what it was even thirty years ago. The farmers and ranchers that still were prevalent in the Valley into the 1950s gave way to engineers and venture capitalists. As agriculture, as the underlying base of the economy, began to give way to high-tech in the 1960s, virtually all of the orchards that had dotted the Valley's landscape when the Macomber Ranch was bought in 1939 were gone by the mid-1970s.

With the loss of agriculture, community involvement and support for the annual fair also began to change. The fair, which in the 1950s grew into an eighteen-day event, would eventually shrink to ten days and then to a three-day run by the turn of the century. By the early 1990s, continuing declines in attendance at the fair and a steadily deteriorating infrastructure at the fairgrounds had led to financial losses that would cause the nonprofit that had historically managed the complex to declare bankruptcy in 1994. At that point, the Santa Clara County Fair Management Corporation (SCCFMC) was created by the County to assume responsibility for managing the complex, and the SCCFMC continues to operate the fairgrounds on behalf Santa Clara County.

But despite the diminishing size and popularity of its fair, the Santa Clara County Fairgrounds still serves an important mission in the region. Last year, the complex attracted more than 850,000 visitors to trade and consumer shows, ethnic festivals, craft and hobby shows, pet shows and an array of other popular activities. Part of the fairgrounds' popularity is attributable not just to the space it has reserved for community events but also to its affordability. It is common, for example, to have some of the complex's

The Fair signature arch located at the main gate.

smaller halls rented for events that host between 300 to 2,000 people—events that are sponsored by patrons who might not be able to afford local convention centers and hotel ballrooms. The complex has become especially popular with the Valley's many Hispanic families, who routinely rent facilities to host *Quinceañeras* to celebrate their daughters' fifteenth birthdays. Retirement parties and wedding receptions also are common at the fairgrounds. In addition, the fairgrounds now boasts one of the

more popular destination points in the Valley for recreational vehicle (RV) stays and RV shows. Charitable events, dances, motor cross races and even paint ball operations also now call the fairgrounds their home. The complex additionally serves as an emergency preparedness center for the Valley in the event of an earthquake or other major disaster.

Faith in the future of the fairgrounds led the County Board of Supervisors in 1998 to adopt a revitalization plan for the property, which at that point called for a 7,200-seat indoor theater and a new 150,000-square-foot exposition building. Because of sweeping changes in the musical entertainment industry, plans for a new theater were tabled in 2004. However, the Board of Supervisors recently committed $5 million to upgrade existing facilities at the complex with new heating, air conditioning and plumbing systems. A plan to commit part of the fairgrounds' remaining 150 acres to revenue-producing private development also will be considered during 2008, and that plan may generate income to help finance an expansion of the complex's exposition space.

Arthur Troyer, who has served as the executive director of the Santa Clara County Fairgrounds since 1997, remains optimistic about the complex's future. "The loss of agriculture as the underlying base in the Valley's economy long ago rendered the long-term prospects for a traditional fair problematic," said Troyer. "However, change and reinvention is a core strength in this region, and the Valley's diversity is well represented in the events that continue to be hosted at our fairgrounds. Under the right circumstances, and with the support of our County, the fairgrounds can transform itself into an urban exposition center that meets the varied recreation and entertainment needs of the region well into the foreseeable future."

Expo Hall in the 1950s.

STANFORD UNIVERSITY

One of the world's leading research and teaching institutions, Stanford University, in Palo Alto is a private university located thirty-seven miles southeast of San Francisco. It is one of the most highly regarded universities worldwide for its institutions, traditions, community, academics, and rankings.

In 1876 former California governor and railroad magnate Leland Stanford purchased 650 acres of Rancho San Francisquito for a country home and began the development of his famous Palo Alto Stock Farm for trotting horses. He later bought adjoining properties, bringing his farm to more than 8,000 acres—land that eventually became the Stanford campus. The university is named in honor of his and wife Jane's only child, Leland Stanford, Jr., who died of typhoid just before his sixteenth birthday. The morning after his son's death, Leland Sr. turned to Jane and said, "The children of California shall be our children." And so Stanford University was born.

The university's founding grant, written on November 11, 1885, stands today as the university's constitution. The university officially opened on October 1, 1891, to 559 students, with free tuition and fifteen faculty members, seven from Cornell University. Among the first class of students was young president-to-be Herbert Hoover.

When Leland Stanford Sr. passed away, his wife Jane was faced with closing the university. Appealing to President Cleveland in 1894 to release her estate from government claims growing out of construction loans, Mrs. Stanford, won the battle two years later when the Supreme Court released the estate. Mrs. Stanford turned over $11 million to the university trustees and made sure the Outer Quadrangle was completed, as well as a chemistry building and the magnificent Memorial Church.

The 1906 San Francisco earthquake destroyed parts of the Main Quad as well as the gate that first marked the entrance of the school. Stanford's first president, Dr. David Starr Jordan, stayed on to help

Stanford University campus from above. View from Hoover Tower observation deck of the Quad and surrounding area, facing west.

rebuild and was followed by: geologist John Casper Branner in 1931; the dean of the School of Medicine, Ray Lyman Wilbur in 1933; alumnus Donald B. Residder in 1943; and J. E. Wallace Sterling in 1949, who boosted Stanford from regional to national prominence by adding buildings and outstanding researchers.

The next president, Kenneth S. Pitzer, served a short term during a period of disruption on campus over the conflict in Southeast Asia. In 1970, Richard Lyman, a British history expert, became Stanford's seventh president at a time when Stanford saw an increase in the numbers and influence of women and minorities in both faculty and students. In 1980, under Donald Kennedy, Stanford completed the $1.26 billion Centennial Campaign, raising the most money collected in the history of institutional fundraising. Gerhard Casper presided over physical infrastructure improvements and additions, including restoration of buildings damaged in the 1989 Loma Prieta earthquake. Current president, John L. Hennessy, focuses on science and is a pioneer in computer architecture.

As the university embraces its second century, campus planning and develop-

ment continues. The list of academic departments is long and includes a School of Medicine, Electrical Engineering Department, Graduate School of Business, Law School, Department of Mathematics, Aeronautics & Astronautics, Art & Art History, Biochemistry, Computer Science, Drama, Economics, Geological & Environmental Sciences, Linguistics, Mechanical Engineering, Molecular & Cellular Physiology, Philosophy and Music.

Affiliated with the university is the world renowned Stanford University Medical Center which has been the home of scores of groundbreaking technologies and treatments.

The university's list of famous alumni is long and includes U.S. Poet Laureate Robert Pinsky, Pulitzer Prize-winning author Douglas Hofstadter, playwright David Henry Hwang, novelist Ken Kesey, poet and author Vikram Seth, Nobel prize-winner for literature John Steinbeck, astronaut Sally Ride, thirty-first President of the United States Herbert Hoover, U.S. Senator Dianne Feinstein, Secretary of State Condoleezza Rice, NFL quarterback John Elway, Heisman Trophy winner and NFL quarterback Jim Plunkett, and golf champion Tiger Woods.

The dream conceived by Leland and Jane Stanford lives on. The official motto of the university, selected by the Stanfords, is the German "Die Luft der Freiheit weht," which means "The wind of freedom blows."

SANTA CLARA VALLEY WATER DISTRICT

For many, it is easy to take for granted the water that we use every day. But what if this life-sustaining resource wasn't available and clean when we needed it? The history of how water has been collected, conserved and protected in California's Santa Clara Valley offers a glimpse into the evolution of a water system that now is a model for other states to follow.

During the early 1800s, it seemed like there was more water in the bowl-shaped and flood-ridden Santa Clara Valley than could be used. Rain and floodwater seeped thousands of feet below the ground to create aquifers. Wells, windmill pumps, and dams were used freely. By 1915 approximately 8.1 million gallons of water were taken each year from the valley's ground. Farmers soon noticed that the water replenished itself at a slower rate than it was being used. As a result, in 1920 they joined with business leaders to form the Santa Clara Valley Water Conservation Committee to protect the groundwater supply. The committee commissioned engineers to

Anderson Reservoir

Uncontrolled flooding in San Jose in 1911

conduct a survey of the valley's water system, which indicated that a formal water district should be developed to maintain the water supply.

With the growth of the agriculture business in the 1920s, the importance of guaranteeing a water supply became even more important. In 1929 voters approved the Santa Clara Valley Water Conservation District, which pioneered the water conservation program that engineers recommended in the previous decade. The program included acquiring, preserving and storing water. The Conservation District directed the winter storm flows into the ground reservoir of the valley. This activity quickly raised the groundwater level and created sufficient water for irrigation and domestic needs. The Conservation District was located in the north-central part of the county and by the mid-1930s annexed or merged with other water districts in the county to build six reservoirs to recharge the underground aquifers.

The 1940s brought a drastic postwar population increase. With the population on the rise and more agriculture, industry and construction, the major droughts the area endured, limited the local water resources. Under the authority of the South Santa Clara Valley Water Conservation District, two more dams were built to increase water storage. Soon after, the county board of supervisors formed the

Santa Clara County Flood Control and Water Conservation District. The District protected the area from floods and imported water from outside of the Santa Clara Valley.

In the mid 1950s, central coastal counties made water importation a priority, forming a Tri-County Water Authority, which conducted importation studies. The studies indicated that the proposed federal San Felipe Project was ideal for supplementing water for the central coastal counties. San Felipe became part of the federal Central Valley Project, which was created to transfer water from northern California into the dry valley. Additional imported water supply came from the State Water Project through the South Bay Aqueduct.

In 1968 the Santa Clara Valley Water District was officially created by the state legislature, merging the water conservation and flood control districts with a board of directors to steer policy making. This single agency was charged with integrating water management by protecting the land from floods and providing a safe, adequate, water supply to Santa Clara County.

A constant challenge for the agency, droughts plagued the area in the late 1970s. As a result, the State Water Project, which annually supplied up to

100,000 acre-feet of water through the South Bay Aqueduct during the previous decade, provided less water deliveries. The water that was delivered was too salty to be percolated into local aquifers. Water conservation efforts were introduced and yielded a 22 percent drop in water usage.

Environmental regulations were the focus for the agency during the 1980s. After discovering potential underground contamination from storage tanks, the organization worked with biologists and environmental specialists to protect water quality. The San Felipe Division of the Central Valley Project delivered 152,500 acre-feet of water to Santa Clara in 1987, during the period when the valley began to experience a seven-year drought.

With the damage from the droughts, in the 1990s the agency looked for new sources of water supply. Recycled water projects, water banking and increased water conservation were a few methods. The Integrated Water Resources Plan was created to ensure a long-term water supply. The Plan showed that future severe

South Bay Water Recycling transmission pump station

droughts could have resulted in a near 100,000 acre-feet water shortfall. In response, the Water District focused on other viable solutions: water conservation, water recycling, water banking and long-term water transfers. As part of its environmental commitment, the district upgraded its three water treatment plants to meet state and federal water quality standards.

Today the Water District, with nearly 800 employees, proactively manages the water system that nearly 2 million individuals rely upon every day. According to Olga Martin Steel, water district CEO, the biggest challenge for the District is maintaining clean and ample water sources. While early water planners focused on a stable water supply, today they must not only supply water, but also make sure that it is safe through watershed practices and treatment technologies.

In 2001 and 2002, the Water District hosted a Land Use and Water Summit to

Guadalupe flood protection project

gather business leaders and environmentalists to discuss land use issues in preparation for a major population growth. The Water District has adopted a "smart growth" method for sustainable development, which includes supporting a prosperous economy, a high-quality environment and social equity. Continued water recycling, groundwater recharge, and water conservation are key strategies to maintaining the area's water supply, while keeping in mind cost efficiencies.

More than 100 years ago, the concept of integrated water management was in its initial stages. Today, certified through the Green Business Program of Santa Clara County as a "green business" in 2005, the Santa Clara Valley Water District continues to be committed to comprehensively managing water resources that are vital to individuals who depend on it every day.

FRANK SURIAN & SONS, INC.

There are a variety of general contractors in the area surrounding San Jose, California. Frank Surian & Sons, Inc., a family business of three generations in operation since 1946, is one of the smaller ones, but nevertheless one that continues to serve the community skillfully, working on schools, historical renovations, and other projects.

In 1919, Frank Surian, in his early twenties, arrived in New York from Italy. He traveled across the United States, stopped in Las Vegas and worked in the lead mines for a week before moving to California. He next spent a few months in Santa Barbara picking lemons and other fruit; then traveled to the San Francisco area and worked on a power plant in the Shasta area as well as in the lumber industry, and later in the San Francisco shipyards.

Working in construction one day on a cousin's grocery store, he was asked by an agent of the California General Contractor's License Board if he had a license. Since he did not, he immediately went to the board office and applied for one. When Frank learned shortly thereafter that Santa Clara County was booming economically, he moved there with his new license.

For the next few years he worked on many small jobs himself as well as for Bay General Contractor. One project was the bridge over Los Alamitos Creek below Almaden Dam. He also did

Jose Higuera Adobe

Frank Sr. at the family home, 1971.

repair work on Old St. Anthony's Church, the old Redwood Cabin Bar, and Café del Rio (known today as La Foret). From 1941 to 1945 he and his son, Frank Jr., worked at Hunter's Point Shipyard.

In 1946 father and son formed Frank Surian & Sons, which they continued to develop until Frank Sr. retired in 1965. Frank's sons Edward and Frank Jr. and Frank Jr.'s wife Winnie comprised the second generation. Some of the local projects that Edward and Frank Jr. have developed include Orchard Supply Hardware at Branham Lane, and a new commercial building at Almaden Expressway and Branham Lane.

Frank Jr. passed away in 1995 and Edward Surian retired in 2005. At that time Frank Sr.'s grandson David became chief owner and operator, running the company with his wife Paula.

Paula had known the Surian family since she was a child. David's uncle was married to Paula's aunt so, as Paula says, "We were related by marriage even before we were married in 1983." Paula began working for Surian & Sons in 1991. An

essential part of the company's everyday affairs, in addition to handling the phones and all correspondence, she manages the bidding process, notary work, and picks up and delivers supplies.

Today, the company continues the work of David's grandfather by doing its own framing and finish carpentry. The company has built many schools and remodeled others for such customers as the San José Unified School District and the Evergreen School District. It has also constructed numerous fire stations for the City of San José, as well as churches in the area.

Edward, David and Paula are proud to have also worked on several historical renovations, including that of Luis Maria Peralta Adobe, which is the only structure from the era of the Spanish and Mexican land grants that still survives in the Santa Ana Canyon area. The building has survived more than 200 years of life in a rapidly changing city and is the oldest building in San José, as well as the only remaining structure from the original Pueblo de Guadalupe. The Peralta Adobe was reopened in April 2006 as an official museum, featuring historical exhibits that include artifacts excavated on-site.

Another Surian renovation is the Jose Higuera Adobe building, in the city of Milpitas, whose history dates back to sixteenth century Ohlone Indians. The historic adobe house is situated on five-and-one-half-acres park site with barbecue pits, tables and play equipment.

In Santa Clara, Surian & Sons renovated the Santa Clara Women's Club, La Pena Adobe, originally built about 1790, which was one of thirty houses in five parallel rows constructed for married neophyte Indian couples. It is the only surviving structure of the third mission complex and one of the oldest adobes in California. Purchased in 1913 by the Women's Club, it has served as their headquarters ever since, renovated by Frank Surian & Sons in 2004. The house links Franciscan padres labor with

La Pena Adobe

the California of today and is registered as a California historical landmark.

As a union contractor, to remain competitive, the company also works on public buildings. The Santa Clara area is continually growing and expanding and competition continues to be challenging. Bidding is never easy and always varied.

David Surian says that in 1948 Edward's check for a forty-hour week totaled $48.00. Today carpenters earn $87.50 per hour. These days, David, wife Paula and another carpenter are the only permanent employees; the company hires extra carpenters as required. On a recent summer project, there were twelve carpenters working on one of their projects. Says David, "We have no aspirations to grow into having a need for hundreds of employees. We are a longtime single-family business and enjoy dealing personally with owners and making sure that we're there, on the job, and that work is being done to our satisfaction. This kind of thing is easier to accomplish when you're small."

Has construction changed over time? Tools have changed, David says. There are more pneumatic, air-filled tools and power tools. Battery-operated tools used today are far more convenient than the hand tools of yesterday, but, he says, "We still use hand tools for detail work. The days of craftsmanship of my father and grandfather's eras are pretty much gone, but we still work to carry them on. We're proud of what we do and always want to aim for quality work. Many young carpenters today don't know what a handsaw is. Power tools are great, but for fine trim, there's nothing like a hand tool. Buildings today don't require the delicate woodwork that older buildings used to require," he adds. "Wood frame buildings are what we prefer," he says. "There are always new products—plaster, acrylic paint, stucco and glass—but basic wood-framing has not changed for us."

The way business is done has also changed. In today's marketplace, David says, one has to be a politician. "In my grandfather's era," he recalls, "we shook hands, did the work, got paid and moved on. Now, in any business today, there are lengthy contracts, construction management firms and a lot more paperwork. The construction management firms serve as go-betweens. We personally prefer to be our own middleman since we have a vested interest in any project we take on. We believe that if we can't manage what we're doing, we shouldn't be doing the job."

Will there be a fourth generation Frank Surian & Sons? David thinks it may not be likely since his and Paula's daughters appear to be interested in other fields. David, who calls himself a frustrated chef, hopes that someday he and Paula can retire and pursue a quiet life of good food and wine. As a former art student at Casper College in Wyoming, he has an eye for beauty and design, which is apparent in the work he's done all these years for the company. It's important to him that Frank Surian & Sons sustain the legacy of his grandfather—doing a good job at a reasonable price. "All you need," says David, "is a good architect and an honest general contractor."

St. Anthony's Church

UNITED GENETICS

Though the Santa Clara Valley is well known for technological advancements of the computer variety, the Valley is home to notable innovations of all types. While other companies are working on the latest computer processors and online data platforms, another company is refining something even smaller and even more vital—plant seeds. United Genetics Seeds Company was founded in 1990 by Italian native, Remo Ludergnani and his wife, Norma Echeverria, as a small business. Combining the founder's years of experience and drive to nurture the best products for his customers, United Genetics is now a multi-million dollar international enterprise.

United Genetics breeds and markets hybrid and proprietary open-pollinated varieties of ten major classes of vegetable crops. United Genetics employs nine top-notch scientists who specialize in eight classes of products: tomato, cantaloupe/ melon, watermelon, squash, pepper, cucumber, eggplant, and onion. Meticulous research is undertaken to refine the quality of the seeds so that they produce consistent and high-quality crops that are more resilient and resistant to disease. All of the work at United Genetics is done through active traditional breeding with absolutely no transgenic activity. This means that all seeds are created as a result of skillfully combining ideal

Remo Ludergnani (top left) and Mario Martinelli, general manager, Unigen, Italy, (bottom right) selecting new HY Watermelon with International Seedsmen.

plant traits through natural pollination procedures, not through any genetic engineering or the insertion of DNA into a plant species. "What nature could have done naturally in 500 years, we will do in five," Ludergnani claims to his customers. The resulting seeds produce superior fruit and vegetables, better suited to the needs of the end user.

Much of the work of the members of the United Genetics team is inspired by current market needs. This is a point that owner and founder Remo Ludergnani takes great pride in. The results of this research can be seen in the plants themselves. Tomatoes of all varieties grown from United Genetics seeds are plump and ruby red, ready to be sold at market or to be utilized in processing of other tomato products. Likewise, melons and watermelons grown from United Genetics seeds have the sweetest and the highest interior quality with unique characteristics that make them ideal for different market needs.

Resiliency is a word that perfectly describes not only the seeds cultivated by United Genetics, but its founder as well. As a boy growing up in Italy, life was challenging for Remo Ludergnani, who was born into a family of well-respected cattle dealers. When he was just three years old, the occupying German forces took over his family's recently built home, forcing them out into the countryside. After nearly a year of constant moving, they finally found a single home for the whole family once again.

Normal schooling was not possible during World War II, and Remo's first lessons were taught by an old priest, who introduced this young boy to Latin. When the war finally ended, and life returned to normal, it was possible for Remo to attend regular school, a pursuit that he excelled at from the beginning. After graduating from technical school, Remo Ludergnani continued his studies at the University of Parma, one of the oldest universities in Italy. He graduated with the title of doctor of economy and commerce, then served as an officer in the 78.0 Regiment, *Lupi di Toscana* (Wolves of Tuscany).

Remo Ludergnani began his business career in a bank, after which he moved into the tomato processing industry. These two experiences would lay the groundwork for his ultimate foray into the seed business. While Remo was working in a famous tomato processing company in North Italy, Petoseed, one of the leading tomato breeding companies in the United States began offering its product to Italian tomato factories. It was at that time that the entire approach to tomato production was revolutionized. To that point, processors were at the mercy of growers for their supply. If the processor had special requirements for his tomato crop, these would often be left unmet.

Remo quickly saw the potential of having the demand dictate the supply. When Petoseed began looking for a sales manager for the Italian market, Remo was the ideal candidate. His knowledge of the

Norma, Remo standing and son Diego.

Italian tomato processing industry helped him excel, and within a year he was named general manager. He spent the next several years building up not only the European market but the Central and South American venues as well.

A promotion to vice president of all international sales brought him to California in 1977, where he was able to gain first-hand experience into the research techniques employed to refine seeds to produce healthier plants and bigger crop yields. In 1984 he and two seedsmen, old colleagues from Petoseed, took on the challenge of a new seed venture called Sunseeds, which was located in Hollister, California.

In 1990 he was ready to branch out on his own, along with the help of his wife, Norma, who was a chemical engineer with terrific international experience in sales and management. From the beginning, Norma Ludergnani handled the administration of the company, freeing Remo to devote himself to breeding and selling their products. The company's motto is "New Ideas for Better Seeds," and the founders find that this is the best approach to selling their product.

The concept is realized in this sentence: "We ask our clients to allow United Genetics to make money for them," says Remo. If United Genetics' seeds can't produce a profit for dealers,

Costa Rica—a moment of relaxation. Remo and a giant leaf on the Poa Vulcan.

importers and their customers, then Ludergnani takes this as a challenge to continue to improve and innovate until they achieve the best varieties on the market.

When United Genetics began, the company focused strictly on tomato seeds, specifically, a processing tomato for Europe and the *saladette* tomato for Mexican markets. With the success of this product line, the company branched out into watermelon and melon lines in 1993, followed by squash, cucumbers, and onions. Soon, United Genetics was able to develop with its traditional breeding techniques very good hybrids in cucumber and squash species, as well.

The next step was to take United Genetics onto the international stage. An

Aerial view of the corporate location of United Genetics, Hollister, California.

Italian branch of the company was formed in 1995, which is now a leading seed company in Europe, followed a few years later by branches in Chile and later, India. The company is slated for even more international expansion.

As the need for a robust and healthy food supply continues to grow, so will United Genetics. Given its important place in its agricultural industry and its forward-thinking scientific methods, United Genetics fits in well with Santa Clara's culture of innovation.

A new melon for Europe.

VALLEY OIL

Business works a little differently in the petroleum industry. Unlike in many other industries, the product one petroleum company has to offer is exactly the same as that of its competition. What makes the difference between the two is the human touch, the ability to understand each customer's needs and to meet those needs efficiently and effectively in today's changing industry. That is the difference that has made Valley Oil Company an outstanding member of the Mountain View business community for over sixty years. As company president Bob Christiansen explains, "We don't refine the oil; we refine the service."

Valley Oil was founded by Arnold Peter ("Pete") Christiansen, a northern California native and longtime citizen of Petaluma, in 1947. Originally from a chicken ranching background, Pete had made his start in the petroleum business years before as a mail clerk with Shell Oil. He was quickly promoted from his starting position to that of a truck driver and spent several years delivering petroleum to farms and other locations (such as the Hearst Castle) throughout the area.

By the time he opened Valley Oil in August 1947, Pete had already formed

One of Valley Oil's stations.

relationships with many farmers throughout the area, and these relationships undoubtedly helped him make his own start in the industry. For many years he continued to deliver petroleum to farmers all over the region, along with various chemicals they used in their operations. Meanwhile, he began to raise a family with his wife Dorothy Buchser, a primary school teacher, with whom he built a home in Los Altos in 1941.

Pete's son Bob grew up to work in his father's business for several summers

Pete and Dorothy Christianen's four children, Jean, Bob, Ann and Carol, with Pete in May 1953.

during high school and college. After graduating from the University of the Pacific with a degree in Business Administration in 1970, Bob decided that he'd had enough of petroleum and headed south instead to do graduate work at San Diego State. But he didn't stay in Southern California long.

"I knew my dad was getting to the point where he wanted to get out of the business," Bob explains, "and I didn't want to miss the opportunity [to own it]."

In the interest of taking advantage of a good opportunity, therefore, Bob returned to the family business in 1972. Two years later he convinced his old college friend Bob Buck, who was studying to become a dentist, to join him. It was the beginning of a business partnership that has lasted over thirty years.

When Bob Christiansen rejoined his father in 1972, Valley Oil was still mostly in the business of delivering petroleum to construction companies, farmers, and service stations. The company was run entirely by four employees who did sales, accounting, delivery, customer relations, marketing, and general office work—

most of the time, as Bob jokes, "all of the above."

One major advantage of such an operation was that Bob and his father, along with Bob Buck once he came on board, were able to develop personal relationships with their customers. As time passed, the company took on more accounts and was able to hire more drivers, but those personal relationships remained as the core of the family business.

"It's a fun business because the people involved are fun people, good people," Bob says, referring not only to his

Original 20,000 gallon tanks, still in use today, next to the new office (right) built in June 2000.

customers, but also to his employees and—perhaps surprisingly—to the competition. "You end up being in friendly competition, getting along well with other distributors because we're all in the same boat together."

The people, he explains, are what attracted him and Bob Buck to the business in the first place. He considers it a privilege to have been able to own Valley Oil and thereby have the opportunity to

meet and work with them. "We make a profit by accident," he says. "We're really here because we enjoy the industry and the tradition of service to our customers."

The partners' enjoyment has led to exceptional growth in the business, from four employees at the time of their joining together in the early 1970s to almost forty today. Many of those employees were added to help support one of Valley Oil's most innovative new services: a twenty-four-hour onsite refueling service that specializes in fueling diesel-powered construction equipment. One of only a few companies in the Silicon Valley that offers such a service, Valley Oil provides fuel for tanks anywhere from 50 to 20,000 gallons in size.

In addition to the onsite refueling service, Valley Oil continues to provide fuel to construction companies, municipalities, service stations, hospitals, and other large operations throughout the San Jose-San Francisco Bay Area. At one time, provider to many different industries, Valley Oil serves such well-known clients as Pacific Gas and Electric Company, AT&T, and Stanford University. Some of the company's longtime distributors in the Santa Clara Valley who are still around today include Herb Richards of Coast Oil Company and Tom Lopes of Western States Oil Company.

Other longtime customers include O'Grady Paving, Tollner Painting, Devcon Construction, Peninsula Building Materials, Cap Concrete, McCarthy Ranch, and South Bay Construction.

Valley Oil's commitment to service doesn't stop at its clients, however. Following the community-oriented approach of his father Pete, who served on the board of directors for Los Altos High School, Foothill College, and De Anza College for many years, Bob Christiansen has served on the board of directors of Alliance Petroleum Corporation since 1978. Alliance Petroleum is a cooperative effort of 125 distinct fuel distributors in California, Nevada, and Arizona to address the common problems and regulations that help keep the "small oil jobber" alive in the rapidly transforming petroleum industry.

"To be able to survive in this industry, you've got to be able to keep up with whatever the needs are," Bob explains. For sixty years, Valley Oil has been able to do precisely that. Today's petroleum industry is about much more than selling oil: it's about providing comprehensive energy solutions for the world in which we live. With a focus on service and an eye for innovation, Valley Oil will continue to provide these solutions to the Santa Clara Valley for many years to come.

VALLEY VIEW PACKING CO. INC.

When Pietro Rubino departed his native Italy in 1886, he settled in San Jose, where he purchased a fertile eighteen-acre prune orchard in the heart of the Almaden Valley. While tending fruit trees, he and his wife Petrina raised three sons, Sam, Leonard, and Joseph. Pietro worked the orchard until the 1920s. When his health began to fail, his sons had to leave school to support the family. To enhance business, they opted to expand into commercial spraying, pruning, tractor work, and sharecropping of local ranch properties.

Around this time, the brothers tried hand-packing prunes, which were then steamed until they were soft (and very hot), and molded by hand to resemble the more commercially popular figs. The prunes were placed in ten to twenty-five-pound wooden boxes for shipment. The process, which was extremely slow and labor intensive, created a challenge to experiment with better ways to process and pack dried fruit.

In 1935 the Rubinos helped design and finance a tunnel method for dehydrating prunes that revolutionized the industry. It was a two-story, above-ground tunnel

Sam and Leonard.

Original label.

overseas, the Rubino brothers purchased a small packing operation from J. L. Mosher on a farm close to theirs, increasing their area of operation to more than thirty-five acres.

When the war ended, Leonard Rubino traveled across the U.S. and Europe opening new markets and establishing a broker and customer base that remains today. Sam Rubino looked for land and developed bonds with many farming families. Partners and Pietro's grandchildren—Sal Rubino, the company's president and Sam's son, and Patricia Rubino Brunetti, the company's secretary/treasurer and Leonard's daughter—continue those bonds today. Valley View now owns some of the finest orchard land in California. Many of these orchards were first planted by

First office, current office.

that dried prunes with a uniform flow of heated air. These tunnels are still used today. A year after developing this new invention, traveling in their 1936 Chevrolet truck from store to store between San Francisco and Los Angeles, Sam and Leonard sold 1,500 tons of prunes—a record first year.

World War II was gearing up in Europe by 1938. The Rubinos began hauling sacks and bulk containers of prunes to the San Francisco docks to be shipped overseas, where food was in short supply. As they expanded operations to match the increased need for food

Leonard and Sam in the early 1950s. Sam's wife Rose, and Leonard's wife Grace, were among Valley View's first employees. They helped pack prunes by hand and used a tire hung from the ceiling to glue and seal the twenty-five-pound boxes of prunes. From these humble beginnings Valley View Packing Company was born and has gone on to become a firm with domestic sales from coast to coast and international sales to almost every country in the world.

"Everything was done with a handshake," says Patricia Rubino Brunetti. "And everything our fathers developed—the land, brokerage/customer base and farmer relationships—still exist today."

From the 1950s through the 1990s, Valley View Packing Company was one of the largest growers and packers of dried fruits, fruit concentrates, fruit nectars, prune concentrate and prune juice. At the same time, the company helped to perfect methods and machinery to pit prunes, make prune concentrates and juice, can prunes with different flavor essences and pasteurize fresh fruit to make nectars. Valley View has always had a reputation for being both innovator and quality producer.

Sal and Patty are still running Valley View Packing Company today with the same ideals forged by their fathers, but with twenty-first- century goals. In 1998 they made the difficult decision to close the San Jose Plant. At a time when many companies are looking to expand and grow, Valley View Packing Co. Inc. has done the exact opposite, and for a good reason: family. Both Sal's wife, Becky Lozzio Rubino, and Patty's husband, Michael Brunetti, are from long-standing Santa Clara Valley families. Becky's family was involved in ranching since the turn of the century, while Michael's family has its own century-old business, California Monumental. Family values and interests are number-one priorities.

San Jose was once called "Valley of Heart's Delight." At that time, all fruit-packing companies were in San Jose. In the 1960s and 1970s, the area became better known as Silicon Valley. Over the years it became expensive and impractical to run a plant in San Jose. As the population exploded in San Jose, the Rubino Family was pressured to turn their local acreage into land for housing.

"Also," says Patty, "we have changed the scope of our business. While we once packed dried fruit for the world, our focus today is only on prunes and prune concentrate and business is mostly wholesale. My cousin and business partner, Sal Rubino and I noticed that most of our employees, some who had been with us for decades, were nearing retirement age. That's when we decided it was time to slow down."

The Rubino cousins decided to use Sal's machinery expertise to design and build a state-of-the-art prune concentrate operation to complement the ongoing

Sal and Patty.

orchard and drying operation in Yuba City after closing the San Jose plant. Today, Valley View is basically self-contained, using its own prune crop from its own orchards. The company sells prune concentrate in 620-pound drums, and "natural condition" prunes in twenty-five-pound boxes.

"We are still using the same network of brokers, developed by our fathers, who sell all over the world," Patty says. Valley View has up-to-date machinery these days to enable the company to respond to special-order specifications for any company and country. Prunes are used in a variety of ways—from an ingredient in sauces, bakery products, nutritious snacks and juices to pet foods and cosmetics.

Today, the fourth generation of the Rubino family is involved in Valley View Packing. While the third generation continues in agribusiness, Sal's son and daughter—Sal Rubino Jr. and his wife Kelly—and Kim Rubino Kelley with her husband Jeff, and Patricia's children Michael Brunetti and Tricia Brunetti are following in the footsteps of their great-grandfather when he bravely left his native country to begin a new life in a new land.

Together these cousins are developing and investigating new ideas and exciting ventures for family business interests.

"It's truly a family business," Patty adds. "We shrank Valley View in the twentieth century to involve our families. We are now growing—all together—with twnety-first century enthusiasm. We have state-of-the-art machinery. We never forget the importance of a handshake. People don't get a second chance to make a first impression, and a single action can ruin a name for a long time. The most important things our family has is its trust in each other and our family's good name and reputation. We feel blessed and very fortunate."

The landscape of Valley View Packing Co may have changed but the lessons learned, the memories kept, and the friendships forged from each previous generation will live on with the fifth generation of Rubinos—Nico, Jake and Lisa.

Plant before closing.

A TIMELINE OF SANTA CLARA COUNTY'S HISTORY

Over a thousand years before the Spanish arrive, the Ohlone, a Penutian speaking people, settled in small villages in the valley.
1602
Sebastián Vizcaíno discovers a "great bay" he names Monterey.
1769
Gaspar de Portolá leads the Sacred Expedition from Baja California to establish a mission in Monterey. Missing the "great bay," they cross the mountains becoming the first Europeans to see San Francisco Bay. They camp under El Palo Alto.
1776
Fray Tomás de la Peña establishes Mission Santa Clara de Thamien along the Guadalupe Creek near the Taris' (Ohlone) village of So-co-is-u-ka.
1777
José Joaquín Moraga establishes El Pueblo de San José de Guadalupe.
1779
Guadalupe Creek floods the mission.
1781
Mission rebuilt at present-day Martin Avenue and de la Cruz Boulevard.
1784
Fray Junipero Serra dedicates the third mission on the site of the present-day railroad station.
   Peña Adobe, now the Santa Clara Women's Club, built to house married neophytes.
1797
San Jose moves one-mile south due to flooding.
1798
Captain George Vancouver describes Santa Clara Valley in *A Voyage of Discovery*.
1810
Revolution against Spain and civil war in Mexico halt supplies. *Californios* trade hides with foreign ships.
1814 or 1815
John Cameron Gilroy, a Scott, is the first non-European to settle in the valley at San Ysidro, now Gilroy.
1817
Antonio María Suñol arrives. He becomes an influential citizen in San Jose.
1820
Thomas W. Doak, first U.S. settler in California (1816), marries into the Mariano Castro family, holders of two south county ranchos.
1822
Mexico gains independence from Spain and gives land grants in California.
   Two earthquakes destroy the mission. It is rebuilt at the current location of Santa Clara University.
1826
Suñol becomes first postmaster of San Jose.

Antonio María Suñol, an educated Spaniard, arrived in the Pueblo de San José. He became the first postmaster, the sub-prefect, and was the most influential citizen in the pueblo. Courtesy, History San José

1826–1827
Jedediah Strong Smith travels over the Sierra Nevada, opening California to American settlers.
1828
Mexico allows foreigners to settle, providing they pledge allegiance and become Catholics.
1832
James Alexander Forbes becomes majordomo at the mission. Later he builds Forbes Mill in Los Gatos.
1835
San Jose has about forty homes and 700 settlers— forty are non-Hispanic.
1836
Californios, led by José Castro, a prominent valley citizen, with Isaac Graham and his band of fur trappers, overthrow Governor Nicholás Gutiérrez.
1841
Bidwell-Bartelson overland party arrives in San Jose. Later, Josiah Belden becomes first U.S. mayor of San José.
   Population of the valley reaches 935.
   George Ferguson builds a flour mill on the Guadalupe north of San Fernando Street later operated by Pierre Sainsevain and Suñol.

1844
Martin Murphy, Sr., Dr. John Townsend, and Captain Elisha Stephens brought the first wagon train across the Sierras. They settle throughout the valley.
1844-1845
Manuel Castro organizes an army in San Jose and overthrows Governor Manuel Micheltorena.
1845
Nine hundred settlers live in San Jose; most are from the United States.
   Captain Andres Castillero, identifies the red ore used by the Ohlone to paint their bodies as cinnabar or quicksilver. It is processed into mercury and used to separate gold from ore.
   A "Call to Foreigners" is issued for a 4th of July meeting in San Jose to discuss secesssion from Mexico.
1846
James F. Reed and his family, members of the ill-fated Donner Party, arrive in San Jose. He becomes a successful real estate developer.
1847
Battle of Santa Clara, the only battle in northern California during the Mexican-American War, ends with no casualties.
   William Campbell builds a sawmill on the Saratoga Creek above present-day Saratoga. Logging remained a major industry into the twentieth century.

James F. Reed, a native of Ireland, fought alongside Abraham Lincoln during the Black Hawk War. He was an organizer and chronicler of the ill-fated Donner Party. Reed, banished from the wagon train after killing a member of the party, traveled over the Sierras to Sutters Fort for supplies, but was unable to make it back due to heavy snow. He took part in the Battle of Santa Clara before returning with supplies and helping to rescue survivors. Reed settled in San Jose where he became prosperous in real estate. Courtesy, Sourisseau Academy

The Battle of Santa Clara, the only battle in northern California during the War of 1846, was fought on January 2, 1847 near where present-day el Camino Real crosses el Arroyo Quito. It ended with no casualties to either side. This watercolor was painted by William H. Meyers a sailor on the USS Dale who did not participate in the event but heard about it from his shipmates. Courtesy, Franklin D. Roosevelt Presidential Library

1848
United States wins the Mexican-American War and secures California.

1849
Valley population approaches 4,000.

John Whisman establishes the first stage service in California between San Jose and San Francisco. In winter, the stage connects with ships in Alviso.

1849
Judge Peter H. Burnett of San Jose is elected governor. First legislative session, nicknamed "the legislature of a thousand drinks," was held in the Sainsevain home on Market Plaza.

1850
California enters the Union and San Jose is the first capital.

1851
Several colleges established: Santa Clara College (Santa Clara University); California Wesleyan University (University of the Pacific), originally located in Santa Clara, moved to San Jose in 1870, then to Stockton in 1924; the College of Notre Dame in San Jose became the first women's college in California; it moves to Belmont in 1923.

1852
County population reaches 6,764. Population of San Jose is 2,500.

First county road built between Saratoga and Alviso. County supervisors also authorize toll roads.

Bernard S. Fox establishes the Fox Nursery, the largest on the West Coast.

Santa Clara incorporates.

1855
County Infirmary opens in San Jose. In 1871 county purchases 114 acres for what becomes Santa Clara Valley Medical Center.

1856
Louis Pellier introduces the French prune to the valley.

1857
Minns' Evening School, the oldest public institution of higher education in California, opens in San Francisco. It moves to San Jose in 1870 as the State Normal School (San Jose State University).

1859
Gilroy becomes the "Tobacco Capital of America."

1860
County population reaches 11,912. San Jose has 3,430 residents.

1860
Chinese build the San Francisco & San Jose Railroad. They remain as farm workers and help build the South Pacific Coast Railroad.

1861
Settler's Revolt occurs when Antonio Chabolla forces Yankee squatters off Rancho Yerba Buena. 1,000 armed settlers arrive in San Jose with a cannon donated by Saratoga citizens. Chabolla and the squatters reach a monetary agreement and bloodshed is averted.

1862
Charles Lefranc makes wine from French cuttings at the New Almaden Vineyard.

1864
Battle of Almaden Road, the only Civil War action in California, occurs when a gang of Confederate sympathizers rob a Wells Fargo stagecoach and flee to Santa Clara County. A posse led by Sheriff John H. Adams captures them after a gunfight.

1865
Pierre Sainsevain began making red table wines at the Belle Vue vineyard.

First oil well in California dug in Moody Gulch above Los Gatos.

1867
County Courthouse, designed by Levi Goodrich, in St. James Park is completed.

Civil War General Henry Morris Naglee, establishes a winery and brandy distillery. His brandy won a special award at the Centennial Exposition of 1876.

1869
Central Pacific Railroad establishes service from San Jose to Sacramento.

1870s
Board of Supervisors and the San Jose City Council authorize horse drawn railroad

---

The first Chinese arrived in the valley in 1860 to build the San Francisco & San Jose Railroad. After completing the railroad in 1861, they stayed in the valley working on farms and helped build the South Pacific Coast Railroad from Oakland to Santa Cruz in the 1870s. This is the Bassett Street Station in 1912. Courtesy, Sourisseau Academy

companies. They eventually merge into the Peninsular Railroad Company.

1870
Phoenixonian Institute, a school for African American children, is established at 4th and William Streets. The African American community is centered on San Antonio and 3th Streets.

A. P. Giannini, founder of the Bank of Italy, (Bank of America), was born in San Jose, grew up on a family farm, and attended school in Alviso.

Gilroy incorporates.

1870s
Board of Supervisors and the San Jose City Council authorize horse-drawn railroad companies. They eventually merge into the Peninsular Railroad Company—The Interurban.

1871
Dr. James M. Dawson establishes the first cannery in the county.

At the age of 14, Tiburcio Vasquez stabbed a constable and by the time he was an adult, he was one of California's most notorious bandits. After serving two sentences in San Quentin between 1857 and 1870, he returned to horse thieving, moving to the Tejon Pass area of southern California, where he hid in the rock formations known as Vasquez Rocks. In 1874, he was captured and stood trial in San Jose for two murders committed in San Benito County. Hundreds visited him in the Santa Clara County Jail where he posed for pictures and gave out autographs. Sheriff John Adams hung him on March 19, 1875. He was buried in the Santa Clara Mission Cemetery. Courtesy, Edith C. Smith Collection (McKay), Sourisseau Academy

When the county supervisors decided to build a new courthouse, they wanted a building that would remind Californians that San José should have remained the capital as the statehouse in Sacramento was far from completion and that city was prone to flooding. The Santa Clara County Courthouse, designed by Levi Goodrich, remained the center of several attempts to relocate the state capital over the next four decades. Courtesy, Sourisseau Academy

1872
Vincent Picchetti discovers one of the finest wine-growing areas in the world, the Chaine d'Or in the Santa Cruz Mountains.

1875
Tiburcio Vasquez, the bandit, was tried and hung in San Jose.

1876
Garden City Gas Company established a gas plant for illuminating homes. It is later purchased by PG&E.

1878
Clara Foltz wrote the verbiage that allowed women to practice law in California. She was the first woman: to graduate from Hastings Law School; admitted to the State Bar, attorney in San Jose, San Francisco, and San Diego; appointed to the Board of Charities and Corrections; to prosecute a murder; deputy district attorney in Los Angeles. She also proposed the idea for paid public defenders.

1880
South Pacific Coast Railroad operates between the cities of Alameda and Santa Cruz until 1940.

1883
John Bean establishes the Bean Spray Pump Company in Los Gatos. After moving to San Jose in 1915, and merging with the Anderson-Barngrover Manufacturing Company in 1929, it becomes the Food Machinery Corporation.

1885
California Fruit Union is established. By 1889 it produces two-thirds of the fresh fruit consumed on the East Coast.

1886
Senator Leland and Jane Lathrop Stanford establish Leland Stanford Jr. University in memory of their son.

Clara Foltz wrote the law that allowed women to become attorneys in California. She also wrote the California law that gave women the right to vote in 1911 Courtesy, Bancroft Library

1887

Chinatown, on Market Street (where the Fairmont Hotel is located), burns down. The San Jose City Hall (1889) and Post Office (1892) are built on the site to force the Chinese out of downtown. They move to 6th and Jackson Streets (Heinlenville Chinatown).In the 1890s, Japanese immigrants settle between 1st and 8th and Jackson and Taylor.

Los Gatos incorporates.

Campbell establishes the first free rural mail delivery in California.

1888

Lick Observatory, featuring the largest telescope in the world, opens on Mount Hamilton.

1892

Stanford wins the first "Big Game" against the University of California.

1896

Paul Masson establishes the Paul Masson Champagne Company in the Mount Eden

---

About 15,000 people watch John Joseph Montgomery fly the glider, Santa Clara, *to a predetermined site and safely land. This was the first controlled landing of a heavier-than-air craft and earned Montgomery the title,"The Father of Basic Flight." Montgomery died in a crash-landing in 1911 in Evergreen Valley. Courtesy, Edith C. Smith Collection (McKay), Sourisseau Academy*

Anna Virgil Stokes McCall, was born in Georgia in 1879 one of at least sixteen children. She was one of the founders and first treasurer of the Garden City Colored Women's Club in 1908, now known as the Garden City Women's Club. She was also very active in the local Women's Christian Temperance Union. After she passed away in 1949, the Garden City Women's Club created a scholarship in her memory. Courtesy, History/San Jose.

District of Saratoga.

1898

Sunset Magazine, the first magazine devoted to Western living, begins publishing. In 1929 Lawrence W. Lane purchases it and shifts the emphasis to western travel, cooking, gardening, and home design.

1900

Pierre Klein won the gold medal at the Paris Exposition for his Santa Clara County Mira Valle Cabernet.

Andrew P. Hill, a noted artist and photographer, and Josephine Clifford McCrackin, a well known author, establish the Sempervirens Club of California. They lobby the state Legislature to establish Big Basin Redwood Park in Santa Cruz County.

County population reaches 60,216.

1902

Mountain View incorporates.

1905

John Joseph Montgomery, "The Father of Basic Flight," flew the glider, *Santa Clara*, in the first controlled landing of a heavier-than-air craft. Montgomery crashes and dies in 1911.

1906

Earthquake collapses Agnews State Hospital killing 117 patients and staff; Stanford University campus and the Stanford Memorial Church suffer damage; the tunnel at Wrights Station is closed for three years.

Morgan Hill incorporates.

1907

Garden City Bank, on the corner of 1st and San Fernando Streets, is the first reinforced concrete skyscraper in the county.

1908

Anna Stokes McCall establishes the Garden City Colored Women's Club and is a founding member of the San Jose Chapter of the NAACP.

1909

Palo Alto incorporates.

Stanford graduate, Cyrus Elwell, forms the Federal Telegraph Company in Palo Alto. It moves to New Jersey in 1931. Several engineers remain and later establish Litton Industries and Magnavox.

Charles D. Herrold broadcasts from the world's first radio station, KQW, in the Garden City Bank Building. In 1949 the station moves to San Francisco changing its call sign to KCBS.

1912

Sunnyvale incorporates.

1917

County farmers organize the California Prune and Apricot Growers Cooperative packing fruit under the Sunsweet label.

1919

Herbert Hoover donates $50,000 to Stanford University to establish the Hoover Institution

on War, Revolution and Peace.

1921
San Jose City College opens in downtown. It moves to the present location in 1953.

1926
Fourth mission burns; it is rebuilt in 1929.

1929
Voters approve the Santa Clara Valley Water Conservation District to recharge groundwater under the valley floor.

1930
Santa Clara County citizens purchase land, once a Posolmi village, and sell it for $1 to the Navy (Moffett Field).

1931
Valley farmers establish Orchard Supply Hardware.

1933

Below:
On October 11, 1922, readers of the San Jose Evening News learned that the Milano Hotel at 101 North Market Street and the Swiss-American Hotel in Gilroy were the first establishments in California to be closed for a year for violating prohibition. Several other hotels in the county faced similar fates including the Saint Charles Hotel at 31 N. Market Street and the Pederson resort on the Monterey Highway, where $16,000 of booze was seized in one haul. Courtesy, Edith C. Smith Collection, Sourisseau Academy

Above:
On Friday, April 26, 1918, at 2 p.m. thousands of citizens from throughout the county gathered along 1st and Santa Clara

Streets to see the Liberty Day Parade and to support the anniversary of America's entry into WW I. Seven bands, including the Santa Clara, the Agnew, the Chinese-American, the Municipal, and the San Jose High School Band, shown in this photograph, as well as Army Bands from the Eighth Infantry and the Fifth Regiment helped those marching keep in step. In addition to six companies of Regular Army, soldiers from Camp Frémont, politicians, fraternal orders, students from Santa Clara University, University of the Pacific, San José Normal School, the San José High School Cadet Corps, and several other high schools and grammar schools participated.

Brooke Hart was kidnapped and murdered. After his murderers were captured, a mob broke into the jail and hung them in St, James Park. This was the last lynching in California.

1935
Upon the death of County Supervisor Henry Melville Ayer, Louise Schemmel Ayer, his widow, serves out the remaining term becoming the first woman supervisor.

1938
Interurban is abandoned. Passengers switch to automobile or bus service until the Light Rail opens in 1987.

1939
David Packard and Bill Hewlett, Stanford

graduate students, develop audio oscillators for stereophonic sound in Walt Disney's *Fantasia* in a Palo Alto garage.

1940
County population reaches 174,949.

1943
IBM locates a plant in San Jose. It builds several facilities throughout the county.

1944
Supervisors and San Jose City Council each give $35,000 to the Chamber of Commerce to promote the valley.

1945
County was the 10th largest county in the U.S. in agricultural annual income ($65 million).

San Jose population reaches 80,734.

1946
Stanford establishes the Stanford Research Institute.

1949
A Southwest Airways (Pacific Airlines) DC-3 becomes the first commercial flight from the San Jose Municipal Airport.

1950
A.P "Dutch Hamann appointed San Jose city manager. The city has a population of 95,280 and a total area of seventeen square miles. When he retired in 1969, the city had a population of over 400,000 and covered 149 square miles.

George F. Haines establishes the Santa Clara Swim Club. His teams win thirty-five AAU Championships. He coaches four U.S. Olympic teams.

County population reaches 290,547.

1951
Stanford University establishes the Stanford Industrial Park in Palo Alto. Varian Associates are the first tenants.

1952
Felix Bloch, a Swiss physicist, becomes Stanford's first Nobel laureate.

Joseph Eichler sells homes in Palo Alto for $11,000 to $14,000. The California Modern homes feature radiant heating, glass walls, open floor plans, and atriums designed to "bring the outside in."

1952
Campbell and Los Altos incorporate.

1954
Milpitas (Spanish for "little cornfields") incorporates, stopping San Jose from annexing it.

1955
Ford assembly plant opens in Milpitas. It builds 4.7 million vehicles in twenty-eight years.

Cupertino incorporates on land surrounding Cali Brothers feedlot to stop developers. By the mid-1980s, the farms were subdivisions and the Cali property was developed.

1956

In 1943 International Business Machine Corporation (IBM) located its West Coast headquarters in San Jose. IBM became a high-tech industry mainstay in the latter decades of the century with facilities throughout the county and the world. Courtesy, Edith C. Smith Collection (McKay), Sourisseau Academy

Valley Fair Shopping Center opens, signaling the demise of downtown San Jose.

San Jose Redevelopment Agency is formed to create jobs, develop housing downtown, improve neighborhoods, and build public facilities.

First computer to use disk storage, IBM 305 RAMAC (Random Access Method of Accounting and Control) developed in San Jose.

Los Altos Hills incorporates to preserve the foothills.

Saratoga incorporates.

1957
Monte Sereno incorporates.

Foothill College, "the most beautiful community college in America," opens.

1960
County remains the world center for fruit and vegetable processing.

1961
Milpitas halts annexation to San Jose. The city seal becomes the 1776 Minutemen.

1963

In 1886 Senator Leland and Jane Lathrop Stanford established Leland Stanford Junior University in memory of their son. Herbert Hoover, a member of the first graduating class in 1895, donated $50,000 to Stanford University to establish the Hoover Institution on War, Revolution, and Peace in 1919. He became the thirty-first president of the United States in 1928. This photo shows the Hoover Archives and Tower. Photo by Kevin Sterling Payne

West Valley College opens in the Campbell Grammar School and in 1976 moves to Saratoga.

1967

National Semiconductor moves to the City of Santa Clara.

De Anza College opens as part of the Foothill-De Anza Community College District.

Mission College opens as part of the West Valley-Mission Community College District.

1968

Tommie Smith and John Carlos, of the San Jose State University Track Team, win Gold and Bronze medals at the Mexico City Olympics. During the medal ceremony, each raised a gloved fist to protest the way black Americans were treated at home. Peter Norman, the Australian Silver medalist, wears the Olympic Project for Human Rights badge. San Jose State erected a statue commemorating the event in 2003.

Robert Noyce and Gordon Moore found Integrated Electronics Corporation (Intel).

1970

Xerox establishes the Palo Alto Research Center in Stanford Research Park.

1971

Don C. Hoelfer coined the term "Silicon Valley" in his tabloid *Microelectronics News*.

1972

Voters establish the Santa Clara County Transit District and fund county parks.

Complaints by Native American students, force Stanford to drop its Indian mascot name for "The Cardinal."

Mark Spitz, a Santa Clara High School graduate, won seven gold medals in the ill-fated Munich Olympics.

1974

Geraldine Steinberg is appointed to the Board of Supervisors, filling out Victor Calvo's term upon his election to the state assembly. In 1976 Steinberg became the first woman elected to the Board and, with Janet Gray-Hayes' election as the first female mayor of San Jose in 1974, began a new era for women leaders.

1975

Evergreen Valley College opens in the San Jose-Evergreen Community College District.

1976

Steven Wozniak and Steven Jobs sell Apple I computers at the Homebrew Computer Club in Palo Alto.

Marriott opens the Great America Theme Park. In 1983 the City of Santa Clara purchases it for $93.5 million.

1979

Gilroy, "The Garlic Capital of the World," holds the first Garlic Festival.

1980

Not to be outdone, Morgan Hill, "The Mushroom Capital of the World," holds the annual Mushroom Mardi Gras Festival.

County (population 1,295,071) is largest in Bay Area. San Jose reaches 629,442.

1982

San Jose Mercury News reporter Susan Yoachum described how storage tanks at the South San Jose Fairchild plant leaked toxic carcinogens into the drinking water supply. Ten years later the *Mercury News* reported that the plant sat abandoned, "a scar on the placid suburban landscape ... the place where Silicon Valley lost its innocence."

Adobe Systems founded in San Jose by John Warnock and Charles Geschke, two former Xerox Palo Alto Research Center researchers.

Sun Microsystems established by Stanford graduate students Andy Bechtolsheim, Vinod Khosla, Scott McNealy and UC Berkeley graduate student Bill Joy.

1984

Construction of the Valley Transit Authority Light Rail system starts. By 1987 the first section was operating. It currently serves San Jose, Santa Clara, Sunnyvale, Campbell, and Mountain View.

A 6.2 magnitude earthquake on the Calaveras Fault hit Morgan Hill, injuring twenty-four people and causing $10 million in damage.

Len Bosack and Sandy Lerner, a married couple working at Stanford University, establish Cisco Systems in San Jose.

1985

Only seven canneries remain in the valley.

Stanford hosts Super Bowl XIX; San Francisco 49ers defeat Miami Dolphins.

1987

San Jose redevelopment effort opens the Pavilion Shops and Fairmont Hotel. In 1989 Market Plaza and the Convention Center also open.

1989

Bay-Bridge World Series delayed by the Loma Prieta Earthquake. Damage ranged from cracks in chimneys to major structural damage. Landslides cover large portions of Highway 17, the main artery between Santa Clara and Santa Cruz Counties.

1990

Renovated St. Joseph's Church reopens as a cathedral.

San Jose opens the Children's Discovery Museum

Pacific West Outlet Center (now Gilroy Premium Outlets) opens with sixty stores.

County has 1,682,585 residents;

San Jose (population: 782,248) becomes the third largest city in California.

1991

Congress approves the closure of Moffett Field Naval Air Station. NASA Ames took over the facility in 1994 and supported the Pioneer Spacecraft Missions and conducts aeronautical, space science, and technology research.

1992

Business executives and public officials establish Joint Venture: Silicon Valley.

1993

San Jose renames the old plaza in honor of farm worker leader and civil rights advocate César Chávez, who began his career in San Jose.

San Jose Arena (HP Pavilion) opens attracting the Sharks (National Hockey League).

1994

Jim Clark and Marc Andreessen establish Mosaic Communications (Netscape) in Mountain View.

Stanford holds six World Cup Soccer

Now fully recovered after the 1989 Loma Prieta earthquake damaged business and residential buildings in eight blocks of down-town Los Gatos, the Gem of the Foothills has a new parking garage to support its revitalized business district, sporting boutique shops and trendy restaurants. Photo by Kevin Sterling Payne

games. Los Gatos hosts Brazil the eventual champion.

Great Mall Milpitas opens at the Ford assembly plant.

1995

Stanford University graduate students, Chih-Yuan ''Jerry'' Yang, and David Filo, incorporate *Yahoo!*

eBay (originally AuctionWeb) the online auction site was founded by Pierre Omidyar in San Jose.

Saratoga was once known for its lumber, flour, and paper mills that lined the Arroyo Quito (Saratoga Creek), the city now known for its outdoor cafes, wine tasting rooms, and fine restaurants along with attractions such as Villa Montalvo, the Hakone Gardens, and the Mountain Winery Summer Concert Series. Photo by Kevin Sterling Payne

The Downtown Courthouse, pictured above, is one of twelve courts in the county. It sits on the same block as the 1867 Old Courthouse, where the most important case to be tried in the county was held. The 1886 case of Santa Clara County v. Southern Pacific Railroad *determined that the 14th Amendment gave corporations the legal status of persons. Photo by Kevin Sterling Payne*

San Jose Earthquakes (Major League Soccer) play at Spartan Stadium through 2005.

Sybase Open (SAP Open) tennis tournament, the second oldest U.S. tennis tournament (1889), moves to the Arena.

San Jose SaberCats (Arena Football League) play at the Arena.

1998

Larry Page and Sergey Brin establish Google.

1999

Mexican Heritage Plaza opens in San Jose. The cultural center sponsors the annual International Mariachi Festival and Conference.

Netflix, a DVD rental-by-mail business, is founded by Reed Hastings in Los Gatos.

2000

Census shows Santa Clara County the most ethnically diverse in Bay Area.

2001

San Jose Airport is renamed Norman Y. Mineta San Jose International Airport after Norman Yoshio Mineta, former council-member, mayor, congressional representative, and secretary of transportation.

Bonfante Gardens opens in Gilroy.

2002

Arena Bowl XVI held at HP Pavilion; SaberCats defeat Arizona Rattlers.

2003

Martin Luther King Library, the first cooperative library between a city and university and the largest public library west of the Mississippi, opens

A ten-mile-long underground plume of contaminated well water is discovered at the site of the former Olin flare plant in Morgan Hill.

San Jose Stealth (National Lacrosse League) play at the HP Pavilion.

2004

California Theatre reopens and is home to Opera San Jose and Symphony Silicon Valley.

San Jose (population: 904,522) becomes the tenth largest city in the nation.

For the fifth consecutive year San Jose is the safest big city in America.

2005

San Jose City Hall moves back downtown to the corner of East Santa Clara and 4th Streets.

Guadalupe River Park, a massive flood control project and park, is complete.

Initial running of the San Jose Grand Prix Champ Car World Series.

2006

U.S. District Court ruled that the department of the interior must explain its decision to require the Muwekma Ohlone Tribe to complete a procedure that other tribes have been allowed to bypass in its effort to be recognized as a tribe.

Inaugural Amgen Tour of California, a professional cycling race, travels through Santa Clara County.

2006–2007

City of Santa Clara and the San Francisco 49ers football team discuss moving the team to a new sports stadium.

BIBLIOGRAPHY

COUNTY HISTORIES

Foote, Horace S., ed., *Pen Pictures from the Garden of the World or, Santa Clara County, California* (Chicago, 1888).

Laffey, Glory Anne, and Robert G. Detlefs, *County Leadership: Santa Clara County Government History* (San Jose, 1995)

Munro-Fraser, J. P., *History of Santa Clara County, California (San* Francisco, 1881).

Sawyer, Eugene T., *History of Santa Clara County* (Los Angeles, 1922).

Thompson & West, *Historical Atlas Map of Santa Clara County* (San Francisco, 1876). Reprinted (San Jose: Smith McKay, 1973).

HISTORIES OF INCORPORATED AREAS

Arbuckle, Clyde, *Clyde Arbuckle's History of San Jose* (San Jose, 1985).

Beilharz, Edwin A. and Donald O. DeMers, Jr., *San Jose: California's First City* (Tulsa, Oklahoma, 1980).

Bruntz, George G., *History of Los Gatos: Gem of the Foothills* (Fresno, 1971).

Garcia, Lorie, et al, *A Place of Promise: The City of Santa Clara* (Santa Clara, 2002).

Hall, Fredrick, *The History of San Jose* and *Surroundings: With Biographical Sketches of Early Settlers* (San Francisco, 1871). Indexed by Everett and Anna Marie Hager, *An Index to Hall's, 1871 History of San Jose* (San Jose State University: Sourisseau Academy, Occasional Paper No. 2, 1974).

Henderson, Judith, ed., *Reflections of the Past: An Anthology of San Jose* (Encinitas, 1996).

James, William F. and George H. McMurry, *History of San Jose* (San Jose, 1933).

Salewske, Claudia Kendall, *Pieces of the Past:A Story of Gilroy* (Gilroy, 1982).

Trounstine, Philip J., and Christensen, Terry, *Movers and Shakers: The Study of Community Power* (New York: 1982).

Winslow, Ward, *Palo Alto: A Centennial History* (Palo Alto, 1993).

Winther, Oscar O., *The Story of San Jose, 1777-1869* (San Francisco, 1935).

HISTORIC BUILDINGS AND LANDMARKS

Butler, Phyllis F., *The Valley of Santa Clara Historic Buildings, 1792-1920* (San Jose, 1975).

Pace, Pauline, *Santa Clara County Heritage Resource Inventory* (San Jose 1975).

Wyatt, Roscoe D. and Clyde Arbuckle, *Historic Names, Persons and Places in Santa Clara County* (San Jose, 1948).

HIGHER EDUCATION

Gilbert, Benjamin F. and Charles Burdick, *Washington Square, 1857-1979: The History of San Jose State University* (San Jose, 1979).

Hunt, Rockwell D., *History of the College of the Pacific, 1851-1951* (Stockton, 1951).

McKevitt, Gerold, S. J., *The University of Santa Clara: A History 1851-1977* (Stanford, 1979).

GENERAL REFERENCES

5:05 p.m.: The Great Quake of 1989, (Santa Cruz, 1989).

Allen, Rebecca and Mark Hylkema, eds., *Life Along the Guadalupe River*. (San Jose, 2002).

Arbuckle, Clyde and Ralph Rambo, *Santa Clara County Ranchos* (San Jose, 1968).

Bancroft, Hubert Howe, *The History of California*, Vols. I-IVV (San Francisco, 1886).

Beal, Richard A., *Highway 17: The Road to Santa Cruz* (Aptos, 1991).

Belser, Karl, *The Making of Slurban America,Cry California* Fall 1970.

California History Center, *Historias: The Spanish Heitage of Santa Clara Valley* (Cupertino, 1976). *Water in the Santa Clara Valley: A History* (Cupertino, 1981).

Castellanos, Teresa, et al, *KIN: Knowledge of Immigrant Nationalities in Santa Clara County* (San Jose, 2001).

Horn, Gloria S., ed., *Chinese Argonauts: An An-thology of the Chinese Contributions to the Historical Development of Santa Clara County* (Foothill College, 1971).

Lanyon, Milton and Laurence Bulmore, *Cinabar Hills:The Quicksilver Days of New Almaden* (Los Gatos, 1967).

Lukes, Timothy J. and Garry Y. Okihiro, *Japanese Legacy: Farming and Community Life in California's Santa Clara County* (Cupertino, 1985).

Margolin, Malcolm, *The Ohlone Way: Indian Life in the San Francisco-Monterey Bay Area* (Berkeley, 1978).

Mars, Amaury, *Reminiscences of Santa Clara Valley and San Jose* (San Francisco, 1901).

MacGregor, Bruce A., *South Pacific Coast* (Berkeley, 1968).

Payne, Stephen M., *"A Howling Wilderness:" A History of the Summit Road Area of the Santa Cruz Mountains, 1850-1906* (Cupertino, 1978).

Pierce, Marjorie, *East of the Gabilans* (Santa Cruz, 1976).

Santa Clara County Pioneer Papers, 1973 (San Jose, 1973).

Sullivan, Charles L., *Like Modern Edens: Wine-growing in Santa Clara Valley and Santa Cruz Mountains, 1798-1981* (Cupertino, 1982).

Sullivan, Leo, *Sunshine, Fruit and Flowers, Santa Clara County and its Resources, A Souvenir of the San Jose Mercury* (San Jose, 1895).

Young, John V., *Ghost Towns of the Santa Cruz Mountains* (Santa Cruz, 1979).

THESES AND DISSERTATIONS

Armstrong, David Robert, "The Inter-City Council: An Experiment in Intergovern-mental Cooperation in Santa Clara County" (San Jose State University, 1966).

Claus, Robert J., "The Fruit and Canning Industry in the Santa Clara Valley" (San Jose State University, 1966).

Detlefs, Charlene, "Flour Milling in Santa Clara County, 1840-1898" (San Jose State University, 1985).

Nelson, Truda Cooling, "John Gilroy: A Biography" (San Jose State University, 1981).

Williams, James Calhoun, "The Role of Defence Spending in Recent Economic Growth of the San Francisco Bay Area" (San Jose State University, 1971).

PAMPHLETS

Bernstein, Alen, Bob DeGresse, Rachael Grossman, Chris Paine, and Lenny Siegel, *Silicon Valley: Paradise or Paradox* (Mountain View, 1977).

Corr, Jack and Fred Keeley, *The Community Theater and the Fiscal Irresponsibility of the San Jose Establishment A Civic Lesson* (Los Angeles, 1975).

Eakins, David W., ed., *Businessmen and Municipal Reform: A Study of Ideals and Practice in San Jose and Santa Cruz, 1896-1916* (San Jose, 1976).

Rambo, Ralph, *Pioneer Blue Book of the Old Santa Clara Valley* (San Jose, 1973).

Simon, Patricia Snar, *Henry Miller: His Life and Times* (Gilroy, 1980).

Williams, James C., ed., *Sketches of Gilroy, Santa Clara County, California* (Gilroy, 1980).

INTERNET SOURCES

Ackerman, Elise, *"Google emerges as a valley powerhouse," Mercury News*, April 11, 2006

City of Santa Clara http://www.ci.santa-clara.ca.us/about_us/u_history_index.html

Joint Venture: Silicon Valley, Annual Reports at: http://www.jointventure.org/

Leventhal, Alan, et al, *"The Muwekma Ohlone Tribe of the San Francisco Bay Area,"*www.islaiscreek.org/ ohlonehistcultfedrecog.html.

McAllister, Sue, "Entry-level Buyers are Finding it Harder," *Mercury News*, May 17, 2007

Rogers, Paul, "Perchlorate Suit Fails." *Mercury News* and *Monterey County Herald*, August 13, 2005.

Russell, Kiley, "Bay Area Project Aims to Ease Congestion," *MediaNews*, December 14, 2006

Santa Clara Valley Water District at www.valleywater.org.

Santa Cruz Mountains Winegrowers Association (www.scmwa.com)

Swift, Mike, "Diverse county tries to find common voice," *Oakland Tribune*, March 23, 2007

"Where we live," *San Jose Mercury News* series:
"Milpitas," August 27, 2006.
"Morgan Hill and Gilroy," November 12, 2006.
"Campbell," April 24, 2006.
"Los Gatos," May 21, 2006.
"Mountain View," February 25, 2007.
"Santa Clara," June 26, 2005.
"Palo Alto," August 28, 2005.

MISCELLANEOUS

Various student term papers in the San Jose State University Archives.

INDEX

GENERAL INDEX
Italicized numbers indicate illustrations